D1090961

ARCHITECTURE AND PLANNING OF GRAHAM, ANDERSON, PROBST AND WHITE, 1912–1936

CHICAGO ARCHITECTURE AND URBANISM

A series edited by
Robert Bruegmann
Joan Draper
Wim de Wit and
David Van Zanten

Other volumes in the series
Joseph Connors, *The Robie House of Frank Lloyd Wright*
Joseph Siry, *Carson Pirie Scott: Louis Sullivan and the
   Chicago Department Store*
John W. Stamper, *Chicago's North Michigan Avenue:
   Planning and Development, 1900–1930*

SALLY A. KITT CHAPPELL

ARCHITECTURE AND PLANNING OF GRAHAM, ANDERSON, PROBST AND WHITE, 1912-1936: TRANSFORMING TRADITION

THE UNIVERSITY OF CHICAGO PRESS
Chicago and London

Works in Chicago Architecture and Urbanism are
supported in part by funds given in memory of Ann
Lorenz Van Zanten and administered by the Chicago
Historical Society.

This publication has been supported by a grant from
the Graham Foundation for Advanced Studies in the
Fine Arts.

SALLY A. KITT CHAPPELL is a professor in the
Department of Art at DePaul University.

The University of Chicago Press, Chicago 60637
The University of Chicago Press, Ltd., London
© 1992 by The University of Chicago
All rights reserved. Published 1992
Printed in the United States of America
01 00 99 98 97 96 95 94 93 92 5 4 3 2 1

ISBN 0-226-10134-7

Library of Congress Cataloging-in-Publication Data

Chappell, Sally Anderson.
    Architecture and planning of Graham, An-
  derson, Probst and White, 1912–1936 : trans-
  forming tradition / Sally A. Kitt Chappell.
        p.   cm.—(Chicago architecture and
      urbanism)
    Includes bibliographical references and index.
    1. Graham, Anderson, Probst, White.   2. Ar-
  chitecture, Modern—20th century—United
  States.   I. Title.   II. Series.
  NA737.G7C48   1992
  720′.92′2—dc20   91-9162

This book is printed on acid-free paper.

Cover: Graham, Anderson, Probst and White,
  Wrigley Building, sheet 8, elevation.
  Courtesy of the Chicago Historical Society

TO WALTER

CONTENTS

ILLUSTRATIONS

CATALOGUE RAISONNÉ
LIST OF ENTRIES

ACKNOWLEDGMENTS

IN BOTH THE DEVELOPMENT of my knowledge and the writing of this book I am most indebted to my friend and colleague Robert Bruegmann, associate professor of architectural history at the University of Illinois at Chicago. Professor Bruegmann's autonomy of vision, his profound knowledge, and his unstinting line-by-line critiques sent me back to the library, to more fieldwork, and to the word processor on many occasions. At other times my fledgling notions seemed to take wing after a conversation with him. I valued his contributions as evidence of his devotion to the history of architecture and collegiality, and I received them with gratitude. The book is better for Robert Bruegmann's work. The faults that remain are entirely mine.

Professional help and friendship went hand in hand as other colleagues contributed to various chapters or sections, especially Carl Condit, my former teacher and lifelong mentor, whose books on Chicago architecture have educated us all. I thank him specifically for his perspicacious and indispensable review of this manuscript. Joan Draper's thorough reading of the manuscript and helpful suggestions led to further research in some important areas. Encouragement and help from Kevin Harrington, David Van Zanten, John Zukowsky, Neil Harris, and Wim de Wit came generously on several occasions.

Without the unfailing courtesy and help of William Surman, president of Graham, Anderson, Probst and White, this book would not have been possible. His staff, especially Gerald Eisel and Robert Surman, helped frequently with requests for materials or information. Several former employees of the firm allowed me to interview them for hours, especially Charles F. Murphy, Clifford Noonan, and Edward Histed. Christine Susman-Histed preserved one of the two original watercolors known to be by the hand of Peirce Anderson; Barbara Graham Jaffee, the other. Patrick Shaw donated materials from the Alfred P. Shaw Papers to the Art Institute of Chicago. Most of all, Carter Manny, Jr., architect, architectural historian, and director of the Graham Foundation for Advanced Studies in the Fine Arts, led me to invaluable original materials and offered continuous encouragement.

ACKNOWLEDGMENTS

Architectural circles overlap in rich profusion in Chicago. On any given evening there may be two or three opportunities for an exchange of ideas—before or after lectures and exhibitions, during presentations or panel discussions, or at informal dinner meetings. Authors can be certain that their works in progress will elicit critical care and response from colleagues. I presented some of the sections of this book in their early stages at local chapter meetings of the Society of Architectural Historians and the American Institute of Architects, where they were met with helpful objections and suggestions. On the national level, some chapters were read by jurors or editors whose high standards forced the growth of my ideas before related articles reached print.

Scholars and architects in other cities were swift and accurate in giving me data, escorting me on guided tours, and opening doors to libraries and archives. Among them are Lloyd C. Engelbrecht in Cincinnati; Wallace G. Teare, Walter C. Leedy, Jr., and Wilma Salisbury in Cleveland; Thomas J. Schlereth in South Bend, Indiana; Allan Greenberg in New Haven; Edward Teitelman, M.D., in Philadelphia; Mark M. Brown at the University of Pittsburgh; Ruth Harpold Basner in North Canton, Ohio; Reginald Watters at Coe College; Lynn Meyer in Omaha; Bradford Breuer in San Antonio, Texas; Sue Meldman in Chicago; Frank Perez at the Mount Wilson Observatory; and Jacqueline Babe and Joseph Grella in Detroit.

Fieldwork in Chicago was more productive and enjoyable thanks to the cooperation of John Powers and Rebecca Grill of Commonwealth Edison; Peter Mansbacher of the Stevens Company; Dino d'Angelo, enlightened owner of the Civic Opera Building and the Straus Building in Chicago; and many other persons as well.

Insightful editors Fannia Weingartner, Todd Marder, Sharon Irish, Robert Post, and Meg Moss helped to shape my ideas as well as to polish my prose.

The aesthetic sensibilities of Joan Sommers, the book's designer, enhanced the architectural imagery on every page.

I used several libraries, and I wish to express my thanks for the privileges I enjoyed at DePaul University, the Chicago Historical Society, the Art Institute of Chicago, Harvard University, Loyola University, Centre Canadien d'Architecture, and the Library of Congress. Countless people in local libraries and in the offices of architects and building managers preserved materials that would otherwise have been lost to history. They are too numerous to mention, but my gratitude to each one is profound. I owe a debt to students who worked as research assistants, including Kevin Latham, Marc Waters, and Amy Gold. Linda Lombardi and John Gestautas helped with the typing and word-processing of the manuscript. Their cheerful consideration and ability to anticipate the needs of others smoothed the way on many occasions.

I dedicate this book to my husband, Walter Kitt, M.D. From its beginnings he understood what it is to work on a large, decade-long project. He knows what support means, and his good-humored patience and affection sustained me and are part of this book. My sons Jonathan and David were helpful to me in countless ways that make the years involved in producing a book warm and fulfilling. An energizing sense of the continuity of love and work has come from the relationships I have with my daughter, Jennifer; my daughter-in-law, Mary Chappell; and my three granddaughters, Jennifer, Katherine, and Lauren, and my grandson, Ryan.

P R E F A C E

FASCINATED BY CHANGE, architectural historians of the modernist generation usually filled their accounts with new developments—Doric capitals became Ionic volutes, rounded arches sprang into pointed Gothic vaults, masonry walls gave way to steel-cage skyscrapers, Frank Lloyd Wright changed our idea of what a house should be. Descriptions of stylistic evolution, the role of technological discoveries, the spell of great epochs of building, and the influences of works of geniuses were the warp and woof of these historians' interpretive material. None of these concerns justifies this study.

As successors to Daniel Burnham, the principals of one of the largest American firms of the turn of the century, Ernest R. Graham, Peirce Anderson, Edward Probst, and Howard White, were architects in the mainstream. At the center of the movement that produced big offices through the building boom decades of the 1920s, they were neither conservative nor avant-garde. They embraced tradition without question. Yet within the canons of good architecture

handed down to them, they modified forms and made creative adaptations to solve some of the largest architectural problems of their times in railroad stations, in civic monuments, and in hundreds of banks, offices, department stores, and other building types. Some of their works were beautiful; a few were masterpieces.

Even competent architecture on such a large scale in a boom period deserves careful perusal by the specialist, for it has many lessons to teach about planning, design, construction, and materials. But the success of these architects in the prevailing current of their era also provides insights into broader aspects of history, such as the use of "commercial classicism" and what this rather typical approach to the art of building tells us about American life. It shows the way in which tradition is a source of strength to the architect facing new problems, often providing solutions as worthy as those invented by more innovative practitioners, the so-called "hero" architects like Frank Lloyd Wright or Ludwig Mies van der Rohe.

The range of Graham, Anderson, Probst and White's work and the variety of building types that the firm designed in a period of rapid economic change required the adoption of corporate techniques in architectural practice. More importantly, as inheritor of the architectural practice of Daniel H. Burnham, the firm was involved with the design of large urban schemes, notably in Cleveland, Philadelphia, and Chicago. In these cities, where the architects built several buildings, their work altered the urban hierarchy and reflected the changing values of the society around them. Since none of the partners wrote down any of the thinking underlying these changes, the art historian must interpret the images in the light of other work and the literature of the period. By examining the work of this firm we gain an insight into the changing cultural values of a crucial twenty-five-year period in American life.

Looking at the many buildings designed by a firm based in Chicago, we also learn something about the adaptability of classical Beaux-Arts principles to such new building types as railroad terminals and power stations; we sharpen our discrimination of traditional practices by observing what can be retained and what must be rejected to meet new circumstances. To be validated and make sense, these concepts must be examined in concrete circumstances, and the works of Graham, Anderson, Probst and White provide a living laboratory of examples.

The Thirtieth Street Station in Philadelphia and Union Station in Chicago are superb adaptations of Beaux-Arts planning principles to a new building type, both in subordinating the stations to a larger plan for the whole city and in making them key elements in its future development. The Cleveland Terminal complex marks the reemergence of the idea of the urban group in the heyday of soaringly individual skyscrapers.

A case study of the uniquely American approach to museum building through public-private collaboration is unveiled in the accounts of the construction of the Field Museum of Natural History and the John G. Shedd Aquarium in Chicago. Three other works reflect the private basis of social welfare efforts in the 1920s—the British Old Peoples Home in Riverside and Baby Village in Mooseheart, both in Illinois; and the Hoover Suction Sweeper Community Building in North Canton, Ohio. The specially created feminine world of the department store mirrored many facets of the position of women in the society of the 1920s, while Filene's department store in Boston reflected contemporary visions of a utopian city life.

Occasionally, several of these factors come together in one building. The confluence of Old World principles, the legacies of the Chicago commercial style of the 1880s, developments in the terra-cotta industry, the challenge of contemporary architecture in New York, the habit of civic-mindedness in the clients of the business world, and post–World War I optimism all merge in one of Chicago's most popular structures—the Wrigley Building on Michigan Avenue.

Smaller insights are offered by examining the workings of a design team and the relationships of client and architect, some unique to the firm, others typical of the era, and others still simply good examples of time-honored universal practice.

Since the firm's work has been of consistently high quality throughout its history, its buildings have had continued and long use. They have also been adaptable to change, enlargement, or modification, another factor in their longevity, and one that provides occasional glimpses into the preservation movement that began in the 1970s, as in the conversion of the Chesapeake and Ohio Railway Station in Ashland, Kentucky, into a contemporary bank.

When we ask, "What endures and why?" we enter a different dimension than when we ask "What's new and why?" There is perhaps more to be learned from what people cherish and refuse to part with than there is to be gleaned from what they are willing to sacrifice or change radically. What they conserve has a far more pervasive influence and is at least as telling an aspect of their underlying values as what they discard in favor of the novel, the fashionable, or the avant-garde. Shifting our focus from what is timely to what is timeless in our lives allows us at once a more intimate and a more substantial view of ourselves.

As if opening a never-ending nest of boxes, a researcher goes on exploring one question after another, until some arbitrary stopping place declares itself. Caught in something like Zeno's paradox, a scholar must reach halfway on a given course before arriving at the end, and because the halfway point advances with each step, there are an infinite number of halfway points along a path of inquiry. One never reaches the end. Many more questions remain for those who follow to answer, but I trust I have advanced our knowledge of Graham, Anderson, Probst and White and thus made the work of later historians easier.

INTRODUCTION

PART ONE OF THIS BOOK is devoted to a discussion of changes in the various building types the firm designed, and shows how they reflect the accompanying changing values in the civic hierarchy. Since this section is typological, many of the buildings discussed are among the firm's finest achievements, and they are analyzed in further detail in the chronological study in Part II, the Catalogue Raisonné, which includes other important examples. However, in reading Part I the reader may wish to refer to the Catalogue Raisonné List of Entries, which is in approximate chronological order. Part III is devoted to a history of the ownership of the firm and biographical studies of each of the partners and several other members of the staff. It is intended to show what influences had a part in the architects' creative decisions, the role of their mentor Daniel H. Burnham, and the respective education of each of the partners and their experiences before and after coming to Chicago to work for the firm. Finally, Part IV lists the works of the firm under two names from 1912 to 1936. Following Burnham's death in 1912, his associate Ernest R. Graham, and Burnham's two sons, Hubert and Daniel H. Burnham, Jr., formed Graham, Burnham and Company. In 1917, the two sons left and the firm Graham, Anderson, Probst and White was incorporated, a name it bears today under the presidency of William Surman.

The illustrations in Part I are arranged according to building type categories, but within each category they appear chronologically. In Part II, all the works are illustrated in chronological order without regard to building type, except when a slight deviation allows related groups of buildings, like the Cleveland Terminal Group, or the structures for the Mooseheart orphanage, to be placed together. Illustrations in Part III accompany the biographies.

HISTORIC OVERVIEW: A MAINSTREAM ROLE IN THE CHANGING VALUES OF THE EARLY TWENTIETH CENTURY

Some aspects of a city seem immutable, others change slowly and only under special circumstances. There are some moments when the whole urban fabric rapidly takes on a new form. These shifts in the material world can only occur when there are concomitant changes in the political, social, and economic life of the community. In the period 1912 to 1929, ideas about civic order changed radically. The commercial world impinged on the cultural world as it never had before. Graham, Anderson, Probst and White, one of the most prolific architectural firms of this period, erected hundreds of buildings in cities from New York to Pasadena, providing a microcosm of a larger metamorphosis in American history.

Ernest R. Graham and Peirce Anderson were both working for Daniel H. Burnham while he was developing a new vision of the city in the Plan of Chicago of 1909. Based on City Beautiful ideals and their experiences at Chicago's World's Columbian Exposition of 1893, where the Court of Honor dazzled visitors with the possibilities of Beaux-Arts planning, the Plan of Chicago was, like the fair, based on the hierarchical vision that was deeply rooted in Western tradition. Elements of the larger idea of civic order and the myriad refinements that the classical tradition had undergone were handed down to the principals of the firm to their great enrichment.

Privileged to work in one of the great building periods in American history, they in turn modified and created new elements within the larger civilization of which they were a part. Because Graham, Anderson, Probst and White was a large firm with many commissions for commercial buildings in large cities, its members played a major role in changing the character of the American city in the two decades between 1910 and 1930.

Although never overtly stated (as social mores tend not to be), importance was assigned in a descending order to various types of buildings. Whether consciously or subconsciously, the members of the firm had clearly incorporated this hierarchy into their vision of the role of architecture in the built environment.

Looking back on cities and built works of this time, we can rank civic values as follows:

1. Public buildings, cultural institutions, and public parks
2. Joint public-private buildings and spaces
3. Private banks, office buildings, and department stores
4. Loft buildings and light manufactories
5. Factories, warehouses, and other industrial buildings

The Plan of Chicago is a manifestation of the hierarchical thinking of this period. Grandest of all in the scheme to which planners, businessmen, and citizens alike subscribed were public buildings such as the great Civic Center, intended to be to Chicago what the Parthenon was to Athens, or St. Peter's to Rome (fig. 1). On the same level but lower in value were the Field Museum of Natural History and Grant Park, Chicago's formal front garden. Below these came railroad stations, where private interests cooperated with government authorities in the creation of majestic buildings within generous open plazas.

At the middle level one finds a cluster of buildings that might be designated as borderline. In the Plan of Chicago, Daniel H. Burnham (mentor of his junior associates, the future partners of Graham, Anderson, Probst and White) had deliberately made only outline sketches for buildings whose place in the hierarchy was as yet undetermined. In later years the partners developed some of these sketchily indicated sites with a variety of buildings. The most striking example is the Merchandise Mart, which in the original hierarchy would have been placed at the very bottom as a warehouse, but which by the 1920s had risen to the middle level. It is important to note that it was the client's perception of his building as part warehouse, part store that led the architects to design a higher level of building in form and detail.

This is but one example of a situation in which a client had special requirements. Some businessmen might have wanted their corporate headquarters in the same building as their factory. Many Chicago architects proved ingenious at creating forms that accommodated these new multipurpose buildings to their older neighbors. Also within the middle levels of this graded series were works outside the central city, plans for colleges and universities, modest businesses, charitable endeavors, and suburban stores.

Ranked below the middle level in the original scheme were industrial lofts, manufactories, laboratories, warehouses, and garages. Differentiated in rank, these buildings were related to each other by their respective positions in the overall scheme. In Chicago, buildings of the highest level were near the lake; those at the lowest

[1] CIVIC CENTER, *THE PLAN OF CHICAGO* (1909), DANIEL H. BURNHAM AND EDWARD H. BENNETT, CHICAGO, ILL.

Dominating the western skyline, the Civic Center was meant to fulfill a twofold purpose: to give Chicago an urban focus and to symbolize the city. With such a majestic crown, Daniel H. Burnham believed Chicago would take its rightful place in the galaxy of world-renowned cities that included Rome, London, and Paris. Although a domed state building was never constructed, the vision of a powerful building as the focus of a unified cityscape composed of lower-scaled buildings expressed the planning philosophy of the era.

level were northwest or south of the Y-shaped Chicago River. In between were middle-level buildings. Domestic architecture was in a category by itself.[1]

By the nineteenth century, the traditional dominance of religious and public structures in Western civilization had already been challenged by commercial buildings. In addition, new cultural institutions, such as museums and libraries, had found a place in the order of the city. These changes of meaning and shifts in community values show in the Plan of Chicago of 1909, where churches do not appear at all. The city as Burnham envisioned it was dominated by the high dome of the Civic Center and, next down in the hierarchy, the Field Museum, appropriately

adorned in the original design with a smaller dome. (The dome was left out in the final plans.)[2]

PUBLIC BUILDINGS, CULTURAL INSTITUTIONS, AND PUBLIC PARKS

In public buildings and cultural institutions the firm was more likely to honor the traditions of the past, to adhere more closely to the precedents of its heritage, than to experiment with new forms. Basically symmetrical, organized along an axis, with traditional ornament, each public building was well related to its site, composed of a sequence of spaces with climactic, ceremonial public areas which were decorated with fine art appropriate to the purpose of the building and to its time and place. Despite these shared characteristics, each of the buildings was unique. The distinctive qualities of each emanate from the specific problems involved in its design. No two buildings were alike because each had a different site, context, client, and program. Only in cases where these elements were the same, as in the Federal Reserve banks in small towns, built in the 1920s, did the buildings resemble each other closely.

United States Post Office, Washington, D.C. (1911–14)

For a democracy, the scale of Washington, D.C., strikes just the right balance between impressiveness and friendliness. Its open spaces, green vistas, and sparkling white buildings are monumental, yet appear approachable and inviting to the ordinary citizen. Two city plans ensured this: Pierre L'Enfant's design of 1792 and the Senate Park Commission Plan of 1901–2, in which Daniel H. Burnham and Peirce Anderson played significant roles.

Crucial elements in the 1902 Plan were the removal of railroad tracks and buildings that had cluttered the Mall in the nineteenth century and the erection of a union railroad station north of the Capitol, which would eventually be known as Union Station, to bring together the seven railroads serving the city. Burnham believed the railroad entrance to the city should be, more than utilitarian, an adornment of the capital. As a civic vestibule, it was as important for the northern view as the Mall was for the western approach. It needed to be august, yet it should not vie for attention with the Capitol Building itself.

Soon after the completion of the railroad station, pressure mounted for a larger post office to serve the city's growing volume of mail. Burnham was chairman of the Commission of Fine Arts at the time and seized this opportunity to complete his vision of the plaza in front of the station.

A link was missing in the frame around the railroad station and the plaza to the northeast of the Capitol. It could be filled handsomely by a

new post office on Massachusetts Avenue just west of the station. Burnham's aesthetic preference was supported by the United States Postal Service's practical argument that since trains carried most of the nation's mail, a great percentage of which was generated by the government, the post office should be located near both government offices and the chief means of mail transportation. Since members of Congress were already agitated about the unseemly appearance of this area so near the Capitol, there was little opposition to Burnham's plan. Soon after funds for the post office were appropriated in 1911, Peirce Anderson, who had designed Union Station, moved back to Washington to work on the new building.

[2] UNION STATION AND UNITED STATES POST OFFICE, WASHINGTON, D.C.
A visitor arriving in Washington by train passes through the triumphal arches of Union Station to see the sparkling white of the Capitol beyond the green foreground of the plaza park. Acting as a backdrop screen, the post office to the left and an office building to the right give this space the scale and sense of closure needed to complete a ceremonial space for such events as the arrival of a visiting chief of state. The flat roof and the simple colonnade of the post office ensure that, like an honor guard, the building plays a subordinate part in the larger civic whole.

The Washington post office should thus be seen as one part of the urban complex designed first for Union Station with its attendant semicircular plaza in 1908. The post office closes the northern edge of the plaza, defining the area and giving it emphasis. The building plays the role of the part in classical relationship to the whole: it is an end in itself, yet subordinate to the larger urban plan (fig. 2). Still resplendent in the interior are the original rose marble floors, golden marble wainscoting, granite columns with composite capitals, and the elaborate stucco ceiling decorated with swags of oak leaves, meanders, leaf masks, and crests, a testament to the high place in the hierarchy accorded civic buildings.

Two museums very near each other in Chicago make the same point. Similar in essentials, different in aspect, the Field Museum of Natural History and the John G. Shedd Aquarium are both in the "cultural arc" of the city envisioned

[3] FIELD MUSEUM OF NATURAL HISTORY, JOHN G. SHEDD AQUARIUM, AND ADLER PLANETARIUM, CHICAGO, ILL.

The sublime union of Lake Michigan and the Chicago skyline is adorned by the city's museums. The Shedd Aquarium, the Field Museum, and the Adler Planetarium (Ernest A. Grunsfeld, Jr., 1931) are set in the southern half of Chicago's frontyard, to greet the many sailboats and tourist vessels that ply the waters nine months of the year. Sited to take advantage of its lakefront location, the symmetrical Field Museum crowns the vista along Lake Shore Drive from both the north and the south. (Field Museum of Natural History, Neg. GN83127A)

[4] FIELD MUSEUM, EXTERIOR
Elevated twenty feet above the spacious landscaped park, the Field Museum sits on a broad terrace overlooking the harbor. The templed facade, stately columns, and gleaming white marble of the building express the importance of a cultural institution envisioned at the top of the urban hierarchy.

in the Plan of Chicago of 1909. Each has a strong, separate identity, yet each is subordinated to the role it plays in shaping the form of the city according to the hierarchical vision embodied in the Plan (fig. 3).

Field Museum of Natural History, Chicago (1911–19)

On its elevated base, the Field Museum provides a sense of closure at the south end of Chicago's cultural mile, which extends from the Chicago Public Library past the Art Institute, Orchestra Hall, and the Auditorium and beyond the Field Museum to the Shedd Aquarium and the Adler Planetarium to the east. From all directions, the museum is a key element, providing a climax to the urban vista. Just as the Louvre sounds the coda of the Champs-Élysées, or the Victor Emmanuel Monument crowns the Via del Corso in Rome, so the Field Museum gives monumental form to South Lake Shore Drive (fig. 4).

The grassy lawn relates the building to its parklike surroundings, and the balustraded terrace unites the whole complex. Classical, with many orthodox features of the Ionic order—plinth, flutings, volutes, and a continuous frieze—the museum is symmetrical in plan. The expression of the interior spaces is clear on the exterior. The entrance pavilion in the center and the colonnaded wings on either side serve as guides to the interior, where the exhibition spaces follow the same symmetry (fig. 6). This fusion of the exterior appearance of the building with its interior circulation pattern is one of the great strengths of the design. In addition, the large scale of the building is made more comprehensible by the symmetrical disposition of its parts.

Place in the hierarchy determined every aspect of a building, from choice of materials to the proportions of the interior spaces, the nature of the ornament, and the quality of the fixtures. Every detail of the Field Museum attests to its high place in the hierarchy. In the James Simpson

[5] FIELD MUSEUM, STANLEY
FIELD HALL
At the heart of the museum, Stanley
Field Hall is grandly proportioned
for its role as both a ceremonial
space and a focus in the circulation
scheme. The combination of columns and arches is the architects'
homage to the past, an appropriate
bow to tradition in the spirit of a
scholarly institution.

[6] FIELD MUSEUM, PLAN
The symmetrical plan indicates the
"architectural walk" through the
Field Museum. Although visitors
may stroll in and out of the adjacent galleries, they always return to
the tall central space of Stanley
Field Hall, reassured of their location on the route through the exhibitions.

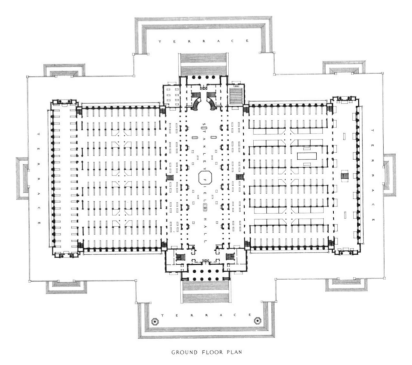

GROUND FLOOR PLAN

[7] FIELD MUSEUM, JAMES SIMPSON THEATER
The James Simpson Theater marks the end of a vista within the museum. Its lofty illuminated ceiling sets an appropriate tone for the activities that take place in the theater.

[8] FIELD MUSEUM, STANLEY FIELD HALL, DETAIL
The airy vaults of Stanley Field Hall, with their coffered ceilings and star ornaments, invite visitors to further exploration in the second-floor galleries.

[9] JOHN G. SHEDD AQUARIUM, CHICAGO, ILL.
From any direction the Shedd Aquarium shows itself and Chicago to great advantage, whether against the infinite waters to the east, Lake Shore Drive to the north and south, the Field Museum to the west, or the city skyline across the harbor. Since marble is translucent in its upper surfaces, the cladding catches the light as it sparkles and reflects back from the lake. At sunrise and sunset, the warm glow in the stone reminds the visitor of Michelangelo's remark, "Clay is life, plaster is death, marble is resurrection."

Auditorium (fig. 7), Doric columns pay homage to the classical past; marble is used on all exterior and interior walls; the proportions of Stanley Field Hall are grand (300 feet long, 70 feet wide, and 75 feet high). The allegorical figures were designed especially for the museum by New York sculptor Henry Hering (figs. 5, 8).

John G. Shedd Aquarium, Chicago (1925–30)

A galaxy of cultural institutions forms the southern peninsula of the Chicago harbor. At the transition between shore and peninsula just east of the Field Museum, the South Park District created a circular platform for the Shedd Aquarium.

Several feet above the grade of the surrounding park it commands a magnificent view of the harbor and the skyline (fig. 9). Carl Condit, peerless historian of Chicago architecture, wrote: "No setting for a major civic building could compare to this, and when Graham, Anderson, Probst and White received the commission . . . they rose fully to its magnificent promise."[3]

The white marine-veined marble and the clear geometry of the octagon unite the sea and the land (fig. 10). From the west, the sparkling form marks the beginning of the peninsula; from the east, it seems to light the opening of the harbor at the breakwater. Meeting the land, a circular walkway curves along the shore, and a broad terrace leads to the Doric order that firmly anchors the entrance of the building (fig. 11).

[10] SHEDD AQUARIUM, ELEVATION

In this presentation drawing the architects suggested the active role that the Shedd Aquarium would take in the life of the city at the lakefront. Elevated above ordinary traffic and set off by an emerald green park with trees and plants, it is a delightful place for visitors or families to spend Sunday outings.

[11] SHEDD AQUARIUM, ENTRANCE

Bold Doric columns proclaim the entrance to the museum, while the surrounding terrace invites visitors to linger and enjoy the natural marine setting.

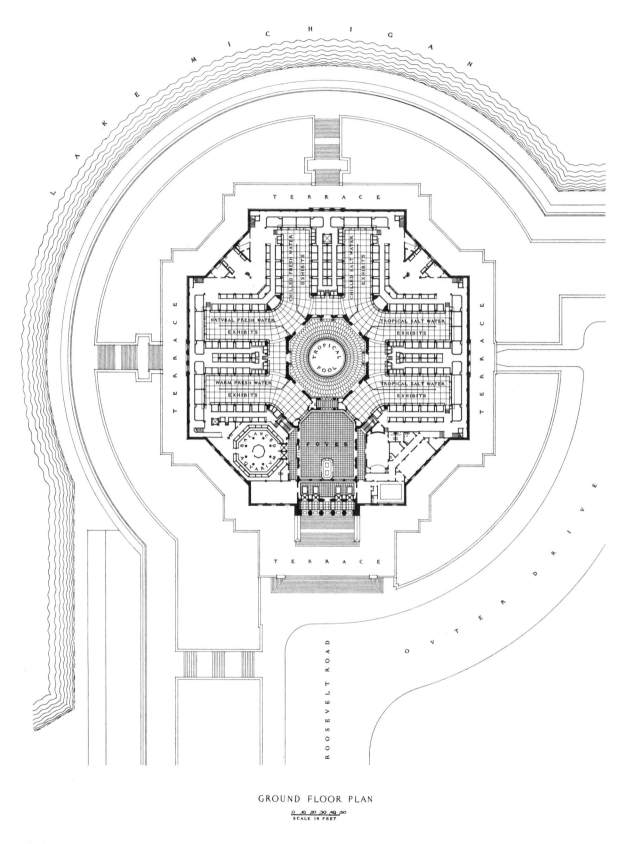

GROUND FLOOR PLAN

0 10 20 30 40 50
SCALE IN FEET

[12] SHEDD AQUARIUM, PLAN
Guests may wander at will in the symmetrical plan of the Shedd Aquarium without giving a thought to where they are, for the unfolding of the spaces guides them through the building.

12

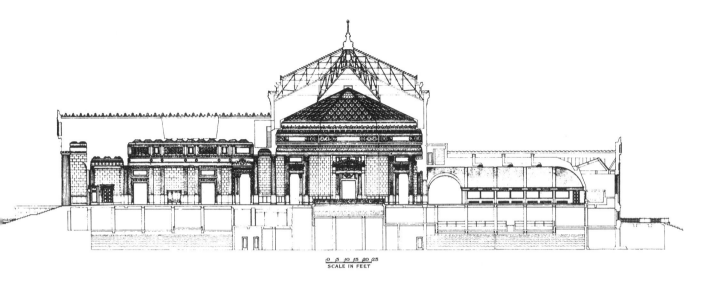

SCALE IN FEET 0 5 10 15 20 25

[13] SHEDD AQUARIUM, SECTION
The section drawing of the Shedd Aquarium reveals the progression from the broad steps of the porch to the tall entrance hall through to the lofty heights of the central dome, and then off to the dark tunnels that house the fish.

A Greek cross within an octagon within a circle, the ground plan (fig. 12) contrasts with the rectangular design of the Field Museum across South Lake Shore Drive. The rhythm of this group of buildings, the orderly progression from the temple-fronted rectangle of the Field Museum, to the temple-fronted octagon of the Shedd Aquarium, to the circle of the Adler Planetarium (Ernest A. Grunsfeld, Jr., 1931), makes a stately closure to the cultural core of the city. As cultural institutions, the buildings are at the top of the civic hierarchy, yet they are subordinated to the larger whole—the city itself. In this role they work as a cohesive link in the urban vista.

Inside the aquarium, the symmetrical plan provides a continuing sense of direction, guiding one along the architectural promenade. One moves from the Ionic marble columns of the grandly proportioned foyer to the Corinthian capitals of the climactic dome and then to the darkened corridors where the fish are exhibited (fig. 13). Throughout, a wealth of original ornament in costly materials adorns the surfaces (figs. 14, 15).

[14] SHEDD AQUARIUM, DETAIL
Bronze dolphins, turtles, starfish, and other specially designed marine animals play on the wall surfaces of the Shedd Aquarium.

[15] SHEDD AQUARIUM, FOYER
Light from the glass dome is visible from the adjacent galleries, and visitors can see it wherever they are in the exhibition tunnels. Since the galleries themselves are darkened to create an underwater atmosphere, this periodic return to the light gives a gentle rhythmic accent to a walk through the museum.

Civic Opera Building, Chicago (1927–29)

In the late 1920s, designer Alfred Shaw adapted the new motifs of the Art Deco era for the ornament of the firm's cultural buildings, but retained the underlying planning principles of the Beaux-Arts classical tradition. Chicago's Civic Opera House is masterful. Dominating the western skyline of the city, the monumental structure was conceived as an opera house–office building (fig. 16). Considerations about diluting the cultural importance of the musical institution with commercial considerations and the idea of a hierarchical order in the city were cast aside. Like many Americans of the times, the client and the architects believed that what was good for business would be good for opera.

"Big Business, Grand Opera" ran the headline in the *Economist* when Samuel Insull completed the purchase of the plot. The structure would "surpass in magnificence any similar building in this country and will compare in beauty with the famed Grand Opera House of Paris." There would be no stinting because a commercial office building was to rise on top of the auditorium. On the contrary, Chicagoans were proud that they could turn their own lusty skyscraper know-how to support the venerable musical traditions of the civilized world in the finest architectural style.[4]

The reporter was expressing the hopes of Samuel Insull and the other subscribers that the Chicago Civic Opera (unlike European opera companies) would not have to depend upon gov-

[16] CIVIC OPERA BUILDING (TWENTY WACKER DRIVE BUILDING) AND CHICAGO DAILY NEWS BUILD-
ING (HOLABIRD AND ROOT), CHICAGO, ILL.
Together with the Chicago River, these two buildings exude a sense of place and time that is quintessentially Chicago.
The terrace of the Daily News Building looks out over the river, facing the theatrical richness of the Civic Opera on
the opposite bank.

[17] CIVIC OPERA, ELEVATION

The soaring office tower gives monumental grandeur to the broad auditorium of the Civic Opera, held in the arms of the lower office wings. Sometimes compared to a throne, the structure is lavishly ornamented with musical motifs at the crown of each section.

ernment subsidies. Ultimately it would not only own its home but also profit from the rental of the offices above its stage spaces. This, indeed, was the rationale for combining two building types—the office building and the opera house. It seemed that almost all building types could be combined with a skyscraper in the world of the 1920s. It was a period when banks, churches, colleges, department stores, libraries, meeting halls, and monuments were frequently tucked into or on top of a steel-framed office building.

The site of the Civic Opera Building, also called the Twenty Wacker Drive Building, is directly across the river from the nearly contemporary Chicago Daily News Building (Holabird and Root) with its river plaza embankment. Together the two structures give the Chicago River at this location the kind of grandeur that Queen Hatshepsut's temple and the desert cliffs give the Nile at Dayr-al-Bahari (fig. 17).

The four principal parts of the Civic Opera Building stand out clearly from the riverside—the high central tower, the two wings at either end, and the protected auditorium in between. The massing inevitably invited comparisons to a chair, and the building was soon dubbed "Insull's Throne." If it recalls a throne, it is indeed a magnate's throne. At the street level, at the crown, and in its interior spaces the building is decorated with distinctive original ornament, restrained on the exterior but lavish on the interior in the Chicago manner.

The eastern elevation is distinguished by the colonnade along Wacker Drive. Seventeen bays long and thirty-five feet high, this grand entrance was designed to allow passengers from forty taxicabs to alight while the traffic signal changes on Madison Street and the policeman blows his whistle for the next block-long queue to come in.

Inside, the magnificent Grand Foyer is sumptuous (fig. 18). Lofty in its proportions (52 feet by 119 feet and 39 feet high), the room is flanked by fluted marble piers surmounted by lyre capitals decorated with gold. A frieze of stylized leaves eases the transition to the glowing rose and gold ceiling, with its geometric decorations

designed by Jules Guerin. The walls are faced with Roman travertine marble, the floors with pink and gray Tennessee marble, and all fixtures are of bronze. Broad stairways lead to a wide balcony that surrounds the foyer on three sides, and on one of these sides it becomes a broad promenade giving access to the boxes.

The auditorium is lavishly decorated in a glowing color scheme. Gold covers most of the elaborately carved surfaces with touches of a palette of subtle mixtures of cadmium red and cadmium yellow light blended with vert emeraude. On the ceiling, the rose-colored floral ornament on a soft green background is bordered with stylized leaves. As the ceiling drops, wide mouldings with open grille panels are lit by concealed indirect lighting within the deep semicircular mouldings that lead down to the next panel and to the proscenium arch. Along the sides, red and gold leaves border four descending panels, while elaborate octagonal medallions hold sunbursts of golden lyres, trumpets, and laurel leaves in high relief. The predominantly rose color scheme of these panels gives way to gold and green at the proscenium arch. Thus, the linear scheme moves toward the stage, warmed by golden colors and given additional drama by indirect lighting. Finally, the effects come together at the brilliant proscenium arch, itself a great gold frame around a thirty-five-by-fifty-foot painted curtain, also by Guerin (fig. 21). Greatly loved by all visitors, this magnificent panorama (which serves as a fire curtain) depicts characters and scenes from more than forty operas.

To walk the razor's edge between grandiose and grand, Guerin chose an intimate color scheme, raised the scale of the detail, insisted upon using rose and gold without any abrupt transitions, and specified that the colors of the carpets and all fabrics be chosen to help unify the space.

To see and be seen in this dazzling setting were strong social motives for going to the opera. For some, it offered a chance to act out a chapter in the drama of their own lives: to catch the eye of a certain gentleman or lady, or to be introduced to

[18] CIVIC OPERA, FOYER AND DETAIL

The grand proportions, sumptuous materials, magnificent colors outlined in gold, and original ornament of the brilliant foyer express the aspirations of an opera house intended to achieve international significance. The designer brought the classical pilasters up to date with the sharp edges of the Art Deco era.

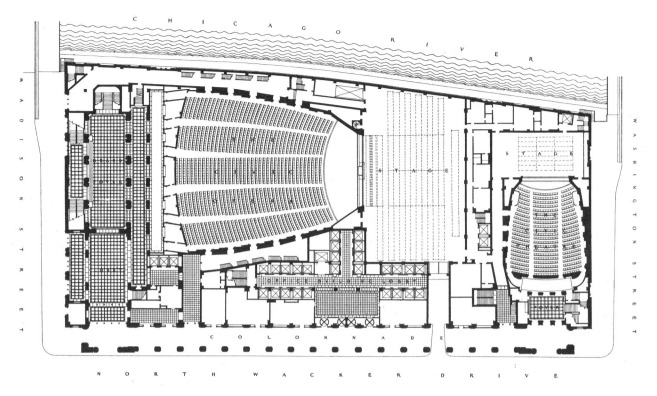

FIRST FLOOR PLAN

0 10 20 30 40 50
SCALE IN FEET

[19] CIVIC OPERA, PLAN

The plan reveals the relationship of the Civic Opera to the Civic Theatre to the north, with the office building lobby in the center.

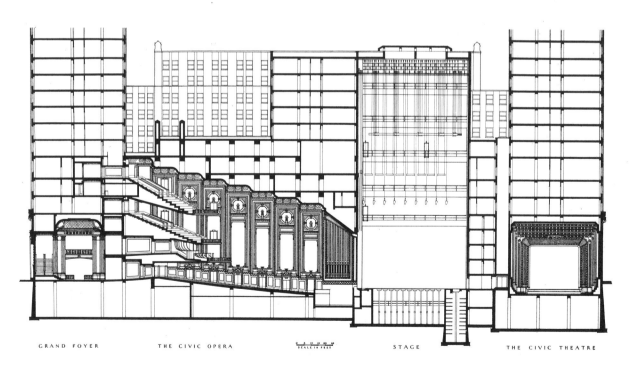

GRAND FOYER   THE CIVIC OPERA   STAGE   THE CIVIC THEATRE

0 5 10 15 20
SCALE IN FEET

[20] CIVIC OPERA, SECTION

The grand foyer, the various levels of seating, the intricate substructure of the stage, the flies above, and other thespian paraphernalia are illustrated in this section drawing. Also evident is the location of the smaller Civic Theatre and the Civic Opera under the office building.

[21] CIVIC OPERA, FIRE CURTAIN
Nowhere are Jules Guerin's gifts more apparent than in the main stage's fire curtain, with its rich, lively panorama of the world of opera—a fitting climax to the decoration of the majestic auditorium.

a powerful business or political figure, or to assert their position in the social hierarchy by sitting in the orchestra or the dress circle. Just as the architecture and its sumptuous decorations indicated the lofty position of the arts in the hierarchy of the city's values, so one's social status was indicated by where one sat at the opera. Chicagoans were quite aware that in this they were emulating the Parisians and the elites of other grand European cities.

As the prospectus put it, "In the new building will consequently be embodied the best features of the world's most renowned opera houses. At the same time the foyers, lounges and main auditoriums, while echoing the gorgeous conservatism that the best of Europe has to offer, will have a distinctive character entirely their own." [5] This

was also true of the smaller Civic Theatre in the northern portion of the building (fig. 22). With daring originality the designers synthesized classical and Art Deco motifs. The volutes of Ionic capitals become stylized lyres. The great chandeliers and the torches along the travertine marble walls of the Grand Foyer combine the jazzy frosted glass of Art Deco with classical masks in a manner that is not merely additive but a logical unification of the two styles. The whole is stately and majestic.

The most impressive of all the skyscrapers erected during the stock market boom, for its cultural institutions and its structural intricacy as much as for its architectural design, is the Civic Opera Building. . . . [It] is

[22] CIVIC OPERA, CIVIC THEATRE
Masks of comedy and tragedy, the lyre of Apollo, and other theatrical motifs adorn the Civic Theatre.

[23] CHICAGO HISTORICAL SOCIETY, CHICAGO, ILL., EASTERN ELEVATION

Walkways curve through the lawns and gardens of Lincoln Park providing a spacious setting for the Chicago Historical Society. The original main entrance faced the lake, the traditional location of the front door in all buildings situated on the water. The steps of the Georgian-style building rise to the *piano nobile,* the grand floor, which originally contained the chief ceremonial and exhibition spaces.

the leading example among large commercial buildings in Chicago of great richness of color and surface material disciplined by the geometry of plan and section (figs. 19, 20). . . . The whole intricate complex of spaces, all of it superbly planned for handling great crowds of people concentrated in short periods of time, makes it one of the skyscraper classics of America.[6]

Chicago Historical Society, Chicago (1930–32)

A more modest cultural institution, the Chicago Historical Society enhances its graceful setting in Lincoln Park on the North Side of the city. The site plan provided a landscaped plaza at the western entrance on Clark Street and a ceremonial entrance facing Augustus Saint-Gaudens's statue of Abraham Lincoln on the east (fig. 23). From here a flight of steps led up to the temple-fronted main entrance portico. The building's Georgian style recalled the traditions of colonial America and expressed its purpose as a museum. Many institutions, especially libraries and museums, adopted the Georgian style for their new buildings in the 1920s.

As a guide prepared for the opening noted, the interior spaces were laid out for a specific purpose (fig. 24):

The new building of the Chicago Historical Society has been designed to depict by means of period rooms the chronological history of the United States from the days of Columbus to the present time. It is probably the first attempt of an historical museum to do this sort of thing. If we succeed in thus presenting history dramatically before the people of Chicago, we shall have made one of the greatest steps forward in the field of visual education and historical museum technique that has been made for many years.[7]

Coming through the park and arriving at the Chicago Historical Society on the east, the visitor ascended the broad staircase that led up to the *piano nobile,* or "noble floor." Enhancing the grand sense of entrance, Foyer Hall (fig. 25) is a careful reproduction of the foyer in Independence Hall in Philadelphia (Andrew Hamilton, 1732–41), except that in Chicago the two archways on either side were left open according to an earlier plan of 1729. With its arched openings,

between fluted Roman Doric columns, the Palladian design of the interior culminates in the Doric frieze at the top, where the sparkling crystals of the chandeliers illuminate the circular medallions on the ceiling. The classical Beaux-Arts "architectural promenade" began in the dramatic vestibule. It was a walk through history.

From the Spanish Exploration Room in the south, to the French Alcove, and on to the British Colonial Room, the various periods of American history were represented with typical interiors and artifacts of each era. The Washington Room, New Republic Room, Civil War rooms, and exhibitions devoted to Chicago's history filled the spaces. A reading room, library, the stacks, and offices took up the top floor.

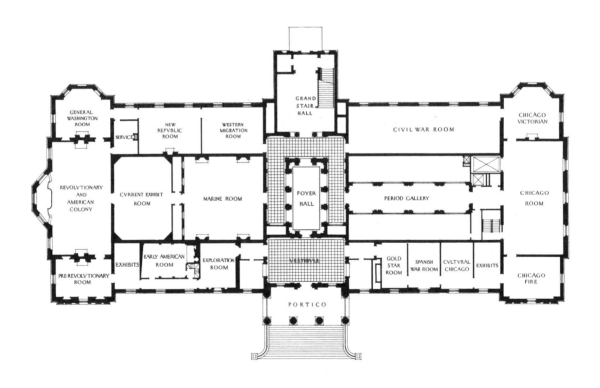

FIRST FLOOR PLAN

SCALE IN FEET

[24] CHICAGO HISTORICAL SOCIETY, PLAN
The plan indicates the original circulation pattern from the east plaza up to the covered portico and then to the vestibule, the foyer, and beyond. The symmetrical placement of the galleries invited people to walk through the history of America from colonial times to the present.

[25] CHICAGO HISTORICAL SOCIETY, FOYER
The stately dadoes, graceful columns, and ornament in the foyer were inspired by Independence Hall in Philadelphia.

United States Mail Building, Chicago (1921)

Seven years after finishing work on the post office in Washington, the firm began the United States Mail Building in Chicago.[8] Because it was not in the capital and functioned primarily as a sorting depot, an adjunct to the main post office in the Loop, the Mail Building was lower in the hierarchy. Its only formal entrance served the public at its eastern end. Embellished with four Doric columns, which formed a giant order embracing the first two stories, this facade also had a frieze, decorative spandrel panels, and a cornice with a flagpole on the top (fig. 26). The two long sides, on the other hand, were utilitarian in character, similar to the loft buildings in the vicinity, and appropriate to their use as portals for mail trucks along the entire 700-foot length at the street level.

[26] UNITED STATES MAIL BUILDING, CHICAGO, ILL., ELEVATION
Reserved for package mail only and located in the southwest part of the city, the U.S. Mail Building in Chicago was not a major public building. But even buildings at a lower level in the hierarchy were accorded the dignity of a strong entrance portal, a tripartite division, and original sculpture.

[27] FEDERAL RESERVE BANK OF KANSAS CITY, OMAHA BRANCH, OMAHA, NEBR., EXTERIOR
A small treasure chest, the Omaha Federal Reserve Bank combines sturdy proportions with the elegant arched windows of its two-story public Banking Room.

Federal Reserve Banks

In the 1920s, the firm designed seven banks for the Federal Reserve System. Seeking to continue the successful model set under Burnham's aegis,

> it was a happy thought of the architects to transplant from the medieval city of Siena a palace of the Piccolomini family to the modern city of iron and steel. . . . This palace combines beauty with strength, and is, therefore an appropriate prototype for a modern bank building in which these ideas predominate. The architects have improved on the ancient palace, note the treatment of the long windows which form a conspicuous feature of the new building.[9]

Federal Reserve Bank of Kansas City, Omaha (1925)

Every small Federal Reserve bank of the 1920s that the firm designed follows this Italian Renaissance prototype. Although each was different, the Omaha Branch of the Federal Reserve Bank of Kansas City may be regarded as typical. The deeply raked joints of the base serve to set it off from the smooth masonry of the second floor, which is treated as a *piano nobile* housing the great arched windows of the Banking Room (fig. 27). Marble pilasters with Corinthian capitals articulate the public spaces, which are decorated with luxurious materials and elaborate ornament everywhere—in the brass fixtures, the brackets supporting the balconies, the doorways, and the tellers' cages. Thus, symbols of beauty and strength borrowed from the European aristocracy lent status to public bank buildings in the American republic of the early twentieth century.

Federal Reserve Banks of Chicago and Kansas City (1919–21)

Two similar Federal Reserve banks in Chicago and Kansas City (fig. 28) combine banking functions with office buildings. In the opening-day brochure issued by the Kansas City bank we can read between the lines and see the architects and client struggling to assert the high status of the Federal Reserve Bank, despite its incorporation into an office building.

> The architectural treatment . . . was chosen with a view to producing in this building an effect such that the passerby, including the youngest school boy, would realize in viewing the building that here stands a building representing something bigger and greater than an ordinary commercial institution.[10]

Henry Hering added the following explanation in his account of the allegorical figures he sculpted for the bank.

> Industry holds in her hands a sheaf of wheat and a distaff representing respectively the industries of the soil and manufacture. Over her head is the beehive of indefatigable industry against a background showing the sun casting its rays over the universe. Commerce wears a coat of mail signifying security. She bears in either hand the torch of progress and the caduceus of Mercury, god of Commerce. Above her head is the ship of Transportation, against a background of stars and the moon.[11]

Embellished with these allegorical figures, the bank took its place as a national institution at the top of the hierarchy of buildings in Kansas City—or at least that was the intention. The office building portion above the bank premises was also given added distinction: each story is

[28] FEDERAL RESERVE BANK OF KANSAS CITY, KANSAS CITY, MO., ELEVATION
On the exterior, the Federal Reserve Bank of Kansas City is a tall office building, distinguished from commercial structures by the heights of its floors and the symbolic references embodied in its sculpture.

higher than the average floor in an ordinary commercial office building, so that although it is only sixteen stories high, it looks like a twenty-two-story building. At the time of its erection, it was the highest structure for miles around.

It is clear that both architects and clients had to deal with economic pressures that made it necessary to disregard the traditional hierarchy to some extent in order to subsidize the less profitable civic or cultural buildings by adding commercial space. To ensure the superior status of these mixed-use buildings within the city, architects adapted the kind of approach evident in Graham, Anderson, Probst and White's Kansas City bank building: they increased the height of the buildings, and they added elaborate sculptural programs. Similar modifications were made in the Federal Reserve Bank Building in Chicago.

By the late 1920s, the fading of the notion of architectural hierarchy in civic life and the increasing domination of the commercial over the cultural and the civic were reflected in architectural projects throughout the country. In Graham, Anderson, Probst and White's buildings of the period, we see this process in microcosm. Mainstream firms were likely to adhere longer than others to the idea that hierarchy should be preserved, especially at the highest levels, and so we see the canons of tradition prevailing more strongly in Graham, Anderson, Probst and White's designs than elsewhere. By the end of the decade, however, the importance accorded both cultural institutions and public buildings was eclipsed by the larger role assumed by commercial institutions.

JOINT PUBLIC-PRIVATE BUILDINGS AND SPACES

Railroad Stations

By 1900, railroad stations had earned a position just under civic and cultural institutions in the urban hierarchy. Having first merely provided spaces for passengers in transit, stations had gradually attained more cultural value in American life and had become focal points for the expression of civic and personal values. The nerve centers of the country's continental transportation system, they also acted as the interface between that system and the local and suburban

systems of the various cities they served. By providing connections to other railways, as well as to riverside docks, underground freight passageways, and taxicabs, streets, and sidewalks, railroad stations knit the different systems together into a complex working unit. Often they served as catalysts for the economic development of the surrounding area and as a means to complete key elements of an overall city plan. Nearly all of the large terminals constructed by Graham, Anderson, Probst and White had significant long-range effects on the economic life of the cities they served.[12]

Two of the four most influential designs in the development of the American railroad station had stemmed from the office of Daniel H. Burnham—the Terminal Station at the World's Columbian Exposition of 1893, designed by Charles Atwood, and Union Station in Washington, D.C., designed by Peirce Anderson (1903–7) while the firm was still under Burnham's name. The other two were New York's Pennsylvania Station (1902–11) and Grand Central Terminal (1903–13).[13] American architects were strongly influenced by these structures, and the many major terminals that followed showed their influence. Later designers adapted and modified the archetypes to take advantage of new developments in technology and to meet new demands arising from the increasingly important role that stations played in the changing fabric of large cities. Peirce Anderson himself showed remarkable growth in this process, as his work in Union Station in Chicago (1913–25) shows. Two later examples in the firm's work illustrate this continuing evolution—the Cleveland Terminal Station, designed partially by Anderson, and the Thirtieth Street Station in Philadelphia, designed by Alfred Shaw.

Masterful works of architecture, these stations exemplify the hierarchical planning tradition of the École des Beaux-Arts where Peirce Anderson had studied. The ordering of new (and often vast) ensembles of buildings into the city fabric was part of the French tradition of the nineteenth century, and Anderson absorbed the lessons of the built environment around him. In his student days, he had seen dozens of projects by his fellow students and visited several built complexes. Not far from his room in Paris were Victor Baltard's Halles Central (1845–70, demolished in 1973, commonly called Les Halles), the Gare d'Orsay (1897–1900) of Victor Laloux, and Louis Duc's Palais de Justice (1852–69). Duc's building, for example, made a unified urban unit out of a scattered area by filling out the site between the Place Dauphine, the Boulevard du Palais, and the banks of the Île de la Cité and by including many existing older buildings in a new context. Also, when Anderson arrived in Chicago in 1899, the memory of the Terminal Station at the 1893 World's Columbian Exposition was still vivid in the minds of his new midwestern colleagues.[14]

In 1902, Burnham was selected as a member of the four-man commission to revise and expand Pierre L'Enfant's 1792 plan for Washington, D.C. A document in the Graham, Anderson, Probst and White archives describes the role the architects envisioned for the station and its forecourt in integrating the railroads with the city itself. "Through these converging avenues large bodies of people can leave or enter the station without difficulty, while the plaza, with ample space for massing troops and spectators, affords adequate space for those public ceremonials that take place in front of the gateway of a city."[15]

Washington's Union Station was designed in a period when nearly everyone arrived by train, and when the station was finished, the character of the nation's capital changed—physically, kinetically, and symbolically. Graham and Anderson would go on using the railroad station complex to serve a variety of urban purposes: as an entrance symbol, as part of a larger transportation network, and as a visual link between the gateway to the city and the city itself.

Union Station, Chicago (1913–25)

When Burnham died in 1912, one of the jobs at hand was to work with the Chicago Plan Commission on the city's new Union Station. The Enabling Ordinance, passed nearly two years later

on March 23, 1914, embodies the results of many meetings involving architects, railroad men, and government representatives. In accord with the spirit of the Plan of Chicago of 1909, the group agreed on restructuring a thirty-five-acre complex of streets, bridges, and other public works to create a new west-side area. To accomplish the work the railroads spent $75 million in the next nine years, and the municipal and federal governments spent the same amount, for a total of $150 million.[16]

Private interests were partly motivated by the prospect of improved real estate values in the ad-

[29] CHICAGO UNION STATION, CHICAGO, ILL., ELEVATION
Open and generous, the broad expanses of windows and the airy colonnades of Union Station in Chicago greet people moving from taxis to trains. In the 1920s, the station also marked the edge of the commercial city and the beginning of the industrial city along the west bank of the Chicago River.

jacent area. Everyone was dazzled by the profits New York developers had enjoyed in land and building speculation on Park Avenue after the completion of Grand Central Terminal (Reed and Stem; Warren and Wetmore, 1903–13). Since the Chicago and North Western Station (Frost and Granger, 1906–11) two blocks to the north of Union Station was already in use, many Chicagoans hoped that the West Side of Chicago would experience a similar boom when plans for Union Station reached their final development in the early 1920s.[17] Knowledgeable Chicagoans were aware that other planned urban areas with amenities at the street level, like the arcades along the Rue de Rivoli in Paris, or the sculptural decoration in plazas like the Piazza Navona in Rome, assured a long and profitable economic life for nearby landowners and tenants. Both the architects and the clients responded to these favorable circumstances.

The Chicago Union Station does not have the obvious organic relationship to the city plan that Washington's Union Station has, situated as the latter is at the edge of a park to the north of the Capitol. Nevertheless, the present infrastructure of the surrounding bridges and streets is evidence that even if its forms were not exactly the same as indicated in the Chicago Plan, the Chicago Union Station contributed to the completion of the Plan in spirit. Initially the station had been envisioned as a connecting element between the riverfront and government buildings to be erected on Congress and Halsted streets, but Burnham never intended that the Plan of Chicago be followed in every detail. The station's new role in providing a key focus along the west bank of the Chicago

River may be viewed as a kind of transplant within the same organic whole of Burnham's vision. (fig. 29).

World War I interrupted work on the station. When construction recommenced, the architectural profession faced new problems, not in designing and engineering but in meeting new economic and organizational demands. The Experience Exchange of the National Association of Building Owners and Managers, a recently formed professional organization, brought pressures for economy and efficiency. The 1920 design for Union Station indicates Anderson's response.

He suggested that a twenty-story office building in the form of an open rectangle rise around the rectangle surrounding the Headhouse. Tenants in the upper stories would provide income and also help upgrade the area by ensuring steady occupancy in the years ahead. The station itself retained the time-honored signs of railroad travel—the portal with a semicircular or lunette window indicating the Concourse (fig. 30) and a colonnade leading to the Waiting Room, an urban amenity that graces the street to this day. (The main building was built only to the fifth story, and the Concourse Building was later demolished.)

The trilevel design was ingenious (fig. 33). This was the first large station where passengers and baggage were handled separately. Travelers left their vehicles at the street level and took stairs down to the main level while porters carried their baggage down to the third or lowest level. Walkways to the trains and the river adjoined the baggage platform. Chauffeured Parmalee Company limousines met people arriving at all stations. Other connections to public transportation lines were close by, and there were broad sidewalks. In addition, U-shaped internal drives, the first of

[30] CHICAGO UNION STATION, CONCOURSE EXTERIOR
An end in itself as well as part of a larger whole, the Concourse was a symbolic entrance to the city—like a triumphal arch. This part of the complex was demolished in the 1970s.

[31] CHICAGO UNION STATION, WAITING ROOM
Columns, arches, vaults, grand proportions, and luxurious materials proclaim the Waiting Room as a place appropriate for both public and personal occasions of note.

their kind, gave trucks, taxicabs, and other vehicles space in which to unload and turn around without crowding the city streets. There were connections to small-gauge railroad tunnels for moving freight to warehouses and stores in the Loop. The station's other important feature was its double stub-end plan, which made it possible for trains to move in both directions at both ends.

Once in the middle level of the station, patrons could move about with ease from the moment they bought their tickets, and on through the experiences of dining, buying a book or magazine, waiting to board, and walking to the trains. To express the technological precision of the railroads, the architects used unadorned steel-truss columns where the passengers met the locomotives—in the Concourse (fig. 32). All the

rooms in this efficient layout were of grand proportions and executed in lavish materials. One entered the lofty, arched Waiting Room through composite columns embellished with glowing volutes and acanthus leaves (fig. 31). Below, rows of brass lamps decorated with vines and birds showed Anderson's taste for elegant architectural detail. Henry Hering's sculptural figures and Jules Guerin's color scheme of rose, ivory, and gold further enriched the design. Station spaces were often the setting for communal and personal rites of passage, such as greeting visiting dignitaries at an inauguration or leaving home. The architects expressed this symbolic role through the Beaux-Arts classical style and by means of materials like marble, travertine, limestone, and granite that conveyed a sense of importance.

[32] CHICAGO UNION STATION, CONCOURSE INTERIOR
Efficiency and speed emboldened the spirit of train travelers in the 1920s. Exposed steel trusses highlighted the technological drama of that moment when the passengers climbed aboard.

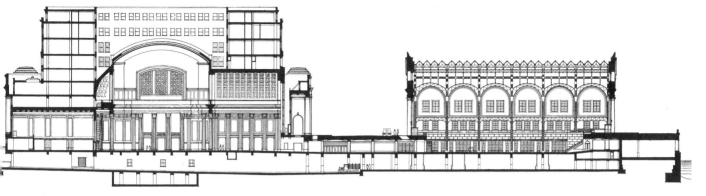

MAIN HEADHOVSE AND WAITING ROOM   MAIN CONCOVRSE

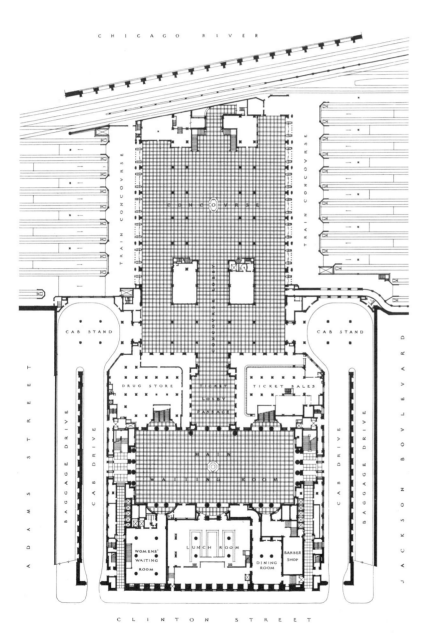

[33] CHICAGO UNION STATION,
SECTION AND PLAN

It is in the plan and section of
Union Station that we see the logical arrangement of the spaces—
places for buying a ticket or a newspaper, having a meal, reading while
waiting for the train, going to the
drugstore or the barbershop, or visiting the chapel. Various kinds of
traffic were clearly separated from
one another. Taxis and trucks entered at the sides without interfering with city vehicles; baggage went
down to the lowest level; all the
traveler's needs could be satisfied
on the same floor.

Cleveland Terminal Group (1917–30)

What did the firm do in a different city, in Cleveland? Chicago and Cleveland had many things in common. Both cities where transfer points for railroad and Great Lakes traffic, and were manufacturing centers as well. At the turn of the century, Cleveland also had a confusing tangle of tracks. Daniel H. Burnham and others had been called in to devise a plan for the area along the lakefront and extending into the core of the city. The resulting Group Plan of 1903 called for public buildings around and adjacent to a mall crowned by a unifying station on the lakefront.

The ensuing story is complex, but ultimately two Cleveland businessmen who were trying to develop the suburban community of Shaker Heights—Oris Paxton Van Sweringen and his brother Mantis James Van Sweringen—persuaded their fellow citizens to abandon the Group Plan and to build a station on Public Square instead to connect with the rapid transit lines to the suburbs.[18]

The earliest (1919) proposal (fig. 34) has a taut coherence; each part is an end in itself, yet it is subordinate to the larger whole. The separate functions of the different parts are made clear by the architectural imagery. Arched windows express the grand lobby space of a hotel. Prominent display windows at the sidewalk level on the other side proclaim the department store, and the triumphal arches and clock at the center unmistakably say "railroad station—gateway to the city." The grid of windows above indicates an office building.

The railroad station and its adjacent parts form a microcity, like Grand Central Terminal in New York, but since the Cleveland complex ultimately encompassed nine buildings, and more were planned, it is clear that it was conceived as an urban group. Anderson's design, published January 6, 1919, in the *Cleveland Plain Dealer*, establishes a claim that the Cleveland Terminal Group was the first of this new version of the urban group, which had fallen into neglect in a period of increasingly high individual skyscrapers.

It came before Eliel Saarinen's 1923 plan for the center of Chicago, before Benjamin Wistar Morris's proposal for an opera complex in New York a few years later, and well before work on Rockefeller Center was begun.

Local citizens were well aware of the thinking behind the plans. On November 19, 1928, when the Chamber of Commerce moved into its new quarters in the Terminal Tower, the *Cleveland Plain Dealer* published the plans for what it called the "Vans' Super-City." From the vantage point of the 1990s, the cluster of nine buildings on Public Square with its connections to local, suburban, and national transportation systems in a seventeen-acre complex with links to the existing park on Public Square, had all the characteristics of a modern urban group. Conservative only stylistically, in every other respect the complex was ahead of its time (figs. 35, 36, 37).

Many changes in the city accompanied the new station, including the erection of a mile-long bridge, the reworking of the existing street plan, and the building of several viaducts to raise the level of the station on the sloping site to be contiguous with the streets in the business district.[19]

Urban groups were not new in the history of architecture, for they had evolved from classical cities in a great variety of forms throughout European history and included the Court of Honor at the 1893 World's Columbian Exposition in Chicago. But this was a new form of the old archetype, following a temporary abandonment of the concept in the early twentieth century by architects preoccupied with erecting individual towers of ever-greater height. As Henry-Russell Hitchcock noted, for a time verticalism had eclipsed the urban group. "The second skyscraper age came to a belated close with the erection of the Empire State Building" (1929–31). Just at the time a new approach was being seen in Rockefeller Center, "a more urbanistic grouping . . . replaced the earlier ideal of building single structures of ever greater height."[20]

What is startling about the Cleveland group in the context of the firm's designs is that after Anderson's death, Graham and his clients added

[34] CLEVELAND TERMINAL GROUP, CLEVELAND, OHIO, PROPOSAL
Peirce Anderson's Hotel Cleveland on the right was the starting point for this urbane complex proposed in 1919 that focused on the railroad station in the center, but also included a department store (on the left), and offices.

a fifty-two-story tower to the original low-rise scheme. To them an urban group with a sky-scraper seemed like a natural focal point for the city's skyline, and the logical place for it was right above the hub of the city's transportation system, the railroad station. It was partly the clients' decision, of course, and the Van Sweringens announced to the public on Valentine's Day 1925 that the new tower would be "the land-mark of Cleveland like the Woolworth Building in New York."[21] In subsequent years the Termi-nal Tower did in fact become the civic symbol of Cleveland, fulfilling the promise of its owners.

We can look at this in several ways. A rail-road station was once a building for private use. With increased government intervention and fi-nancing it became a joint public-private building and thus at the second highest level of the urban hierarchy. When the Cleveland Terminal Group became the symbol of the city it took on some of the functions formerly reserved for religious or civic buildings. Does it then ascend to the highest level? Or, conversely, does the hybridization with a lower-level form, an office building, demote the status of the railroad station? The answer cannot be a little of each; rather the answer is that the idea of hierarchy was giving way.

[35] CLEVELAND TERMINAL
GROUP, ELEVATION
A gateway to a commercial midwestern city in the railway age, the
Terminal Tower soon became the
symbol of Cleveland to that city's
inhabitants. The soaring tower was
added and the entrance portal expanded in this final version of the
design.

[36] CLEVELAND TERMINAL, CONCOURSE
Gleaming marbles reflected the sunshine streaming through the arched vaulted skylight of the Concourse.

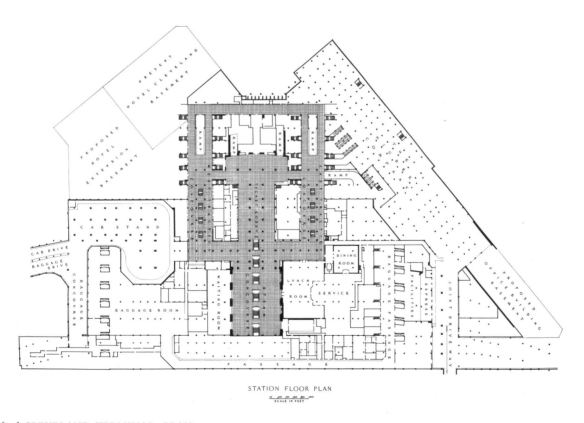

STATION FLOOR PLAN
SCALE IN FEET

[37] CLEVELAND TERMINAL, PLAN
The railroad station itself was a model of efficiency. Connections were provided to taxicabs, to the Cleveland rapid transit system, and to the Hotel Cleveland. The routes to the transit lines' concourses were laid out in an open square. This was intersected by a broad rectangle containing the train Concourse and leading to the Waiting Room and dining and baggage facilities.

Thirtieth Street Station, Philadelphia (1927–34)

As we have seen, complex motives were involved in the erection of railroad stations, and the Pennsylvania Railroad station at Thirtieth Street in Philadelphia is no exception. Its arches symbolized a civic entrance to the old city to the east, but were also envisioned as a link and a gateway to the expanded city across the river to the west. Connected to the widened Pennsylvania Boulevard (now John F. Kennedy Boulevard) by a plaza, the station thus faced the main route to the Broad Street Suburban Station (One Penn Center

at Suburban Station) under an Art Deco office building (also designed by the firm). Envisioned as forerunners of further commercial development, the two stations were part of a complex plan of related city improvements, including riverfront beautification and new, wider streets, plazas, and thoroughfares from different sections of the city, all joined to the electric suburban lines.

The aerial view shows the architect's early conception of this future development in Philadelphia (fig. 38). Alfred Shaw, chief designer for Graham, Anderson, Probst and White after Peirce Anderson's death, gave the central portion a crisp classical entrance, and the wings, stripped pilasters (fig. 39). Adaptations of certain features of the late 1920s, such as simplified rectilinear piers and sharp verticals, were used as decorative motifs, but the planning department of the firm, under the direction of Sigurd Naess, continued to use Beaux-Arts principles for the disposition of the space. Since a five-story office building was wrapped around, and not above, the station, and since there was a smaller volume of traffic in Philadelphia than in Chicago, the two architects were free to combine the Concourse and the Waiting Room into one monumental room (fig. 40). With the Burnham tradition behind them, and the Pennsylvania Railroad's preference for large-scale design, they drew up a vast space supported by columns. It enclosed more cubic feet

[38] PENNSYLVANIA BOULEVARD DEVELOPMENT PROPOSAL, PHILADELPHIA, PA.
Two stations for the Pennsylvania Railroad gave the architects an opportunity to further a related boulevard development. The Thirtieth Street Station forms one corner of a central urban triangle which has City Hall as its apex. Near the angle formed by John F. Kennedy and Benjamin Franklin boulevards is the Suburban Station. Logan Circle, midway along the second arm, was already in place on the route which ends at the Philadelphia Art Museum. A scenic drive along the Schuylkill River completed the surface beautification scheme. Underneath, a complex network connected the various levels of transportation.

[39] THIRTIETH STREET STATION, PHILADELPHIA, PA., ELEVATION
Like a resounding chord, six Corinthian columns and two broad spreading wings proclaim Philadelphia's time-honored status and mark the culmination of John F. Kennedy Boulevard (formerly Pennsylvania Boulevard) at the Thirtieth Street Station.

than the Waiting Room in Pennsylvania Station in New York and was decorated lavishly with marble.[22]

The Waiting Room combined with the Concourse (still in use) is 639 feet by 327 feet in area and 116 feet high. The ends are dominated by six great columns and banks of windows with walkways in between, emulating Grand Central in New York. Rays of sunlight stream in on the north and south, and nubbed glass diffuses the light. The interior has a grandeur and radiance that passengers still remark on with great feeling, attesting to the role the space has played in their communal identities and personal lives.

Although the areas around Union Station in Chicago, the Cleveland Terminal Group, and the Thirtieth Street Station in Philadelphia may not have been realized in full as the architects hoped, the larger intention behind each has in some measure persisted and influenced the subsequent history of each city. In the 1920s, the Chicago Union Station was seen as a gateway to a "south central city" development, and in the 1980s, rehabilitation and new construction at the eastern edge of the station complex has seen the fulfillment of part of this vision. Plans for a "tower city" on the other side of the Cleveland Station have been part of a large-scale effort there to develop the riverfront and to "save the urban group." In Philadelphia, the boulevard scheme was finally developed in the 1950s and 1960s.

It is clear that the railroad station played a vital role in urban development in the United States. In dealing with the underlying issues, the architects, engineers, government officials, and railroad managers faced some serious questions. The railroad station was both public and private; it had a role to play in the hierarchical ordering of the city; and it was a structure that was both useful and ceremonial. Graham, Anderson, and the others involved in the construction of railroad stations believed that not only must stations

[40] THIRTIETH STREET STATION, WAITING ROOM
The vast windows admitting streaming sunlight and the luxurious materials of the Waiting Room express the important missions fulfilled by train travel, whether undertaken for economic, cultural, or personal reasons.

play a role in completing the national transportation networks of which they were a part, they must also provide an interface with local transportation systems. Beyond this, the railroad station must express communal values with a monumental setting appropriate both to the civic functions it honors and to the personal rites of passage it symbolizes.

The architects gave expression to the ceremonial importance people placed on travel by train in the 1920s. Whether one arrived in a city to conduct government or business negotiations, or for such personal reasons as the wedding of a family member, or the funeral of an old friend, the spaciousness of the railroad station provided an appropriately grand setting for one's arrival and departure. Over the years, the buildings, streets, bridges, and small parks or squares erected in this spirit may have suffered from neglect, misinterpretation, and abuse, but the vision of a hierarchically ordered city embodied in the railroad station, both technically up-to-date and culturally meaningful, has persisted.

PRIVATE BANKS, CORPORATE OFFICE BUILDINGS, AND DEPARTMENT STORES

Over the course of thirty years, from the death of Daniel H. Burnham in 1912 to the death of Edward Probst in 1942, Graham, Anderson, Probst and White built more than forty large office buildings and eleven major department stores. In a period when big business radically altered the fabric of American society, architects had to meet new demands from clients and respond to escalating social and economic pressures. Developing new images to rise to the challenges of corporate advertising, the firm put together a repertoire of various styles. But style is just a surface matter. It is never the sole or even the most important issue in architecture. In all other aspects of their art, in the planning of spaces, the selection of materials, and the supervision of construction, the architects continued to draw from the classical tradition. It continued to serve them well in spite of pressures for more lucrative floor-area ratios, taller buildings, and other cost-cutting measures.

All of the firm's office buildings designed during the three decades after 1912 are tripartite in their horizontal divisions. Each building has a beginning, middle, and end—a base, shaft, and capital in classical terms. Ornament of some kind, usually classical, articulates and adorns every structure. Giant orders are often used to unite the lower two stories, and giant pilasters at the top bring harmony and a sense of completion to the ensemble. Durable materials at the base, such as granite and limestone, frequently give way to terra-cotta on the upper stories, where ornament is sometimes also presented in a lighter vein with more delicate mouldings. In the middle section, or "shaft," the even rhythm of the windows and repetitive detail indicate the warren of tenant spaces within.

Consistent in plan and section, the buildings' lower stories are usually given over to public spaces underneath a central light court; the upper stories to private clubs, board of directors' headquarters, and meeting rooms; and the remaining middle stories to rental offices. In practices going back to Burnham's days, an office building was itself hierarchically ordered, and places in the hierarchy were distinguished by changes in materials and amounts of detail. Pride of position was given to the great public lobbies, or banking rooms, which were lavish in proportions, materials, and original detailing. Club spaces for executives at the top of the building were smaller, but adorned with wood-paneled walls and carefully chosen fixtures. In the middle, in the office rental section, double-loaded corridors were wainscoted in Vermont or Tennessee marble, not in the imported marbles of the lobbies; the doorways were oak, not mahogany; mouldings were simple; and the stair railings were cast iron. Every step in the scale had its appropriate accoutrements. Just as one expects to find damask tablecloths, fine porcelain, fresh flowers, and original artwork in a three-star continental restaurant, but cotton, china, a rose, and a print or two in a one-star inn, and bare tables, armless chairs, and do-it-yourself oil and vinegar at a bistro, one knows what one will find and where in any one of the buildings designed by Graham, Anderson, Probst and White.

Honoring the traditions of architecture, the firm's architects respected the way in which aesthetic and practical considerations had been worked out over a period of time. Polished granite looked appropriate for the base of a tall, block office building; figuratively it expressed sturdiness, literally it threw off stains from mud splashes and withstood years of ground-level scuffing. Although this was just one of countless aspects of the building art that members of the firm inherited from the past, learned in school, or observed on travels or during apprentice years, there were many others.

The architects did not, however, rely solely on traditional solutions. New ordinances regarding height limits or building codes, new developments in technology, a client's change in fortune, the addition of a talented young designer to the staff, a major shift in public taste, different climatic conditions, or plain do-it-better-next-time intentions all contributed to change in the firm's designs. The buildings discussed below will illustrate the course of this development and reveal the architects' creative responses to new pressures, as well as their continued reliance on many features of their traditional practice.

*Insurance Exchange Building (1911–12);
Illinois Merchants Bank Building (1920–24;
now Continental Illinois Bank and Trust
Company); Federal Reserve Bank of Chicago
(1920–22), Chicago*

Comparing the Insurance Exchange in Chicago with its near contemporary, the Equitable Building in New York, one is struck by the rightness of the former for its place in the urban fabric of Chicago as opposed to the Equitable's somewhat awkward relationship to its site in New York. In Chicago, the conservative building codes and the Plan of Chicago tradition of a cohesive city (with uniform cornice lines and sites filled to the lotlines with flat-roofed rectangular buildings) was coupled with a general preference for a tripartite division in a building. These factors gave unity to the urban context, and since many of the already existing buildings were designed by Burnham and his followers, or other architects who shared his vision, the Insurance Exchange harmonized with the surrounding buildings in every respect (fig. 41). Its pedestrian level window-colonnade and cornice height conformed to the scheme as nearly as the parade of businessmen in their similar three-piece suits conformed to each other. The interior court was like an enclosed urban plaza (fig. 42).

Two buildings a block away from the Insurance Exchange, the Federal Reserve Bank and the Illinois Merchants Bank (now the Continental Illinois Bank and Trust Company), occupy unique places in the city plan. The Chicago Loop is generally an unmitigated grid, but at its junction with Jackson Boulevard, LaSalle Street stops and shifts half a block to the east, creating a dramatic spot for a closure to the vista of the street as viewed from the river to the north.

The old Board of Trade Building originally occupying the site was destined for demolition, and when Anderson designed the two buildings on the northern corners of the intersection he envisioned a new Board of Trade also along the usual tripartite lines of the firm's work. The three buildings together, he must have thought, would provide a fitting crown to Chicago's financial district (fig. 43). To Anderson, the two banks at the end of LaSalle Street were subordinate parts of a larger urban whole that culminated in the Board of Trade. In the end, Holabird and Root won the commission for the new Board of Trade in 1929, and Anderson's dream was only partially realized.[23]

To Peirce Anderson, a door relates to an entrance, which relates to the scale of the whole building as the building relates to its larger setting. Accordingly, Anderson's buildings met LaSalle Street with pedimented entrances, uniform cornice lines, and flat roofs—a way of expressing their penultimate status just before the grand climax at the closure of the long vista. To the sides, on Jackson Boulevard, the buildings were endowed with long colonnades to meet the sidewalks along the streets to the east and the west (fig. 45). Anderson's goal was for these buildings to be "part of" rather than to stand "apart from" the city, as shown in the exterior of the Illinois Merchants Bank Building (fig. 44).

Although the exteriors were restrained in a similar manner, the interiors of the two banks were remarkably different. The Federal Reserve Banking Room is sedate, severe, and somewhat overbearing, but the Illinois Merchants Bank Banking Room is in an elegant *piano nobile*, a hall 167 feet wide, 200 feet long, and 53 feet tall. The mature design of this great interior is revealed by the carefully scaled relationships of the parts that break it down gradually to human scale: balconies, columns, railings, mouldings, lamps, and furniture. Warmth suffuses the whole, from the rosy, painted frieze by Jules Guerin to the colors of the imported marbles (fig. 46).

Going to the bank was a ceremonial occasion in those more formal days when ladies always

[41] INSURANCE EXCHANGE BUILDING, CHICAGO, ILL., ELEVATION
The Insurance Exchange in Chicago meets the street with an urbane combination of shop windows and a colonnade.

[42] INSURANCE EXCHANGE,
ATRIUM
The atrium, bordered by restaurants and small shops and illuminated by a skylight, serves as a lively meeting place for shoppers and office workers at all hours of the day.

[43] BOARD OF TRADE
BUILDING, CHICAGO, ILL.,
PROPOSAL
Had the firm won the commission for the Board of Trade Building, its vision for the hub of Chicago's financial district on South LaSalle Street would have been fulfilled. Just across Jackson Boulevard from the Illinois Merchants Bank (Continental Illinois Bank and Trust Company) on the northeast corner and from the Federal Reserve Bank of Chicago on the northwest corner, the Board of Trade Building illustrated here would have completed the trio of Beaux-Arts buildings. The two "side" buildings had flat roofs, but the main building would have been topped by a circular temple on a pedestal rising four stories higher.

[44] ILLINOIS MERCHANTS BANK BUILDING (CONTINENTAL ILLINOIS BANK AND TRUST COMPANY) CHICAGO, ILL., EXTERIOR

Colonnades along both LaSalle Street and Jackson Boulevard relate this bank building to the streets of the banking district, as the tripartite division, flat roof, and classical ornament unite the building with the other structures in the center of the city.

[45] ILLINOIS MERCHANTS BANK, DETAIL
Orthodox in their classicism, the Ionic capitals of the colonnade are topped by a continuous frieze.

wore hats and gloves and gentlemen donned waistcoats and gold watchchains. The architects provided an appropriately reassuring setting for transactions that were seen as the foundation of the whole economy. The iconographic theme for the murals in the Merchants Bank was "the general commercial activity of the international community." Holland holds a basket of tulip bulbs, England a great ocean liner, and Russia the fur pelt of an animal. The quotations separating the allegorical paintings are supposed to convey "finance in epigram"; for example, "Private credit is wealth, public honor is security—Junius" or "A fertile soil, with industry and easy transportation for men and things from place to place, make a nation strong and great—Bacon."

In addition to these expressions of the iconography of the building's program, the Ionic columns suggest strength, the lavish materials wealth, the vast spaces power, and the classical vocabulary an international exchange of art and architecture. Other bank-office buildings by the firm were like other denominations of the same currency. In office buildings that were not connected with banks, the firm emphasized the public lobby instead of the banking room. One of the best examples is the Conway Building.

Although the long tree-lined avenues of ivory buildings with a uniform cornice line that Burnham, Graham, Anderson, and the others envisioned did not materialize even years after the publication of the *Plan of Chicago* in 1909, the Insurance Exchange and the two banks were conceived as building blocks of that grand design. They exist today as a living embodiment of the older ideal.

[46] ILLINOIS MERCHANTS BANK, BANKING ROOM
Bankers of this period wanted to be seen as cultivated men of affairs. Paintings and learned quotations along the top of the Banking Room were added for the pleasure of the entrepreneur with a taste for the finer things in life.

David Whitney Building, Detroit (1915–16)

One of the firm's loveliest and most unusual buildings of this period was designed for a lot of an unusual shape. Located on three of Detroit's leading thoroughfares, on a direct line of travel between downtown and the residential district, the distinctive Whitney Building must have inspired high hopes when it was erected (fig. 47). The green park setting in the foreground and the gleaming white terra-cotta cladding of the tall sil-

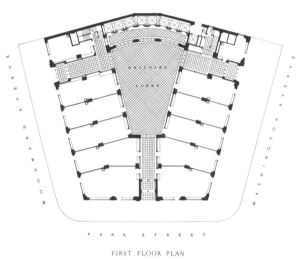

FIRST FLOOR PLAN

[48] WHITNEY BUILDING, PLAN
After entering on Park Street, the visitor walks to the dramatically expanding atrium space of the lobby.

[47] DAVID WHITNEY BUILDING, DETROIT, MICH., ELEVATION
The Whitney Building makes the most of its setting on Woodward Avenue. The slightly splayed white walls and the delicate ornament herald the extraordinary power of the courtyard within.

houette against the blue sky were an invitation to even greater charms within.

Four floors of shops open their doors to corridors encircling the large "rotunda" space under the polygonal light court (fig. 48). Elegantly proportioned pilasters form a colonnade at the first level, then rise to a giant order ending in a rich arcade that circles the upper floors. The upper surface of gleaming white tile is enriched by geometric and floral ornaments surrounding the generous semicircular arched openings at the top. Globe fixtures at every pilaster at every floor and a stringcourse of lights at the springing of the vaulted glass roof give sparkling illumination to the whole (fig. 49).

The Whitney is a work of unusual delicacy in the handling of proportions and details, and extraordinary felicity in the shaping of interior space. It has all the hallmarks of the firm's work, showing the enormous variety within the parameters of the tripartite, flat-roofed building, even in the very early years of their work. Within four years, the architects would design another delicate, white terra-cotta building with a very different silhouette, destined to become the most popular of their creations.

[49] WHITNEY BUILDING, COURT LOBBY

This multilevel court lobby is one of the firm's masterpieces. Photographs merely suggest the possibilities of the space, which must be experienced while walking up and down and in and around the arcades above. Recalling the gallerias of the nineteenth century, the many levels of the Whitney interior are lit by the globes of streetlamps, enhancing the glow of the creamy terra-cotta cladding.

[50] WILLIAM WRIGLEY, JR., BUILDING, CHICAGO, ILL., EXTERIOR
Beloved by all Chicagoans, the Wrigley Building combines classical monumentality with soaring height, making the most of its prominent site at the intersection of Michigan Avenue and the Chicago River.

William Wrigley, Jr., Building, Chicago (1919–24)

Had Daniel H. Burnham realized that Chicago would grow toward the north instead of to the south, he certainly would have put an important civic or cultural plaza at the junction of Michigan Avenue and the Chicago River. Michigan Avenue turns at a diagonal here, and the polygonal site (fig. 52) thus commands a dominant view in all directions. After the Wrigley Building was finished one contemporary noted, "At a distance of about a mile one becomes suddenly conscious of the new presence. . . . One can see the tower in all the airy grace of its many pinnacles and turrets, much as one might glimpse the towers of some distant castle set on a rock." [24] Another observer wrote that "from Roosevelt Road the tower is like a phantom castle in a fairy tale. At Adams Street it becomes recognizable as the boulevard's climax. Beyond Madison it dominates the whole picture, stealing admiration from its companion wonder, the link bridge." [25] From the north, wrote another, "the building seems a huge, sharp, dominating prow. . . . It seems to cut the air and be slowly bearing down on the spectator with an awful majesty quite overpowering." [26] The location has few equals in the city, and the river doubles its impact by reflecting the image to the west and by providing a generous foreground to the southeast (fig. 50).

The Wrigley is at once something new and the embodiment of a number of traditional elements. It shows the heritage of Beaux-Arts canons of design, the legacy of the Chicago commercial style of the 1880s, the influence of the World's Columbian Exposition of 1893, developments in the terra-cotta industry especially seen in the architectural detail (fig. 51), the challenge of contemporary architecture in New York,

and the habit of civic-mindedness prevalent among the clients of the Chicago business world. But the quality that breathed life into the confluence of these many traditions, the spirit that transformed the structure from an additive mixture to a new synthesis, was the inspired pen of the gifted Beaux-Arts-trained designer Graham assigned to the project, Charles G. Beersman. [27]

Structurally the building is like the older Chicago models, and the base is also articulated in the usual tripartite manner. But the Wrigley is no longer in the old Burnham mode of burly blocks. Wedding the love of white that came after the success of the World's Columbian Exposition of

[51] WRIGLEY BUILDING, ENTRANCE DETAIL
Light plays over the profusely decorated surfaces of the Wrigley Building, enhancing the rich effect of its many wreaths, festoons, pinnacles, and medallions in various shades of white.

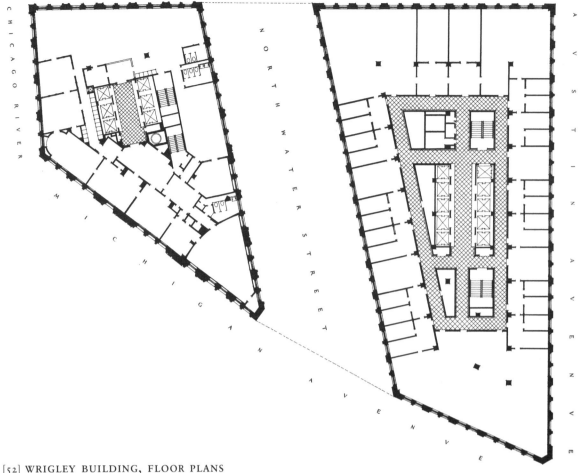

[52] WRIGLEY BUILDING, FLOOR PLANS
At its narrowest along the Chicago River, the plan of the Wrigley expands as it goes north. As Michigan Avenue bends slightly at North Water Street, the smaller section is seen as the apex of Michigan Avenue viewed from the south, and the larger section as the apex viewed from the north—both unparalleled urban vistas.

1893 (also known as "The White City") to the perception of the big city as a metropolis of towers (derived from New York), the Wrigley's shimmering, airy form challenged the old ways and introduced a new note. A special, painterly attention to the glazing added to both the refinement and the dazzle. Six different shades of a special enamel finish were baked on the terra-cotta, varying from gray to pale cream, getting progressively lighter toward the top, so that the Wrigley seems "to soar from mists and fog to clear skies." [28] Add to this the effects of dramatic nighttime illumination (fig. 53), "projected by powerful x-ray reflectors, using 500 watt lamps for a total of 70,750 watts," [29] and the continued dominance of the Wrigley Building in Chicago's skyscape, as well as in the hearts of its citizens, was assured.

What else moved the firm to develop in the direction of towers in their office buildings? Allowing the "Beaux-Arts boys from the East" free reign in the design studio had been part of Burnham's practice, and Graham did not alter the pattern. No doubt Graham also felt that New York's Woolworth Building (Cass Gilbert, 1913), with its slender tower, demonstrated a successful eclectic Gothic combination of the office building and the tower, but Anderson, who was still chief designer, could not accept eclectic Gothic. Perhaps when William Mitchell Kendall of McKim, Mead and White designed New York's Municipal Building in 1913, with its combination of Beaux-Arts classicism and a tower, Anderson decided it was possible to have the best of both worlds—dignity and great height, a synthesis of aspiring monumentality.

[53] WRIGLEY BUILDING, NIGHT VIEW

Electricity promised a new way of life in the 1920s, and the nighttime illumination of the Wrigley Building reflected the optimistic expectations of the period. Today the floodlights on the Wrigley mark the beginning of the expanded "Magnificent Mile" of Michigan Avenue to the north, a nexus of city lights and city life both day and night.

Koppers Building, Pittsburgh (1927–29)

After Anderson's death in 1924, Alfred Shaw became the chief designer, and the style of the firm's work took on still another aspect. Both Shaw and his chief, Graham, were eager to earn a reputation for keeping up with the times without being avant-garde: they wanted an image that captured the best of the old and the best of the new.

With its green copper chateau roof, the Koppers Building recalls the earliest of the metal-frame skyscrapers in New York, such as Richard Morris Hunt's Tribune Building (1873), but its setbacks and the sleek verticality of its uninterrupted piers are up-to-date stripped classicism (fig. 54). Like many other contemporary structures by several of the nation's leading architects, the Koppers Building was embellished with flat, geometricized ornament, sometimes called Art Deco after the "modernistic" decor popularized by the Paris Exposition of Decorative Arts of 1925 (fig. 55).

In the lobby of the Koppers, the spatial volumes suggest the same judicious mixture of the new and the old. Balconies intersect the tall, sleek proportions of the four-storied lobby, like the overhead bridges in the latest assembly-line manufacturing plant, but the materials are the finest tradition has to offer—Italian cremo and premier breche centella marble (fig. 56). Accordingly, the interior of the Koppers has a warm beige glow, enriched by the marine patterns of rose and brown. The parquet design of the floor is made of pink and gray marbles, with panels of red Spanish alacanate. Ceiling mouldings of gold, dark green, and maroon are lit by chevron fixtures in the Art Deco style. While the circles, squares, diamonds, and interlocking rectangles suggest the modernity of the Jazz Age with its love of machinery, the marble piers and capitals and the color serve as reminders of tradition. The end result, considered by some to be a masterpiece of the era, is an appropriate combination for a city aspiring to be congenial to both an automated Vulcan and a timeless Venus (fig. 57).[30]

This combination of stripped classicism with

[54] KOPPERS BUILDING, PITTSBURGH, PA., EXTERIOR
The uninterrupted verticals of the Koppers Building suggest the soaring speed of the airplane age, but its chateau roof is traditional, so that the building combines the best of contemporary and historical styles. Some critics regard this building as a masterpiece of the Art Deco style.

setbacks and a chateau roof was used frequently by the firm in the late 1920s, with variations on the theme. In San Antonio, Texas, the Alamo National Bank Building (1929) is given a southwestern color scheme of beige piers and brown spandrel panels. In Kansas City, the setbacks of the Hughes Bryant Building (1929–30) are marked by smooth arcs formed by the curves of the pier finials, suggesting the art moderne, aerodynamic forms of the Santa Fe streamliners in the nearby railroad station. The lighted barrel vault of the lobby, on the other hand, was decorated with golden midwestern sunflowers. Similar to the Koppers Building in silhouette but more traditional in every other way is the Pittsfield Building (1926–27) in Chicago.

Field Building, Chicago (1929–34)

The Field Building shows that both client and architect were dedicated to traditional materials while desiring the latest Art Deco imagery. Every part of this building expresses vertical energy. Its five towers mount and unite in one upward surge of massive forms; its windows and piers rise dramatically without interruption, echoing the rapid movement of the forty express elevators in its interior (fig. 58).

At the core of the lobby, these ideals of speed and efficiency, so near the hearts of American entrepreneurs of the period, are embodied in a new icon of the times cast especially for the building—a giant elevator indicator in the shape of the building itself. With its red and green lights flashing up and down the "windows," it is a nerve center and microcosm of the larger macrocosm it serves. Also housing the central mail chute, this lustrous metallic indicator is both practical and symbolic, a kinetic light sculpture expressing the spirit of the place and the times (fig. 60).

The clients had high hopes for this building occupying half a city block in the heart of the financial district.

Places, like people, have their destinies which time fulfills. LaSalle Street has been

[55] KOPPERS BUILDING, DETAIL
Triangles, chevrons, rectangles, and other geometric ornament in the entrance of the Koppers Building reflect a love of machine forms.

from its beginning the financial heart, not only of Chicago, but of the great Middle West.... Banks, investment houses and other financial interests have long been drawn to LaSalle Street as by an irresistible magnet of gold, until today it is Wall Street's only rival for concentrated activity. The "Canyon of Gold," this great money mart has been called, but canyons are old and dead, whereas LaSalle Street is young and teeming with life. Its vast monuments of finance and commerce are symbols of the

[56] KOPPERS BUILDING,
LOBBY
Inside, the railings, walkways, clock,
and light fixtures of the Koppers
Building have a shipshape austerity,
warmed by the rose and amber of
the traditional marble cladding.

[57] KOPPERS BUILDING, NIGHT VIEW
At night, the floodlights illuminating the roof dispel the darkness and animate the city sky.

[58] FIELD BUILDING, CHICAGO, ILL.
The largest office building in the heart of Chicago's LaSalle Street area glistens in polished granite and white bronze, reflecting the center of financial activity in the "Wall Street of the West."

tireless energy of our people. . . . The Field Building dedicates itself to the future of LaSalle Street and Chicago.[31]

The building was also within easy access of restaurants and hotels and close to the State Street shopping district. Five railway terminals—the LaSalle Street Station, the Dearborn Street Station, the Grand Central Station, Union Station, and the Chicago and North Western Station—were within a five- or ten-minute walk.

There were other reasons for optimism. The Field Building was Chicago's largest office building and the fourth largest in the United States. Attracted by the prestige of the name, the convenience of the location on the "Wall Street of the West," and the advertising possibilities associated with its record-breaking size, many public utilities, investment bankers, law firms, and insurance companies leased space at an early date.

The thin, rectangular slab of the central tower, forty-three stories high, was flanked by a

[59] FIELD BUILDING, ENTRANCE

Sleek and soaring, the entrance to the Field Building was illuminated by searchlights, evoking the glamour associated with opening nights in Hollywood.

twenty-two-story tower at each of its four corners. "Five towering edifices in one," the grouping of the narrow shapes created unusually generous light wells, giving the offices on the periphery access to daylight and air. As with other late 1920s designs, the architects avoided ornament and suppressed the spandrel panels so that the vertical piers and windows dominated the pattern on the exterior. The four-story base of polished black granite inset with white bronze doors and aluminum window frames, throws the doorways into dramatic relief. The renderings accompanying the rental brochure evoked Hollywood premiers of the 1920s, showing elegant limousines drawing up to the building at night, with searchlights illuminating a setting fit for the arrival of movie stars (fig. 59).

The interior lobby, 27 feet high and 350 feet long, carries out the promises of the exterior. A two-story arcade at the ground floor stretches the entire length of the building, with shops on either side. Bridges with nautical railings connect the upper levels in the Art Deco style. Striking staircases lead to the upper level, or continue to the lower-level arcade where more shops are located. Like the exterior, the bi-level lobby is clad in luxurious materials. White Colorado yule marble pilasters are modeled with zigzags, an updated version of classical flutings, and the intervening recessed panels are of vibrant beige Italian loredo chiaro marble. The floors are white mosaic terrazzo, and the exposed metalwork is nickel silver bronze. The Italian marble and the softly glowing bronze create a warm overall effect. To heighten the drama, each pilaster is illuminated by a floodlight. Tiered prismatic glass fixtures fill the elevator lobbies with light.

Aware that "the modern office building comprises a little world all its own," the designers of the Field Building provided a fleet of forty high-speed elevators, enclosed radiators, and alternating current generators, as well as central air-conditioning on the first four floors. Amenities offered to the Field Building tenants on all floors included safety deposit vaults, general storage space in one of the sub-basements, a laundry and towel service, and three restaurants reflecting the

[60] FIELD BUILDING, ELEVATOR INDICATOR
The elevator indicator is an image of the building itself. With its kinetic energy, the elevator system is both sign and cynosure of the skyscraper.

usual hierarchy of the business world—an executive dining room, a middle-management grill room, and a coffee shop for secretaries and file clerks.[32]

At the time of its construction, the Field Building was one of the few major skyscraper office buildings being erected in the United States. Planned in September 1929, when the country's mood was one of exuberance and optimism, and finished in 1934, in a period of massive unemployment and depression, the Field Building is clearly a product of the late 1920s and the early 1930s. In this it teaches us something about the distinction we usually make between the two decades. The change from the lively style of the Jazz Age to the subdued social realism of the 1930s was not as abrupt as is commonly believed. Far from rejecting the promises of the machine, the designers of the Field Building clung to its forms and symbols even after the stock market crash of October 1929. Since Americans' faith in their economic system was shaken, they turned their hopes for better lives all the more to the wonders of technology, to electricity, and to science. It was twenty-five years before another major building went up in Chicago's Loop, so that the Field Building remains one of the last, one of the richest, and one of the best repositories of the dreams of the era.

When the stock market crashed in October 1929, the firm of Graham, Anderson, Probst and White was offering five different styles: a sedate version of the old Burnham Baroque—the State Bank, Chicago; a setback with Egyptian motifs—the Chase National Bank, New York; a chateau-roof vertical Gothic—the Pittsfield Building, Chicago; an example of severe stripped classicism—the First National Bank, St. Paul; and a version of conservative Art Deco style—the Foreman State National Bank, Chicago. Clearly, finding its own "signature style" was not a concern. Needing to develop a style that would look modern but not show its age for many years to come, while also turning a profit for the titans of commerce who were its clients, the firm moved from its Beaux-Arts-oriented architecture to an architecture that selected what seemed best from a variety of sources.

If the architect's vision of a hierarchically ordered city had been adumbrated earlier by commercial skyscrapers, it had been totally eclipsed by the late 1920s. Electric lights, air-conditioning, sleek towers, and the hard-edged geometric motifs of the Art Deco symbolized the dreams of a new era, a period when religious, government, and cultural buildings took second place to commercial structures. Graham had shared with his contemporaries—both clients and other architects—the problems of finding new images to express the hopes of the period. The Field Building, with its telescoping forms, its fleet of high-speed

elevators, its "man-made weather," and its multileveled lobby, signaled the firm's major break with its Beaux-Arts vision and announced a distinctly new direction. But before its completion, the depression deepened and with it the firm's chances to erect any more buildings.

But if hierarchy had faded in the exterior design of office buildings and in city planning, it remained a valid ordering principle for interior planning throughout the period from 1912 to 1929. Cultural institutions, like the Civic Opera Building in Chicago, government buildings like the firm's Federal Reserve banks, and railroad stations like the Thirtieth Street Station in Philadelphia, retained a division into parts of decreasing importance in their interiors as one moved from the grand public rooms to the purely utilitarian sections. However, one building type in which the architects could create a hierarchically ordered utopian microcity was the department store. In his lifetime Ernest R. Graham supervised the design and construction of twenty-two department stores.[33] Three examples will suffice.

Wm. Filene's Sons Company, Boston (1911–12); Marshall Field and Company Annex, Chicago (1914); Gimbel Brothers, Philadelphia (1926–27)

No doubt it was a Frenchman who visited the Great Exhibition of the Works of Industry of All Nations, the world's fair in London in 1851, who founded the first department store in 1852, the Bon Marché in Paris.[34] It resembled a multilevel marketplace full of specialty shops where a buyer could find a melange of goods—from carpets and paintings to jewelry to spices and coffee—under a single roof. The Bon Marché was a world's fair for shoppers, but controlled by a single owner. Peirce Anderson must have visited it during his student days in France, for his designs for Marshall Field's main department store (1904–7) in Chicago incorporated many of its features.

Instead of simply using the horizontal loft spaces Louis Sullivan had employed for Schlesinger and Mayer's store (1891–94 and 1899, now

[61] WM. FILENE'S SONS COMPANY BUILDING, BOSTON, MASS., EXTERIOR
Decorously ornamented, Filene's is sedate—in every way a proper Bostonian department store.

[62–64] FILENE'S, INTERIOR DRAWINGS

The interior of Filene's was conceived as a microcity for women. Street lamps and park benches lined the aisles, and every effort was made to satisfy the needs of shoppers for whom a day in town was often a social occasion as well as a day of errands. Places to enjoy luncheon with friends, to listen to music, to buy a steamship ticket, or to send a telegram were all available to Filene's patrons, as were all kinds of clothing, from the finest of furs to basement bargains.

Carson, Pirie, Scott and Company) a block down State Street from Marshall Field's, Anderson designed three vertical spaces for Field's: a six-story urban square, a twelve-story arcade, and a four-story restaurant. This work, carried out under Burnham's aegis, served as a model for various department stores built during the two decades following his death. Clad in gray limestone, Marshall Field's was sedate, orderly in its horizontal tripartite divisions, and completely at home among the commercial buildings in the Loop. In keeping with the building's subordinate place within this larger urban scheme, the design was restrained, adorned only by four Ionic columns at the entrance and simple mouldings at the stringcourses. Unlike the exteriors of department stores in other cities that resembled those of an Italian palace or a mansarded French chateau, the outside of Marshall Field's conformed to the conservative businesslike aspect of its neighboring buildings in the Chicago Loop.[35]

Anderson's design for Filene's in Boston is also a three-part, horizontal structure (fig. 61) but much more lavishly decorated than Field's. In the interior Anderson developed the idea of a hierarchically ordered city. Taking advantage of the resemblance of the steel-cage grid to city streets, he worked with the interior designers to

develop "the streets of Filene's."[36] Each department was presented as a specialty shop on an enclosed street, and the store itself as a "Store of Shops." To simulate an outdoor atmosphere, carefully decorated shop windows traversed each floor in both directions. Furnishings included lampposts, mailboxes, and other street accoutrements (figs. 62, 63, 64). This air of sprightly urbanity was enhanced by a telegraph office, a travel bureau, and a beauty salon all located on a long balcony overlooking the main floor. The effect was of multilevel streets in a minicity, reminiscent of European gallerias.

Filene's handsome elevator lobby offered another opportunity for a stroll. Here the average Boston housewife might encounter people from all walks of life, from the city's first families to visiting celebrities. Thus the promise of adventure was added to the allure of shopping, and every woman became part of a glamorous world.

The contrast with the Marshall Field Annex (Store for Men) in Chicago underscores the point. There the interior shopping space clearly resembled the lobby of an office building, while the Grill Room on the sixth floor emulated a men's club (fig. 65). On the exterior, the tall, broad, volumetric men's building is clad in gray limestone, and its tripartite division is rigorously articulated by simple pilasters, sober stringcourses, and an Ionic colonnade that supports the crowning cornice. The bulk of the building was given over to office spaces, another example of the commercial building type devouring almost all other forms in this period (fig. 66).

After World War I, Graham, Anderson, Probst and White designed the L. S. Donaldson Company Building in Minneapolis; W. A. Wieboldt and Company in Chicago; O'Neil's Department Store in Akron, Ohio; and Higbee's in Cleveland. The firm's last downtown department store commission was done for the Gimbel brothers in Philadelphia. Since the large store Anderson had designed for Gimbel's in that city in 1908 was still in use, the 1926 commission was for a seven-story store topped by a five-story office building in the same area. Once again, the department store was submerged in the office building. Although the whole-block structure that the architects first designed was never built, a much smaller version of it was erected. It contained a great arcade that ran through the building from Chestnut Street to Market Street (fig. 67). Its lofty two-story central space with its combination of pillars and arches recalled the old center of Roman city life, the baths, and even its descendant, the modern railroad station.

[65] MARSHALL FIELD AND COMPANY ANNEX, THE STORE FOR MEN, CHICAGO, ILL., INTERIOR ELEVATION
A worldly atmosphere for male shoppers crowned the sixth floor of the Marshall Field Annex, the Store for Men. Evoking the main salon of the Ritz in Madrid, the domed glass ceiling and splashing fountain of the Men's Grill brought the elegance of the Old World to the Midwest.

[66] MARSHALL FIELD ANNEX, ELEVATION

Two building types—the office building and the department store—merge in the Marshall Field Annex. On the exterior, its vertical proportions and tripartite divisions mirrored the commercial structures in the Loop, but parts of the interior were as ornate as the dining room of a Parisian men's club.

Gimbel Brothers drew upon this old urban imagery in the brochure prepared for opening day, calling the building "Gimbel City" and quoting lines from Revelation 21:16, "and the city lies foursquare and the length is as large as the breadth," a quotation Ernest R. Graham no doubt enjoyed.[37]

Within Gimbel Brothers' walls the shopper found such services as a bank with safe deposit vaults, beauty parlors, restaurants, a public auditorium, a pet shop, a florist, a men's barbershop with a lounge to add "the final touch of clubiness and masculine exclusiveness," radio station WIP, fur storage vaults, and a travel bureau. Declaring the store "the market place of the world," the new owners voiced another aspect of department store civic life—its cosmopolitanism.

For a hundred years camel-laden caravans plodded over a thousand diverging paths bringing their merchandise to the great market of Nijni-Novgorod. . . . In 1927 the best that every land provides finds its way by boat, by rail, by aeroplane, or motor, to GIMBEL BROTHERS . . . . Flaming shawls from Kashmire—hand-tooled leather from Tuscany—filmy lace from old Seville— dainty porcelain from Sevres—sturdy woven woolens from England—spicy condiments from far Madras—silver filagree from Venice—ruby goblets from Czechoslovakia—pungent tea from ancient China—quaint novelties from Hamburg— gay fads and fashions from Paris—silk from Japan—rugs from Ispahan, and, last but not least, all that is finest that our own dear nation provides—everything from everywhere—the cornucopias of the world onto the shelves of GIMBEL BROTHERS.[38]

In Filene's in Boston, in Marshall Field's in Chicago, in Gimbel's in Philadelphia, or in any of the firm's other department stores, strollers could avail themselves of numerous services and eat lunch in a fine restaurant while enjoying a con-

[67] GIMBEL BROTHERS BUILDING, PHILADELPHIA, PA., INTERIOR ELEVATION
A classical version of a galleria, the arcade in Gimbel's combines the advantages of a street with the protection of a roof.

cert. Each store was endowed with a kind of rotunda or central space containing a "civic-center" or information center. At Marshall Field's in Chicago, phone books from every major city in the country are still to be found just off the rotunda on the third floor.

One could walk down and around the central rotunda of a department store on the inner staircases, just as one could promenade in a piazza; or one could pause in accented, climactic spaces as if on a balcony in Venice or by a fountain in Versailles (fig. 68). The whole store, like a great world's fair or an urban utopia, was hierarchically organized so that each part had a meaningful relationship to the whole. Destinations could be reached in a logical manner; there were waiting rooms, toilet facilities, and first aid stations. As in an ideal city there were courtesy, safety, art, music, entertainment, diversity, luxury, and a seemingly inexhaustible supply of goods from all over the world.

For Daniel H. Burnham, Ernest R. Graham, Peirce Anderson, and other architects, the department store was a miniaturized version of a perfect city. As the hierarchical vision of the larger city began to break down in the 1920s and many other building types came to be subsumed by the commercial office building, the department store managed to retain many characteristics of the earlier vision.

[68] DEPARTMENT STORE, PROJECT
In this department store rotunda project, the architects adapted the atrium design of the office building for use as an indoor city square for women. Complete with fountain and dome, its purpose was to cater to the cosmopolitan tastes of its customers.

LOFT BUILDINGS AND LIGHT MANUFACTORIES

Ernest R. Graham had the benefit of knowing intimately two of Chicago's contributions to nineteenth-century city planning: Solon Spencer Beman's (1853–1914) company town for George M. Pullman, begun in 1880, and the World's Columbian Exposition of 1893. Like other Chicago architects of his era, he adapted the underlying principles of the company town and the exposition for buildings lower down in the urban hierarchy. As a result, high architectural standards for loft buildings and light industry sites became a hallmark of Chicago's manufacturing neighborhoods.

Unlike the structures of earlier decades—unarticulated boxes with rough elevations that might have had windows on the street side, but were otherwise blind[39]—the industrial buildings in Chicago began to take on some of the architectural character of the rest of the city, especially after the fire of 1871. In 1883, George H. Edbrooke designed a warehouse for Hiram Sibley and Company with a horizontal tripartite division articulated vertically with piers crowned by capitals to harmonize with the Chicago office buildings nearby. Unlike the office buildings, which were usually clad in limestone, the warehouse was clad in red brick with terra-cotta trim. So seemly, so satisfying was the result that it set a precedent.[40]

In less than a generation, several buildings of this type were put together in an ensemble called the Central Manufacturing District, located in the southwestern section of Chicago.[41] The buildings in this industrial park had uniform cornice lines, were clad in red brick, and were ornamented with limestone and terra-cotta trim. All utility lines were buried, and manufacturers in the district enjoyed the advantages of centralized shipping facilities, a union freight station, attractive landscaping, a dining club for executives, a bank, a Western Union office, a medical station, and other services.[42]

*Crane Company Corwith Plant (1914–26);
Western Union Telegraph Building (1917–
19), Chicago*

When Graham, Anderson, Probst and White designed an entire plant for the Crane Company, manufacturers of plumbing fixtures, the architects were clearly influenced by these models. Planning a total of thirty-three buildings, including manufacturing lofts, warehouses, shipping centers, train sheds, offices, and service buildings, the designers wove the details together in a complex that was erected between 1914 and 1926.

The Administration Building took its regular form directly from the underlying columns and beams of its structure. Around the corner on Pershing Road the twenty-five bays of a manufacturing section had the same width and fenestration pattern as the bays of the Administration Building, but the much longer side elevation was articulated with four entrance portals, each with overhead arches adorned with circular medal-

lions. When viewed from the northeast, the ensemble, stretching along both streets and coming to a climax at the corner, created a satisfying effect. The no-nonsense practicality of the relationship between structure and form would be greatly admired by later architects. With harmony provided by the rectangular form and the materials, and special distinction accorded by the 130-foot clock tower, the ensemble has both unity and variety (fig. 69). A few buildings of the complex remain on the site today.

A few blocks south of the Chicago Loop, a structure to house the electrical equipment of the Western Union Telegraph Company suggests its transitional role between the office and the loft building. When it was first erected, the building housed enormous quantities of electronic communications gear and equipment, including support facilities and backup, but it also provided space for over a thousand operators handling messages twenty-four hours a day, many of them delivered to Loop buildings through a complex

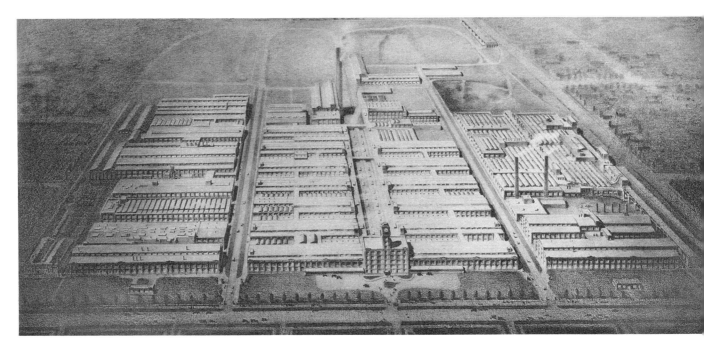

[69] CRANE COMPANY CORWITH PLANT, CHICAGO, ILL., AERIAL VIEW
Emulating a microcity, the buildings of the Corwith Plant were organized on a grid. They resembled other lofts and manufactories in the area, each building being divided into three parts horizontally, while protruding pavilions at the ends articulated the parts into a meaningful whole vertically.

[70] WESTERN UNION TELE-
GRAPH BUILDING, CHICAGO,
ILL., EXTERIOR
The Telegraph Building reflects the
Chicago industrial style on a
smaller scale. The widely spaced
piers allow for large windows, and
a central bay emphasizes the entrance portico.

system of pneumatic tubes under the streets. In addition, there were office facilities for supervisory personnel.[43] Everything about the building speaks of a mediating role between warehouses and offices. Clad in brick with limestone trim like the lofts to the south and west, the structure is also adorned with pilasters and stringcourses like the office buildings to the north (fig. 70). The bases of the pilasters are especially expressive of the hybrid character of the building (fig. 71).

[71] TELEGRAPH BUILDING, DETAIL
The base of a pilaster on the Telegraph Building shows that the architects exercised great care in creating a vocabulary that would give dignity to their industrial buildings.

FACTORIES, WAREHOUSES, AND OTHER INDUSTRIAL BUILDINGS

Sometimes changes in the hierarchy itself could be precipitated by a radical change in the technical or social order, or a warehouse would take on a transitional role, as is evident in the following examples.

Butler Brothers Warehouses (1912–13; 1917–22), Chicago; Crawford Avenue Generating Station (1924–25), Chicago; State Line Generating Station (1921–29), Hammond, Indiana

In Chicago, two bold, sturdy warehouses for the Butler Brothers now stand as powerful parts of the wall of buildings that articulates the west bank of Chicago's riverfront. Just across the river from the commercial city, their four-square format is a brawny version of the Burnham office buildings in the Loop (fig. 72). In the original hierarchical vision of the city they had had two transitional functions to perform: mediating the passage from the city's office area to the light industrial area that was to be located further north and west, and forming a closure to the urban gateway made by Union Station which was planned to the south. The barges, steam locomotives, and boxcars in the foreground indicate this vital junction between industry and commerce. In fact, the city did not grow in the manner depicted in the drawing. The original intention survives only in fragments, but the civic spirit remains clear.

The workaday character of these hefty buildings has the dignified air of a carpenter in well-pressed overalls. There are the touches of tradition—the division of the design into base, shaft, and capital. The Chicago businessman's preference for the flat roof is respected. The ornament on the cornice is not top-hat classicism, it is a cap of Tuscan arcading. The designs of these buildings along the river reflect the relationship of the architectural hierarchy to Chicago's contemporary social hierarchy with its implicit understanding that separate activities were carried on

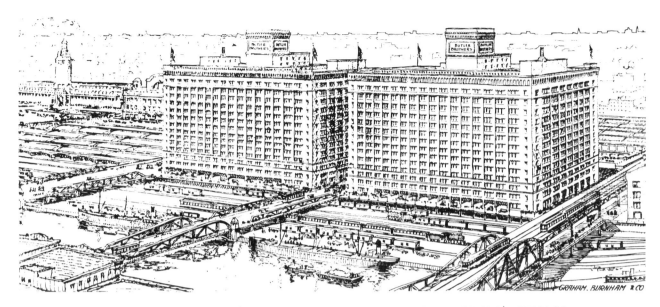

[72] BUTLER BROTHERS WAREHOUSES (ONE NORTHWEST CENTER AND RIVER CENTER), CHICAGO, ILL., ELEVATION

Workmanlike in their strong simplicity, the Butler Brothers Warehouses took their place in the midst of the railroad tracks that lined the north bank of the Chicago River at the time of their design. In 1913, the architects envisioned a different version of Union Station to the west.

in different parts of the city. For overall harmony's sake, the cladding and trim are the same as those of the industrial plants nearby, though the latter have many large windows, and the warehouses fewer, smaller ones.

In July 1915, architect Andrew Rebori called the first Butler Brothers building a "striking and unchallenged" success.

> I do not know of a more expressive and enlightened work in its own kind by its author or by any other architect. It attains a very noble largeness and simplicity which is due in a measure to the structural emphasis that makes the fronts independent of extraneous ornament. The building relies on means of support that are in this case made visible by the frank and expressive treatment of its long piers. . . . It is the vertical lines of the super structure, however, that thrill me the most, for here indeed is a solution of the problem in high design that would be commercially practicable even if this were an office building instead of a warehouse![44]

In 1927, critic Lewis Mumford included the Butler Brothers Warehouses in his very short list of the best modern buildings in Chicago.[45] Both Rebori and Mumford admired the Butler Brothers Warehouses for their structural expressiveness, which would have surprised their more traditional colleagues at Graham, Burnham and Company, whose motives had probably been to provide a utilitarian structure with an appropriate cladding for its place in the urban fabric of the city.

A major change in the hierarchy came when Samuel Insull, president of the Chicago Edison Company, wanted new buildings for his electrical generating plants. By 1912, Insull had bought out or merged with a number of utility companies, creating a monopoly that was technologically efficient, economically operated, and served all of Chicago.[46] Insull wanted structures that not only would express the power of electricity, but would also proclaim its new place in civic life. No longer would industrial lofts, however dignified, suffice. As early as 1903, he commissioned Daniel Burnham to build the Fisk Street Station, and as his empire and the demands on it grew, he commissioned the larger Crawford Avenue Generating Station as well in 1924–25.

The machinery dictates the dimensions, pro-

[73] CRAWFORD AVENUE GENERATING STATION, CHICAGO, ILL., EXTERIOR
A palace of industry, the Crawford Avenue Station is distinguished by rhythmic massing, textured brick cladding, and terra-cotta architectural detail.

portions, and arrangement of a power station, but the architects used every device at their command to endow the emerging building envelope with individual character (fig. 73). Protruding pavilions that rise above the roofline break up the mass of the southern elevation into five parts—a center, two sides, and two ends—adapting a time-honored Palladian villa concept to industrial Chicago. In addition, white terra-cotta horizontal accents give rhythm to the broad bays filled with industrial glass, and changing patterns in the brickwork catch the light at different angles to provide textural contrast within the rhythmically articulated walls.

While the wall surface of the interior of the boiler room had the utilitarian character necessary to resist coal dust, the turbine room had, and indeed still has, the air of an industrial palace. The white tile pieces that make up the cladding are of three different sizes: the largest at the bases of the supporting piers, smaller ones on the

piers themselves, and the smallest in the walls in between. Balconies and geometric ornament further attest to the showplace quality of this immense space and the attention paid to architectural detail. Samuel Insull was so excited about the installation of the first turbine generator that he chartered a special Illinois Central train to bring guests to the plant for the opening ceremonies.

> The entire property, inside the station and out, was in orderly, spic and span condition. The clean white tile walls of the turbine room and the operators in their white duck uniforms, the total absence of disorder and dirt, all must have made a favorable impression on the guests.[47]

Seen from the air, the majesty of the conception evokes the era when it seemed that electricity would transform a landscape turned dingy and dreary by the byproducts of manufacturing into a clean, shining space. If utilities magnates were ranked by their power to generate the kilowatt hours to effect these wondrous results, then Samuel Insull of Chicago was global emperor in 1928. The generating capacity of the Crawford Station, 360,000 kilowatts, was the largest in the world.[48] Before the year was out, client, architect, and engineer came together again to build yet another plant, where imagery befitting a prince of industry would emerge on the shores of Lake Michigan at the State Line Generating Station. When Insull contemplated the erection of the largest unit in history for his plant at State Line, he must have felt himself at the pinnacle of his career.

To Insull, and many others of his generation, electricity and progress were synonymous. Technology inevitably would make the world a better place. Zigzags and thunderbolts became the icons of the Art Deco age; they adorned the literature of the period in great profusion, as demonstrated by the title page of the State Line Generating Station brochure. The foreword to the brochure accompanying the opening of the station sounded a typically optimistic note:

In Chicago and adjacent territory in northeastern Illinois and northwestern Indiana there is one of the great interconnected electric power systems of the world. All of the

[74] STATE LINE GENERATING STATION, HAMMOND, IND., EXTERIOR
A triumphal arch proclaims the entrance to the largest power generating station of its times, the State Line Generating Station. The arches in the stepped massing of the station to the east echo the motif, simulating the power of electricity in their reverberating forms.

[75] STATE LINE, DETAIL

Each arched window was further emphasized by a checkerboard pattern in the brickwork. The great Turbine Room, decorated with terra-cotta medallions and illuminated by vast arched windows, often served as the setting for elaborate luncheons at tables set with the finest linen and crystal.

electric generating stations in what is known as the Chicago Metropolitan District are interconnected in one system. They have a total capacity of 1,517,700 kilowatts or 2,034,450 horse power. The various companies in this district serve nearly 1,300,000 customers. In the midst of this great power system stands the new generating station of the State Line Generating Company, operating a turbine unit of 208,000 kilowatts or 278,000 horse power—the largest generating unit ever built. . . . The station is planned for five units with a total ultimate capacity of at least 1,000,000 kilowatts. The present station, therefore, is about one-fifth of its eventual size.[49]

Only some of these predictions came true. Indeed, the generator was the largest of its kind, and it remained so from 1929 to 1954, but the expansion never extended to five times the original size of the generator. At the time, however, Graham and Insull must have found special satisfaction in the ensemble with both its triumphal arch entrance and the even greater triumphal arch of the turbine room. With the addition of the office building, two towers, the great smokestacks, and a cluster of smaller buildings in a landscaped yard, the plant was a citadel of electricity, an appropriate holding for a prince of electricity (figs. 74, 75).

When the stock market crashed a few months later, and the dreams of the 1920s dissolved into the depression of the 1930s, Insull's personal history became a nightmare, but the palace for industry on the lakefront remains as testimony to the optimism of the preceding decade.

Two areas of the firm's practice were outside the urban hierarchy: domestic architecture and buildings for charitable institutions. The few residences designed by the firm were competent but undistinguished, but its commissions for religious and community organizations were often sensitively designed, although they are almost

unknown. They include Baby Village in Mooseheart, Illinois, and the Hoover Suction Sweeper Community Building in North Canton, Ohio.

CONCLUSION

When Graham took over the office, the old version of the hierarchically ordered city had already been significantly altered, but the process of change accelerated even more in the course of the next two decades. Cultural and civic institutions that had once stood alone, set off by terraces or parks, were subsumed in whole or in part into office buildings. Office buildings had climbed from the lowest levels of the urban hierarchy to the middle as early as the nineteenth century. The railroad station, a public-private ensemble within the cityscape, retained its penultimate position for a while, but even here the office building climbed aboard in a dominating way, as seen in Cleveland and in the Broad Street Suburban Station at Seventeenth Street in Philadelphia. In this push and pull of circumstances there were always pluses and minuses. The office building benefited in Cleveland; the suburban railway station suffered in Philadelphia. Naturally, some of the new hybrids were more effective than others. As the decline in rail traffic deepened, the point about railroad stations became moot because rarely were new stations constructed. Some structures at the bottom of the hierarchy—such as electrical power plants and warehouses—began to move upward. In this way, the architectural world reflected changes in society at large.

At the same time, the firm continued to adapt and change the canons of architecture taught in the schools to meet the needs of new building types and to take advantage of new developments in technology—speed of elevators, air-conditioning, heating, lighting, and engineering discoveries. In response to the new demands, inspired design emerged in the plans for the Wrigley Building, the Shedd Aquarium, Union Station, the Field Building, and the Civic Opera Building, to mention only the Chicago examples.

The principals of the firm were influenced, consciously or unconsciously, by the widespread belief that a unified order of ideas and values could be made manifest in physical form. This belief continued to lose its original power, and the decline in its force was accompanied by a blurring of the old distinctions in the corollary idea of hierarchy. The architects at Graham, Anderson, Probst and White did not deliberately set out to cast aside Daniel H. Burnham's vision of a unified city ordered by public buildings and cultural institutions. But new economic pressures, the firm's focus on downtown buildings, and the sheer number of its built works led to their playing a major role in this historic change.

Skyscrapers and buildings from a formerly lower level began to dominate the built environment, obscuring church steeples and civic domes. Distinctions between building types that had been obvious in an earlier era and easily recognized by silhouette and location were now differentiated by less obvious, smaller-scale characteristics like ornament. From a few blocks away the Civic Opera of Chicago looks like an office building. Only at close range do the symbols of a cultural institution, the colonnade and the building's original ornament, become prominent. The building's specific function as an opera house does not become apparent until one enters.

A characteristic quality of American architecture in general during this period was the great freedom with which architects and their clients reorganized the old categories. Peirce Anderson, chief designer for Burnham and Graham, had certainly learned the principles of hierarchy at the École des Beaux-Arts, and that approach was common among all major architects of the time. But just as the architects at Graham, Anderson, Probst and White modified such classical canons as axiality, order, and ornament to meet their clients' taste for "Commercial Classicism" or for circulation in a new building type like the railroad station, so they accommodated requests to apply the polite and marketable veneer of columns, triumphal arches, and tripartite divisions to warehouses and power stations. Without any

grand proclamation of new principles and directions they and other architects of their era challenged the assumptions underlying Burnham's urban hierarchy.

The firm was by no means conservative. It did not rely solely on the adaptation of past models or cling to outmoded beliefs. But neither could its members be characterized as avant-garde, like the European modernists who placed housing and social needs at the top of the urban hierarchy and invented a new architectural vocabulary to express their theories. The architects of Graham, Anderson, Probst and White were in the mainstream, trying to preserve what was valuable in the old tradition, while embracing the best that new discoveries had to offer and responding to pressures from clients and the economy. They were successful partly because Graham (and Burnham before him) had grasped the importance of operating an architectural office as a big business. Few firms were able to handle the large, complex, multifunctional structures that Graham, Anderson, Probst and White could manage with its large, specialized staff of over two hundred men. Creative adaptation in technical, aesthetic, and social matters marked every aspect of the firm's major works. The minor works, some of them admittedly rather pedestrian, sustained the office and made it economically possible to keep the large staff constantly at work. As the architects of Graham, Anderson, Probst and White went along, they abandoned both some of the virtues and some of the vices of the older hierarchies, while maintaining others, and they also pursued some new directions.

The process by which the interplay of social, cultural, and economic factors is reflected in the work of the architects, engineers, and developers who shape our physical world is never-ending. Today we do not look for a return to the hierarchical order of Burnham, Graham, Anderson, and the others, nor to the social spirit of the times they expressed. We may regret the subsuming of so many aspects of our public and cultural worlds under commercial life. In looking for the best in past traditions—preserved in buildings and fragments of older hierarchies still extant in some of our cities—we also seek an architectural expression of the more fluid, pluralistic values of the social order of our own time.

NOTES

1. *The Plan of Chicago* (1909) was enormously influential, but Burnham's city-planning vision was not wholly original or unique. Burnham himself acknowledged the influence of several older cities on the classical Renaissance or baroque models in the first chapter of the *Plan,* and other architects were drawing up similar views for other contemporary cities (e.g., Otto Wagner's work in Vienna).

2. See *The Plan of Chicago,* plate 128. The subsequent design for the Field Museum did not have a dome.

3. Carl W. Condit, *Chicago, 1910–29: Building, Planning, and Urban Technology,* p. 196.

4. *The Economist,* January 2, 1927, p. 1.

5. Brochure for prospective tenants, n.d., GAPW archives, Chicago, Ill.

6. Condit, *Chicago 1910–29,* pp. 125–29.

7. Tour guide notes, September 26, 1932, Manuscript Collection, Chicago Historical Society, Chicago, Ill.

8. Burnham to Anderson, August 27, 1908, Letters of Daniel Burnham, Art Institute of Chicago, Chicago, Ill.

9. *The First National Bank of Pittsburgh,* n.d., GAPW archives.

10. Opening day brochure, n.d., Federal Reserve Bank of Kansas City archives, Kansas City, Mo.

11. Ibid.

12. Sally A. Kitt Chappell, "Urban Ideals and the Design of Railroad Stations," pp. 354–75. I am grateful to Carl W. Condit for a letter responding to the article. The present offering incorporates most of his suggestions, including a reference to William J. Wilgus, "The Grand Central Terminal in Perspective," pp. 1028–29. According to Condit, Wilgus was the first to recognize the importance of the railroads as an interface between various modes of transportation. Condit's "Bibliography of the Design, Construction, and Operation of Railroad Passenger Stations, 1875 To Date" is a helpful compendium of the literature. *See also* Carl Condit, *American Building Art: The Twentieth Century,* which contains an invaluable chapter on the metropolitan railway terminal.

13. Pennsylvania Station, Seventh Avenue at Thirty-second Street, New York City, 1903–10, McKim, Mead and White, architects, Charles W. Raymond, chief engineer; Grand Central Terminal, Park Avenue at Forty-second Street, New York City, 1903–13, Reed and Stem and Warren and Wetmore, architects, William J. Wilgus, chief engineer.

14. Carroll L. V. Meeks, *The Railroad Station,* p. 128. Meeks illustrates all major railroad stations and provides an in-depth building-type study of the form. Sir Nikolaus Pevsner, *A History of Building Types,* has a chapter on railroad stations that includes photographs of several using the combination of arches and the lunette window. Subdivided into three lights by two vertical mullions, the window was revived by Palladio in the sixteenth century and is a feature of Palladianism. The Gare de L'Est in Paris (Francois Duquesney, 1847–52) is perhaps the first railroad station to use the form, although King's Cross Station in London (Lewis Cubitt, 1851–52) is nearly its contemporary. Other examples followed in the Gare du Nord in Paris (J. I. Hittorff, 1861–65) and the Gare du Quai d'Orsay in Paris (Victor Laloux, 1898).

15. "Notes on the New Union Station at Washington, D.C.," n.d., GAPW archives, p. 1. Similar in style to Peirce Anderson's known writings, this document was probably written by him. Many European expressions of these ideas antedated even the fair of 1893—the stations in Frankfurt, Bucharest, Geneva, and Milan to mention four cited by Meeks. Charles Atwood's design for the station at the Chicago World's Columbian Exposition of 1893 was, of course, known firsthand to Americans and hence was the most direct influence. Meeks was the first to see the influence of this station not only on subsequent designs by Burnham, Graham, Anderson, Probst, and White, but also on stations by other architects in Kansas City, New York, Chattanooga, Detroit, and Toronto (Meeks, *The Railroad Station,* pp. 127–29). *See also* John R. Stilgoe, *Metropolitan Corridor: Railroads and the American Scene,* which examines the place of railroads in American culture.

16. The situation in Chicago was complicated in the early stages of planning around 1912, however, by a number of narrow bottlenecks in the street pattern. Taking advantage of the opportunity to remedy the situation, the Chicago Plan Commission induced the Chicago Union Station Company to undertake a program of improvements at its own expense. There was to be a thirty-five-acre complex of streets within private property lines with connections to the public transit system and other railroads. Plans for new freight terminals and a new post office were also included. Improvement agreements included the following: to connect Canal and Orleans streets uniting the north and west parts of the city; to widen and elevate Canal Street between Washington Street and Roosevelt Road to make a direct artery to the new Illinois Central Terminal; to open Monroe Street as a through east-west viaduct over the tracks that ran from Lake Street to Roosevelt Road; to erect a Congress Street viaduct; to help the city in the straightening of the Chicago River; and to abandon freight plans that interfered with circulation in the southern portion of the city (Rexford Newcomb, "The New Chicago Union Station," *Western Architect* 35 [January 1926]:4).

17. In addition, the Union Station Company contracted to pay the city $3 million for vacated streets and to relocate all utilities at its own expense (A. B. Olson, "Chicago Union Station Company," *Railway and Locomotive Historical Society Bulletin* 49 [May 1939]:103).

18. Eric Johannesen, *Cleveland Architecture 1876–1976*, p. 131. Johannesen's bibliography is an invaluable source of other references on the Cleveland Terminal Group. Especially noted are Taylor Hampton, "Cleveland's Fabulous Vans," *Cleveland News,* August 2–August 20, 1955; Joseph G. Blake, "The Van Sweringen Developments in Cleveland" (senior thesis, University of Notre Dame, 1968); Cleveland Terminal Company, *The Cleveland Union Station, A Description of the New Passenger Facilities and Surrounding Improvements,* brochure, 1930; James Marston Fitch, *Grand Central Terminal and Rockefeller Center: A Historic-Critical Estimate of Their Significance;* Winston Weisman, "The First Landscaped Skyscraper," p. 54. Also pertinent are Jim Toman and Dan Cook, *The Terminal Tower Complex: 1930–80* (Cleveland: Cleveland Landmarks Press I, 1980) and Carol Herselle Krinsky, *Rockefeller Center.*

19. The complexity of the process involved in integrating the new station into both the national railroad network and the Cleveland street and transit system and its contiguous streets is indicated by a map in Walter S. Lacher, "Dedicate New Cleveland Station Today: Electrification, air-rights development and many innovations in design feature great terminal just completed," *Railway Age* 88 (June 28, 1930):2. Trains from other railroads reached the station in a complex of lines from all directions. The terminal traction tracks and the New York Central and St. Louis lines from the southwest pass under West Twenty-fifth Street, Chatham Avenue, and Abbey and Lorain avenues and then over Franklin Avenue and the river on the Cuyahoga Valley Viaduct into the city where they enter the station. From the east, similar adjustments to the network of city streets were made.

20. Henry-Russell Hitchcock, *Architecture: Nineteenth and Twentieth Centuries,* p. 401. The plan for the Cleveland terminal was criticized at the outset because of the obstacles to construction imposed by the topography both of the station site and its approaches. Anticipating enormous expense, Cleveland citizens debated the plans extensively. Two documents that recount the situation are *Interstate Commerce Commission Reports* and Robert Morss [*sic*] Lovett, "A Non-Union Union Station."

21. Walter Leedy, Jr., "Cleveland's Terminal Tower—The Van Sweringens' Afterthought."

22. Neal D. Howard, "Philadelphia Improvements of the Pennsylvania Near Completion," *Railway Age* (July 28, 1934):92. Built on the site of the old West Philadelphia Station, the new station was already connected by tracks to the surrounding region, but a number of problems had developed making extensive changes necessary.

23. Alan Greenberg, "Urban Detail and the Urban Street," develops this idea in more detail.

24. "New Wrigley Building, Chicago's Tallest Structure," *Fort Dearborn Magazine,* March 1921.

25. F. K. Plous, Jr., "The Dowager of Michigan Avenue," *Chicago Sun-Times,* July 23, 1972.

26. "X-Ray Projectors," *Architecture and Building* 53 (December 1921):95.

27. Sally A. Kitt Chappell, "As If the Lights Were Shining: Graham, Anderson, Probst and White's Wrigley Building at the Boulevard Link." Beersman's role was affirmed by Charles F. Murphy, a long-time member of the firm, who said, "The Wrigley was Charlie Beersman's," in an interview June 22, 1981.

28. "X-Ray Projectors," p. 95.

29. Ibid.

30. Franklin Toker used this metaphor in an address to the Society of Architectural Historians in April 1985.

31. Brochure, n.d., Field Building archives, Chicago, Ill.

32. Ibid.

33. Among them Marshall Field's in Chicago, which together with the Wanamaker's and Gimbel's stores in New York and Philadelphia, secured the reputation of Daniel Burnham and Company as a leading designer of department stores in the country. For a study of this building type, see "Shops, Stores and Department Stores" in Pevsner, *Building Types*, pp. 257–72.

34. Russell Lewis, "Everything Under One Roof: World's Fairs and Department Stores in Paris and Chicago."

35. Neil Harris, "Shopping—Chicago Style," in John Zukowsky, ed., *Chicago Architecture 1872–1922: Birth of a Metropolis* (Munich: Prestel-Verlag in association with the Art Institute of Chicago, 1987).

36. Brochure, n.d., Filene's archives, Boston, Mass.

37. Opening day brochure, n.d., Ameribass Realty archives, Philadelphia, Pa.

38. Ibid.

39. Harold M. Mayer and Richard C. Wade, *Chicago: Growth of a Metropolis*, pp. 48, 52.

40. Carroll William Westfall, "Chicago's Wholesale Markets, 1885 to the Present."

41. Condit, *Chicago 1910–29*, pp. 139–42.

42. Michael J. Herschensohn, "Idealism in Industry: Chicago's Pioneering Contribution to American Urban Planning History in the Central Manufacturing District."

43. D. A. Brown, in-house report on the condition, history, and present usage of the building, Telegraph Building archives, Chicago, Ill.

44. Andrew N. Rebori, "The Work of Burnham and Root, D. H. Burnham, D. H. Burnham and Co., and Graham, Burnham and Co."

45. Lewis Mumford, "New York vs. Chicago in Architecture."

46. H. A. Seymour, "History of Commonwealth Edison Company," n.d., Commonwealth Edison Company archives, p. 200, quoted in Thomas P. Hughes, "Electrification of America: The System Builders."

47. Commonwealth Edison Company, *Round Table*, June 1, 1925, p. 1.

48. *Crawford Station*, brochure, n.d., GAPW archives, Chicago, lists the capacity of each of the units at 51Mw, 60Mw, 75Mw, 88Mw, and 100Mw respectively.

49. *State Line Generating Station*, brochure, n.d., GAPW archives.

PRINCIPAL WORKS: A CATALOGUE RAISONNÉ

In 1912, Peirce Anderson was at work on the United States Post Office in Washington, D.C. At this period in the firm's history, the place a building occupied in the hierarchical ordering of the city was of primary importance, and nowhere was it more important than in the nation's capital. Other buildings of this period too, such as the department store for William Filene's Sons Company in Boston, the David Whitney office building in Detroit, and an industrial structure for the Crane Plumbing Company in Chicago, were all conceived from the viewpoint of the appropriate place each would occupy in a larger civic order.

As the years went by, however, the notions of what was appropriate within the civic context changed, and clear shifts in emphasis followed.

Since this Catalogue Raisonné is roughly chronological, these changes, as well as the accompanying design solutions—some subtle, some daring and imaginative—become apparent in every building type. The various reasons for the changes are indicated when known, for they reflect the complex cultural, economic, social, financial, and political processes that affect the art of architecture in all periods.

UNITED STATES POST OFFICE

1911–14; north section, 1931–33
Massachusetts Avenue, North Capitol, G and First streets NE
Washington, D.C.

Cost in 1933: $2,911,082.77

Status: extant; landmark, Washington, D.C., Inventory of Historic Sites, 1966; eligible for National Register of Historic Places, June 16, 1983

The exterior of the post office in Washington, D.C. (fig. 76), and its relationship to the rest of the Capital City is discussed at length in Part I. The interior of the building is divided into three main spaces—a formal public service lobby which extends the full width of the building along Massachusetts Avenue, office spaces, and work areas to the rear for carts, baggage, and the sorting of mail (fig. 77).[1] The public areas are sumptuously adorned in marbles of various colors, with elaborately decorated ceilings (fig. 78).

Apparently, an extension had been intended from the beginning, for the 1911 structure was not completed on the north. When it was made by Graham, Anderson, Probst and White in 1931–33, the area of the building was expanded by one-third. The corner pavilions were knocked out for the extension, but their replacements were exactly the same as the originals except for one circle in the connecting frieze that is slightly larger. Like the original, the extension is a steel cage, clad in Italian marble on a granite base. Today the building retains its stately Ionic colonnade on the principal entrance and an arcade of windows on the other three elevations.

[76] UNITED STATES POST OFFICE, WASHINGTON, D.C.

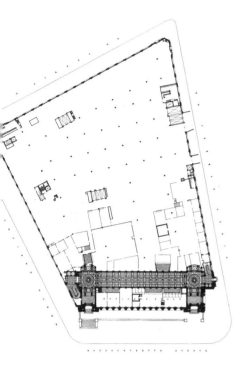

[77] UNITED STATES POST
OFFICE, PLAN

We may take Burnham's own
words for it, that he would have
been pleased. In 1908, in a letter
to Anderson, he had indicated
that in order to insure a treatment that would harmonize the
line of buildings around "Capitol
Plaza," thereby providing a fitting setting for the cultural jewel,
the Capitol Building itself, he
wanted the post office next to the
railroad station.[2]

1. Approximately two hundred
drawings for the United States Post
Office in Washington, D.C., are in
the archives of the General Services
Administration.

2. Burnham to Anderson, August 17, 1908, Letters of Daniel
Burnham, Ryerson and Burnham Libraries, Art Institute of Chicago,
Chicago, Ill.

[78] UNITED STATES POST OFFICE, INTERIOR

FIELD MUSEUM OF NATURAL HISTORY

1909–20
Roosevelt Road at Lake Shore Drive
Chicago, Illinois

Cost in 1920: $7 million
Status: extant, restored 1988

At its inception, the Field Museum was caught in the middle of a conflict: Chicago's need for cultural institutions versus its need for open spaces. Daniel Burnham wanted a museum in Grant Park at the west end of Congress Avenue, a focal point in his 1909 Plan of Chicago, but A. Montgomery Ward, founder of the mail order company and civic leader, wanted no buildings there at all. The history of this complex battle, with its many lawsuits, has already been told, but the important point is that the conflict was waged between two goods.[1] People need contact both with the natural world and with the civilized world, but in such a way that one does not diminish the other. In 1911, there seemed no way to accomplish this, no way for Chicago to have both a grand, free green space *and* a distinguished museum in its flagship park along the lakefront. It was Stanley Field who broke the deadlock. He suggested to the Illinois Central Railroad (IC) that it give the city two blocks of the land it had reclaimed from the swamp near Twelfth Street just south of the park, and build its new station elsewhere. Since the IC was eager to rid itself of the onus of causing more lakefront clutter, it agreed to make the gift and sited its new station west of the park (fig. 79). Thus the Field Museum was begun in 1914 on private property given to the city—a compromise hailed by everyone. Young Stanley Field's energies brought Chicago more green space and the distinguished museum that bears his family's name (figs. 3–8).

The plan (fig. 6) exemplifies Beaux-Arts canons of design. Symmetrical, with identical north and south elevations, the aisles are arranged on bilateral cross axes running the entire 706-foot length and 438-foot depth of the

[79] FIELD MUSEUM OF NATURAL HISTORY, CHICAGO, ILL., EAST PAVILION COLONNADE

[80] FIELD MUSEUM, STANLEY FIELD HALL

sumptuous marble surfaces, the grand proportions, the sculptural figures, and the sunlight streaming through the skylights into the vaulted upper aisles gave the effect of a proud building. The James Simpson Theater on the first floor of the west wing is still one of the finest classical rooms in the city (fig. 7). The seating area, which accommodates about a thousand, is surrounded by a Doric colonnade that connects it to a continuous lobby on all three sides. The other places for study, collections, and classrooms, as well as the traditional exhibition and lecture halls, also express the idea that a museum involves its visitors in active participation and is not merely for passive viewing. The idea of doing research in a museum is as old as the Mouseion in Alexandria, with many other examples throughout history, and the presence of facilities for this purpose in the new structure placed Chicago firmly in this venerable tradition.[2] The combination thus expressed in this building embodies the highest civilized values: civic pride and an active cultural life. In the 1920s, Chicagoans considered such surroundings appropriate to their emerging cosmopolitan status.

By the 1950s, however, the classical style of the Field Museum seemed an anachronism to critics who thought Chicago should pride itself only on its modern achievements, its architectural innovations, and its skyscrapers, or on the works of geniuses like Frank Lloyd Wright and Mies van der Rohe. In the next two decades, the classicism of the Field Museum seemed *retardataire,* especially to genera-

building, but a sense of terminus comes from the long rooms that form the wings. An auditorium, research laboratories, storage spaces, offices, and public service areas were planned in accordance with practical considerations of traffic and other requirements.

World War I delayed the opening of the museum as the War Department commandeered its nearly completed space for a military hospital. After that, it took a year to put in the fixtures and another two and a half years to move the thousands of exhibits from the old Fine Arts Building in Jackson Park to the new structure.

On opening day, May 4, 1921, the public entered a museum devoted to more than the mere reposition of objects (fig. 80). The

tions of visitors in blue jeans. The building was on few lists of the best in Chicago. And it should be said that the building is not without imperfections. Its vast scale can be overwhelming, its extensive acreage tiring, its severity utterly devoid of the lighthearted moments appropriate to a holiday or a day off. In later reflection, however, most ordinary visitors recall an impressive architectural experience from their visit to the Field Museum.

Recently the building has seemed more likely to recapture acclaim due to the new attitude toward our past and the increased attention to our history through the works of the revisionist historians and the historic preservation movement.

1. Lois Wille, *Forever Open Clear and Free*, pp. 71–98.

2. Nikolaus Pevsner, *A History of Building Types*, pp. 111–38. Great vaulted exhibition halls appeared in the Renaissance, and the Field Museum also borrows elements from Guy de Gisors and J. F. Delannoy, eighteenth-century French architects who won the Grand Prix for their large-scale museums. Nineteenth-century museums, such as the Munich Glyptothek and the Altes Museum in Berlin, were also fertile fields for inspiration, especially in the severity of their cubic massing. *See also* William Burger, "Field Museum as Architecture," *Field Museum Natural History Bulletin*, March 1982, pp. 3–5; Alma Stephanie Wittlin, *The Museum* (London: Routledge and Kegan Paul, 1949).

[81] DIME SAVINGS BANK BUILDING, DETROIT, MICH., EXTERIOR

DIME SAVINGS BANK

1912–13
Fort and Griswald streets, NW corner
Detroit, Michigan

Cost in 1912: $1,919,957.93; pcf $0.362
Status: extant, renovated 1983–84

At 304 feet, the Dime Savings Bank was the tallest office building in Detroit in 1913. Combining two office towers around a U-shaped court, the structure incorporates a low, four-story, temple-fronted bank in its center (fig. 81). An early example of the

use of white terra-cotta cladding in Detroit, the building recalls the Reliance Building in Chicago.

Inside, the four-story Banking Room (fig. 82), originally the Peoples Wayne County Bank, was surrounded by Ionic columns with a running frieze of palmettes above and a skylight ceiling admitting light to the marble floors and walls and the brass tellers' cages below.

Like other buildings in the financial district of downtown Detroit, the bank suffered a decline after World War II. Recently it has undergone a major renovation under the direction of John Stevens Associates. The lobby has been completely changed by alterations in a "more contemporary spirit." The corridors on the ground floor of the U-shaped plan were converted into a circular alcove lobby, a change that also included lowering the ceiling five feet to nine and a half feet, a height out of character with the original design. Other aspects of the renovation are more successful, such as the removal of wall marble installed in the 1940s and its replacement with Italian marble. The cleaning and restoration of the building's exterior terra-cotta was an important step in preserving the historic significance of the building.[1]

Two aspects of the design are typical of traditional Chicago building—the expression of the steel-cage frame and the historic references in the classical details. On the other hand, two aspects are innovative for Graham, Anderson, Probst and White—the tall twin towers and the U-shaped plan. The building is thus an important transition work for the firm, whose members, while

[82] DIME SAVINGS BANK, INTERIOR

retaining some old solutions, were preparing to enter the age of the tall skyscraper.

1. Don Durocher, "Major Renovation, New Name Bring New Look to Commonwealth Building," press release, January 21, 1984, Dime Savings Bank archives, Detroit, Mich.

WM. FILENE'S SONS COMPANY BUILDING

1911–12
Summer, Washington, Hawley, and Franklin streets
Boston, Massachusetts

Cost in 1912: $1,751,096.36; pcf $0.308
Status: extant

Proportioned for respectable Bostonians of the period, Filene's is a substantial, heavily ornamented example of Peirce Anderson's adaptation of Beaux-Arts design to a New England department store (fig. 83). Windows on three sides give the shopping floors a liberal amount of light on the periphery, originally supplemented in the center by bronze hanging fixtures which threw electric light up against the ceiling and then down on the merchandise. While not as advantageous as sunlight, this indirect lighting was better than direct electric light, which caused sharp contrasts and heavy shadows and "did not allow color to appear to its best advantage."[1] At the time, the lighting system was state of the art, as was the ventilation system. Fresh air was taken from the roof, cleaned of impurities, and channeled to the basement for a complete change of air every six minutes. Now, of course, air-conditioning has replaced the old system.

The aisles were treated as streets (figs. 61–64), but the finest materials clad the interior walls: American walnut, imported mahogany, and various marbles. The architects also designed a setting for Filene's fa-

[83] WM. FILENE'S SONS COMPANY BUILDING, BOSTON, MASS., DETAIL

mous Automatic Bargain Basement. Every item in this system of markdown bore a price tag indicating the first date it was put on sale. After that the reductions were automatic: after twelve days, 25 percent was taken off; after eighteen days, 50 percent; after twenty-four days, 75 percent; and after that, the item was given to charity.

This added a sporting element to shopping, the element of chance. And the buyer who discovered a designer dress for half the price could be counted on to talk. "As the typical yankee was enthusiastic about thrift," the bargain hunters who flourished in Filene's made "a persuasive group of traveling ambassadors."[2] After World War I, the Automatic Bargain Basement became a resounding success. The average Boston housewife found herself at the Filene's gaming tables with the Cabots and the Lodges, show business personalities, baseball players, famous actresses, and other stars. Adventure was added to shopping.

1. Stacy Holmes, *Filene's* (n.p., 1972). The book can be found in the archives at Filene's along with photographs of the progress of the construction taken almost daily, of the restaurant on opening day, of the library for employees, and of the show windows decorated for opening day with the fashions of 1912. Close-ups show the exterior terracotta, the cast-iron marquee, and the skylit restaurant bedecked with ivy and potted palms. There are also photographs of all elevations and of many details.

2. Gerald Johnson, "A Liberal's Progress," manuscript of a biography of the founder's son, Edward A. Filene, Filene's archives, Boston, Mass.

[84] INSURANCE EXCHANGE BUILDING, CHICAGO, ILL., ELEVATION

INSURANCE EXCHANGE BUILDING

North section, 1911–12; south section, 1927–28
175 West Jackson Boulevard
Chicago, Illinois

Cost in 1912 for the north section: $3,962,610; pcf $0.365
Cost in 1928 for the south section: $6,349,851; pcf $0.597[1]
Status: extant

Located in the heart of Chicago's financial district just west of the Board of Trade Building at Jackson Boulevard and LaSalle Street, the Insurance Exchange, with its 1,320,000 square feet of rentable area, was one of the largest office buildings in Chicago until the late 1960s. The building was owned by an association of businessmen, including Ernest R. Graham, and earnings derived from the offices rented to insurance agents, downtown railroad ticket offices, and others formed the greater part of Graham's private fortune.

The stately aspect of the design is due chiefly to the handsome proportions and the dignified giant-order Ionic columns at the top that echo the Ionic colon-

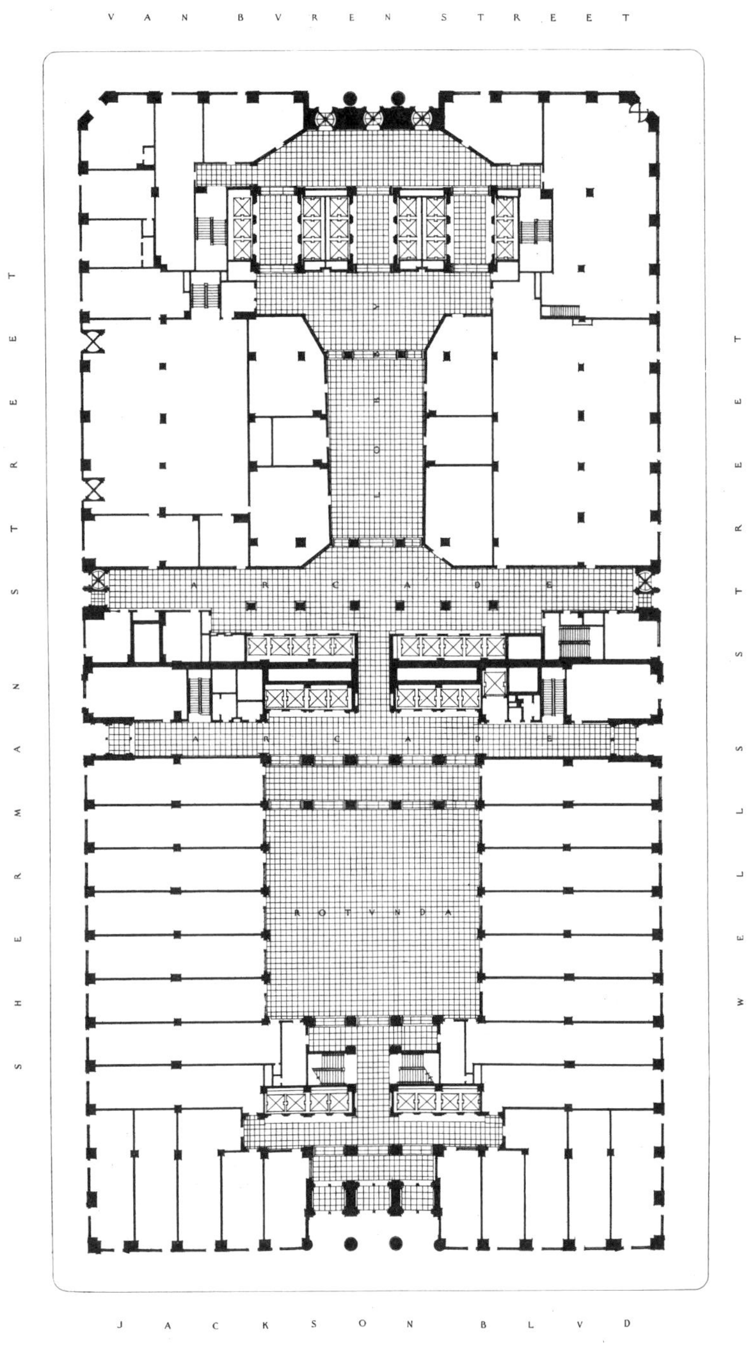

VAN BUREN STREET

STREET

SHERMAN STREET

JACKSON BLVD

WELLS STREET

[85] INSURANCE EXCHANGE, FIRST FLOOR PLAN

ered adding a broad sixteen-story-tower, and caissons were sunk with this future bearing capacity in mind.

Although fifteen years separate the two sections of the building, the second section was similar enough to the first that the outside became a unified rectangle a block in area. The entrances were drastically remodeled after World War II. Four of the Ionic columns and the cast-iron spandrel panels were ripped out of the center of each of the four elevations to make room for slick gray granite portals. The original elegance is still apparent in the northeast corner, however, where the Citicorp Bank has a branch office.

Originally, three public spaces opened up from the ground floor—a rotunda, an elevator arcade, and a lobby (fig. 85). As visitors walked from Jackson Boulevard to Van Buren Street, they passed through these spaces articulated by great Doric piers, which also carried mezzanine stories. The rotunda was lit from above by a great skylight measuring seventy-two by seventy-three feet. It was reported that a suicide in this space prompted its closing, and its remains are now only discernible from the nine lights that mark its former outline. The Grand Trade Room has been divided up, and the marble staircases removed. Without its climactic center and denuded of much of its historic ornament, the building has lost some of the grace and strength of its original spirit. Perhaps this accounts for its underrating in critical accounts of Chicago architecture. Although devoid of its skylight, the interior lobby is still spacious and the arcade full of the activi-

nade of the base. Circular medallions adorn transition stories, and a restrained cornice of anthemia and palmettes pro- vides the finishing touch (fig. 84). When the design for the southern section was being drawn up, the architects consid-

ties of two restaurants, a florist, a shoe store, and two tailors.

Even during the depression, the low maintenance and the high occupancy rate made the building one of the few in the Loop not forced into receivership. For Chicago, and for Ernest R. Graham and the other stockholders, the Insurance Exchange balanced civic-suitability and the profit motive.[2]

1. Square footage from black book of cost records and other statistics in GAPW archives.

2. Other information on the building is available in Carl W. Condit, *Chicago, 1910–29: Building, Planning, and Urban Technology*, p. 93; *Architectural Record* 38 (July 1915): 110–11; *Brickbuilder* 21 (April 1912): 106–9.

COLUMBUS MEMORIAL

1912
Capitol Plaza
Washington, D.C.

Status: extant

The site plan for Union Station in Washington, D.C., made around 1908 when Burnham was head of the firm, included a memorial park at the main entrance just north of the U.S. Capitol. Although the station buildings were completed in 1908, the park, architectural setting, and sculpture by Lorado Taft were not finished until more than three years later. The heavy monumentality of the central cenotaph and the severe geometry of the base with its spare swag-and-wreath ornament are characteristic of the designs of Peirce Anderson (fig. 86).[1] Daniel Burnham also played an active role in the design decisions for this important portion of the urban fabric of Washington, D.C.[2]

1. In the twenty-fifth anniversary record of the Harvard class of 1892 published in 1917, Anderson lists the setting for the monument as one of his works.

2. Burnham to Anderson, August 27, 1908, Letters of Daniel Burnham, Art Institute of Chicago.

[86] COLUMBUS MEMORIAL, WASHINGTON, D.C.

ALFRED DECKER AND COHN BUILDING

(Society Brand Building)

1912–13
416 South Franklin Street
Chicago, Illinois

Status: demolished

The Alfred Decker and Cohn Building was typical of many built in the decade after the turn of the century in the manufacturing districts on the periphery of the Loop. A combination of office block and factory, it used the wide-bayed steel framing common to both, but the red brick cladding with limestone trim was usually reserved for buildings on the lower levels of the urban hierarchy (fig. 87). The firm also used this utilitarian mode for other buildings of this type, such as the Western Union Telegraph Building (*q.v.*) in Chicago.

STARKS BUILDING

1913; addition, 1926
455 South Fourth Avenue
Louisville, Kentucky

Cost in 1913: $666,476.10;
    pcf $0.2739
Cost in 1926: $2,071,006.00;
    pcf $0.57
Status: extant; landmark,
    National Register of Historic
    Places, July 11, 1985

An anchor of the area around Fourth Avenue and Walnut Street, the Starks Building is a major architectural landmark in

[87] ALFRED DECKER AND COHN BUILDING (SOCIETY BRAND BUILDING), CHICAGO, ILL., EXTERIOR

the central business district of Louisville and an important part of its busy retail sector. Four factors have contributed to the long-term success of the building—its design, its location, its mixed use, and its maintenance.

The wide openings of the department store windows were designed to meet the street with elegant displays of clothing and other merchandise.[1] The designer (perhaps Sigurd Naess) remembered his lessons in classical ornament, for he marked the transition between the base and the

[88] STARKS BUILDING, LOUISVILLE, KY.

suckle, and acanthus leaves. (The cornice is no longer extant.) The exterior is Vermont granite at the base with cream-colored vitreous Kittanning pressed brick with terra-cotta trim above (fig. 88).

The principal features of the plan are the marble L-shaped arcade that extends from Fourth Avenue to Walnut Street and

the largest and best light court possible, at a great sacrifice in space, but at a corresponding gain in the desirability of the offices facing this large light court ... with relief from the hum of the traffic and the dust and distractions of the street. . . . It is natural for businessmen to desire to do business with groups of highly respected and successful businessmen. The more such men are housed together the easier it is for them to meet and do business one with another. . . . The Starks Building offers all of the advantages—the most centrally located and the largest and most complete office building in the South.[2]

The upkeep of the building has kept current with maintenance needs and changing times. Carrier Weathermaster air-conditioning was installed in 1955. The center light court was enclosed, and retail space, with an illuminated fountain, trees, fabric hangings, and window boxes, was added there on the second floor in 1984.

1. See the twenty-by-thirty-inch presentation drawing in tempera and pencil in the office of the building, which also contains original blueprints, eighteen drawers of other drawings in flat storage, and others in rolls in wood cases.

shaft of the building with a strong horizontal. As clearly as a Greek painter made a band between the foot and the body of a decorated vase, the leafy spandrel panels, urns, and scrolled mullions of the fourth floor indicate a pause before the uninterrupted rise of the vertical piers begins at the fifth floor. At the thirteenth floor, spandrel panels of bold swags and lions' heads prepare us for the transition to the top of the building, the cornice itself, with its elaborate display of anthemia, or honey-

2. Rental brochure, n.d., Starks Building archives, Louisville, Ky. Other information may be found in the Kentucky Heritage Council Inventory. *See also* "Bids Soon to be Taken for Work on Skyscraper," *Louisville Courier-Journal,* June 18, 1912; Jefferson County (Ky.), *Deed Book;* Andrew N. Rebori, "The Work of Burnham and Root, D. H. Burnham, D. H. Burnham and Co., and Graham, Burnham and Co."; "Starks Building," rotogravure section, *Louisville Courier-Journal,* November 7, 1936. A book of the architect's specifications is also in the office of the building.

CONTINENTAL AND COMMERCIAL NATIONAL BANK BUILDING

(208 South LaSalle Building)

1912–14
208 South LaSalle Street
Chicago, Illinois

Cost in 1914: $5,775,203.50; pcf $0.379
Status: extant

In the mid-nineteenth century, Chicago was laid out on a grid composed of blocks 325 feet by 380 feet, which were intersected by alleys in both directions. The alley between Jackson and Adams streets, however, was wider than the others and seemed to deserve a street name. As all the names of the presidents had already been used up (this was during the tenure of Martin Van Buren), the city council chose the middle name of the second Adams—Quincy Street. Although only half a block wide, the Continental and Commercial National Bank thus has four street elevations (fig. 89).[1] Its stately proportions—approximately 305 feet long, 116 feet wide, and 287 feet tall—give the building a certain elegance.[2]

Today the main entrance of the 208 South LaSalle Building is still distinguished by the immense polished granite columns of its loggia. Inside, an uninterrupted arcade of shops stretches the length of the building. A broad staircase once ascended to a lofty Banking Room, expressing the vaulted halls of a great financial institution (fig. 90). Enhanced by the abundant daylight that streamed through the barrel vault seventy-five feet overhead, the interior reflections were fur-

[89] CONTINENTAL AND COMMERCIAL NATIONAL BANK BUILDING (208 SOUTH LASALLE BUILDING), CHICAGO, ILL., EXTERIOR

[90] CONTINENTAL AND COMMERCIAL NATIONAL BANK, INTERIOR

ther intensified by the white marble mosaics on the floors, the shining brasses, and the lustrous columns that articulated the space.[3]

Although some of the original materials have been preserved, the great glory of this interior space was destroyed by a remodeling in the 1960s. The seventy-five-foot space was divided into two stories, the lofty skylight encased in scaffolding, and the giant columns removed. A modern plastic skylight now covers the office space in the lower half. Plans are underway for renovating the upper half by restoring

the old skylight and developing new office space. But the old skylight will cover a space only half as tall as it did originally.

1. *The Making of a Modern Bank*, rental brochure, c. 1914, the office of the 208 South LaSalle Building, Chicago, Ill.

2. Transverse and longitudinal sections drawn to scale appear in Peter B. Wight, "The Continental and Commercial Bank, Chicago," *Building Progress* 3, no. 10 (October 1913).

3. Rebori, "The Work of Burnham and Root," pp. 136–43, contains illustrations of the original interiors.

FIRST NATIONAL BANK BUILDING

(First Wisconsin National Bank Building)

1912–14
735 North Water Street
Milwaukee, Wisconsin

Cost in 1914: $1,805,717
Status: extant

An elevated terrace adorned with boxes of flowers originally lined the 120-foot frontage on North Water Street and the 209-foot frontage on Mason Street that separated the First National Bank Building from the Milwaukee River.[1] Responding to the prominent place the building has in Milwaukee, near the center of the city and just one-half block from City Hall, the site has long been an urban focal point (fig. 91).

Like many structures of this period by Graham, Burnham and Company, the bank's elevation is tripartite, with classic ornament. The U-shaped plan allowed natural light to reach offices off an interior court fifty-nine feet square in area. On the ground floor, English-veined Italian marble decorated the spacious Banking Room, and the long, narrow lobby on the south side was treated as an interior sidewalk.

In the late 1950s, the entire interior was remodeled to accommodate air-conditioning ducts and to provide modern lighting.

[91] FIRST NATIONAL BANK BUILDING (FIRST WISCONSIN NATIONAL BANK BUILDING), MILWAUKEE, WIS., EXTERIOR

At this time the original skylight was also closed to increase the rentable square footage.[2]

1. Observable in the original drawings in the offices of the owners. A book of specifications is also there.

2. Costing $7.5 million, the modernization in 1959 also added eight new elevators to the original eight and remodeled the Banking Room floor. Sue Meldman, interview, July 1987.

CONWAY BUILDING

(Chicago Title and Trust Building)

1912–15
111 West Washington Street
Chicago, Illinois

Cost in 1915: $3,471,301.79;
    pcf $0.36
Status: extant; landmark,
    National Register of Historic
    Places

The Conway Building marks the busy intersection of Clark and Washington streets in Chicago's Loop. Unlike the four-square office blocks pictured in the Plan of Chicago, the Conway has rounded corners and is clad in creamy terra-cotta (fig. 92). The designer, Frederick P. Dinkelberg, went even further and projected the curves slightly from the planes of the adjoining buildings, giving the Conway a soft prominence in the streetscape. Elaborate architectural ornament once adorned the entrance (fig. 94), but was removed in a later remodeling.[1] Since this design for the estate of Marshall Field was begun before Burnham's death, and no doubt had

[92] CONWAY BUILDING (CHICAGO TITLE AND TRUST BUILDING), CHICAGO, ILL., EXTERIOR

his approval, we may deduce that the stretch of similar buildings in the Plan was a general sketch only and never meant to be followed literally.[2]

In the original interior (fig. 93), the vestibule space continued into a two-story rotunda, which provided daylight for the shops on the first floor and the offices that opened on a balcony off the second floor (fig. 96). The space continued to flow to the south elevator lobby (fig. 95),[3]

99

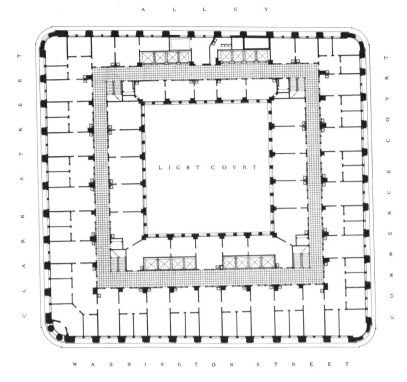

[93] CONWAY BUILDING, PLAN

and all of these public rooms were sheathed in ornamented white terra-cotta, which was replaced with black and white marble slabs in a 1945–47 remodeling by Holabird and Root.

A fine example of the firm's work during the transition between the Burnham era and the work of Graham, Burnham and Company, the Conway is among the most sophisticated Chicago office buildings of the period. At the time of its opening, the new managers boasted that the mechanical equipment was "all of the best modern type in each line," the power and lighting "up-to-the-minute," with a switchboard that was the last word and an automatically fed furnace. There was a barbershop, a shower room for employees, and a gymnasium, and the rental office itself was furnished as a model for the "cosmopolitan character" of the occupants of the building—"executive offices and branch offices of manufacturing concerns; real estate offices; architects; insurance companies; law offices; building contractors; lumber producers' headquarters; public accountants; mercantile agencies; and public service corporations."[4]

Over its seventy-year life, the Conway Building has proved remarkably adaptive to changing needs, and even to changing tastes. Fortunately, major remodeling efforts have been in the hands of skilled architects. A shopping arcade was erected between the Conway and the adjacent Foreman State Bank in

[94] CONWAY BUILDING, ENTRANCE LOBBY INTERIOR

[95] CONWAY BUILDING,
ELEVATOR LOBBY

1933. This "Washington Arcade," still extant, is certainly a rare, and perhaps the only, instance of cooperation between Graham, Anderson, Probst and White and Holabird and Root, who between them built much of Chicago's Loop. Although the 1945–47 alterations of the main lobby by Holabird and Root changed the character of the interior, making it contemporary in feeling rather than keeping to the spirit of the original, the outcome was in the best of the modernist tradition. The octagonal pillars were resheathed in travertine, and the skylight was re-

[96] CONWAY BUILDING,
ROTUNDA

moved, as was the glazing on the mezzanine office windows, but the new ceiling was coffered and given indirect lighting, and new mezzanine railings appropriate to the new character of the space were added. The 1983 remodeling by Jack Train Associates added bay windows to some offices in the interior court and landscaped the area over the old skylight.[5]

The building retains the dignity of its exterior proportions, color, and texture, and the interest of its airy central space, though some of its charm has been sacrificed. Its own character, strong to begin with, and the perceptiveness of its successive owners and architects, have ensured its long, valuable life as a member of Chicago's business community. The long tree-lined avenues of buildings with uniform cornice lines, but some variety in their individual facades, that Burnham, Graham, Anderson, and the others envisioned did not materialize. The Conway, a building block of that grand de-

sign, remains as an embodiment of the ideal.

1. John Zukowsky, "Frederick P. Dinkelberg and the Chicago Architectural Club," *Chicago Architectural Journal* 5 (1985): 32.

2. Marshall Field (1834–1906) was born in Conway, Massachusetts, hence the name of the building. At his death his estate was valued at over $83 million; his will called for the funds to be invested, particularly in Chicago real estate, until 1943, when all funds were to be transferred to his grandson, Marshall Field III, on his fiftieth birthday. The executors purchased many existing buildings, but they also undertook two major construction projects in addition to the Conway: the Pittsfield Building and the Field Building, also by the firm and discussed later. See the Landmark Nomination by Nancy Hubbard and Dana Hubbard, 1983, for a careful description and history of the Conway. Hubbard and Hubbard also highlight the difficulty of attributing the building. Two sales brochures, for example, identify the architect differently; the 1912 brochure names D. H. Burnham and Company as the archi-

tect, and the 1915 version names Graham, Burnham and Company. Thomas S. Hines, *Burnham of Chicago: Architect and Planner,* Appendix A, p. 383, has a useful list of buildings designed before, but completed after, Burnham's death in 1912. The drawings for the Conway Building were signed by Ernest Graham, Peirce Anderson, and Edward Probst on April 30, 1912, almost two months after the Continental and Commercial Bank Building drawings were completed.

3. Ground plan, n.d., Conway Building archives, Chicago, Ill., which also includes an estimated two thousand drawings, blueprints, ink and watercolors, hectographs, hectographs with colored pencils, and colored inks. Two presentation drawings, one looking west by day (17" x 37") and signed "C. B. del." and one looking north by night (17" x 37"), and one full-view sepia lithograph(?) (22" x 32") are included.

4. Brochure, 1915, Conway Building archives.

5. *Chicago Title and Trust Building,* rental brochure, c. 1983, Conway Building archives.

CRANE COMPANY CORWITH PLANT

1914–26
3900 South Pershing Road
Chicago, Illinois

Costs: Archival records at Graham, Anderson, Probst and White contain costs for all buildings.
Status: partially demolished

An industrial complex with manufacturing lofts, warehouses, shipping centers, train sheds, and office and service buildings, the group included a total of thirty-three buildings for the Crane Company, a manufacturer of plumbing fixtures (fig. 69). Like most of the industrial architecture that began in the late nineteenth century in Chicago, the Crane buildings all express their structural frames directly, and all are clad in red brick with limestone and terra-cotta trim (fig. 97). Put together in a complex united by uniform height and cornice lines, the cluster of Crane buildings was part of the early industrial park movement, which included two other complexes going up at the same time: the new Western Electric Plant at 2200 South Cicero Avenue (1918–21) and the Central Manufacturing District at 3900 South Pershing Road (S. Scott Joy, 1914–26). Unlike George M. Pullman's company town, these complexes included no workers' housing, but focused on centralized facilities, including such executive amenities as dining rooms, barbershops, and other services.

Most of the Crane buildings have been demolished, and the area, now owned by the Santa Fe Railroad, is used as a parking lot for large trucks. Extant, but

[97] CRANE COMPANY CORWITH PLANT, CHICAGO, ILL., AERIAL VIEW

missing the large clock originally at the top of its eight-story tower, is the five-story Administration Building on the southwest corner of Kedzie Avenue and Thirty-ninth Street, which has been modernized with bronze aluminum windows. Also extant is a three-story warehouse twenty-five bays long to the north, which has been altered with additions, and a one-story blind brick warehouse twenty-two bays long on Pershing Road (see Part I).

LEHIGH VALLEY COAL COMPANY BUILDING

(King's College Administration Building)

1913
133 North River Street
Wilkes-Barre, Pennsylvania

Status: extant

Facing the Susquehanna River, the Lehigh Valley Coal Company Building was given a landscaped setting between its entrance and the street (fig. 98). The facade is further distinguished by three divisions, with three arches at the ground level which open into an entrance lobby clad with boldly grained marble and leading to a spacious library,[1] today a reception area for the president of King's College.

1. Drawings in King's College Library, Special Collections. *See also* description in the Wilkes-Barre, Pa., *Chamber of Commerce Journal*, July 1913, p. 23; Michael Conner, letter to the author, June 15, 1984.

[98] LEHIGH VALLEY COAL COMPANY BUILDING (KING'S COLLEGE ADMINISTRATION BUILDING), WILKES-BARRE, PA.

EQUITABLE BUILDING

1912–15
120 South Broadway
New York, New York

Cost, architect's figures, probably in 1915 dollars: $11,706,904. In his history of the Equitable Life Assurance Society, R. Carlyle Buley states that the client, Thomas Coleman duPont, paid $13.5 million for the site and $14.9 million for the building.

Status: extant; landmark, National Register of Historic Places Inventory

The day after the January 9, 1912, fire that destroyed the old Equitable Life Assurance Society Building in New York, Ernest R. Graham was on the 2:30 train to arrange to make the ruin safe until it could be razed.[1] The Equitable called in Graham as its representative because it had been discussing plans for a new building on the site with the Burnham firm off and on since 1909.[2]

More than painters or sculptors, architects are caught in the forces of change. Sometimes unusual opportunities come their way because they are in the right place at the right time; sometimes accidents and other mishaps no fault of their own mar otherwise creditable work. Graham was fortunate in most of his buildings, but this first commission after the death of Daniel Burnham was fraught with political and social ordeals no one could have anticipated. Before it was all over, the best efforts of Graham, Anderson, and the others would be invested in a building soon called a "monstrous parasite on the veins and arteries of New York"[3] and destined to occupy, somewhat unfairly, an infamous place in the history of American architecture. Designed to mitigate the very evils of

which it was accused, the skyscraper was caught in an ideological crossfire that has made a balanced judgment impossible until now.

Soon after Burnham's death in June, Graham set about the tasks involved in designing a new building on the site, which was sold to Thomas Coleman duPont, an heir of the duPont chemical fortune, the same summer. Graham wanted a model of safety and efficiency in the elevator system, state-of-the-art heating and ventilating systems, and fireproofing that met the highest standards of the National Board of the New York Fire Insurance Exchange. He ensured his client special arrangements for a new kind of construction schedule so that no time or materials would be wasted, a hard promise to keep for a wagon-fed job in lower Manhattan. He entrusted the design to the man in whom he had the most confidence in the office, Peirce Anderson. While these arrangements were being carried out, social pressures for zoning regulations were mounting on all sides in a New York increasingly frightened by the hazards of large buildings.

In the meantime, before the Equitable Building was even laid

out in plan, Graham faced the first problem: speed of elevator service. In his early days with Burnham, the main object in designing a skyscraper for revenue, or a speculative office building as we would call it today, was to add as many stories as possible without going so high as to lose too much space to elevators and stairways. Graham knew that if the Equitable was to attract tenants in an area with plenty of available spaces for rent, it had to do so by providing better service than its competitors, and nowhere did service count as much as in the elevator system. As a contemporary writer put it, "a man will stop while buying a cigar to chat with the clerk; he will wait ten minutes, if the bartender is busy, to get a cocktail this particular bartender only can mix; he will spend an hour at the manicurist's table after his shave . . . but he can't wait one second for an elevator. If he waits more than a second he is losing money . . . and he goes to the starter and expatiates on the . . . funereal elevator service in the building."[4]

Accordingly, Graham visited Charles E. Knox, one of the leading consulting elevator engineers in New York. He put the matter directly: "We want the new Equitable Building to have the name of giving the best elevator service of any building in the world. It is up to you to show us how to do it. We want the answer in four days. The elevator service will determine the height of the building."[5]

Knox's previous dealings with architects had been of the oppo-

[99] EQUITABLE BUILDING, NEW YORK, N.Y., ELEVATION

site kind. Usually they came to him and said, "We have a twenty-five-story building on a plot 150 feet by 150 feet, and only so much space is allotted for elevators, fit them in."[6] He had to do what he could, irrespective of the quality of the service, the number of clients, or the type of use expected. To Knox, the situation was comparable to a tailor saying to his customer, "This cloth will not make a suit for a man your size, but I can snip a few inches off your legs and arms and fit you nicely."[7] Graham, on the other hand, understood the relationship of technology and service and gave the elevator engineer an opportunity to make use of his skills, even if he had only four days in which to do it!

Knox had been collecting data on elevator use for years. His survey of office buildings in lower Manhattan told him the relative percentage of occupancy in such buildings by stockbrokers, lawyers, and businesses, floor by floor. By collecting data every hour of each workday he was able to predict the number of people who would use a floor occupied by a certain type of tenant. Accordingly, he had developed a system for elevator planning. After four days he provided Graham with his recommendations. He could not give adequate service for the forty-two-story building that the client wanted, but he could fulfill every speed and safety requirement for fifty thousand people a day with seven banks of forty-eight elevators, each with a maximum rush-hour capacity of 300 people every fifteen minutes; that is, he could provide the best service in the world for a thirty-six-story

building. Thus the height of the Equitable Building was determined.

Just as important as the elevator problem were Graham's orders that the Equitable be the first building in Manhattan to conform in every way to new fireproofing standards. At the time these included furnishing ample means of escape and warning for those in the danger zone; confining the fire not only to the floor on which it originated, but to a section of that floor; allowing easy access by the fire department to all points around and above the blaze; providing adequate fire walls and fire doors; using high-temperature-resistant materials, such as terra-cotta; and installing an automatic sprinkler system in especially vulnerable areas and an extensive fire alarm system.

Equally pressing were the demands for speed and economy of construction. The high land value and the labor costs made it desirable for the building to stop costing money and start earning rental income as soon as possible. In 1912, general contractors usually obtained bids from various subcontractors and parceled out the work. It was a system fraught with profit-padding and excessive delays, and delays had a domino effect. If one subcontractor was behind in his work, other work that was affected by it came to a halt. If the plumbing was not installed, for example, work on the interiors could not be finished on schedule. Under this system, the various subcontractors were in competition with each other, duplication of work was frequent, and few had a genuine interest in

the operation as a whole. Soon everyone began to realize the cost of this absence of cooperation. The owner was paying two profits on all branches of the work, one to the general contractor and one to the subcontractor.[8]

Graham, duPont, T. R. Tinsley (superintendent of construction), and Louis Horowitz (the contractor), created an organization to oversee the Equitable Building's construction to ensure the greatest speed, efficiency, and profit for the owner, architect, and contractor. Coordinating the work of thousands—quarrymen, stonecutters, steamship and railroad workers, drivers of horses and trucks, riveters, bricklayers, draftsmen, excavators, architects, engineers, and superintendents—was essential, and this was accomplished by an official plan, the so-called Method of Procedure to which everyone involved agreed.[9]

Formulated before the first spade of earth was dug, the Method of Procedure provided for any exigency by designating the responsibilities of everyone involved, by developing a time schedule, and by identifying the relationship each of four principals—owner, supervisor, architect, and contractor—had to each other and to the whole. It provided what modern managers would call a flowchart. Recommendations went down from the owners to the supervisors to the architects to the contractor, and reports went upward in the opposite direction. Meetings were held every Wednesday with the heads of the various departments, and they were official. Nothing could be done unless the action had been approved by this body. Minutes were taken and copies sent not only to duPont, Tinsley, Graham, and Horowitz, but to the twenty other men usually in attendance.

In lower Manhattan, the Equitable Building had to be a "wagon-fed job," that is, there was no place to store materials, so the time schedule was especially important.

There were 32,500 tons of steel in the skeleton of the building and the steel for the foundation for each floor was to be delivered on a certain date. If the foundation was not ready for the placing of its steel and the steel arrived on the day set what was to be done with it? It couldn't be stored on the sidewalk. It couldn't be stored in a building, there being no building to store it in. So, the foundation work simply had to be ready for its steel when that steel arrived. And it was.[10]

More than twenty-five hundred men worked nearly every day on the Equitable beginning June 10, 1914, and it was completed February 1, 1915, according to schedule.

For his part, Peirce Anderson drew up formal solutions adapting Beaux-Arts canons to the needs of modern skyscrapers. On the surface, the Equitable is a classical, tripartite design (fig. 99). Visitors entering from Broadway find themselves on an interior east-west street a block long, arcaded and lined with shops. The coffering twenty feet above, in octagons and diamonds, adds to the richness of the scene, and marble pavement leads to an intersection with a north-south arcade, which also acts as a foyer for the elevators

[100] EQUITABLE BUILDING, ARCADE

(fig. 100). This urbanistic enclosure responds to the streets of lower Manhattan, an adaptation to a twentieth-century office building of the Galleria in Milan or the Rue de Rivoli in Paris.

In plan the Equitable forms the letter H, and the shape of the exterior thus clearly reflects the working divisions of the building, for the elevator lobbies are in the short middle section of the H

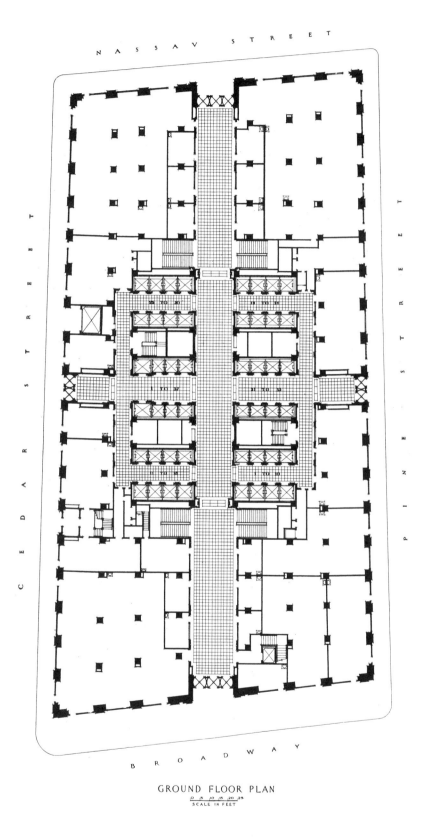

GROUND FLOOR PLAN

0 5 10 15 20 25
SCALE IN FEET

(fig. 101). In elevation the Equitable is a solid rectangle up to the seventh story, where the two large light courts open to reveal twin towers. Below, arches and Corinthian pilasters give a quiet dignity to the entrances on all street sides. To respond to the stone of the Equitable's Broadway neighbors, Anderson selected granite for the cladding of the first three stories, but granite-colored terra-cotta for the upper stories. Anderson must have envisioned the building as an American classic, a sedate addition to lower Manhattan, the interior arcades providing a continuation of the life of the street.

Unlike Chicago, New York in 1912 did not have a widely accepted published vision of what the city would look like in the future. New Yorkers were sharply divided on the subject of skyscrapers. Many may have imagined the city of the future dotted with towers like Metropolitan Life's, while others thought the Flatiron Building (D. H. Burnham and Company, 1902) a more suitable model. With the pictures in Burnham's *Plan of Chicago* and their own experience as their guides, Graham and Anderson developed the Equitable Building in the Chicago image. In the end, however, the architects created neither an icon of big business like the Metropolitan Life Tower (Napoleon Le-Brun and Sons, 1909), nor a restrained office building of the type pictured in the *Plan*. The Equitable was neither an individualistic tower nor an urban building block. The demands for

[101] EQUITABLE BUILDING, PLAN

profits had resulted in a floor-area ratio over thirty times the size of the plot—1.2 million square feet on a lot just under one acre.[11] The Equitable was tall but without the redeeming slender, spirelike quality of a tower, and yet its height prevented it from having the urbanistic decorum of an office block. It was neither the one nor the other.

When the movement toward public control of building height and size came to its climax and orators sought a harrowing case in point, there were nine other buildings in New York taller than the Equitable,[12] but they were such favorites as the Woolworth Building (Cass Gilbert, 1913) and the Metropolitan Life Tower, and therefore not good objects for negative political rhetoric. Seemingly without redeeming features, and with its bulk added to its height and its sedate imagery, the Equitable became a favorite target of reformers, and the invective heaped upon the building has obscured its other merits until today.

In his admirable study of the movement toward public control of land use, Seymour Toll states that "the Equitable Building carried the development of the skyscraper to such intolerable extremes that, beyond any other structure, it may be isolated as the one building which was a final cause of the zoning law."[13] This opinion has echoed throughout the profession and has sifted down to popular accounts such as the *AIA Guide to New York City,* which characterizes the building as the "behemoth that triggered the 1916 zoning law ... more famous for what it caused than what it

is.... The hue and cry after Equitable's completion led to the adoption of the first zoning resolution in 1916."[14]

Yet opposition to buildings of extreme height had begun as early as 1894 when the Architectural League of New York sponsored a symposium on the question of height limitation for office buildings. Little support was gained for the idea of public control of building height in the next decade, which saw the erection of Daniel Burnham's Flatiron in 1903 and Cyrus L. W. Eidlitz's Times Tower in 1904. By 1908, however, three more tall buildings by Francis H. Kimball—the Trinity Building, United States Realty Building, and the edifice at 165 Broadway—were in place, Ernest Flagg's 600-foot Singer Building was completed, and plans for the 700-foot Metropolitan Life Tower were announced. Alarmed, a group of private citizens formed the Committee on Congestion of Population in New York, and the Heights of Buildings Commission of the New York Board of Alderman Building Commission began hearings.[15] On December 23, 1913, when this committee issued its report, the acknowledged blueprint for zoning,[16] the excavation work for the Equitable Building had only just begun.[17]

Careful study of testimony before the Building Commission of the New York Board of Aldermen, of letters to the editor of the *New York Times,* and of the 1913 *Report of the Heights of Buildings Commission to the Committee on the Height, Size, and Arrangement of Buildings of the Board of Estimate and Ap-*

portionment of the City of New York reveals that the professional planning for the control of building height, size, and apportionment was complete by 1913. Although the ordinances were not enacted into law for another two-and-a-half years, these thirty months were filled largely with public hearings, publicity, political rhetoric, and elaborate discussions about boundary changes. On May 23, 1914, the *New York Times,* for example, reported that it was generally conceded that regulation of building height was desirable. At that time the steel work for the Equitable had not yet reached the twelfth floor.[18] The Equitable could not have been the single cause of the zoning laws. If one had to point to a single force, it would be fairer to name the coalition of architects and planners, Fifth Avenue property owners, and reformers who had drafted and fought for the ordinance in the years between 1910 and 1913.

For those appearing before the commission in the last year before passage, however, the Equitable's monumental presence was a convenient common reference. It was said that the Equitable blocked ventilation, dumped thirteen thousand users onto nearby sidewalks, choked the local transit facilities, and created potential problems for firemen.[19] The Equitable's noon shadow, someone complained, enveloped six times its own area. Stretching almost a fifth of a mile, it cut off direct sunlight from the Broadway fronts of buildings as tall as twenty-one stories. The darkened area extended four blocks to the north.

Most of the surrounding property owners claimed a loss of rental income because so much light and air had been stolen by the massive new building, and they filed for a reduction in their assessed valuations.[20] The rhetoric was strong, and by 1915 the zoning ordinance faced little general opposition. A few scattered conservatives spoke up in the last few days of hearings before the 1916 zoning ordinance passed, but most of the testimony was taken up with requests for minor changes and alterations in the wording. On June 27, for example, the Brooklyn Board of Real Estate Brokers requested that Brooklyn Heights north of Joralemon Street be restored to the 2X Zone. Seventy-seventh Street property owners in Brooklyn opposed apartment houses between Fourth and Fifth streets.

The Equitable Building suffered the full measure of wrath that might have been shared by a few other tall or bulky buildings under different circumstances. But the Equitable was tall *and* bulky. One year after the building was finished, the new zoning ordinance allowed a floor area of only twelve times the area of the site, as opposed to the Equitable's thirty. The Equitable's slab shape would have to have been severely altered to conform to the new rules—requiring two setbacks by the time it reached the eighteenth floor, and confining the whole upper half to a tower. The Flatiron Building, by contrast, would have required no change to be in compliance; and the effect of the regulation on the Woolworth Building would have been insignificant: the setback at the twenty-seventh floor would have been lowered to the twenty-

third, but the regulations would have permitted a larger bulk for the tower, with no limit placed on its height.[21]

In light of this history, it is not surprising that not one contemporary critic found anything positive to say about the building. At that time it would have been tantamount to pointing out that Kaiser Wilhelm had a nice smile. Fifteen years later the Chrysler Building and the Empire State Building, with their crowns above a thousand feet, and several other setback skyscrapers in Manhattan dwarfed the Equitable and made it less offensive. In the 1930s, critic Francisco Mujica stated simply that the principal interest of the Equitable Building lay in "its intelligent interior arrangement and the central location of its 50 elevators."[22] Later writers spoke unfairly only of its causative role in the zoning movement without mentioning any of the positive aspects of the building.[23] The Equitable became a scapegoat, bearing the blame not only for itself, but for others. It became a symbol of the evils of skyscrapers, a "spectre of greed in a megalopolis out of control."[24] History singled it out to symbolize one side of the entire prezoning period. By today's standards the building seems almost a welcome caesura in Manhattan's restless skyline. In any case, the Equitable was clearly not the sole cause of the zoning movement, it did mitigate two of the major evils of skyscrapers, as its fireproofing and elevator service attest, its adaptations of management techniques to building construction were models of the industry, and its arcades continue to provide urbanistic grace.[25]

1. Diaries of Ernest R. Graham, January 10, 1912, GAPW archives, Chicago, Ill. Daniel Burnham died six months after the fire that destroyed the old Equitable Building. It was not until August that Graham and the others completed the arrangements for the new firm, Graham, Burnham and Company, with Burnham's sons, Hubert and Daniel, as junior partners. Probably at some time in the interval it was necessary to assign an architect's name to the project, so Graham used his own name, the only time his name appeared alone on a building. Peirce Anderson was the designer, as he reported to Harvard University Alumni Office on the occasion of the twenty-fifth anniversary of the class of 1892 in *Class of 1892—Report 6,* p. 11.

2. The *New York Times,* January 10, 1912, illustrates the 1909 proposal Burnham filed with the Building Permit Department.

3. Louis I. Horowitz, *Towers of New York,* p. 153.

4. Fred Arnold, "Up Go Fifty Thousand People," *Real Estate Magazine,* February 1915, p. 61. By coincidence the 1870 Equitable Building had been the first office structure to use elevators to make rental of upper stories desirable. This fact, together with its five-story height, has earned it the title of the world's first skyscraper in the minds of many scholars. The site at 120 Broadway thus marks two key moments in the history of elevator technology and its role in skyscraper design. See Winston Weisman, "A New View of Skyscraper History," in *The Rise of an American Architecture,* ed. Edgar Kaufmann, Jr. (New York, 1970).

5. Weisman, *American Architecture,* p. 61.

6. Ibid., p. 60

7. Ibid.

8. Louis I. Horowitz, "The Modern Building Organization," *Real Estate News,* February 1915, p. 26.

9. F. A. Austin, "Team Work Built the New Equitable," *Real Estate Magazine*, February 1915, pp. 29, 31.

10. Ibid., p. 34.

11. Carol Krinsky, "Sister Cities," in John Zukowsky, ed., *Chicago and New York: Architectural Interactions*, p. 59. *See also* Paul Goldberger, *The Skyscraper;* M. Domosh, "The Symbolism of the Skyscraper: Case Studies of New York's First Tall Buildings."

12. *Report of the Heights of Buildings Commission to the Committee on the Height, Size, and Arrangement of Buildings of the Board of Estimate and Apportionment of the City of New York*, December 23, 1913, p. 15.

13. Seymour I. Toll, *Zoned America*, p. 48. For other relevant discussions of the zoning movement, see R. Babcock, *The Zoning Game;* John Delafons, *Land Use Controls in the United States;* Carol Willis, "Zoning and *Zeitgeist.*"

14. Norval White and Elliot Willensky, *AIA Guide to New York City* (New York: Collier Macmillan, 1978), p. 20.

15. Typescript of testimony before the New York Board of Aldermen Building Commission, 1908, New York Municipal Library, New York, N.Y., also contains relevant material.

16. Toll, *Zoned America*, pp. 146–54.

17. Construction photographs, GAPW archives, Chicago, Ill.

18. Ibid.

19. *Report of the Heights of Buildings,* note 19, p. 17; Toll, *Zoned America*, p. 71; Helen Christine Bennett, "The Greatest Builder of Skyscrapers in the World," *American Magazine* 89 (April 1920): 177–78; statement of Lawson Purdy, May 8, 1916, in "Commission on Building Districts and Restrictions," *Final Report, June 2, 1916* (New York: City of New York Board of Estimate and Apportionment, Committee on the City Plan, 1916), p. 168; statements of Herbert S. Swan and George W. Tutle, March 15, 1916, ibid., p. 177.

20. Toll, *Zoned America*, pp. 143–210.

21. *Report of the Heights of Buildings*, Diagram 6, p. 77.

22. Francisco Mujica, *History of the Skyscraper* (Paris: Archaeology and Architecture Press, 1930).

23. Horowitz, "The Towers of New York," *Saturday Evening Post*, March 28, 1936, pp. 49–50.

24. Ibid., p. 49.

25. Sally A. Kitt Chappell, "The Equitable Building Reconsidered," *Journal of the Society of Architectural Historians* 49 (March 1990): 90–95.

MOUNT WILSON OBSERVATORY

1914–17
Pasadena, California

Cost in 1917 for instrument and housing: $600,000
Status: extant; landmark, American Society of Mechanical
   Engineers, June 1981

During the first half of the twentieth century, the scientific world was astonished by the work of astronomers. Huge galaxies—whole universes at incredible distances from our own Milky Way—were seen for the first time. Sunspots were photographed with a new instrument called a spectroheliograph and a supernova was recorded on photographic plates.

Harvard University had installed the first permanent telescope on Mount Wilson in 1889, but removed it eighteen months later because of the mountain's lack of water, overabundance of rattlesnakes, and inaccessibility. In 1904, George Ellery Hale of the University of Chicago's Yerkes Observatory chose Mount Wilson as the site for the Snow Solar Telescope, and thereafter the steep sloped peak with its thorny chaparral covering began to bristle with the towers, derricks, and domes of astronomers doing their celestial work.[1]

Throughout the early period of Mount Wilson's development as an astronomical observation post, the narrow access path and the capacity of pack animals placed severe limits on the designers of the housings of the telescopes. A burro can carry cement, lumber, steel, glass, bread and butter, and water, but only in small amounts. No structural member of the Snow Telescope building, for example, exceeded eight feet in length. To bring the heavy and fragile parts of the Snow Telescope up the hazardous ten-mile-long road with its forty-four hairpin turns, Hale had to design a special steel cart that could be steered from both ends and pulled by mules. When a sixty-inch telescope was installed between 1906 and 1908, the road had to be widened to ten feet and a unique gasoline-electric-mule-powered truck specially built to carry the more cumbersome parts.[2]

This road was still in use when

the decision was made to erect an even larger instrument. Ernest R. Graham won a supporting role in this dramatic history because California had a limited capacity for steel fabrication in 1914, and the scientists turned to a Chicagoan familiar with the processes necessary to build the housing for the 100-inch solar telescope.

Optical specialists, of course, handled the complex problems of the lens. In those days before Pyrex, the glass with the best temperature stability was made by the French wine bottle manufacturer at St. Gobain, and the disk, designed by George Ritchey and W. L. Kinney under the guidance of Francis G. Pease, astronomical engineer, was shipped from France to Pasadena where the grinding and polishing took six years.

While this tedious, painstaking work was going on, the heavy castings for the mount, which were designed by George Ritchey, were made in Quincy, Massachusetts. The working drawings for the dome and its foundations were made in the Chicago office of Graham, Anderson, Probst and White, who also supervised the steel work construction (fig. 102). After the completion of the huge concrete piers, the rivets and the steel were transported in sections up the infamous road. To move the 4.5-ton telescopic mirror up the mountain, the road had to be widened in 1917 to twelve feet.[3]

The supports for the telescope itself and the dome were sepa-

rate. The telescope mechanism, weighing seventy-two tons, was floated on mercury so that the bearings could be small, accurate, and steady. After it was put in place, the dome, weighing 500 tons, was moved by two separate 7.5-horsepower motors.

Years ago there were both stellar and solar research activities at Mount Wilson, but much of its earlier usefulness as an observatory of galaxies and other faint sources of light was ruined by the smog and lights of Los Angeles. The telescope was closed to observational work due to lack of funds in July 1985.

Although the instrument itself and all the key movable parts had been designed by the astronomers and Graham had played only a minor part in its erection, he must have been very proud that winter just before his death

in 1936 when a supernova ten times brighter and fifty times hotter than our sun, and 7 million light-years away, was scientifically recorded and photographed every night on Mount Wilson until it faded from view.

1. George Ellery Hale, *Ten Years at a Mountain Observatory* (Washington, D.C.: Carnegie Institute, 1915). *See also* Helen Wright, *Explorer of the Universe: A Biography of George Ellery Hale* (New York: Dutton and Company, 1966).

2. John W. Robinson, *The Mount Wilson Story* (Glendale, Calif.: La Siesta Press, 1973).

3. Working drawings, construction pictures, and other photographs documenting the history of this structure are extensive and are stored in albums and scrapbooks in the archives atop the mountain and in the observatory office in Pasadena.

[102] MOUNT WILSON OBSERVATORY, PASADENA, CALIF., EXTERIOR

CHARLES A. STEVENS BUILDING

1912–13
17 North State Street
Chicago, Illinois

Cost in 1913: $1,901,599.07; pcf 0.283
Status: extant

In 1923, a Chicago journalist likened the story of Aladdin's lamp to the history of State Street, where property turned into money for local retailers.

When you consider that within an easy night's ride of Chicago is one-third of our nation's population as well as one-half of the nation's industrial and commercial activity, you realize what this . . . means. . . . This great district possesses an all powerful magnet to attract shoppers, for here in unequalled assortments, they find just what they want, assembled from every corner of the earth, through the unlimited purchasing power of these great houses, by highly trained experts risen to their positions by virtue of their superior taste, judgment and efficiency. Here, where competition is extremely keen, price is fixed, not by asking "How much will it bring" but by asking "How low can we sell it and obtain our desired percentage of profit?" The east side of State Street, from Randolph south to Monroe, where the finest of everything is shown in the greatest variety, is controlled now by only four firms— Marshall Field & Company; Carson, Pirie, Scott & Company, Mandel Bros. and Charles A. Stevens & Bros.[1]

Had the reporter extended his vision three more blocks to the south he could have added Leiter Brothers', Rothschild's, Lytton's, and Wieboldt's to his list. Walking up the east side of State Street today one still sees one large store after another.

Most of these structures were already in place when Charles A. Stevens and his brothers asked Graham, Burnham and Company to design an L-shaped building to fit into the space between Wieboldt's and the proposed Marshall Field Annex. Seven floors were to be reserved for their women's clothing goods store, the other eleven above were to be used for rental income. In the optimistic atmosphere of the times, there seemed no end to the need for retail space on State Street or to the increasing demand for specialty shops and related services. Street-level space was taken up by the prestigious large stores with their sidewalk display windows, but more space in the Loop for smaller businesses was essential. In their conversations, client and architects hit upon the idea of creating more levels of State Street or "streets in the air" like the Republic Building erected at the southeast corner of State and Adams streets by Holabird and Roche,[2] or the Cleveland Arcade, or the Galleria in Milan where rows of shops on several floors opened onto balconies surrounding a covered courtyard. Adapting the concept to a narrow eighteen-story building required

[103] CHARLES A. STEVENS BUILDING, CHICAGO, ILL., EXTERIOR

only the necessary elevators.[3] In its commercial work, the firm had often created a ring of shops around the open lobby of an office building; in its department stores, it had created interior streets. The problem, it seemed was to combine these two ideas and execute them in tall, vertical proportions (fig. 103).

In display windows on the ground level "street" that ran along the south side of the building from State Street to Wabash Avenue, larger tenants in the inner corridors of the upper floors could show their wares and attract customers from below (fig. 104). Above, a shoprow atmosphere with large windows enticed the visitor to the jewelry shop to pause before the "fronts" of the antique dealer, the custom shirtmaker, and the millinery designer. The usual practice of stenciled signs on the State and Wabash side windows added another lure.

These combined efforts were, however, only partially successful. Only one side of the upper eleven levels can be occupied, because the other side had to be given over to elevators; thus the arcades are only half-streets. More importantly, there is no dramatic, unifying spatial element, such as a dome or a staircase. An arcade at its best combines the virtues of the light court, the shopping street, and the elevator. Given imaginative architectural treatment, it can have the busy market atmosphere where small dealers band together to garner some of the advantages and glamour of the big department store.[4] Since the Stevens Building had no spacious dome and only half a street on each floor, it lost much of the potential urban magic of an arcade. Eventually it became a side street of cobblers, used book dealers, and manicurists.

Streets in the air, it seems, need their squares or plazas to give them life, just as terrestrial streets do. The fate of the women's clothing section of the Stevens Building was happier. The business itself celebrated its hundredth anniversary in 1986, before its demise in 1989. The high ceiling of the main floor and the airy stories above provided a suitable atmosphere for the sale of fine merchandise on which the company built its reputation over many years in the city.

1. *Economist Special News Bulletin,* November 29, 1923.

2. Robert Bruegmann, *Holabird and Roche, Holabird and Root,* Chapter 7.

3. See drawings in the archives of the store, which also contains photographs, brochures, architectural ornament, and other materials.

4. Mary-Peale Schofield, "The Cleveland Arcade," *Journal of the Society of Architectural Historians,* December 1966, pp. 281–91, quoted in Eric Johannesen, *Cleveland Architecture 1876–1976,* p. 34.

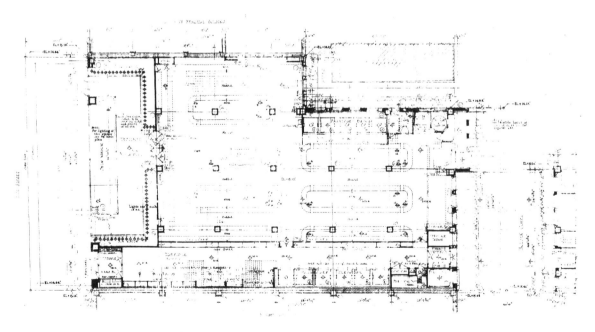

[104] CHARLES A. STEVENS BUILDING, PLAN

DAVID WHITNEY BUILDING

1915–16
1553 Woodward Avenue
Detroit, Michigan

Cost in 1915: $1,528,543;
     pcf. $0.37
Status: extant

Marking a major point on Detroit's leading thoroughfare between the center of the city and the residential district, the stone, light brick, and white terracotta–clad Whitney Building has a distinctive six-sided shape (figs. 47, 48). Designed to take advantage of the three-way intersection facing a public park, the building creates a charming interlude in this urban vista in Detroit (fig. 105).

The interior, one of the firm's best, is formed by four floors of shops on corridors encircling a large "rotunda" space (fig 49) under a polygonal light court.[1] The four-story arcade space is shaped by generous arched openings set off by gleaming white enameled brick. Rich geometric and floral ornaments surround the semicircular arched openings at the top. Globe fixtures at every pilaster on every floor and a stringcourse of lights at the springing of the vaults give sparkling illumination to the whole, showing the work of an unnamed designer to be unusually delicate in the handling of proportions and details, and unusually felicitous in the shaping of interior space (see Part I).

1. See drawings, hectographs, and blueprints pasted on linen in the archives of the building. A rental brochure with a reproduction of a color presentation drawing, signed Daniel H. Burnham and Company, a blackline drawing and two framed color photographs, and a gray book of *Specifications* (417 pages) dated November 24, 1913, are also there.

[105] DAVID WHITNEY BUILDING, DETROIT, MICH., EXTERIOR

BETHLEHEM STEEL COMPANY BUILDING

1916
700 East Third Street
South Bethlehem, Pennsylvania

Status: extant

Daniel Burnham and Charles Schwab, president of Bethlehem Steel, were friends, and Schwab also knew Graham as a business associate. As both men were staunch supporters of the "Bethlehem beam" or the "Gray beam" manufactured by Bethlehem Steel, which was responsible for the growth of the company, it seemed appropriate when a new building for the original plant (Cope and Stewartson, 1906) was needed to give the commission to Graham, Burnham and Company (fig. 106).[1] In 1928, the firm added six more stories, and a remodeling was done later by McKim, Mead and White (1948–51).[2]

The interior decor of the Directors' Room is a good example of the power imagery associated with steel magnates in 1916—thick carpeting, an over-scaled table, upholstered leather furniture, mahogany wood paneling, and a fireplace marked by Corinthian pilasters. The elaborate plasterwork on the ceiling recalls the Sun-King ornament of Louis XIV, and the armchairs at the head of the room are of regal proportions (fig. 107).

1. Robert A. Hessen, *Steel Titan: The Life of Charles Schwab* (New York: Oxford University Press, 1975).

2. Nicholas Adams to author, March 28, 1984.

[106] BETHLEHEM STEEL COMPANY BUILDING, SOUTH BETHLEHEM, PA., STEELWORK

[107] BETHLEHEM STEEL COMPANY BUILDING, DIRECTORS' ROOM

MAY COMPANY BUILDING

1914–15; addition, 1931
158 Euclid Avenue
Cleveland, Ohio

Cost in 1915(?): $2,225,965.70;
 pcf: $0.191
Status: extant

Every element of the May Company Building is exuberant—its white terra-cotta cladding and the festive roofline, with its wavy ornament, four-sided clock, standing lights with shining globes, flagpoles, and the bold lettering of the company name (fig. 108). Enlivening the eastern corner of Public Square, one of Cleveland's two principal public spaces, the broad, low proportions and the wide windows invite the passerby to view the merchandise on display. Underlying this spirited mood is a handsome tripartite facade, dominated by "Chicago-style" windows.

Modernist alterations to the building at a later date have somewhat diminished the spirit of the original by substituting black polished granite around the entrance, but above, the star-spangled spandrel panels and the decorative belt courses are still intact. Installation of air-conditioning ductwork and the addition of acoustical tile and mirrored piers have also changed the appearance of the interiors throughout.

[108] MAY COMPANY BUILDING, CLEVELAND, OHIO, EXTERIOR

EATON COMPANY MAIL ORDER BUILDING ONE AND MAIL ORDER BUILDING TWO

1916;1920–21
Hargrave Street and Graham Avenue
Winnipeg, Manitoba, Canada

Cost of 1916 building: $815,106.29; pcf: $0.177
Status: extant

Both standard warehouse designs, the first was designed for twelve stories, but only eight stories were built. The second (fig. 109) was also designed for twelve stories, but only nine were built. Both warehouses were connected with the Eaton Company Department Store by a subway. The firm did some other projects for the Eaton Company, but none of them was ever built.[1]

1. Drawings for the warehouses are in the Archives of Ontario, Toronto, Canada. Drawings for the projects are in the Canadian Center for Architecture in Toronto, Ontario, and in the Art Institute of Chicago.

[109] EATON COMPANY MAIL ORDER BUILDING TWO, WINNIPEG, ONTARIO, CANADA, ELEVATION

[110] YOUNGSTOWN SHEET AND TUBE COMPANY ADMINISTRATION BUILDING, YOUNGSTOWN, OHIO, EXTERIOR

YOUNGSTOWN SHEET AND TUBE COMPANY ADMINISTRATION BUILDING

1917
State Street and Walton Avenue, SE corner
Struthers, Ohio

Status: extant

Scaled low and spread out, this four-story administration building seems proportioned for its place on the Ohio plain (fig. 110). The simple form is varied by changes in the materials— brick, concrete, stone, and terra-cotta—by different patterns in the light beige brick, and by stringcourses and moulding accenting the giant order enclosing the main two floors (fig. 111). The generous interior spaces of the L-shaped plan included a ladies' dining room, an officers' dining room, an employees' dining room, vaults, and offices of the engineers employed by the company. The ten-foot-eight-inch ceilings, marble corridors, and wood paneling lend a quiet dignity to the principal floor.[1]

1. *American Architect* 112, no. 2168, July 11, 1917. Plates 17–23 include photographs of the exterior, rear, and interior, and drawings of the first, second, and third floors, all elevations, and some details.

[111] YOUNGSTOWN SHEET AND TUBE COMPANY ADMINISTRATION BUILDING, DETAIL

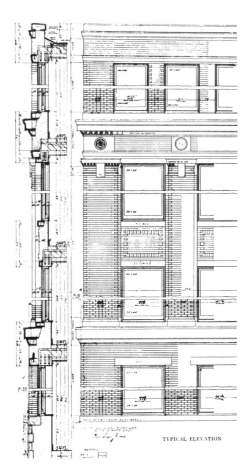

TYPICAL ELEVATION

WESTERN UNION TELEGRAPH BUILDING

1917–19; 1926–27
427 South LaSalle Street
Chicago, Illinois

Cost in 1919: $1,497,350.54;
  pcf: $0.428.
Cost in 1926–27:
  $1,515,148.54; pcf $0.432
Status: extant, many remodelings

Today, old multi-story inner-city structures like the Telegraph Building are being abandoned gradually by the electronic service industry and replaced by continuous single-story buildings in outlying areas. But the Telegraph Building houses such complex electronic communications equipment, built up and changed over the decades with myriad parts and connections, that it would be much more costly to move than to stay put. Electronic components are easily routed over several floors, and the costs of erecting a new structure, completely duplicating existing equipment, both argue in favor of maintaining the south Loop building.[1] Thus this reminder of Chicago's industrial lofts of the 1920s remains in what otherwise is becoming an extension of the financial district south of Jackson Boulevard.

On the northeast corner of the intersection of two of Chicago's major thoroughfares, LaSalle Street and Congress Parkway, the seven-story building (fig. 70) is structurally capable of an additional six stories. Its facing is of limestone and brick with terracotta trim, typical of the industrial lofts of the period (see Part

I). Unusually handsome pilasters of limestone articulate the first floor and the mezzanine, and separate spandrel panels of acanthus leaves add grace notes to this utilitarian building in the center of the city (fig. 71).

During the early 1950s, the city of Chicago tore down the two south bays, approximately thirty-five feet of the building, in order to facilitate the widening of Congress Parkway. At this time the building was given a new facade on the south side.

1. D. A. Brown, in-house report on the condition, history, and use of the building, n.d., Telegraph Building archives, Chicago, Ill. *See also* Frank A. Randall, *History of the Development of Building Construction in Chicago* (Urbana, Ill.: University of Illinois Press, 1949), p. 255.

[112] MARSHALL FIELD AND COMPANY ANNEX, THE STORE FOR MEN, CHICAGO, ILL., FIRST FLOOR

MARSHALL FIELD AND COMPANY ANNEX

(Store for Men)

1914
Washington Street and Wabash Avenue, SW corner
Chicago, Illinois

Cost in 1914: $3,101,607.34; pcf: $0.44
Status: extant, remodeled in 1939 for air-conditioning and extensively remodeled in 1985–86 after Field's sold the building

The Marshall Field Annex is a good example of the subsuming of one building type into another—a specialty store for men into an office building.[1] Six floors of the structure were devoted to men's clothing, and the remaining upper floors to rentals. The four-square proportions and gray limestone cladding seemed suitable for both functions (fig. 66). Inside, the broad columns of the main floor, the heavy braces on the entrance portals, and the restrained ornament of the frieze all combined in an atmosphere of dignified masculinity (fig. 112).

The plan revealed four entrances, two to the men's store and two to the office building

above. Two banks of elevators were similarly divided, five cars on the west served the store; eight on the south, the offices. A special feature of the Annex was the Grill Room on the sixth floor (fig. 65). When the Merchandise Mart was sold to Joseph P. Kennedy, Marshall Field's corporate offices were moved from there to the sixth floor of the Annex, and the Grill Room was closed.[2]

The ground floor once had the classical grandeur provided by its tall, fluted columns and a balconied periphery articulated by pilasters, with a honeysuckle frieze gracing the change from column to lintel, but this was all destroyed in a recent remodeling.

The lobby to the office building has not suffered so much from the change in ownership, and the handsome elevator doors, ceiling mouldings, and bronze fixtures retain much of the spirit of the original.

1. In 1902, when D. H. Burnham and Company built the new Marshall Field Store on State Street, another Field building from 1893 on the southeast corner of the same block, also by Burnham (designed by Charles Atwood), was incorporated into the complex and named the Annex. When the new store for men was finished in 1914 it was named the Annex, probably because it was across the street from the older complex, and the 1893 building was renamed the South Wabash Building.

2. The Marshall Field Archives is a rich source of information containing over a thousand file drawers, boxes, and open shelves with materials relating to the history of the firm.

FIRST NATIONAL BANK BUILDING

1915–17
300 South Sixteenth Street
Omaha, Nebraska

Cost in 1917: $812,917;
    pcf: $0.407
Status: extant; landmark,
    Nebraska Historic Buildings
    Survey and National Register
    of Historic Places Inventory

The 210-foot-tall twin towers of the First National Bank form a major element in the skyline of downtown Omaha. At the hub of

[113] FIRST NATIONAL BANK BUILDING, OMAHA, NEBR., ELEVATION

the central business district, the building's proud sturdiness seems to embody the confidence the city experienced in the boom of the second and third decades of the twentieth century.[1] Focused by the giant-order pilasters that embrace the large windows of the lower stories, the composition at the pedestrian level is satisfying. At the top, the massive proportions are given a graceful vertical rhythm by piers extended above the roofline, opening a pierced parapet to the blue of the sky (fig. 113).

Columns that divide the Banking Room into a vaulted hall surrounded by a bi-level aisle mitigate its vast proportions. A sense of richness and success permeates the space, where a luxurious profusion of vines and leaves, meanders, egg-and-dart mouldings, rosettes, palmettes, swags, and other ornaments adorn the ribs, coffers, and other surfaces. Although unused at the present time, the logic of the room's spatial arrangement is apparent.[2] Deposits, withdrawals, and other business transactions were carried on in the public area in the two-story space, and the circumambulatory balconies led to the working spaces set aside for bookkeepers, clerks, the transit department, the clearinghouse, and the mailroom (fig. 114).

In the offices on the upper floors, the view from one tower to another is delightful, for the architects provided generous windows and the spectacle of spandrel panels with light green arcs festooned with ribboned garlands and flowers. The windows also offer a view of the city for those offices on the outside corridor of the building. One of the best bank office buildings designed by the firm, the First National exemplifies Graham, Anderson, Probst and White's commitment to solid building, logical planning, tasteful ornament, and grand public spaces.

1. Arthur C. Wakeley, *Omaha: The Gate City and Douglas County Nebraska* (Chicago: S. J. Clarke Publishing Company, 1917), pp. 198–200. Other information in Landmarks Heritage Preservation Commission, City of Omaha, *A Comprehensive Program for Historic Preservation in Omaha* (Omaha: Klopp Printing Company, 1980). National Register of Historic Places Inventory, nomination written by Penelope Chatfield and Donna Peschio. *Omaha City Architecture* (Omaha: Junior League and Landmarks, Inc., 1977).

2. Copies of the original drawings are on file in the offices of the Landmarks Heritage Preservation Commission, Omaha Civic Center, Lynn Meyer, administrator; *see also* "Portfolio of Current Architecture," *Architectural Record* 55 (July 1922): 70; "First National Bank is moving to a new home," *Omaha World-Herald,* January 6, 1917, p. 6.

[114] FIRST NATIONAL BANK BUILDING, BANKING ROOM

[115] WILLIAM WRIGLEY, JR., BUILDING, CHICAGO, ILL., EXTERIOR

WILLIAM WRIGLEY, JR., BUILDING

South section, 1919–22; north section, 1922–24
400–410 North Michigan Avenue
Chicago, Illinois

Cost in 1922 for the south section: $3,795,974.46; pcf: $1.228
Cost in 1924 for the north section: $4,535,410.64; pcf: $0.835
Status: extant; under consideration for landmark status as part of
the area at the junction of Michigan Avenue and the Chicago
River

When it was erected, the slender skyscraper tower of the Wrigley Building struck a startling new high note in Chicago (fig. 115). Although there were a few low-mounted towers already in the city, such as the Auditorium Building (Adler and Sullivan, 1887–90), the height limit was then 260 feet, and it had been placed lower at various intervals for years before that. At the time, Chicago was mostly a vast grid of four-square office blocks. Against this older character of the city, the upper part of the Wrigley, the little circular temple together with its cupola, rose to 398 feet, the highest point in the city. To come within the height regulations, the top sections were unrented or purely ornamental. The room just above the clock at the twenty-eighth floor, for example, was just an observation room, but the telescopes offered for viewing the surrounding city were exciting to contemporaries for the "bird's-eye" view of Lake Michigan and the "airplane view," which took in miles of the surrounding landscape. The company also furnished a guide, "prepared to answer all questions" (see Part I).

Although the Wrigley Building was structurally conventional, the play of light brought an unusually lively refinement to its surface. Trained to use watercolors in a painterly fashion in the Beaux-Arts manner, Charles Beersman, the chief designer, created a subtle movement in the cladding. Six different shades of a special enamel finish were baked on the terra-cotta, varying from gray to pale cream and getting progressively lighter toward the top. The result was "as if the sun were always shining on its upper reaches," as one contemporary put it. The effect prompted another writer of the period to exclaim that the Wrigley seemed to soar "from mists and fog to clear skies."[1]

William Mitchell Kendall of McKim, Mead and White had combined a classical building with a tower when he designed New York's Municipal Building in 1913, and the success of this building may have opened Graham's eyes to the possibility of combining what may have once seemed contradictory to him—tradition and height. The tower of the Wrigley Building had the best of both worlds. Like its older model, the Giralda Tower in Seville, it was designed to spring, not from a flat roof, which would have been too abrupt, but from a succession of lesser roofs marked by spires, parapets, and pinnacles for a more vivid effect on the skyline (fig. 117).

After the completion of the original building, the adjacent land to the north was acquired for an annex. When it was finished, the ensemble had such unity that it seemed its parts had been conceived together. How was this accomplished? The new part was drawn up in a similar style, clad in the same glazed terra-cotta, and united to the older building by a decorative three-story screen at the upper Michigan Avenue level. Following the original in its delicate setback at the top of the block section, the annex too has a tower, but one that was deliberately modest, respecting the older building's dominance. The two stand side by side as fraternal, not identical, twins. The taller southern building with its tower seems stately; the shorter northern building seems monumental. In their mutually complementary juxtaposition, each is self-sufficient, but subservient to the life

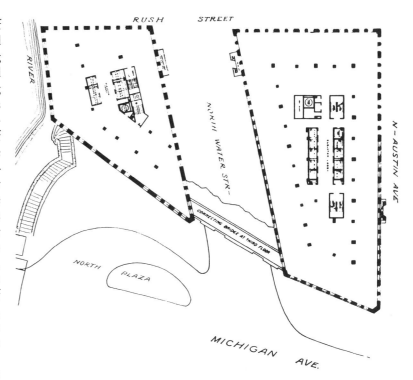

[116] WRIGLEY BUILDING, PLAN

of the whole. This seeming subservience of the "annex" is all the more noteworthy when one learns that it has nearly double the site area of the original—21,000 square feet compared to 11,000.

In addition, by taking advantage of the bi-level street system created by the concurrent construction of a bi-level bridge over Michigan Avenue, the architects designed a plaza for the space behind the glazed screen on the upper level (fig. 116). (North Water Street passes underneath.) Although the plaza was not developed into its present form until 1957, it has always offered a welcome respite from Chicago's weather, an amenity not provided by any other plaza in the "windy" city.

The original building over-

looked another plaza at the river's edge. In the words of a contemporary, Joseph I. Karl, the completed structure fulfilled the dreams of William Wrigley, Jr., for "an impressive and artistic embellishment of [his] commanding property . . . making Chicago his civic debtor. . . . The two diverse plots used, though separated by the width of a street, have, by the wonderful way they have been handled, been united in one improvement of marvelous balance and unity."[2]

In the end, Wrigley sacrificed considerable rental space for a combination of aesthetic, civic, and advertising motives. The north building, although constructed after a 1924 ordinance took effect allowing greater height and volume, was built to conform to the lower cornice line of the south building. Four potential floors were lost. At 16,000 square feet per floor, this space would be worth about $1.6 million in annual rental fees in 1986 dollars.

Wrigley spared no expense in other construction aspects of the building. For comparison, the Federal Reserve Bank Building in Kansas City, a bank–office building the firm built in the same period, cost $0.867 per cubic foot, while the Wrigley Building cost $1.228 per cubic foot for the south section and $0.835 for the north, or an average of $.978 per cubic foot for both. The Builders' Building, another office building constructed across the river from the Wrigley in 1927, also by Graham, Anderson, Probst and White, came in at $0.622 per cubic foot.

In time, the Wrigley Building became a symbol of the city of Chicago. As Philip K. Wrigley explained in an interview, "Something that is interesting is the BOAC [British Overseas Airways Corporation] is using a picture of Big Ben in London and the Wrigley Building clock. There are two pictures and they are reversed. It is a full page ad in magazines which says 'BOAC From Chicago to London,' and vice versa from London to Chicago, and it uses the towers and the clocks as the symbols [of the two cities]." [3]

While the Wrigley has continued to appear as a symbol for Chicago to the present day, there was a time in the 1950s and 1960s when the building's reputation, like that of many other great works of the 1920s, suffered from modernist architec-

[117] WRIGLEY BUILDING, DETAIL OF TOWER

tural criticism. It either was not included or given only slight notice in the architectural books of the period. One writer quipped that it was a building that refused "to go to school—in this case, the Chicago school of architecture," but asserted its uniqueness and charm in spite of that. [4] As late as 1980, a local guidebook declared that "the building achieved fame through traits other than architectural merit." [5]

Comparing the Wrigley Build-

ing to the asymmetrical, flat-roofed, unornamented buildings taking shape during the post–World War I era in Europe, when Continental architects expressed something of the utopian vision shared by those who hoped that art and technology could bring a better way of life for all classes, the Wrigley Building is flagrantly ornamented and given over to consumerist theatricality, not one bit a part of any new social order or new social vision.

Nor is the building without its faults. The lobby space is under-scaled; there are no other major interior spaces for public use, and the river-edge development is minimal. In a balanced judgment, however, these shortcomings are outweighed by the stunning relationship of the building to its site, its grand proportions, the sensitive treatment of its cladding, and the amenities of its interior offices.

If the building's reputation was eclipsed briefly in the heyday of modernism, and if some compromises had to be made over the terra-cotta cladding as the years took their toll, the Wrigley Building's final claim to fame—its dramatic, gleaming nighttime illumination—has improved gloriously over the years. The 1922 rental brochure described the "revolving light at the tower's tip serving as a beacon to the mariners on the lake as well as the navigators of the air," noting that "the building is lighted from hundreds of flood lights on adjacent buildings, as well as its own roof, so that at night, too, it stands forth in an ethereal beauty." A contemporary reporter noted that the lantern carrying the revolving light was visible for twenty miles out on Lake Michigan and from all quarters of the city and explained the nighttime effect:

Light is projected by powerful X-Ray reflectors, using 500 watt lamps mounted on the roof of the Kirk building on Michigan Avenue . . . increasing in intensity with the height until the tower stands out in one blaze of glory. . . . The turrets and other ornamentation on the top of the tower are brought out in relief by

smaller X-Ray reflectors which use 250 watt lamps. In all there are 123 units with 500 watts, and 37 with 250 watts for a total of 70,750 watts. This installation is said by lighting men to be one of the finest of its kind ever attempted.[6]

Certainly it was a great popular success, among the first, if not *the* first, of its kind and hence very influential in the succession of lighted buildings in the 1920s.

Except during World War II and for a brief period during the energy crisis of the early 1970s when the lights were extinguished, the Wrigley has brightened the skyline of the city by day and by night (fig. 53), as well as the spirits of Chicagoans and their visitors.

1. "New Wrigley Building, Chicago's Tallest Structure," *Fort Dearborn Magazine,* March 1921; "Wrigley Building, Chicago, Ill.," *Architecture and Building* 53 (December 1921): 95.

2. Joseph I. Karl, "The Wrigley Buildings Attract Anew," *Real Estate News* 19 (January 1924): 1.

3. Paul McClelland Angle, interview with Philip K. Wrigley, 1966,

Manuscripts Collection, Chicago Historical Society, Chicago, Ill.

4. F. K. Plous, Jr., "The Dowager of Michigan Avenue," *Chicago Sun-Times,* July 23, 1977.

5. Ira J. Bach, *Chicago's Famous Buildings,* 3rd ed. (Chicago: University of Chicago Press, 1980), p. 53.

6. "The Wrigley Building at Night," *Architecture and Building* 53 (December 1921): 95. When the old warehouse supporting the front floodlights was demolished in 1970, a new battery of lamps twice as powerful as the old incandescent lights was mounted on the East Wacker Drive side. The whole structure is now lit by 118 one-thousand-watt metal halide bulbs mounted on Wacker Drive, and the effect of ascending brightness is achieved by placing four more banks of lights near the top. Three of these have sixteen 500-watt quartz lights: one at the seventeenth floor, one at the nineteenth floor, and one at the peak. The fourth, illuminating the west side, is placed on top of the swimming pool of the River Plaza Building. This bank is 1,000 watts because of its greater distance (Robert Bruegmann, "Relighting the Skyline," *Inland Architect* 26 [March/April 1982]: 51–57).

UNITED STATES MAIL BUILDING

1921
Canal Street, between Van Buren and Harrison streets
Chicago, Illinois

Status: extant, remodeled

For the ten years from its completion in 1921 to the erection of the larger United States Post Office (*q.v.*) that wrapped around it (1931–34, also by Graham, Anderson, Probst and White), the U.S. Mail Building was for the exclusive use of U.S. parcel post

service. The northern end, with its four Doric columns, was the public service area, and the rest of the seven-story, seven-hundred-foot-long structure was a sorting depot (fig. 118).

The original building, which straddled a complex of railroad

[118] UNITED STATES MAIL BUILDING, CHICAGO, ILL., EXTERIOR

tracks coming into Chicago, was admirably suited to its purpose. At the center of the nation's complex parcel post system, 120 cars of mail were loaded and unloaded here every twenty-four hours. The tracks below grade had accommodations for forty-two cars, and trains were operated in three shifts a day.

Most unusual is the special truss necessary for the bridging of these railroad tracks. Weighing 364 tons, it provides an unobstructed clear span of 150 feet.[1] Of unprecedented dimensions in Chicago building construction, this feature was the subject of great interest at the time.[2] While bridge and railroad engineers were not astonished by these dimensions, they had not been used before in conventional buildings. When the new building was erected, the north and south facades of the older building were destroyed. Now only the east wall is visible. Long familiarity with railroads and government commissions made Graham, Anderson, Probst and White the logical choice for this job with its special problems.

1. R. F. Imler, "Huge Steel Truss Placed in Chicago U.S. Mail Terminal," *Engineering World,* November 1921, pp. 313–18.

2. "New Parcel Post Building on West Side," *Postal Pioneer* 1, no. 2 (February 1921): 3.

KIMBALL BUILDING

(Lewis Center, DePaul University)

1914–17
25 East Jackson Boulevard
Chicago, Illinois

Cost in 1917: $1,549,078.78
Status: extant, remodeled

Saul Bellow once called the Kimball Building (fig. 119) the "Noah's Ark of stranded European music masters," and indeed the list of those who filled the recital hall with music is cosmopolitan—the Budapest String Quartet, the Fine Arts Quartet, Carol Silver Lems-Dworkin, the Tudor Madrigal Singers, Eva Le Gallienne, Anna Russell, Liberace, the Bali Java Dancers, and the Salzburg Marionette Theater.[1] The first radio broadcasts from Chicago came from this stage,[2] and the first large screen telecast beamed across Lake Michigan— the Army–Notre Dame game of 1947–was received in the same hall.[3]

Supporting all these early efforts was C. N. Kimball, a keen businessman as well as a lover of the arts. When his 1891 building at State and Jackson proved too small for his growing music business, he decided he wanted a taller structure on the same site, but he also wanted to carry on business without interruption. He then looked for architects who would agree to erect a first-class structure with the provision that while the old building was being progressively demolished, space would be provided in the new building with a minimum of disruption to the employees and customers. Graham, Burnham

[119] KIMBALL BUILDING (LEWIS CENTER, DEPAUL UNIVERSITY), CHICAGO, ILL., EXTERIOR

and Company, already reputed for its first-class work, proposed a two-stage construction process and won the commission.

The architects succinctly explained that "The present existing building on the south eighty feet of the lot will remain and be occupied by the Kimball Company until that portion of the new building, lying north of the eighty foot lot line extending to Jackson Boulevard is erected and finished for temporary occupancy by the Kimball Company, after which the South (old) Building shall be wrecked and the new building extended and completed."[4]

Subsequently, the architects required each contractor to lay out his work to meet these conditions. Heating, plumbing, wiring, refrigerating, sprinkling, and other specialists had to install their systems in the first section so that they were complete in themselves and could be put into service immediately, and yet be arranged so that they could be connected to work in the new section without interruption of service. The assignment was completed with such efficiency that the *Wall Street Journal* marveled over the construction planning.[5]

In every other respect the building was also a model of the technology of the period. A perusal of the specification book provides a good cross-section of the state of the building art in 1915. Its 230 pages of printed requirements list among other things that

all wood shall be sound and free from knots, sap, rot, shakes, seams, flaws and other defects. . . . Each and every stone shall ring clear when struck with a hammer[6]. . . . All terra cotta shall be of first class manufacture, made from carefully selected clays, compact and homogeneous in body, carefully fired, burned to a proper degree of hardness, and made perfect in material, workmanship and finish. All surfaces shall be true and out of wind. No warped, over or under-burned, discolored, painted, spawled or cracked pieces will be accepted. A sufficient number of extra pieces shall be made to guard against delay through rejection of faulty material.[7] The plaster work shall be in strict accordance with the details and shall be run perfectly true, straight or curved, as required. All modeling shall be executed by the best and most artistic architectural modelers and sculptors, who may be selected by Architects at their option. Changes in models, or new models, shall be made, changing and rechanging them until they are satisfactory to the Architects in every respect. . . . All models must be executed in Chicago to admit of ready inspection and direction of alterations by the Architects. . . . [The ornamental iron work shall be] especially constructed for strength, with the outer strings provided with angle furrings for anchorage of wire lath . . . newels shall be of cast iron of ornamental design as detailed. Hand rails . . . shall be bronze. . . . All subtreads, risers and platforms shall be secured with tap screws; stove bolts will in no case be permitted.[8]

Bids were let in thirty-four categories: General, Erection of Steel, Painting, Window Shades, Hardware, Mail Chute, Granite Work, Prismatic Lights, Fire Escapes, Ceiling Lining, Ash Removal System, Vault Doors, Sprinklers, Water Cooling Plant, Ejectors, Elevators, Boilers, Fireproofing, Engines, Stokers, Generators, Coal Handling Machinery, Plumbing and Gas, Light Fixtures, Steel Foundations and Masonry, Rubber Mats and Tile, Terra Cotta, Wiring, Ornamental Iron and Bronze, Carpentry, Glass and Glazing, Roofing and Sheet Metal, Heating and Ventilating, and Marble and Tile. More than 240 contractors are listed in the tabulations, some bidding on as many as six different alternatives in the plans. Ten different general contractors submitted estimates ranging from $1,213,349 to $1,700,000, half a million dollars between them. Clearly, Ernest R. Graham had to be a keen businessman himself.

Peirce Anderson, the design partner of the firm, sketched out the form of the building in the style so familiar in other office buildings in that area of Chicago, such as the Lyon and Healy Building across the street, or the Railway Exchange a block to the east. Tripartite in its divisions, the Kimball has a classical base, shaft, and capital. The L-shaped interior lobby, which gives the building access to both Wabash Avenue and Jackson Boulevard, is of buff ceramic tile decorated with stylized floral ornament with touches of loden green. Ornamental bronze meanders and rinceaux distinguish the entrances.

The spacious 500-seat Recital Hall occupying most of the second and third floors was originally light and festive. Golden sunbursts alternated with Apollo's lyres on the balcony, and electric lights surrounded by leafy medallions illuminated the walls and the cross beams of the ceiling, an idea Anderson may have borrowed from Louis Sullivan's Auditorium only two blocks away.

Shortly after Frank J. Lewis purchased the Kimball Building in October 1955, he gave the deed to DePaul University for a downtown education center with this simple dramatic statement: "Of various things I have done or hope to do, I believe this is the best."[9] When the Vincentian fathers, who own the university, purchased the McCormick Theological Seminary buildings along Fullerton Avenue in the early 1980s, some changes were made in how the Kimball Building, renamed Lewis Center, was used. Concerts by European music masters in the recital hall moved with the music school to the uptown campus.

1. Saul Bellow, "Cousins," in *Him with His Foot in His Mouth and Other Stories* (New York: Harper and Row, 1974), pp. 78, 82, 84, 236.

2. Van Allen Bradley, *Music for the Millions* (Chicago: H. Regnery Co., 1957), p. 260

3. *DePaul*, Fall 1955, p. 4.

4. *Specifications*, n.d., p. 7. The Physical Plant Department at DePaul University also contains the tabulation of bids, original blueprints, and some copies of original drawings.

5. Bradley, *Music*, p. 259.

6. *Specifications*, p. 36.

7. Ibid., p. 39.

8. Ibid., p. 63.

9. *DePaul University Newsmagazine* 7, no. 1 (Fall 1955): 3–5. For other materials see: ibid., 8, no. 1 (Fall 1956); ibid., 10, no. 1 (Fall 1959); Bradley, *Music*, p. 258; *Chicago Daily News*, January 29, 1915; John Justin Smith, *Chicago Daily News*, March 1955; *American Architect* 118, no. 2332 (September 1, 1920): 304–10, photographs, and ground plans; News Release to the *Chicago Tribune*, Monday, October 17, 1955.

FEDERAL RESERVE BANK OF CHICAGO

1920–22
230 South LaSalle Street
Chicago, Illinois

Cost in 1922, architects' figures: $7,538,630.21; pcf: $1.08; Federal Reserve figures: $7,493,683.55

Status: extant, with an addition on the lot to the west in 1957. Later alterations included filling in the light court on the north and moving the masonry there to the new exterior to keep the historic fabric of the building intact.

[120] **FEDERAL RESERVE BANK OF CHICAGO, CHICAGO, ILL., EXTERIOR**

[121] FEDERAL RESERVE BANK OF CHICAGO, ENTRANCE

Corinthian capitals embellish this otherwise sedate seventeen-story building designed in the firm's familiar mode of the tripartite division of the office block.

On the LaSalle Street side, the temple front (fig. 121) echoes the temple front of the Continental Illinois Bank and Trust Company across the street. On the Jackson Boulevard elevation, the colonnade of Corinthian columns forms a classical streetscape consonant with Graham, Anderson, Probst and White's Insurance Exchange to the south. This important corner in Chicago's cityscape might have developed completely along classical lines had Holabird and Root not won the commission for the centerpiece, the Board of Trade Building, which it designed in an Art Deco mode (see Part I).

The interior on the first floor has been remodeled extensively, but fluted Doric columns in the two-story Banking Room above retain the original quality of the tall central space. The mouldings are simpler than their counterparts in the commercial banks, and the coffering on the ceiling is restrained. The material is a subdued, plain white limestone. Similar in many respects to its counterpart, the Federal Reserve Bank of Kansas City, Missouri, the office spaces were arranged on the double corridor model to the seventeenth floor, where the recreational facilities provided by the Federal Reserve for its employees were installed.

In the 1920s, Graham, Anderson, Probst and White designed seven structures for the Federal Reserve System: two bank-office buildings in Chicago and Kansas City and five low-story banks in other cities.

At a time when the Federal Reserve System was still new to the national economy, the government was anxious to avoid any appearance of extravagance in this combination bank and office building in Chicago (fig.

120). Although Americans were at that time ordinarily well disposed to the display of wealth and to grandeur of ornamentation in their public buildings such as post offices, the banking system that protects the economic stability of all the rest was held to be accountable to a "basic necessities" appearance even in the 1920s.[1] The Federal Reserve Bank is thus more subdued than its counterparts in the commercial banking world. Only leafy

1. "History of the Building Process," an unpublished book of the minutes of the building committee that met regularly from January 28, 1919, to May 11, 1923. This black leatherette notebook, now in the ar-

chives of the bank, is a month-by-month account of the meetings. On July 19, 1921, a letter arrived from W. G. Harding in Washington, D.C., stating that "there is no wood or marble wainscoting in the Treasury Building," and further words to the effect that the Federal Board would regard it as "unfortunate if any Federal Reserve Bank should spend money merely for ornamentation or display."

Federal architect A. B. Trowbridge wrote to the committee on July 31, 1921, "I have no wish to appear over particular and if it were a private bank I wouldn't spend a minute in questioning it, but the Federal Reserve Board is becoming anxious over big amounts being spent and they would be sure to look with favor on any move to not only actually save money but to act as to avoid the appearance of extravagance. . . . My advice is to omit the high paneling." The committee followed his advice.

FEDERAL RESERVE BANK OF KANSAS CITY

1919–21
925 Grand Avenue
Kansas City, Missouri

Cost in 1921: $3,950,723;
   pcf: $0.867
Status: extant

When it was constructed in 1921, the Federal Reserve Bank was the tallest building in Kansas City. Although actually only sixteen stories high, the bank appears higher because each floor is greater in height than the floors in the average office building (fig. 122).

A colonnade marking the entrance on Grand Avenue produces an effect of simplicity and

[122] FEDERAL RESERVE BANK OF KANSAS CITY, KANSAS CITY, MO., EXTERIOR

dignity, which is underscored by the decorative panels at each end of the entrance. Carrying the seal and the eagle, the support figures symbolize the Spirit of Commerce and the Spirit of Industry.[1]

Within, the great Banking Room is long and narrow (123 feet in length by 73 feet in width),

rising to a height of 38 feet. This space is divided into a central hall and two side aisles by two rows of Doric columns (fig. 123). Above the aisles is a sixteen-foot balcony, which was the working space for the support staff.

Adaptive re-use of the Banking Room space includes using

the lower room for fine arts and travel exhibitions and the balcony for interpretive displays about the Federal Reserve System. The gymnasium and auditorium the architects provided in the original building fell into disuse in the 1940s, but the gymnasium was remodeled in the late 1970s and is today in full use (see Part I).

1. "Federal Reserve Bank of Kansas City," a description given Federal Reserve Bank officials at the time the building was under construction, January 1921, Library Department, Federal Reserve Bank of Kansas City, Kansas City, Mo.

[123] FEDERAL RESERVE BANK OF KANSAS CITY, BANKING ROOM

FEDERAL RESERVE BANK OF DALLAS

1920
400 South Akard Street
Dallas, Texas

Cost of site in 1918: $145,000
Cost in 1920: 1,211,404;
    pcf: $0.71
Status: extant, two additional
    stories added 1939, air-conditioning added and original
    Banking and Directors' rooms
    remodeled in 1958; landmark,
    the City of Dallas,
    May 10, 1979

The Italian Renaissance palace of the Medici banking family in Florence served as the inspiration for many banks in the Midwest, including five that Graham, Anderson, Probst and White built for the Federal Reserve System in the 1920s (see Part I and other catalogue entries). As the nation's central bank, the primary purpose of the system was to provide credit and money to foster growth and stability. Dallas enjoyed a stimulus to its economic development after its selection over Houston, Fort Worth, San Antonio, and El Paso as the eleventh of twelve regional offices. Originally, an eight-story structure was proposed (fig. 124).

Later the Dallas bank was redesigned in the style of many other "strongbox" banks of the period—the New England examples of York and Sawyer or the midwestern examples of Louis Sullivan—except for the openness provided by the many windows, necessary in the hot climate of Texas in the days before air-conditioning (fig. 125).

[124] FEDERAL RESERVE BANK
OF DALLAS, DALLAS, TEX.,
PROPOSAL

The flat roof with the palmette cornice and the four monumental Doric columns of the entrance reflect the ideas of permanence and stability associated with neoclassicism. To underscore the theme, two female figures in Greek togas, representing "Integrity" and "Protection," guard either side of a shield of stars and stripes supported by an eagle at the top of the doorway. Above the stringcourse are just what a Texan might choose from the Roman repertoire—steers' heads strung with garlands.

Two grand spaces once graced the interior—a five-story Banking Room and a mahogany paneled Board of Directors' Room on the fifth floor. Both spaces were remodeled in 1958, but the ceiling frieze in the latter was lowered and preserved. When use of the Dallas branch doubled just after World War I, the board again engaged Graham, Anderson, Probst and White to design more spacious quarters.[1]

1. *Annual Reports Federal Reserve Bank of Dallas,* 1915–22, pp. 36–37. The cornerstone, laid in ceremonies on April 2, 1920, contains the architect's specifications for the building (*Annual Reports,* p. 97). Arthur Trible, an officer of the bank, also provided information for this entry.

[125] FEDERAL RESERVE BANK
OF DALLAS, EXTERIOR

[126] FEDERAL RESERVE BANK OF KANSAS CITY, OKLAHOMA CITY BRANCH, OKLAHOMA CITY, OKLA., ELEVATION

FEDERAL RESERVE BANK OF KANSAS CITY, OKLAHOMA CITY BRANCH

1921–23
West Third Street and North Harvey Avenue, SE corner
Oklahoma City, Oklahoma

Cost in 1923: $447,060; pcf: $0.68
Status: extant, in excellent condition; addition to the east in 1960 by architects Sorrey, Hill and Sorrey of Oklahoma City

Located on a hill in Oklahoma City's downtown, the Federal Reserve Bank exudes an air of security and dignity from its strongbox proportions, gray limestone cladding, and the tall, stately arcading of the windows of the main-floor Banking Room. Tripartite in its horizontal divisions, with a flat roof and originally with a bold overhanging cornice (removed in the 1960s), the three-story structure brings a reminder of the Renaissance palace to the Midwest (fig. 126). The great Banking Room, with its suppressed arch ceiling, was articulated on the sides by piers of slate-colored Belgian marble, which contained the tellers' cages and led to the officers' quarters and the Directors' Room.[1] The original tellers' cages and lighting fixtures were elaborately ornamented brass, so extensive that they required the polishing services of one full-time employee. These were removed during a remodeling after World War II.

When the new addition was contemplated, the architects and the client decided to match the limestone cladding and the floor height of the original Banking Room. The original quarry was found in Arkansas, and the stone acquired. The extra high space required to match the old room height in the new main floor soon proved convenient as it facilitated the bank's conversion a few years later to computer technology.

Like the other buildings Graham, Anderson, Probst and White erected for the Federal Reserve System, the bank in Oklahoma City is in good condition and continues to serve the community.

1. Complete drawings, all dated 1921, are in the archives of the bank in Oklahoma City. In addition, a 143-page book of specifications dated February 21, 1922, and "Building Program: Oklahoma City Branch, Federal Reserve Bank of Kansas City," n.d., are available. The original structure was designed so that three stories could be added. The only known photograph of the original interior appeared in the May 6, 1923, issue of the *Daily Oklahoman.*

FEDERAL RESERVE BANK OF KANSAS CITY, OMAHA BRANCH

1925
1701 Dodge Street
Omaha, Nebraska

Cost in 1925: $430,526.35; pcf: $0.815
Status: extant, a two-story addition made in 1957 to enlarge the
  vault area

Like the firm's other small banks for the Federal Reserve System, the interior public space of the bank in Omaha is smaller than one might imagine after seeing the arches of the seven windows on the exterior. The lobby and Banking Room are unprepossessing in their proportions of only about thirty by thirty feet. The marble pilasters with Corinthian capitals, brass railings, and tellers' cages are still intact, as is the balcony on the west side, which is supported on brackets of acanthus leaves. Especially remarkable is the exquisite detailing of the main doorway.

A special feature of this branch bank (fig. 127) evolved out of necessity. As space was limited, a "round house" was designed for the Dodge Street side in which armored cars loaded with money could deposit their cargoes. The round moving platform is eighteen feet in diameter; the loading room walls are covered with soft green ceramic tile.[1]

1. Drawings are in the archives of the bank in Omaha. A blackline on yellow paper of the presentation drawing is located in the GAPW archives in Chicago. Microfilm of structural drawings only are deposited with the Landmarks Heritage Preservation Commission, City of Omaha.

FEDERAL RESERVE BANK OF KANSAS CITY, DENVER BRANCH

1924–25
Arapahoe and Nineteenth streets,
  NW corner
Denver, Colorado

Cost in 1925: $394,579.27
  pcf: $0.64 (exclusive of vault)
Status: demolished

In Denver, the great Banking Room was elevated to the second floor, the *piano nobile* in the Italian Renaissance tradition (fig. 128). The cornice was simpler than in the other banks, but keystones adorned the main arches and the entrance was on the long side of the three-story rectangular building.[1]

1. Some drawings and photographs are located in the archives of the building that replaced the 1925 structure, others in the GAPW archives in Chicago.

[127] FEDERAL RESERVE BANK
OF KANSAS CITY, OMAHA
BRANCH, OMAHA, NEBR.,
ELEVATION

FEDERAL RESERVE BANK OF CHICAGO, DETROIT BRANCH

1927
160 West Fort Street
Detroit, Michigan

Cost: $1,054,515; pcf: $0.926. These figures do not include a tunnel to the post office at $167,000, which was subtracted before the per-cubic-foot cost was calculated.

Status: extant

Somewhat larger than its counterparts, the four-story Federal Reserve Bank in Detroit is articulated into four horizontal divisions (fig. 129). A black polished granite base supports the principal banking floor and the second floor, and a stringcourse separates them from the third floor, which acts as a transition to the cornice. Above, and recessed on all four sides, is an attic story with rows of office windows on the two main elevations. Vertically the building is defined by the windows, the entrance, and the suggestion of corner bays indicated by octagonal medallions at the corners in the third-story frieze.

The rough marble and limestone cladding, black marble trim, copper window grilles, and the rinceaux and acroteria at the crown are appropriately traditional for a Federal Reserve bank. The planarity of the whole and the restraint of the ornament give the building a somewhat severe quality, no doubt to make it more congenial with the fashionable stripped classicism used on office buildings of the period.

Inside, the Banking Room was destroyed in a later remodeling, but originally, Doric columns divided the room into four areas of equal height. This division was accentuated above by rectangular bands on the ceiling.

[129] FEDERAL RESERVE BANK OF CHICAGO, DETROIT BRANCH, DETROIT, MICH., EXTERIOR

BABY VILLAGE

1919–20
Mooseheart, Illinois

Status: extant

Before government social welfare programs were enacted on a large scale during the Great Depression of the 1930s, care of the poor, the elderly, and the chronically ill was left largely to private charity. Religious denominations, national or ethnic cooperatives, and fraternal groups sheltered orphans, the poor, and the elderly and provided medical facilities and education, sometimes up to the college level.

The Loyal Order of Moose was among the earliest American fraternal organizations to take responsibility for the education of the orphans of its members. As James J. Davis put it in the yearbook of 1914:

A considerable majority of the membership has been drawn from the working people, many of them, who, in their youth, have not had the advantages of education, and as they have grown up have brought to their families their weekly support by the labor of their hands. Such men join fraternal societies, not only for social intercourse and the benefits of an association in time of disaster, but to enlarge their lives and to prepare the way for better opportunities for their children than they have had themselves. To such men the Moose Plan has appealed from the beginning, because the laborious lives which they have been forced to lead makes them eager to insure their children against ignorance.[1]

Each member at that time paid one dollar a year toward planning a campus in Mooseheart, Illinois, to provide a home for widows and children with a progressive educational system. From the outset the men were determined that every building should be done "not in a cheap way and not in a superficial way, but that we should build it from the ground up putting in the best foundation first, to the end that the completed institution might stand forever as a monument to the zeal and fidelity of the order."[2]

The directors also felt from the beginning that the "estate should be made beautiful, and we therefore employed Brother J. A. Young, a landscape gardener of standing and ability to take charge of this feature."[3]

The site on the west bank of the Fox River was laid out on an informal plan, with driveways extending in gentle curves, dividing into branches, and at one point forming a heart (fig. 130). From the earliest days it was thought of as "a Child City" of

[130] MOOSEHEART, ILL., AERIAL VIEW

[131] BABY VILLAGE AND DETAIL

five to ten thousand, except that here fifty people live in each building, not four or five, "and it had all the support services of a small town, an electrical generator, steam plant, laundry and food distribution system."

By 1918, more facilities for babies were needed. "Coddling and petting is just as necessary for a little baby as food," the directors wrote, and the program called for facilities for babies and several adults to live in each building, to come as close as possible to a situation where it would be "as if their own mothers were watching over them." When Graham, Anderson, Probst and White presented its design for five low-scaled, small cottages arranged in an informal circle around a central play area, the complex was named Baby Village (fig. 131).[4]

Suited to their purpose admirably, the houses are U-shaped in plan, with the two wings protecting a terraced forecourt that marks the entrance. Three spacious arched doorways lead into a reception area, and the living-sleeping quarters are off to the sides in the wings. The large windows provide ample air and sunshine. Most of the buildings are made of "Mooseheart granite block," which was manufactured on the grounds by the older boys in the vocational training program. Still in use today, the cribs

in the well-maintained wings and the rocking chairs for the widowed grandmothers who hold the babies are living testimony that the organization continues to fulfill the purposes of its founding fathers. The firm built several other buildings in Mooseheart (q.v.).

1. *Mooseheart Being The Governors First Book*. (Anderson, Ind.:

Mooseheart Press.) Yearbooks from 1913 to 1922 are available at the museum in Mooseheart, along with photographs in albums, frames, and loose files. Included are three large color lithographs of the grounds, other archival materials, and an extensive collection on the Loyal Order of Moose and its history.

2. *Yearbook, 1914*.

3. Ibid.

4. Ibid.

COTTAGE IN BOYS' VILLAGE

(Superintendent's House)

1924
Mooseheart, Illinois

Status: extant

One of the few residential buildings remaining by the firm, this house was no doubt designed by a young architect on the staff (fig.

132). The drawing is signed W. E. Hasball, but it is not clear if he was also responsible for the plans.

[132] COTTAGE IN BOYS' VILLAGE (SUPERINTENDENT'S HOUSE)

Traditional in form, the house fits nicely into the gentle rolling hills of the river valley landscape of Mooseheart. Generous casement windows on the first floor light the living and dining rooms, and gable windows were intended to make the upper stories habitable as boys' bedrooms. Today the house is used as living quarters by the superintendent.

low clubhouse is distinguished by three tall French doors with fan lights, which lead to a porch within an entrance arcade.

Within are a two-story reception lobby, an auditorium, and bedrooms on the second floor. (fig. 133).

WOMEN'S BUILDING

1922
"B" Street
Mooseheart, Illinois

Status: extant

A rectangular building of "Mooseheart granite block" with a red tiled roof, first used as a clubhouse, this building was an early project of the Women of the Mooseheart Legion. The long,

[133] WOMEN'S BUILDING

OHIO DORMITORY

1920s
Mooseheart, Illinois

Status: extant

Following the Greek Revival mode that flourished in the United States during the 1830s and 1840s, the lower portion of the Ohio house has the heavy columns, triglyphs, and the plain frieze common in the American domestic version of this classical style. Here, it has been accommodated to the building material manufactured at Mooseheart— poured concrete granite-faced blocks under a red Spanish tile roof (fig. 134).

Whether this building was originally a dormitory or a clinic is not clear. Taller than the earlier cottages of Baby Village, the building (now called the J. J. Stoehr Big Seven Memorial) is approached by a broad flight of steps. It was named after the Ohio branch of the Loyal Order of Moose which paid for its construction.

NEW YORK STATE BUILDING

1920s
Mooseheart, Illinois

Status: extant

The New York State Building, underwritten by the New York chapter of the Loyal Order of Moose, has a projecting pavilion defined by the two-story Corinthian columns, dormer windows, and side wings often associated with the Georgian revival period. This style enjoyed its greatest vogue in the last decades of the

[134] OHIO DORMITORY

[135] NEW YORK STATE BUILDING

nineteenth century and the first of the twentieth century, and it is still a part of the architectural fabric of most traditional American communities. A commodious dormitory for girls, the large living quarters on the ground floor are provided with two fireplaces and French doors that open onto the terrace along the front (fig. 135).

[136] ILLINOIS MERCHANTS BANK BUILDING (CONTINENTAL ILLINOIS BANK AND TRUST COMPANY BUILDING), CHICAGO, ILL., ELEVATION

ILLINOIS MERCHANTS BANK BUILDING

(Continental Illinois Bank and Trust Company Building, after 1928)

1920–24
231 South LaSalle Street
Chicago, Illinois

Cost in 1924, architects' figures: $12,078,176.18; bank's figures: $13,361,146.47

Status: extant, in excellent condition. Remodelings over the years have preserved the original character of the public spaces.

In the contrast between its exterior and its interior, the Continental Illinois is like the conservative midwesterner of the mid-1920s. With its classical columns and its cornice lined up exactly with the cornice of the Federal Reserve Bank (*q.v.*) across the street, the building is rational and efficient on the outside (figs. 136, 137). The restraint of the gray limestone cladding is as suitable as a businessman's suit for streetwear. Inside, however, the great Banking Room expresses the realm of that higher level of being, the businessman of taste, patron of the arts, sciences, and humanities, and guardian of communal treasures, both financial and cultural (fig. 46).

At the street level the effect of the colonnade along Jackson Boulevard is stately, a major factor in the streetscape of the financial district. In the early 1920s, the firm must have hoped it would receive the commission for the new Board of Trade Building at the southern terminus of LaSalle Street, for it prepared a presentation drawing that showed the district finished with another classical building with a cornice line matching the two banks on the corners opposite, also with a pedimented portal entrance (fig. 43).[1]

The hollow rectangle of the steelwork went up in record time, surrounding a light court from the fifth story up (above the Banking Room) where offices were disposed on both sides of the corridor.[2] Anderson designed a blockwide walk-through space on the first floor to give the building its urbane character, echoing the sidewalks and the grid of the city's streets outside.

The ascent to the second floor, originally by marble staircase, now by escalator, leads to the sumptuous Banking Room. This vast space, 167 by 200 by 53 feet in the center section, and 34 feet on either side, is nearly in its original condition. Matched by the grandeur of the materials that adorn every surface—gilded coffered ceilings, brass fixtures, marble floors and columns, and the elegantly colored murals—it is a salon for the cultivated entrepreneur, the *beau idéal* of the period in Chicago.

The floor is covered with French Hauteville marble, and

the twenty-eight columns are of light Cunard pink marble. The murals that adorn the frieze are the work of the noted painter Jules Guerin.[3] Given to depicting great buildings and groups of people in broad, flat masses, Guerin was clearly influenced by Japanese prints, but his coloring was generally higher in value than that common in Japanese inks of the period. His masterful renderings of buildings made his work prized by contemporary architects. Guerin filled the murals of the Merchants Bank with depictions of the Chicago world's fair, the World's Columbian Exposition of 1893, interwoven with allegorical references to international commercial activity. Countries are represented by symbols—Switzerland holds a clock, Italy a large basket of grapes, and so on. The murals are separated by quotations from the history of banking and economics.

These quotations were chosen by C. W. Barron, who later wrote that he had searched "everything from Adam Smith down" but found that "economic literature did not lend itself to either epigram or proverb." The problem was to find worthwhile sentences with fewer than 115 characters so that the letters might be large enough to be read from the floor more than fifty feet below. Stanley Field, chairman of the building committee, chose the final eight quotations from Barron's twenty submissions. Barron's own wisdom was first on the final list: "All the progress of men and nations is based upon sacredness of contracts." The other messages are equally expressive of the financial ideology of the

1920s: "Capital is what you and I have saved out of yesterday's wages" and "Private credit is wealth, public honor is security." There is also Cicero's "In a family, as in the state, the best source of wealth is economy."[4] In these days of credit cards the quotations may seem to some like the quaint notions of an elderly maiden aunt, but the bank has let them all stand.

Over the years the physical fabric of the building has worn well, needing only the usual air-conditioning and other standard remodeling. The murals were cleaned and restretched in the 1950s, and the incandescent bowl fixtures in the Banking Room were removed in the mid-1960s and replaced by flush flourescent units. Since the designers did not want to puncture the coffers to locate new fixtures, they used 132 narrow-beam, 500-

[137] ILLINOIS MERCHANTS BANK, DETAIL OF ENTRANCE

watt luminaires with black baffle rings to light the center section.[5] In 1980, the plaster-cast indirect light fixtures and bronze chandeliers were refinished and the murals were again cleaned. Other interior features of the original building that have been preserved include the raised paneling throughout all public contact areas and the antique oak-pegged paneling in the private dining room.

1. For further discussion see Sally Chappell, "Another Top: The Board of Trade Proposal."

2. "Steel Workers Set a Building Speed Record," *Chicago Evening Post*, June 17, 1923.

3. Guerin also decorated New York's Pennsylvania Station, the Federal Reserve Bank in San Francisco, the Louisiana State Capitol at Baton Rouge, and the Lincoln Memorial Building in Washington, D.C., and later did more work for Graham, Anderson, Probst and White in the Union Trust Building of Cleveland, Chicago's Civic Opera Building, the Cleveland Terminal Group, and the Merchandise Mart. He was also a color consultant for Union Station in Chicago, director of decorations for the Panama Pacific Exposition in San Francisco in 1915, and an illustrator of books. If they did not meet as young men at the World's Columbian Exposition of 1893 in Chicago, Guerin and Graham surely knew each other as early as 1908–9 when Guerin was at work on some of the drawings for Burnham's *Plan of Chicago. See also* Robert Bruegmann, "Burnham, Guerin and the City as Image," in *The Plan of Chicago: 1909–1979*, pp. 16–28.

4. C. W. Barron, "Finance in Epigram: A Wall Street Sermon," typescript, Continental Illinois Bank and Trust Company library, Chicago, Ill.

5. Lighting system installed by H. J. Chindlund, electrical engineer; Samuel R. Lewis and Associates; and Ole Hill, Commonwealth Edison, 1965. See "Bank Building Text," manuscript, April 14, 1975, Continental Bank library; "Retaining the Elegance of Old Banks," *Illuminating Engineer* 60, no. 7 (July 1965); H. J. Chindlund and Ole Hill, "Relighting a High-Bay Banking Area," *Electrical Construction and Maintenance*, n.d. Surprisingly, there is no contemporary review of this building in any journals indexed by the Burnham Index or the Avery Index.

HOOVER SUCTION SWEEPER COMMUNITY BUILDING

1923
North Canton, Ohio

Status: demolished in early 1970s

Fitting in well with the surrounding neighborhood, the Community Building with its intimate two-story height, brick cladding, and white spandrel panels resembled a midwestern school of the period (fig. 138). In plan the building was two adjoining rectangles. The front held large meeting rooms, four fireplaces, and a kitchen. In the back was a gymnasium that could be converted to an auditorium, complete with projection room, a balcony on three sides, and a large stage. Locker rooms, a small bowling alley, and a poolroom were located in the basement under the gym.[1]

The building was given to North Canton by William H. Hoover, president of the Hoover Suction Sweeper Company, to fill the need for public recreation facilities and to provide opportunities for training and participation in community and welfare work in the vicinity. What the building meant to the community is apparent from the many newspaper items that appeared in its forty-eight-year history. The 1924 slogan for the building, "A Real Place for Real Folks," was repeated in programs for several years. Membership, open to both men and women from the beginning, included services for "tots to tottering elder statesmen."[2]

In those days not everyone had cars or belonged to organizations outside of town. "The Building" was the only place to go and everyone went. . . . The halls and rooms rang with laughter as the young people came and went to their meetings or gym classes. The adult groups enjoyed the meeting rooms too, especially when they had guest speakers. They were so proud of the Community Building—not many towns had such grand facilities.

Many a happy meal was enjoyed in the Legion Room, which had the kitchen adjoining it. The lobbies were large and spaciously appointed with lovely paintings. At the west end of the south lobby was a lighted display case that housed a beautiful collection of rare stuffed birds in all their colorful splendor. Many groups had their beginnings at the Community Building, mainly because it was

[138] HOOVER SUCTION SWEEPER COMMUNITY BUILDING, NORTH CANTON, OHIO, EXTERIOR

a central place to meet and, at that time, was within walking distance of most of the town. It was the hub of most of North Canton's extracurricular activities.[3]

C. B. Williams, director of the Community Building for twenty-six years, wrote a poem about the building in the 1950s.

A Place to Serve
Some think of it as a building, but many of us know
Who have been much about it, that it was not built for show. . . .
For it's much more than a lobby, and it's much more than a gym.

It's much more than a place to meet, and a healthy place to swim.
It's more than bowling alleys, or a place to play baseball
And other games in season, or a club with good for all.

It's a spirit of good fellowship, and a spirit of fair play,
It means good will to others, and a boost along the way.
It's a chance for exploration, along the path He trod,
It's a chance to serve your fellow man, and thereby serve your God.[4]

Ruth Basner said that she spent some of the happiest days of her youth in "The Building,"

and wrote that "When the pear-shaped steel ball on the wrecker knocked down the last wall of the first Community Building years of memories piled upon the heap of rubble."[5]

1. Ruth Harpold Basner, *The North Canton Heritage* (North Canton, Ohio: The Heritage Society, 1972), vol. 1, 1805–1940, p. 174.

2. Ibid., p. 175.

3. Ibid.

4. "Your Community Building YMCA is a Gift," *North Canton Sun*, June 3, 1970.

5. Basner, *Heritage*, p. 174. *See also* "40th Anniversary Edition Community Building YMCA," *North Canton Sun*, March 6, 1973.

BELKNAP HARDWARE AND MANUFACTURING COMPANY COMPLEX

1923
111 East Main Street
Louisville, Kentucky

Cost in 1923: $1,668,335.25; pcf: $0.158
Status: extant; nominated for the National Register of Historic
   Places by the Louisville Landmarks Commission

It is not widely known that Daniel Burnham and Company erected a manufacturing complex for the Belknap Hardware and Manufacturing Company in Louisville from 1905 to 1907, and Graham, Anderson, Probst and White added Warehouse 12 (fig. 139) and a power plant in 1923.[1] The complex is still largely intact and is adjacent to a block of predominately nineteenth-century cast-iron facade buildings, the second largest cast-iron warehouse district in the nation. A comparison of the two complexes shows the changes in scale, materials, and technology in American manufacturing processes during the period.

The earlier buildings reflect the turn-of-the-century trend among manufacturing companies to concentrate their business in large supply depots. This greatly encouraged the sale of goods, for the "carriage-maker, machinist, iron-worker, miner, contractor, farrier, builder or hardware jobber" could then find everything he needed in one place, "from the smallest screw and hinge, to the largest pick or crow-bar that a man can wield."[2] In addition, the firm issued catalogs of several hundred pages and did a large mail-order business in wire, wheelbarrows, hinges, rivets, saws, hammers, and a variety of other hardware items. By the early 1920s, the volume of sales had increased dramatically in response to the building boom after World War I, and a new warehouse and power plant were needed.

Graham, Anderson, Probst and White, no doubt influenced by the powerful industrial forms of the Chicago tradition, designed the eleven-story brick building with brick piers and large industrial multipaned windows and gave it a tripartite division. Thus the building takes its place in the history of industrial architecture, as part of a large complex planned as a unit with inter-related parts (see Part I).

1. *Sanborn Fire Insurance Atlas,* 1972, Louisville Landmarks Commission office, Louisville, Ky. *See also The Industries of Louisville,* n.d., Louisville Landmark Commission office.

2. *Louisville, Gateway to the South,* brochure, Kentucky and Indiana Terminal Railroad Company, 1924.

[139] BELKNAP HARDWARE AND MANUFACTURING COMPANY COMPLEX, LOUISVILLE, KY., EXTERIOR

[140] BUTLER BROTHERS WAREHOUSES, CHICAGO, ILL., EXTERIOR

BUTLER BROTHERS WAREHOUSES

(One Northwest Center and River Center)
South building 1912–13; north building 1917–22
111 and 165 North Canal Street
Chicago, Illinois

Cost in 1913 for the south building: $2,140,408.58; pcf: $0.176
Cost in 1922 for the north building; $3,816,388.98; pcf: $0.313
Status: extant; being converted from warehouse loft space to retail and office space

Bold and strong, the Butler Brothers Warehouses stand as a powerful part of the wall of buildings that articulates the west front of the Chicago River (fig. 72). Their brick facades, sturdy corners, broad piers and spandrels, and heavy parapets express the utilitarian character of warehouses, but they are urbane warehouses, part civic, part industrial, as indicated by the combination of workaday materials and Tuscan arcading (fig. 140).

Almost mirror images of one another, except for details in the roofs, both buildings contain sixteen stories plus a basement and sub-basement and measure more than 12 million cubic feet each. Carl Condit tells us that two buildings were originally constructed in 1912–13 side by side between Canal Street and the river, but that the expansion of the north approach to the new Union Station required the demolition of the east block, and that it was replaced in 1921–22 to the north of its twin, on the block between Randolph and Lake streets.[1]

The floors below grade contained the usual necessities, a

machine room, elevator pits, and a hay room to feed the horses that pulled the wagons of the period. An automatic electric conveyor ran in a tunnel under the street. One hundred twenty feet long and nine feet wide with a five-horsepower motor, the belt operated on the same principle as the moving sidewalk at the World's Columbian Exposition of 1893. The conveyer was built by Link Belt Machinery of Chicago. In its day it carried thousands of packages from the shipping room on the north to the freight and storage warehouse on the south side of Randolph Street.[2]

Above, the stories varied somewhat in function, material, and organization. The first floor contained a vestibule with gray Tennessee marble floors, wooden doors with bronze trim and decorative radiator grilles. The fourth floor, where Mr. Butler had his offices, was also given special treatment and included a fireplace and a bridge connecting the new and the old buildings. Another bridge connected them on the eleventh floor. Otherwise, the upper stories were utilitarian and loftlike in their interior character, except for the fourteenth floor, which held a restaurant, ladies' cafeteria, men's and boys' cafeteria, a public library substation, a sickroom, and a girls' playground with an asphalt roof. This inclusion of social and recreational facilities in a warehouse was not uncommon in the industrial architecture of Chicago.

During the 1970s and 1980s, both buildings were changed significantly. The restaurant in the south building was abolished, six new elevators were added, and new interior decoration was designed to be more compatible with contemporary office space. The underground tunnel housing the conveyor belt was filled and the connecting bridges were removed. The ground floor was converted into retail stores. The north building was painted off-white several years ago, although the south building retains its original brick surface.

Critical opinion of the two buildings illustrates an interesting phase in the history of modern architecture. Traditionally, industrial structures were deemed unworthy of serious artistic consideration and were regarded as the province of the engineer. After the dawn of a new attitude in the twentieth century, today designated "modernism," the architectural community awoke to the beauties of grain silos, manufactories, warehouses, mills, power stations, and a host of other building types. With the zeal of the convert to a new religion, designers cast off all the habits of classicism with its base, shaft, and capital divisions, its vertical and horizontal articulation, its symmetry, and above all its ornament to embrace a new machine-age aesthetic. Some older utilitarian structures designed by canonical architects, such as Henry Hobson Richardson's Marshall Field Wholesale Store and Warehouse (1885–87), were universally admired for their structural expressiveness, and the Butler Brothers Warehouses were among them. Indeed, they are similar to Richardson's work in their massing and articulation, although Richardson's masterful treatment of the windows is lacking.

Shortly after the buildings were erected, Andrew Rebori called them a "striking and unchallenged" success (see Part I).[3] In the mid-1980s, what seems remarkable about the Butler Brothers Warehouses is precisely their blend of the industrial and the traditional styles, a mixture that seems appropriate for their place along the Chicago River, and a mixture that has proved adaptable to the changing character of this part of the city.

The two buildings were remodeled differently. The north building, now called One Northwest Center and owned by Randolph Corporation, has an irregular lobby with mirrored glass windows. The south building, now called River Center and owned by Gregg Builders, was altered by Balsamo Olson Group, Architects. It has a through north-south lobby with fluted walnut columns, a continuation of the city grid, and a spacious east-west lobby due to the sacrifice of the intervening floor space. Both buildings retain the ramps, truck portals, and railroad tracks on the river side that are a carryover from their utilitarian past. The Metropolitan Sanitary Commission has created a narrow park at the river's edge on the south, landscaped with ginkgo trees, evergreens, and flowers that bloom from May to October.

1. Carl W. Condit, *Chicago, 1910–29: Building, Planning, and Urban Technology*, pp. 142–43.

[141] BRITISH OLD PEOPLE'S HOME, RIVERSIDE, ILL., ELEVATION

2. *Chicago Butler Bros. Warehouses*, rental brochure, c. 1912, GAPW archives, Chicago, Ill.

3. Andrew N. Rebori, "The Work of Burnham and Root, D. H. Burnham, D. H. Burnham and Co., and Graham, Burnham and Co."

BRITISH OLD PEOPLE'S HOME

1923
Riverside, Illinois

Status: extant

The welcoming arms of the low-scaled building on the banks of the Salt Creek express the restful accessibility of the British Old People's Home (fig. 141). On eight acres of land, the home accommodates about sixty people, with light and sunshine assured by the three-winged plan. The central pavilion contains the public rooms.[1]

1. Site plan, first and second floor plans, and elevation drawings can be found in GAPW archives, Chicago, Ill.

CHICAGO UNION STATION

1913–25
The complex of buildings, streets, viaducts, tracks, and service structures was all located on the west bank of the Chicago River between Madison and Harrison streets. The two main buildings, the Headhouse and the Concourse, central in the plan, sat between Adams Street and Jackson Boulevard, separated by Canal Street.
Chicago, Illinois

Cost: Various figures are given for the whole complex. The total paid by a combination of municipal and federal governments and the railroads was approximately $150 million. The architects quoted $75 million as the figure for the buildings and related structures. Office records give only a 1919 figure for the Headhouse of $15,523,695.44.

Status: Headhouse is extant; Concourse was demolished in 1969.

"So sovereign a situation," the architects wrote, should have the "most advanced facilities with an architectural dignity befitting the center of the world's railway transportation system."[1] In one of their greatest works, the Chicago Union Station, the architects combined accessibility and convenience, state-of-the-art technology, exterior forms, and interior spaces to express the loftiest aspirations of the railroad age in the United States.

Although seemingly independent of each other above the ground, the Headhouse and Concourse buildings were component parts of a unified scheme below ground where the great sequence of uninterrupted spaces from the Waiting Room to the tracks extended two blocks from Clinton Street under Canal Street to the river. The use of a severe classical style reflected this unity in both buildings as they formed the terminus of the riverbank and

[142] CHICAGO UNION STATION, CHICAGO, ILL., EXTERIOR

acted as a gateway to the West Side of Chicago (fig. 142).

Except for commuters who held season tickets and went directly to the Concourse, most passengers could enter the Headhouse through the great colonnades on Clinton or Canal streets and let the flow of the spaces guide them through the necessary patterns of travel—arrival, checking baggage, buying tickets, waiting, going to the train, and boarding. Taxicabs and baggage trucks could enter at the two west corners of the building on descending ramps, deposit passengers at the main level or baggage on the lowest floor, and exit toward the east (fig. 33).

The Concourse Building was surrounded by a large plaza built on railway property and included street entrances on Adams Street and on Jackson Boulevard. Inclined ramps and stairways led to the space below and were used by the many commuters who walked across bridges over the river on the north and south.

The Concourse Building, approximately 124 feet wide by 204 feet long by about 90 feet high,[2] was much smaller than the Headhouse. Inside, the riveted lattice steel columns that supported the roof were unadorned and uncovered as they rose to support three parallel longitudinal vaults of glass and tile on steel arch ribs (fig. 32).

The distinguishing interior feature of the Headhouse is the

Waiting Room, 100 feet wide by 270 feet long and 112 feet high, lighted by an arched glass skylight. This room also had a restaurant, information stand, telephone, telegraph, drugstore, newsstands, flower shops, and other retail and service areas for travelers. The walls are paneled with Roman travertine, with large openings at each end and on the sides emphasized by Corinthian columns and unified by an entablature that encircles the whole room forty-seven feet above the floor. Above this, the walls are similar to the clerestories in the ancient baths, but here they admit natural light only on the east and west. The distance between this wall and the interior walls of the office building that occupied the fourth to the eighth floors of the Headhouse, however, is sixteen feet, and so this space acts like an interior courtyard. The ceiling is a suppressed arch entirely of skylights except for one tier of coffers around the sides and ends (fig. 31).

The main entrances to the Waiting Room from the street are lobbies forty feet wide by eighty-five feet long fronting on Canal Street, seventy feet ten inches to either side of the east and west axis of the building. These lobbies contain the staircases that lead down to the Waiting Room level, but also function as arcades that originally gave access to the shops bordering both sides. In addition, there were a number of shops within the Canal Street front colonnade. Combining retail convenience with the necessities of travel, the station was a people's palace, following the example set earlier by Grand Central in New York. Containing everything from a ticket office to a first-aid room, these great railroad terminals were also microcities.

The east wall of the Waiting Room opened to the Concourse lobby through a large doorway. In addition, corridors on either side of the two staircases enabled one to pass into the Concourse space at almost any point in the entire length of the east wall. Under the north stairway, baggage service was provided in an enclosure with an elevator, chute, and stairway communicating with the floor below.

Adequate entrances to the office building above the Headhouse were provided where they could be somewhat isolated from the station facilities, slightly above the street level (itself a level above the station) in the center of the block at the Jackson Boulevard and Adams Street sides of the building. A flight of six steps led to a loggia (above the inclined driveway below, with sufficient space to clear the vehicle traffic). On the inside, this loggia led to elevators on the west, or straight ahead to a balcony overlooking the Waiting Room.[3]

The baggage room occupied nearly all the space under the Concourse. Under the Headhouse, the basement was devoted to a variety of purposes—machine shop, fan room, carpenter's shop, and a special room assigned to immigrants.[4]

The train platforms themselves were of two kinds: one for passengers boarding and one for baggage. The latter was screened off from the public and was higher than the passenger platform for safer separation of the two functions and greater ease of loading and unloading the baggage cars. The sheds were an ingenious variation on the Bush Shed,[5] and the complexities of the track layout also led to ingenious solutions, which were incorporated into several agreed-upon improvements to the city's infrastructure.[6]

Construction started in 1916. By the end of 1917, Canal Street had been brought up high enough to clear trains on the two west tracks, the elevated line had been raised over the street and the south tracks, and the old bridge structure had been replaced with a new truss. The construction of approach tracks, subsidiary buildings, and the caissons for the two main buildings was also begun, but the entry of the United States into World War I caused delays in the rest of the construction. A depression for two years after the war caused a slowdown, and work was not started again until 1922. At last, on May 15, 1925, the station officially opened.[7] Alfred Shaw, the designer who took over after Peirce Anderson's death in 1924, expressed his feelings in *Architectural Forum* the next year:

A great terminal of this character, so important in its influence, represents the employment and heroic efforts of many men, men with vision and indomitable optimism, who kept the great undertaking always before their eyes; men who labored under electric lamps, who were relied upon for all kinds of minute mathematical calculations, and the multitude of other men, those disciples of tobacco and fresh air, who swung the hammers and set the rivets and the stones to make the great vision an enduring reality! The Chicago Union Station represents, today, the last word in the world's railroad terminals.[8]

Critical reception was favorable from the outset. Many features in the building were unique at the time. The two passing, or through, tracks to the east were an innovation in the United States, setting an example for speed and efficiency. Also novel were the extremely broad connecting passages between the Headhouse and the Concourse that allowed for ease of traffic during rush hours and holiday periods. Separating the flow of baggage from the passengers greatly improved safety and efficiency. Insisting on the off-the-street facilities mandated by the

Enabling Ordinance of March 23, 1914, members of the Chicago Plan Commission required another unique and frequently praised feature of the station— the cab drives. Another feature noted in contemporary criticism was the promise of a careful relationship between the station and the postal facilities, but this failed to come to fruition exactly as planned. The United States Mail Building *(q.v.),* already erected in 1921–22, was to be at the southern end of the system, with a new post office to be built just north of Union Station, between it and North Western Station. The United States Post Office *(q.v.)* went up years later around the U.S. Mail Building to the south. A powerhouse further south was erected in the mid-1920s (fig. 143).

In the 1920s, the railroad station was more than a place to catch a train. It embodied beliefs in the American way of life; it exuded a kind of national identity. It was an outward symbol of faith in progress, in science, in get-up-and-go determination, in conquest of the wilderness, and in manifest destiny. Entering Union Station today, we see it littered with potato chip bags and chewing gum wrappers, and we can scarcely imagine a time when nearly all the traveling public aspired to gentility in public and in private life, and a trip or going to the railroad station was part of that way of life.

Contemporary photographs testify that ladies wore hats, veils, and white gloves when traveling by train, and gentlemen, their best suits. Rites of passage took place in these spaces. The interiors were lavish and ex-

[143] UNION STATION, POWER HOUSE, ELEVATION

pensive, but no one complained of their cost for they were expressions of communal witness to the importance of what went on there, in public and private matters.

In addition, nearly everyone in 1925 was certain that the use of the station, like the economy of the country, would continue to grow. Shortly after the stock market crash of 1929, however, Chicago's Union Station proved to have been overscaled. When passenger business decreased, the railroads did not spend money on upkeep or improvement of

passenger facilities. It was inevitable that the devastation of the economy during the Great Depression would take its toll on the railroad station.

The classical style of the station fell into disfavor in the same period. Banks, offices, and other facilities needed to attract a wide range of clients and were eager to avoid pretensions of serving only the genteel wealthy. It was not until the United States entered World War II and the nation mobilized its defense system that the railroads, including Union Station, again played a vital part in the life of the country. After the war, the decline began again.

Carl Condit's sagacious interpretation points out the irony of the situation.

At the time of its opening the four constituent railroads of Union Station operated an average of about 390 trains per week-day in and out of the terminal, with a high proportion of these concentrated in the morning and evening rush hours because of the heavy volume of suburban and overnight sleeping-car traffic. The number remained constant throughout the remainder of the decade, having fallen in 1929 to about 365 trains listed in the public timetables. The number declined rapidly during the depression, then suddenly and dramatically turned upward under the enormous demands of the Second World War. The high point of wartime travel came in 1944, but it is doubtful whether traffic at Union Station ever exceeded 400 trains daily. . . . The great irony in the operation of Union Station, however, is that the spacious facility has seldom been used to more than half its capacity. The track system of the north half can easily and safely accommodate 300 trains per day and that of the south half 420, while the concourses, waiting room, and entrance and exit ways provide sufficient area for the comfortable movement of 400,000 passengers a day. As incredible as it seems, after years devoted to the formulation of merger plans, Union, North Western, and the Illinois Central's newly electrified suburban station were all that Chicago railroads needed to handle the city's maximum total of 1,600 daily

trains. In the case of the Canal Street terminals, this enlarged traffic would have required the expansion of coach yard facilities and the rearrangement of connecting tracks, but these would have been simple tasks for a city that had built up the largest metropolitan rail system in the world. It is one of the curiosities of urban technology that city planners and the designers of railroad facilities never recognized the immense reserve capacity available in the big metropolitan terminals that were completed during the years 1899 to 1933 (South Station, Boston, to Cincinnati Union Terminal). That this capacity might some day—even in the late twentieth century—prove essential eventually impressed itself on a few transportation planners.[9]

To many, the interior of the Concourse was one of the greatest spaces in the city, if not the country, and its loss is irreparable. The Waiting Room under the skylight of the Headhouse now alone retains the aura of the building's original grandeur. The great proportions, the rich decoration of the Corinthian columns, the skylight, and the sculpted figures on either side of the entrance portals are still impressive and partially reminiscent of the earlier, complete complex.

The two chief arguments for the preservation of what is left of Union Station, of course, are that it is the only remaining testament to the role Chicago played at the center of American life during the great railroad age, and that it is architecturally distinguished as a planning and design masterpiece (see Part I).

1. *Union Station Chicago*, brochure (Chicago: R. R. Donnelley & Sons Co., 1925).

2. According to Carl Condit's reading of the plans, the Concourse proper was 124 feet wide by 204 feet long; if the aisles were included, the overall width was 260 feet (*Chicago 1910–29*, p. 297, footnote 42; Condit questions Rexford Newcomb's dimensions). Comparing the height of the Waiting Room and the height of the Concourse on the section drawing, we may estimate that the Concourse was about 90 feet high at the crown.

3. *Western Architecture*, January 1926, plates 4 and 5.

4. The description of the station, taken largely from *Concrete and Steel*, January 10, 1927, pp. 15–20, was probably originally provided to the publication by the architects.

5. Carl Condit explains this covering well in *Chicago 1910–29*, p. 281: "They represent a variation on the Bush Shed in which the low vaults with their smoke slots alternate with high light monitors developed into an ogival section like a Gothic arch. The vaults over the tracks and the crowns of the monitors are built up of prefabricated glass-and-concrete panels made by dipping the glass tile in hot asphalt and imbedding it in the concrete frame while the latter was still in a plastic state. The builders sought several ends in the adoption of this relatively costly construction: first, to obtain complete protection of tracks and platforms with maximum light over the latter and exactly the headroom over the tracks necessary for all locomotive smoke to be dissipated through the smoke slots; and second, to provide a form of reasonably attractive appearance when seen from the street. . . . The double necessity of avoiding extremely deep girders . . . and of keeping the tops of the shed at the street level led to the unique framing system of the en-

tire shed structure with its inverted heart-shaped truss." See also Condit, *American Building Art: The Twentieth Century.* The only train sheds that still exist may be seen between Jackson and Van Buren streets. The complexity of the problems of the trackage as it intersected streets and the narrowness of the throat coming into the station also led to ingenious solutions in the signaling system, with signals placed on viaducts and carefully designed interlocking towers. It was actually not until the completion of the freight stations of the Alton and the Burlington on either side of the south approach and the coach yards of the Pennsylvania and the Burlington on the east side near Roosevelt Road (the Burlington was later moved to the west side), and the erection of the United States Post Office in 1930–33 on the air rights over the area between Harrison and Van Buren that this vital part of the city's transportation network was finally completed.

6. As described in the *Voter,* 1925, pp. 22–23, the original enabling legislation called for various boons for the city, outside and beyond the terminal. Improvement agreements included the following: to connect Canal and Orleans streets, uniting the north and west parts of the city; to widen and elevate Canal Street between Washington Street and Roosevelt Road to make a direct artery to the new Illinois Central Terminal; to open Monroe Street as a through east-west viaduct over the tracks that ran from Lake Street to Roosevelt Road; to erect a Congress Street viaduct; to help the city in straightening the Chicago River; and to abandon freight plans that interfered with the circulation in the southern portion of the city. *See also* Rexford Newcomb, "The New Chicago Union Station," *Western Architect* 35 (January 1926).

7. Condit, *Chicago 1910–29,* p. 277.

8. Alfred Shaw, "Chicago Union Station," *Architectural Forum,* February 1926, p. 88.

9. Condit, *Chicago 1910–29,* pp. 283–84.

Additional bibliography:

ARNOLD, BION J. *Report on the Re-Arrangement and Development of the Steam Railroad Terminals of the City of Chicago.* Chicago: Citizens' Terminal Plan Committee, 1913.

ASHCROFT, THEODOR VAN R. "A Great Railroad Terminal and How Chicago Got It." *The Voter,* no. 133 (May 1914).

BROCK, E. "Mechanical Features of the Chicago Union Station." *Journal of the Western Society of Engineers* 30 (December 1925): 527–43.

BRUMLEY, DANIEL J., FREDERICK E. MORROW, and ROBERT H. P. FORD. "Chicago Terminal Improvements." *Transactions of the American Society of Civil Engineers* 87 (1924): 802–10.

Corporate History of the Chicago Union Station Company: Charter Ordinances, Street Vacations, Petitions to and Orders of Illinois Public Utilities Commission, Mortgage, Operating Agreements, Real Estate Transfers, Agreements. Chicago, probably 1925–30, at Chicago Historical Society, Chicago, Ill.

CRANE, JACOB L., JR. "Street Development in Relation to Railroad Terminals." *Transactions of the American Society of Civil Engineers* 87 (1924): 795–801.

D'ESPOSITO, JOSHUA. "Chicago Union Station." *Journal of the Western Society of Engineers* 30 (November 1925): 447–60.

DRUMMOND, WILLIAM. *The Railway Terminal Problem of Chicago.* Chicago: City Club, 1915.

GRAHAM, ANDERSON, PROBST and WHITE. "Chicago Union Station." *Concrete and Steel,* January 10, 1927, pp. 15–20.

HAMMOND, ALONZO J. "Development of Railroad Passenger Terminals: Can Monumental Union Stations Be Economically Justified?" *Civil Engineering* 1, no. 13 (October 1931): 1176–81.

LACHER, WALTER S. "Noteworthy Passenger Station Completed at Chicago," *Railway Age* 79 (July 4, 1925): 7–28.

NEWCOMB, REXFORD. "The New Chicago Union Station." *Western Architect* 35 (January 1926): 6–7.

"New Union Passenger Station, Chicago." *The Bricklayer, Mason and Plasterer,* n.d., p. 45.

NOONAN, EDWARD J. *The Railway Passenger Terminal Problem at Chicago.* Chicago: Committee on Railway Terminals, 1933.

POST, C. W. "Electrical Equipment in the Chicago Union Station." *Journal of the Western Society of Engineers* 30 (December 1925): 543–59.

PUTNAM, RUFUS W. "Modern Rail and Water Terminals, with Particular Reference to the Situation at Chicago." *Transactions of the American Society of Civil Engineers* 87 (1924): 828–60.

SHAW, ALFRED. "The Chicago Union Station." *Architectural Forum* 44 (February 1926): 85–88 and plates 17–24.

WALLACE, JOHN F. *Report of The Chicago Railway Commission.* Chicago: Chicago Railway Terminal Commission, 1921.

WEIDEMANN, E. "Some Features of the Structural Design of Chicago Union Station." *Journal of the Western Society of Engineers* 30 (December 1925): 501–26.

FIRST NATIONAL BANK BUILDING

(Legg Mason Building)

1924
7 East Redwood Street
Baltimore, Maryland

Cost in 1924: $2,222,867.73;
    pcf: $0.745
Status: extant

Handsomely proportioned, the twenty-story gray-limestone-clad First National Bank Building has six three-story arcaded windows

[145] FIRST NATIONAL BANK, BANKING ROOM

[144] FIRST NATIONAL BUILDING (LEGG MASON BUILDING), BALTIMORE, MD., EXTERIOR

on Redwood Street and three on Light Street (fig. 144). Taking advantage of the sloping site, the architects created a special sense of entrance leading down to the three-story Banking Room by providing a small flight of stairs from the elevator lobby. Here four pairs of composite columns define the space, which is lavishly adorned with Roman ornament (fig. 145). The gleaming brasses of the railings and other fixtures set off the lively and elegant color combinations of the gray, maroon, and beige marbles, adorned with rinceaux, cherubs, urns, and rosettes. In full use today, and in its original condition, except for the usual changes necessary for air-conditioning, the building is a good example of the best office-building work of the firm.[1]

1. Hectograph copy of the presentation drawing and construction photographs are located in the office of Raymond A. Mason, president of the bank.

JEWISH HOSPITAL OF ST. LOUIS COMPLEX

Jewish Hospital, 1924–25; Moses Shoenberg Memorial School of
Nursing, 1928–29; Aaron Waldheim Health Clinic, 1930
216 South Kingshighway Boulevard
St. Louis, Missouri

Cost in 1924, architects' figures: $1,823,343.79: pcf: $0.637;
    hospital archives: $1,799,000
Status: extant, in good condition, with several additions
    and remodelings

[146] JEWISH HOSPITAL OF
ST. LOUIS, ST. LOUIS, MO.,
ELEVATION

Terraces overlooking the flowered lawns and wooded hillocks of Forest Park established the character of this hospital, at once residential and therapeutic. In the days before antibiotics, at a time when sunshine and fresh air were the only known treatments for such diseases as tuberculosis, a familial or campus atmosphere was desirable for long-term care of the sick. In the 1920s, religious denominations provided places of sanctuary for those who could not afford medical care at home (the preferred place to be for all who could afford it), and the Jewish Hospital was a result of the social awareness of progressive thinkers in St. Louis during the period. Like its counterparts among Roman Catholics, Baptists, Presbyterians, and Lutherans, this early private hospital was a communal effort, rather than a strictly religious endeavor.

The first Jewish Hospital, erected in 1901, had proved inadequate by 1919, and the board of directors hired Graham, Anderson, Probst and White. The contract called for an architects' fee of 5 percent, but the architects offered a 1 percent rebate as their contribution. The building committee, together with a rep-resentative of the architectural firm, organized a two-week train trip, beginning February 15, 1921, to visit hospitals in New York, Baltimore, Chicago, Cleveland, Boston, and Montreal. Included were visits to Johns Hopkins, Massachusetts General, Peter Bent Brigham, and Mount Sinai.

The Georgian style was chosen for its residential character, since hospital stays of several weeks or months were not uncommon. The designs included many features that responded to the needs of "shut-ins," such as French doors that opened onto cast-iron balconies to provide both better ventilation in a pre-air-conditioned era and cheerful glimpses of the outside world.[1]

E-shaped in plan, the building has wings that are set back at the third floor and terminate at the fifth floor where the center portion rises to eight stories (fig. 146). The first three stories, treated as a base, are clad in limestone, the rest in brick with a limestone stringcourse just below the brick and limestone cornice. A similar treatment tops the penthouses and unifies them with the main portion of the building. Originally, a handsome double-curved driveway with ornate cast-iron lamps led to the entrance pavilion, but it was eliminated in a later remodeling (fig. 147). To the rear, or west side, the base of the building is U-shaped.

Although greatly altered, the interior spaces of the hospital were originally noted for their modern equipment, lavish furnishings, and innovative communications systems. The skylighted operating rooms with their tiled

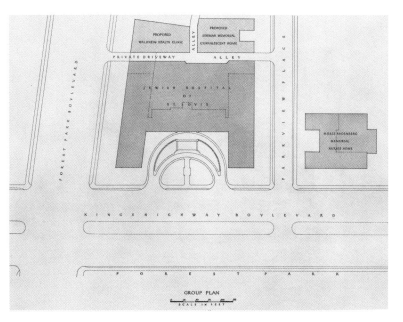

floors have since been converted to delivery rooms, but continue their usefulness. Observation galleries still extant suggest the role the hospital played in medical education at the time.

Pavinazzo marble in the elevator lobby recalls the luxurious atmosphere of an Italian palazzo, and patients enjoyed cheerful dayrooms in the 250-bed facility. The medical staff benefited from such innovations as an audible nurse call system, with speakers

[147] JEWISH HOSPITAL, SITE PLAN

and a hand-held microphone in each room for calling the nurse. One of the first to emphasize electrically operated signaling and communications devices, the hospital won the Modern Hospital Award of the year from the American Hospital Association shortly after it opened.[2]

The Moses Shoenberg Memorial School of Nursing, also Georgian in style, makes a harmonious addition to the ensemble. On the interior, pointed arches in plaster decorate the reception room. Flowers, fruit, and leaves adorn the vaults, and Gothic mouldings add the finishing touches. The nurses also had a small gymnasium-auditorium with a skylight, which has since been covered.

The Aaron Waldheim Health Clinic, to the east of the main building, was originally an outpatient clinic. Also in the Georgian style, it now has two additional stories.

The Kingshighway facade of the main building was severely altered on the west during a rebuilding program from 1951 to 1963, when the institution was transformed from a community hospital to a university-affiliated hospital. Currently the hospital emphasizes its role in an academic institution, once again in a campus setting, in a cluster of buildings that make up Washington University Medical Redevelopment Center.[3]

1. Ink on linen drawings and copies on microfilm are located in the hospital archives.

2. David A. Gee, *A History of the Jewish Hospital of St. Louis* (St. Louis: Jewish Hospital, 1981).

3. Ibid., p. 2.

S . W .   S T R A U S   B U I L D I N G

(Britannica Centre)

1923–24
310 South Michigan Avenue
Chicago, Illinois

Cost in 1924: $8,280,467; pcf: $0.934
Status: extant, Banking Room demolished and replaced by two
    floors of offices

Located on South Michigan Avenue, the Straus Building is an important link in the distinctive streetscape that stretches along the lower part of this famous boulevard from the Chicago River to Seventh Street (fig. 148). Like many of its neighbors, its scale, tripartite form, limestone cladding, and sturdy proportions proclaim its rightful place in the urban fabric of Chicago. After the building reaches the cornice line of its neighbors to the north and south, however, it soars into a tower crowned by a "colonnade" and topped by a stepped pyramid, and then it culminates in a huge beehive.

The tower was made possible by a provision of the Chicago zoning ordinance of 1922 that allowed rental occupancy above the building height limit of 264 feet if the floor area did not exceed 25 percent of the area of the premises or one-sixth the volume, provided there was a setback of one foot in ten from all lines of adjacent property. Towers had been bristling all over New York for decades while Chicago continued to show a preference for four-square, flat-topped, hollow rectangular office buildings since the success of the World's Columbian Exposition of 1893, the Chicago world's fair. The Wrigley *(q.v.)* and the Straus buildings, both by Graham, Anderson, Probst and White, were among the first in Chicago to convert to the tower-like Manhattan image. The Wrigley was more like a traditional New York tower, such as the Municipal Building (McKim, Mead and White, 1914), but the Straus incorporated something of the new view of skyscrapers that began to grow after the passage of the zoning act in New York in 1916.

Although the 1916 zoning laws were conceived out of a desire to limit the height of buildings and to control the location of certain building types, such as warehouses, the new laws stimulated an entirely new vision of the skyscraper. Within another few years they would inspire as well a new vision of the city of the future.[1]

Graham and Anderson were both aware of the dramatic, pyramidal masses that had emerged in Manhattan and knew that these distinctive shapes were regarded by their more progressive colleagues in the profession as embodying the first distinctly modern American style. Wishing to employ new ideas only after they had been tried and tested and wanting to appear up-to-date but not radical, the firm made a characteristic compro-

[148] S. W. STRAUS BUILDING
(BRITANNICA CENTRE),
CHICAGO, ILL., EXTERIOR

mise. The top of the Straus Building is a stepped pyramid, trumpeting its modernity, but the rest of the structure is a traditional office building, richly ornamented with historic references.[2]

The setback of the pyramid at the top of the Straus Building was not only a response to the Chicago zoning ordinance of 1922, but was also a stylistic response to the effect the 1916 New York zoning ordinance had had in making setbacks fashionable, as architects made a virtue of necessity and created new forms to accommodate the new rules.

Also important in the inception of the Straus Building was the conviction in the real estate community in the early 1920s that the south Loop was destined for greater development. The building would be a gateway to this south central district of the city that seemed to be on the verge of a boom. Chicago's growth toward the south had long been stopped by the tangle of railroads and their discouraging daily deposits of black soot. In an ordinance passed in 1919, the Illinois Central Railroad agreed to electrify its trains. This encouraged planners in their efforts to widen the main traffic arteries in the south section of the city, such as Twenty-second and Twenty-fourth streets, Indiana Avenue, and South Park Avenue, and to straighten the Chicago River so that other new streets leading from the Loop to the South Side could be opened.

Heralding the development of suburbs southwest of the city, the planners also hoped to complete the six miles of parkland envisioned earlier in the Plan of Chicago (1909). The enclosed waterways, playgrounds, golf links, yacht harbors, boat landings, walks, bathing beaches, and picnic areas, which all Chicago children had studied in the Wacker manuals[3] distributed in the public schools, seemed about to become realities. All of these factors, some real, some still in the dream stage, encouraged new building in the south part of the Loop, and the Straus was the figurehead. A number of other structures followed, including the Stevens Hotel in 1927 by Holabird and Roche (now the Chicago Hilton and Towers) on Michigan Avenue.

Businessmen told themselves that just as the opening of the Michigan Avenue Bridge increased real estate values in the north part of the city by nearly $100 million, the increase in the south part of the city would be "the creation of realty values approximating one billion dollars, the creation of a new vast city within a city."[4] The dreams for the south Loop crashed, however, with the stock market in 1929.

Many traditional images were incorporated in the details of the original Straus Building. The old beehive at the top, which contained four searchlights pointing in the four cardinal directions, has now been replaced by a prominent blue light, but the four stone bison at the corners of the base of the pyramid were left in place. In the 1920s, the allusion to bees and bison and their thriftiness, industry, and power was widely understood, and their association with a financial firm was deemed appropriate. The bison represented the American continent, the domain of S. W. Straus and Company, according to a prospectus for future tenants. One can imagine some fu-

ture iconographer looking at the Roman arches at the base, the stepped pyramid resembling the pyramid of Papantla or the mausoleum of Halicarnassus, the midwestern buffalo, and photographs of the Beaux-Arts lavishness of the former Banking Room, and concluding that the client and the architect wished to suggest that the institution had the strength, permanence, and breadth of influence of an imperial power.

Originally, a complete set of cathedral chimes played Handel's "Cambridge Quarters" on the quarter hour and tolled the full hours with such a soft, rich, penetrating tone that the sound could be heard for miles under favorable conditions. (The chimes were silent for many years until the present owner, Dino D'Angelo, had them restored in time for Pope John Paul's visit to Chicago in 1979.) Chimes, then and now, are clearly associated with Christian ceremonies. Might our iconographer also conclude that the artists wished to suggest a kind of sanctuary of commerce, or that the powerful financiers of the 1920s liked to think of themselves as having the combined symbols of church and state at their command? The view from the top, in any case, was awesome. As the rental brochure boasted, it was "the highest accessible point in Chicago. Full four hundred and fifty feet above the pavement, it has been estimated that visitors can see from its open windows, even without binoculars, more than three thousand square miles of lake and land."[5]

At the street level, the original

entrance portal with its bronze doorways was "as beautiful as men's dreams."[6] The floor height of this base story was purposely kept low to prevent it from competing with the Banking Room above on the second floor (since removed). Indeed, everything in the entire structure was subordinated to provide the greatest effect for this lost Banking Room. Originally, the entrance to the office building was on Jackson Boulevard so the great arch on Michigan Avenue would be reserved for a dramatic entrance to the Banking Room. Great bas-reliefs depicting Industry and the Arts, Commerce and Agriculture once flanked the sides of the arched bronze doorway, which was cast with figural panels framed with medallions of ancient coins. Today the remaining heavy rustication of the limestone with its deeply raked joints still recalls a palatial urban banking house, a modern Medici palace. But here there are storefronts with expansive display windows set in ornamented crested bronze frames on the first floor.

The visitor entered through a revolving door that led to a broad marble stairway. Starting with a wide flight of six steps, so broad they ascended like terraces across the full width of the Hauteville marble hall, the stairway then narrowed to a flight of fourteen Tennessee marble steps with carved banisters accented with Belgian black marble and divided by a polished bronze railing. At a higher landing about four feet below the main floor, the staircase divided into a double flight leading to the grand space above. Suspended above this stately entranceway was an immense chandelier lighted by lamps with crystal panels and finished in antique gold.

At the top of the stairs the spaces of the three-aisled Banking Room greeted the visitor (fig. 149). Contemporary architect Andrew Rebori wrote that its impressiveness surpassed in grandeur and costliness any work of like character in Chicago.[7] Its scale was in the grand manner of ancient Rome—160 by 170 feet with a ceiling of 45 feet, over four stories by today's standards. Sixteen columns, forty feet high and four feet in diameter, sheathed in Hauteville marble with Corinthian capitals of Belgian black marble, supported an ornamental ceiling decorated with hexagonal coffers painted with touches of bronze, gold, and iridescent blues, reds, and greens. One hundred and thirty-two amber-colored bulbs in two great chandeliers shed a mellow light over the room.

Vaulted arches covered the aisles at the sides, providing appropriate subsidiary spaces. Extending the full length of the room, these arches came to a climax around the exterior windows on the north, with an effect like a great triumphal arch. Centered on the Banking Room floor was a slightly raised platform for the use of bank personnel, enclosed with railings of travertine marble. This floor, in polished Belgian black marble, contrasted strikingly with the light marble of the main-floor spaces. To the rear of this island were the traditional tellers' cages, of polished black Belgian marble to the counter level, with posts of black and gold over the wrought- and

[149] STRAUS BUILDING, BANKING ROOM.

cast-iron parts. Stenciled designs in a deep shade of blue bordered with gold decorated the ceiling between the main room and the aisles on either side. Cast-bronze Italian bracket lights on each pier lit the lower spaces.

Axial, symmetrical, and stately, with its homages to the architectural past, its sumptuous materials, its ceremonial sequence of public spaces setting

up an architectural promenade, the Banking Room was in the best of the Beaux-Arts tradition and was the last work of its designing architect, Peirce Anderson, who died around the time of its completion. Anderson's choice for the climax of this ceremonial space was a stained glass window within the arches on the center axis. Seen through a vista of coffered ceilings and from the rear of the colonnade, this window was executed by Florentine craftsmen and portrayed a full-rigged ship at the center, with figures representing Art and Justice on the sides, and a small scroll at the top with the date of the founding of S. W. Straus and Company and the beginning and ending dates for the construction of the building. As Rebori put it, "Pale amber tones predominate in the color scheme, with reds, blues and greens softly blended. Towards the end of day, when daylight fails, special electric flood lights set back of the window bring out in subdued fashion the full coloring, figures and design."[8]

For the entrance to the office building on Jackson Boulevard, Anderson selected reliefs depicting various aspects of American history. Medallions above the arches of the entrance lobby, by sculptor Leo Lentelli, represented coins from various cities of ancient Greece: a coin from the city of Thruium, showing the head of Pallas Athene; a Greek tetradrachm, showing the head of the young Hercules in lion skin; a coin from Naxos, showing a bearded man with a band around his head; another from Syracuse, showing Persephone surrounded by dolphins and wearing a wreath of corn leaves; and finally a coin showing the lyre of Chalcidice, struck at Olympus after 392 B.C. and before the time of Philip of Macedonia.[9]

The Straus Building was not only the "gateway to the south central district," it was also part of the west wall of Michigan Avenue, which included the cultural complex of the city from the Auditorium Building to Orchestra Hall, and the Chicago Public Library (now the Cultural Center). To the east was the Art Institute, Grant Park, and the lake.

When the devastation of the Great Depression hit the nation in the 1930s, the Straus Safety Deposit Company, as it was then called, went into receivership and was purchased by Northwestern Mutual Life. Throughout the 1940s, the building was over 50 percent empty. William Farnsworth, the leasing agent at the time, reported that he did not make enough money on commissions to make a living. In the 1950s, the building was sold for approximately $4 million, about .05 cents on the dollar of what was owed by the building to various creditors. Sometime during this period, the owners decided that the lavishness of their building was a real hindrance to attracting new clients, or to keeping clients with greatly reduced means. When pressures to modernize were added to these embarrassments, they decided to remodel the building. Sometime in the late 1940s or early 1950s, the bank hired architects to gut the Banking Room, and most of its bronze and gold rosettes, stone carvings, Tiffany favrile glass, marble columns, walnut doors, and the delicate reliefs on the soffits of the arches went to the junkyard in bits and pieces. The room was divided into two floors of offices. Although the loss of its original interior is irreparable, the exterior of the Straus Building remains a vital part of Chicago's "Main Street," cosmopolitan Michigan Avenue.

It was not until the late 1970s and early 1980s that efforts to develop the area began again with the conversion of loft buildings into apartment condominiums and the construction of Bertram Goldberg's River City. The Straus Building, for many decades the anchor of the Loop at Jackson Boulevard, is now also the crown of the newly developing south central district.

1. Carol Willis, "Zoning and *Zeitgeist:* The Skyscraper City in the 1920s."

2. A. Embury II, "New York's New Architecture," *Architectural Forum* 35 (1921): 119–24.

3. Walter D. Moody, *Wacker's Manual of the Plan of Chicago* (Chicago: Calumet Publishing Company, 1916).

4. John E. McEldowney, "South Central District Booms," *Real Estate News,* May 1924, pp. 1, 6.

5. Rental brochure, GAPW archives, Chicago, Ill.

6. Ibid.

7. Andrew N. Rebori, "The Straus Building, Chicago," *Architectural Record* 57, (May 1925): 385–94, 417–23; Leo J. Sheridan and W. C. Clark, "The Straus Building, Chicago," *Architectural Forum* 42 (April 1925): 225–28. *See also* Leo J. Sheridan, "Economic Factors of the Office Building Project," *Architectural Forum* 41, no. 3, (September 1924): 121–32; "Straus Building, Graham, Anderson, Probst and White," *Architecture and Building* 55 (October 1923): 100–101 and ibid. 57 (April 1925): 29–30, plates 70–77, April 1925.

8. Rebori, "Straus Building," p. 393.

9. "Bronze Entrance Doors, S. W. Straus & Co.," *Metal Arts,* February 1929, pp. 19, 101.

L. S. DONALDSON COMPANY BUILDING

1924
Seventh Street and Nicollett Avenue
Minneapolis, Minnesota

Cost in 1924: $1,446,762.38; pcf: $0.468
Status: extensively remodeled and linked together with two other buildings, the Donaldson Glass Block Building (1888) and the Donaldson Office Building (1907) in 1945–48. The whole complex was demolished in 1982–83.[1]

Part of the urbane streetscape of 1920s Minneapolis, this department store had the usual tripartite division and "Chicago windows" used by many Chicago architects of the period. Although the motifs were classical, rinceaux and lions' heads, for example, the decorated spandrel panels echoed the work of Louis Sullivan in their elaborateness (fig. 150).

1. Alan K. Lathrop to the author, February 28, 1984.

[150] L. S. DONALDSON COMPANY BUILDING, MINNEAPOLIS, MINN., EXTERIOR

W. A. WIEBOLDT AND COMPANY BUILDING

1924–25
100 South Ashland Avenue
Chicago, Illinois

Cost in 1925: $2,023,958.26; pcf: $0.363
Status: extant, remodeled

In 1924, Wieboldt's already had two smaller stores in addition to its main downtown department store on Chicago's State Street: one at Lincoln Avenue and School Street and the other at Paulina Street and Milwaukee Avenue. The structure on South Ashland, the only one by Graham, Anderson, Probst and White, indicated the store's further growth into Chicago neighborhoods and was designated Midwest Store number 3. Display windows originally filled all the bays at the sidewalk level (fig. 151), but these have been filled in with the conversion of the building into the Krantzen Studios.

[151] W. A. WIEBOLDT AND COMPANY, CHICAGO, ILL., EXTERIOR

The irregular shape of the lot, caused by the diagonal slice of Ogden Avenue into the Chicago grid, necessitated the erection of the building in three separate sections. Slender cast-iron mullions and sunken panels on the recessed spandrels accent the limestone piers and buff brick cladding. Large circular medallions decorate the stringcourse at the top of the first floor and repeat the circular motif in a lighter spirit and at a faster tempo at the top. The first floor of the interior is much higher than the other floors and was originally one large room articulated by octagonal columns with acanthus leaves. An adaptation of the firm's department store style for a neighborhood setting, it is a tripartite loft building, in marked contrast to the suburban department stores in the Second Empire style that the firm erected later for Marshall Field and Company in Evanston and Oak Park, Illinois.

UNION TRUST BUILDING

(Huntington Building)

1921–24
917 Euclid Avenue
Cleveland, Ohio

Cost in 1924: $12,234,485; pcf: $0.685
Status: extant

Sedate on the exterior, the Union Trust Building underscores a traditional theme with its tripartite divisions and its stately Ionic colonnade. Clad in gray limestone, the bank seems properly businesslike in the urban fabric of downtown Cleveland (fig. 152).

Although conservative on the exterior and expressing a public

[152] UNION TRUST BUILDING (HUNTINGTON BUILDING), CLEVELAND, OHIO, ELEVATION

restraint appropriate for the street, the building on the interior is grandly proportioned and lavishly decorated. The L-shaped Banking Room is three stories high, 50 feet wide, approximately 240 feet long on the Euclid Avenue side, and 320 feet long on the Chester Avenue side. It is immense, quite possibly still the largest such room in the United States (fig. 153). Indeed, the enormity of its proportions suggests a railroad station, or the vast interiors of an imperial Roman bath or basilica. Eleven pairs of giant composite columns define the sides of the Chestnut Avenue Banking Room and six more pairs set off the Euclid Avenue Banking Room. Centered above the main space are barrel-vaulted skylights, while elaborately coffered ceilings top the aisles. At the corner of the L, the granite bases, beige marble columns, palmettes, egg-and-dart mouldings, and dentil friezes are touched with gold. A Greco-Roman combination of colonnade and arched opening rises on two sides.[1] Murals by Jules Guerin[2] decorate the other two, and a climactic domed ceiling covers this pivotal space (fig. 154). The office portion of the building above is outfitted with marble wainscoting, paneled wooden doors, brass fixtures, and other embellishments in fine materials. Lavish dimensions and materials were used in the Directors' Room as well, which also has a classical portico at the end.

Twenty-nine financial institutions had merged to form the original Union Trust Bank, with total assets of $322.5 million, the fifth largest bank in the United States at the time. All of these

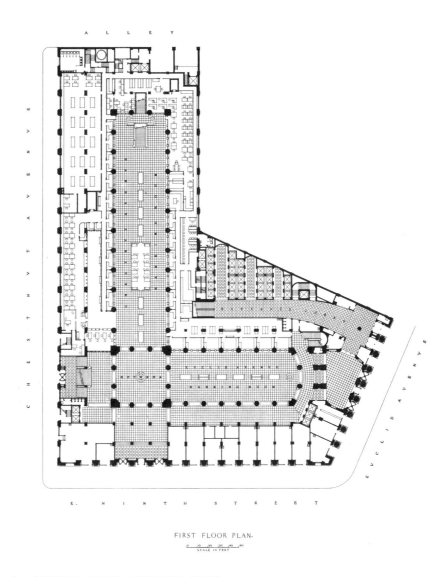

FIRST FLOOR PLAN.

[153] UNION TRUST BUILDING, PLAN

gestures of grandeur, both inside and out, were meant to express the high status of the client in the financial world.[3]

1. Drawings, including presentation drawings, are located in the archives of the building.

2. Jules Guerin did four murals for the bank, two at the end of each wing and two in the dome at the intersection of the two wings.

3. The building, containing more than thirty acres of floor space with a volume of 17,858,716 cubic feet, was claimed to be the second largest in the world at the time. For further information, see Eric Johannesen, *Cleveland Architecture 1876–1976*, pp. 145–46; Mary-Peale Schofield, *Landmark Architecture of Cleveland* (Pittsburgh: Ober Park Associates, 1976).

[154] UNION TRUST BUILDING, BANKING ROOM

CHESAPEAKE AND OHIO RAILWAY PASSENGER STATION

(Third National Bank of Ashland)

1925
1000 Carter Avenue
Ashland, Kentucky

Status: extant, remodeled

The gentle charm of Kentucky and this low, red-brick building with its elegant arched central windows are well suited to each other (fig. 155). The exterior, virtually unchanged, recalls the South of the Federal period, a design choice that helped the railroad relate to the town in a chivalrous way in 1925, and now, for the same reason, assures its continued acceptance and appreciation in a new role.

Because the Chesapeake and Ohio property was also located just west of Ashland's central business district and was easily visible from one of the city's main streets, the board of directors of the Third National Bank of Ashland decided to buy the building with its surrounding acreage in 1977. The building was then fifty-two years old and badly in need of renovation. The result is a good example of adaptive reuse. The triumphal arch windows that once led to the Waiting Room now lead to the Banking Room. In addition, new interior vestibules were placed at the entrances, and thermal windows, selected to match those already on the building, were installed in the interest of energy conservation. Large baggage truck platforms on the east and south sides were removed and replaced by windows to match the older ones. A large elevator penthouse, which was a later addition, was removed. The cast-iron train sheds were refurbished and now create an ornamental covered parking area. Two of the original lightposts were salvaged and placed near the entrance, and the decorative limestone was cleaned.

The Waiting Room, some 2,700 square feet in area, with a twenty-two-foot-high coffered ceiling, became the new lobby. Unconnected in the original design, the two wings on either side of the Waiting Room on the second floor were united by the addition of a fourteen-foot-wide passarelle on the south. The second and third floors were stripped of their old heavy partitions and given new lighter floor divisions more adaptable to the computer operations of the pre-

[155] CHESAPEAKE AND OHIO RAILWAY PASSENGER STATION (THIRD NATIONAL BANK OF ASHLAND), ASHLAND, KY., EXTERIOR

sent. Finally, all paved spaces were relocated away from the building to allow for planting and landscaping of the area. "At completion, a valuable landmark and a viable structure has received a new lease on life ... lending value to the community, strength to the neighborhood,

and purpose to its continued existence. The old depot, preserved to its original splendor, now serves the growing banking needs of Eastern Kentucky." [1]

1. Nomination of the former Chesapeake and Ohio Railway Terminal for landmark designation.

HIBBARD, SPENCER AND BARTLETT COMPANY WAREHOUSE

1925–26
211 North Water Street
Chicago, Illinois

Cost in 1926: $3,788,727.83; pcf: $0.3229
Status: extant

Located directly on the Chicago River half a block east of Michigan Avenue, the Hibbard, Spencer and Bartlett Company Warehouse is a few steps from the Tribune Tower (fig. 156). Today this prominent location seems a more likely site for a high-rise apartment building, but in the 1920s development north of the river was not completely assured. A mixture of industrial build-

ings, railroads, and warehouses occupied most of the river's northern bank. Until the Equitable Building was finished in 1965, the Hibbard, Spencer and Bartlett Warehouse dominated the area east of the Tribune Tower.

Warehouses in Chicago have not always enjoyed such architectural distinction. In the 1860s, the ubiquitous four-story grain

sheds had unarticulated rough walls on all four sides.[1] It was not until after the fire of 1871 and the building period that followed in the 1880s that warehouses took on some of the architectural character of the rest of the city. Soon, architects in the city shared the vision that a warehouse should be clad in brick with terra-cotta trim, have a handsome entrance, and be articulated horizontally into the traditional three-part divisions (base, shaft, and capital) and vertically by broad piers. Like earlier factories, the construction of these new warehouses was of straight-line, serial column-and-beam framing, built for heavy floor loads, but a refinement in their exteriors expressed the new urbanity and a newly cohesive city fabric. One of the first of these new, more urbane structures was the Hiram Sibley and Company Warehouse, designed by George H. Edbrooke in 1883. The Hibbard, Spencer and Bartlett building continued this long tradition.[2]

1. Harold M. Mayer and Richard C. Wade, *Chicago: Growth of a Metropolis*, pp. 48, 52.

2. *See also* "Building for Hibbard, Spencer, and Bartlett," *Western Architect* 36 (April 1927):171–72; Carl W. Condit, *Chicago, 1910–1929: Building, Planning, and Urban Technology*, pp. 143–44; "The Chicago Warehouse," *Architect* 120 (London, 1928): 90–91; Lewis Mumford, "New York vs. Chicago in Architecture," *Architecture* 56 (November 1927): 244.

[156] HIBBARD, SPENCER AND BARTLETT COMPANY WAREHOUSE, CHICAGO, ILL., EXTERIOR

[157] CRAWFORD AVENUE GENERATING STATION, CHICAGO, ILL., DETAIL OF EXTERIOR

CRAWFORD AVENUE GENERATING STATION

1924–25
3501 South Pulaski Road, at the Chicago Sanitary and Ship Canal
Chicago, Illinois

Cost in 1925, architects' figure: $8,036,249; owner's figure for the
whole plant: $22 million
Status: extant

In the early 1920s, an electric power generating station involved a coal handling plant with a conveyor system to transport the coal to a boiler room where steam was produced and conveyed into a turbine housing causing the turbine to rotate, which in turn rotated the generator in the turbine room. Electrical energy produced here was transformed and transferred to the switch house, from which it was sent to transmission terminals and eventually distributed to various substations and to the general public. The elevation (fig. 73) and the general cross section (fig. 158) of the Crawford Avenue Station indicate the interrelationship of this vast system.[1] The plant was designed around the machinery to follow the general format originally established by Fred Sargent, a partner in the construction firm Sargent and Lundy, which specialized in electric utility plants.[2]

It was up to the architects to design the envelope to house these immense structures. Expressing their utility, the power-ful arches, climaxed by the grandeur of the turbine room, the forceful brickwork, and the articulation of the building into pavilions suggests a palace of industry (fig. 157) (see Part I).

Today the interior of the turbine room still has a stately air (fig. 159). Clad in white glazed ceramic, the tiles are larger at the bases of the supporting piers, smaller as they go up, with the smallest in the walls between, showing the attention paid to fine architectural detail. Viewing balconies and geometric ornament further attest to the showplace quality of this immense space. Six turbine generators were eventually installed. The first three were made by three different manufacturers—C. A. Parsons and Company (an English firm), General Electric, and Westinghouse. When Unit 1 was finally en route, it occasioned much excitement. "It is one of the largest and most valuable shipments ever made from Europe to Chicago by an all-water route. Seventy-two English freight cars were required to transport the huge machine from the factory to the docks. The Chicago River is now being dredged at the Fisk Street Station Slip to provide a landing place for the *John Gehm*, a specially chartered 250-foot freighter which has carried the huge turbine down the St. Lawrence and through the Great Lakes."[3]

By 1933, the Crawford Avenue Station generated 40 percent of Chicago's electricity. By 1955, the station turned out an average of 1.75 billion kilowatts per year. In the late 1950s, the first three units were dismantled along with their boilers to make way for the 222-megawatt Unit 7. Two more

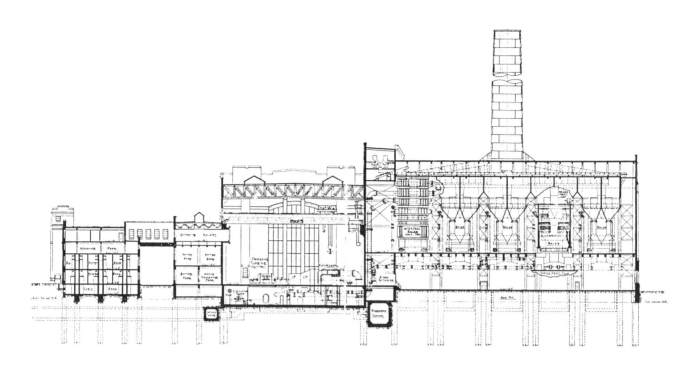

[158] CRAWFORD AVENUE STATION, SECTION

[159] CRAWFORD AVENUE STATION, TURBINE ROOM

units and boilers were dismantled in 1961 to make way for the 347-megawatt Unit 8. In 1967, six new boilers replaced eight old ones to produce steam to drive a 105-megawatt turbine generator. These were gas fired for pollution control, a major concern of the plant in the 1960s and 1970s. Unit 6 was retired in 1976. Today the use of nuclear power has rendered most of the fossil fuel equipment at the Crawford Station obsolete. It remains important to industrial archaeologists and historians of electricity in American culture.

1. Total volume of the switch house, transformer house, and turbine room combined: 14,140,957 cubic feet; total area of station property: seventy-two acres, including five miles of railroad track originally used for handling construction materials and for hauling coal and ashes. The main building, containing the turbine room and boiler house, is 496 feet long and 365 feet wide; the roof 100 feet high. Four steel-plate, brick-lined smokestacks in the center of the boiler room rise

145 feet above ground. Along the south side, the switch house extends 324 by 65 feet, and the transformer house is 456 feet long by 46 feet wide. Ink on linen drawings, dated May 16, 1924, are in flat storage at the station along with two file drawers of construction photographs.

2. Commonwealth Edison Company, "Crawford Ave. Station Goes Into Service Soon," *Edison Round Table,* September 30, 1924, pp. 1–2; Alf Kolflat and Bernhard Schroeder, *The Sargent & Lundy Story* (Chicago: Sargent and Lundy, c. 1961); Commonwealth Edison Company, *Crawford Station Brochure,* n.d.

3. "Crawford Station Highlights," typescript, n.d., Commonwealth Edison archives, Chicago, Ill.

COE COLLEGE

Master plan, 1926; Stewart Memorial Library, 1929–31; Eby Field House, 1930; Greene Hall, 1938
Cedar Rapids, Iowa

Cost in 1929 for library: $175,044.03; pcf: $0.352
Cost in 1930 for gymnasium: $265,639.89; pcf: $0.165. The master plan was probably done without charge.
Status: all buildings extant

Cedar Rapids, Iowa, calls itself the "city of five seasons"— spring, summer, fall, winter, and the time to enjoy the other four. At the heart of the town, the Cedar River opens to encircle a small island, a tiny version of the Île de la Cité in Paris. The people of this community know their setting is especially felicitious, and what is more important, as early as 1910, they knew they should hire an architect to design its development. Accordingly, they secured the services of Edward H. Bennett to draw up a

[160] COE COLLEGE, CEDAR RAPIDS, IOWA, ELEVATION

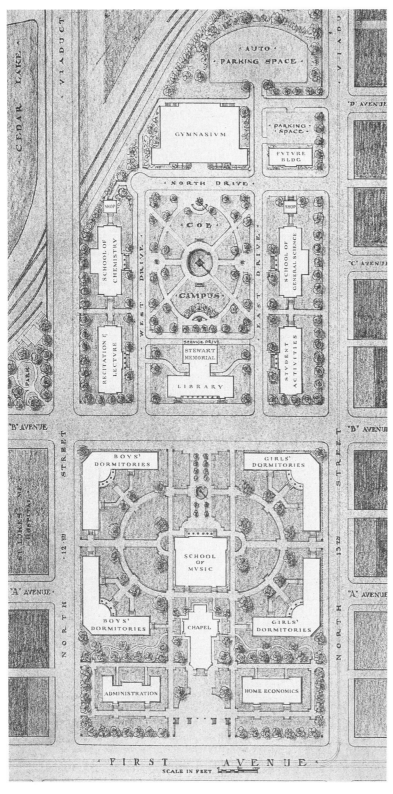

[161] COE COLLEGE, PLAN

master plan. Later Bennett added a riverfront improvement scheme, and the city enjoys the public buildings on the island and the park setting along the river's banks to this day.[1]

Seeing the benefits that planning could provide right in their own frontyard, Coe College trustees sought and accepted a master plan from Ernest R. Graham in 1926. The plan was typical of the symmetrical Beaux-Arts campus plans of the period. Organizing the buildings along the perimeters of two adjoining squares, or quadrangles, the arrangement had three focal points—the chapel to the south (already extant), a new library at midpoint, and a new gymnasium to the north. Along the sides were designs for dormitories and classrooms (figs. 160, 161).

Designed by Mario Schiavoni, the firm's designer responsible for the John G. Shedd Aquarium, the plan included several older buildings.[2] One of them, L-shaped Voorhees Hall on the northeast corner of the first quadrangle, had obviously been conceived as part of a group, and Graham, Anderson, Probst and White continued in its spirit by designing three similar L-shaped structures with semicircular entrance pavilions at the other corners to complete the site. Only one of these, Greene Hall, was built by the firm (fig. 162), on the northwest corner in 1938. The southern half, built after World War II, consists of two buildings by other architects.[3]

The red-brick and limestone neo-Georgian-style Stewart Memorial Library (fig. 163) was built at the base of the north quadrangle in 1929–31. Donated by Col. Robert W. Stewart,

[162] COE COLLEGE, GREENE HALL

this structure forms a climax to the vista from the older quadrangle and sets the tone for the north half of the campus. The neo-Georgian library at the midpoint of the campus responds to the chapel at the south end. Its classical colonnaded porch leads to rooms on either side that are marked by large arched windows. The most distinguishing feature is the main Reading Room, which receives sunlight from five large windows. For reasons of economy, the stacks were incorporated in the rear.[4]

Opposite the library, the closure at the other end of campus is Eby Field House, the large gymnasium (fig. 164) built in 1930. In this part of the campus the corners were left open, the east

[163] COE COLLEGE, STEWART MEMORIAL LIBRARY.

and west sides to be filled in by music and fine arts buildings with temple fronts on both the street and the quadrangle sides.

Eby Field House reveals that here again the architects made

modifications to their original plan while working with the instructors and coaches and under stringent economic circumstances. The gymnasium acts as an enclosing element for the tree-

[164] COE COLLEGE, EBY FIELD HOUSE

173

lined oval surrounded by other red-brick buildings.

Thus, the firm built the library and the gymnasium and one dormitory for Coe College, but the rest of the plan fell victim to the depression. The college remained in its 1938 condition until 1950, when a new building program began. Hickok Hall (Jans Frederick Larson, 1950) and Sinclair Chapel (Jans Frederick Larson, 1951) and Marquis Hall (Larson and Larson, 1959) retain something of the spirit of the firm's master plan, but those built since the 1960s have little, if any, relationship to the original design for the campus.[5]

1. Joan E. Draper, *Edward H. Bennett, Architect and City Planner 1874–1954* (Chicago: Art Institute of Chicago, 1982) p. 51.

2. Old Main (1868 and 1884); Carnegie Science Hall designed by Leroy D. Weld, professor of Physics (1910); Stuart Hall; the Administration Building; Sinclair Memorial Chapel (1911), which burned down in 1947 and was replaced in 1949 with a red-brick chapel designed by Dr. Jans Frederick Larson; and a women's dormitory, Voorhees Hall, built in two sections by Larson and Larson (1915, 1918).

3. Peterson Hall of Science (1967) and Hickok Hall (1950), neither of which conforms to the older design for the quadrangle in shape or materials.

4. A 1987 addition by the Chicago firm Weese, Hickey, Weese now provides much needed space to the library facilities. Sensitive to the original design, the addition continues the cornice line, repeats the arched windows, and uses similar materials.

5. The archives of Coe College contains the original master plan and other documents.

CLEVELAND TERMINAL GROUP

Hotel Cleveland, 1917–19; Terminal Tower and railroad station, 1917–30; Higbee's Department Store, 1928–30; Builders' Exchange, 1926–28; Medical Arts Building, 1928–30; Midland Bank, 1928–30
Public Square, Ontario Street, Superior and Prospect avenues, Cleveland, Ohio

Cost: Architects' cost book lists "Terminal Tower: $9,999,518.63." For the railroad complex around the terminal: "The project represents a total expenditure of $179,000,000, of which $88,000,000 represents the outlay for the passenger terminal, electrification and approach lines provided by the terminal company; $40,000,000 the cost of improvements on the properties of the proprietary railways for additional tracks, improved passenger and freight facilities and engine terminals; $20,000,000 for rapid transit lines; and $31,000,000 for air-rights buildings being built by a separate corporation, the Cleveland Terminals Building Company, over the station site."[1]
Status: extant, under rehabilitation for adaptive reuse

Seen from miles away, the lofty pinnacle of the Terminal Tower dominates the landscape along the shores of Lake Erie, symbolizing Cleveland to its citizens (figs. 165, 166). The original clients, brothers Oris Paxton and Mantis James Van Sweringen, wanted a railroad station on Union Square to connect their real estate development, Shaker Heights, with the center of the city. They had purchased land as early as 1909 for this purpose, but the scheme quickly grew into a larger proposal for a Union Station for Cleveland (see Part I).

The decision to add the fifty-

[165] CLEVELAND TERMINAL GROUP, CLEVELAND, OHIO, DETAIL

[166] CLEVELAND TERMINAL GROUP, ELEVATION

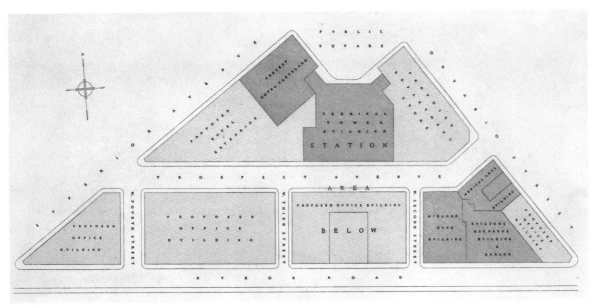

[167] CLEVELAND TERMINAL GROUP, NINE-BUILDING PLAN

[168] CLEVELAND TERMINAL GROUP, SECTION

two-story tower to the original low-rise design of 1919 came about for several related reasons. An amendment to the building code in late 1924 permitted buildings of much greater height than ever before, and it seemed that tall buildings were increasingly popular with the public. The Van Sweringens' promise that the new tower would be the landmark in Cleveland that the Woolworth Building was in New York certainly came true.[2] Completing the key element of the group, the tower of the railroad terminal building rises 708 feet.

The arched doorways below open into a vaulted public lobby lined with Botticino marble adorned with colorful murals by Jules Guerin. Through the outer arches lie the ramps leading down to the through-trains. Beyond these to either side are ramps that lead down to the rapid transit facilities.

The planning of the station below is masterful. In virtually one room, all of the conveniences of travel are efficiently laid out in logical sequence (fig. 37). On the north-south axis the visitor first nears the ticket lobby, passes

shops and service areas, such as the Waiting Room and Dining Room, and finally comes to the Concourse, with its dramatic arched ceiling leading to the trains. (fig. 36). Carefully coordinated into the whole scheme

are facilities for baggage trucks and taxicabs (fig. 168). The unusual amount of retail space in the station influenced the choice of materials—gleaming Tennessee marble floors, Botticino marble walls, and ornamented

[169] CLEVELAND TERMINAL GROUP, HOTEL CLEVELAND, EXTERIOR

[170] CLEVELAND TERMINAL GROUP, HOTEL CLEVELAND, LOBBY

cast-bronze window frames—
which give the air of an elegant
streetscape to the enclosed interior complex (see Part I).

The Hotel Cleveland to the
west was the first of the group to
be finished, a key part of the
clients' dream of a nine-building
hotel–railroad terminal complex
on Union Square (fig. 167).
Knowing that surroundings of
distinction attract discriminating
guests, they desired for Cleveland
the elegance they had seen in the
Claridge Hotel in New York.
Peirce Anderson, the designer of
the Claridge, built in 1910 during the Burnham years, was a
happy choice. A work of his mature years, the Hotel Cleveland
shows Anderson at his best (fig.
169). Especially noteworthy is
the stately vaulted arcade surrounding the majestically proportioned lobby, seventy-five by
forty-five by thirty feet high.
Crystal chandeliers, a splashing
fountain, and other luxurious
appointments give an air of grandeur to the surroundings (fig.
170). An auditorium, with the
winged griffin and swag ornament favored by Anderson, is
still in its original condition. The
hotel rooms above in the E-
shaped plan are also amply proportioned, another reason for
the continued long life of the
building.

The long, broad proportions
of the Higbee Company's department store anchor the urban ensemble on the east. Like the
hotel, the classical tripartite division of the building begins with a
two-story base of display win-

[171] CLEVELAND TERMINAL GROUP, HIGBEE COMPANY, ELEVATION

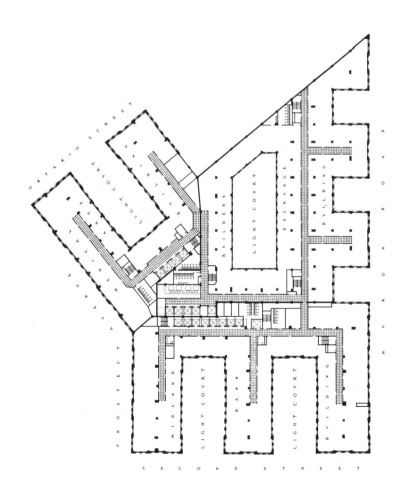

[172] CLEVELAND TERMINAL
GROUP, MEDICAL ARTS BUILD-
ING, BUILDERS' EXCHANGE,
AND MIDLAND BANK, PLAN.

dows and is finished at the top by giant-order pilasters, also similar to the hotel (fig. 171). All of the buildings in the group have a granite water table, limestone cladding, cast-iron window frames, and bronze spandrel panels.

Inside, the principal feature is the main aisle, approximately twenty feet tall, which sparkles with the glint of sixteen chandeliers, each with thirty lights. All the way from Euclid Avenue to Prospect Street the dazzle of three tiers of crystal teardrops and festoons of prismatic octagons fills the room. One can imagine that in the 1930s, the silks and satins of the Higbee fabric department were arranged to reflect this avenue of lights to their mutual advantage.

Sited on the corner of Prospect and Ontario streets, the Medical Arts Building plays a pivotal role in articulating the eastern most of the four blocks envisioned at the rear of the Terminal Group complex (fig. 172). Each of the buildings has a separate identity, yet bears a harmonious, even a strong, family resemblance to the others. Decorated spandrel panels at the second floor and a continuous sculpted frieze at the fifth give the Medical Arts Building a more traditional "base," just as giant-order arcaded windows give it a more traditional sense of "capital" than the other two buildings in the complex (fig. 173). Unifying it with their facades, however, are the uniform treatment of the windows, the broad band of masonry separating the ninth and tenth floors, the capitals of the piers protruding over the roofline, and the similar cladding in granite, limestone, and terra-cotta.

[173] CLEVELAND TERMINAL GROUP, MEDICAL ARTS BUILDING, EXTERIOR

The Medical Arts Buildings is U-shaped in plan, with a landscaped plaza within the arms of the two wings. The central fountain and surrounding benches, handsome pavement, and planted areas form an early example of an urban plaza[3] that encourages pedestrians to pause and rest. The entrance is adorned by two female figures in Greek dress holding emblems of the medical arts, amid vines and rinceaux (fig. 174).

The Builders' Exchange has more up-to-date ornament—the stylized naturalistic, figurative, and geometric motifs of the emerging Art Deco period. Since a garage occupied the lower stories, and a central rotunda or lobby was not possible, the architects designed a double-story skyroom at the seventeenth and

[174] CLEVELAND TERMINAL GROUP, MEDICAL ARTS BUILDING, ORNAMENT

eighteenth levels (fig. 175). Here displays of the building arts and exhibitions of home furnishings were installed to attract people seeking the services of firms with offices in the building.

The Midland Bank Building forms the western terminus of the complex. On the whole, the restrained, flat quality of the exterior, and the Art Deco motifs on the interior are associated with the stripped classicism of the period (fig. 176). But the atmosphere changes with the elaborate peacock and flower doorway four stories high and three bays wide that marks the main entrance to the bank. The Banking Room (fig. 177) on the second floor, with its bronze fixtures and balcony railings, dark wood, fluted pilasters, and floral ornament, is more traditional than the Art Deco exterior. This may have reflected the desire to attract businessmen who wanted the latest fashion in their office buildings, but conservative virtues in their investment bankers.[4]

1. *Railway Age* 88 (June 28, 1930): 2.

2. Walter C. Leedy, Jr., "Cleveland's Terminal Tower—The Van Sweringens' Afterthought."

[175] CLEVELAND TERMINAL GROUP, BUILDERS' EXCHANGE, EXTERIOR

3. Eric Johannesen, *Cleveland Architecture 1876–1976*, p. 131.

4. More than ten thousand architectural drawings are located in the Tower City Properties archives in Cleveland. In addition, Walter C. Leedy, Jr., discovered the existence of dozens of boxes of old papers, photographs, and drawings stored in an abandoned employees' lavatory in the tower and ninety filing cabinets of other materials, then in the possession of Gerald Adams and now in the library at Cleveland State University. Additional references include: *The Cleveland Union Station, A Description of the New Passenger Facilities and Surrounding Improvements* (Cleveland, 1930); Ian S. Haberman, *The Van Sweringens of Cleveland: The Biography of an Empire* (Cleveland: Western Reserve Historical Society, 1979); "Traffic and Building Art: New York City and Cleveland Contrasted," *Architectural Record* 67, no. 6 (June 1930); "Cleveland Union Station Project Far Advanced," *Railway Age* 85, no. 26 (December 29, 1928): 1287–93; Richard Karberg, "The

[176] CLEVELAND TERMINAL GROUP, MIDLAND BANK, EXTERIOR

Terminal Group: A City Within a City," paper presented to the Society of Architectural Historians, 1981; "New Plan for a Union Station at Cleveland, Ohio," *Railway Age* 66 (March 21, 1919): 755–58; "New Station's Facilities Finest in the World," *Cleveland Plain Dealer*, June 29, 1930, Union Terminal Supplement; John R. Stilgoe, *Metropolitan Corridor: Railroads and the American Scene.*

[177] CLEVELAND TERMINAL GROUP, MIDLAND BANK, BANKING ROOM

[178] GIMBEL BROTHERS BUILDING, PHILADELPHIA, PA., PROPOSAL

GIMBEL BROTHERS BUILDING

1926–27
841 Chestnut Street
Philadelphia, Pennsylvania

Status: extant, now an office building

Above all, a department store must display its wares to shoppers passing by, and Gimbel Brothers, in one of the busiest sections of Philadelphia, boasted an uninterrupted band of showcases at the sidewalk.[1] On top of the first seven floors, which were devoted to the sale of goods, five floors were leased as office space (see Part I).

When Gimbel Brothers first gave the firm the commission for the new store, it may have wanted something like Gimbel Brothers in New York, or a new version of the John Wanamaker stores in New York and Philadelphia, which Anderson had designed while Burnham was still

alive. Accordingly, Graham, Anderson, Probst and White prepared a presentation drawing (fig. 178) showing how the whole block would look if the project could be developed on this scale.[2] It would have been a building fit to compete with Wanamaker's, only a few blocks away, but it was not to be. Less than a fourth of the original proposal was erected on the southwest corner of the block (fig. 179).

As if to make up for the loss of their block-long scheme, the architects designed a great arcade that ran through the building from Chestnut Street to Market Street. Like the urban plaza of a European city, the arcade was the

nexus of the store. Above, various departments exhibited their goods. For children, for example, "Uncle Wip's Year-Round Toyland" provided a treasure trove for the seeker of birthday gifts. The dress fabric department displayed "silks from the mills of the world," and a brochure proclaimed the cultivated pleasures the store's music department offered the denizens of Philadelphia:

"The man that hath no music in himself, nor is not moved with concord of sweet sound, is fit for treasons, stratagems and spoils,"—Shakespeare. One of the many proofs of the natural joyousness of the American people is expressed in their love of music. . . . An American home in which some form of melody is not ever-present is unthinkable. Whether by piano or radio, saxophone or violin, phonograph or ukelele, life must be accompanied by some kind of

[179] GIMBEL BROTHERS BUILDING, EXTERIOR

sweet concord. The departments in GIMBEL BROTHERS which cater to this vitally essential part of civilized existence form a harmony in themselves through which the major motif of Service may always readily be heard.[3]

Capitalizing on the advertising potential of the tower of a broadcasting station on its roof, Gimbel Brothers illuminated its building every evening with powerful floodlights. Visible for many miles, the image of the radio station also gave an air of modernity to the office building portion of Gimbel Brothers and proclaimed the progress of the store since the founding days of Adam Gimbel.

Although not built to the grand scale first proposed by the architects, the department store-office building on Chestnut Street was once a shopping mecca for Philadelphians. Since a remodeling in which the arcade was destroyed and the lower floors converted for use as a branch office of the Philadelphia National Bank and other tenants, none of the original character of the department store remains.[4]

1. Edward Teitelman and Richard W. Longstreth, *Architecture in Philadelphia: A Guide* (Cambridge, Mass.: MIT Press, 1981).

2. This drawing is located in the archives of the building in Philadelphia.

3. Opening day brochure, archives of the building.

4. Edward Teitelman to the author, August 25, 1986.

HEYBURN BUILDING

1927
Louisville, Kentucky

Cost in 1927: $1,175,125;
    pcf: $0.534
Status: extant

Lighter in feeling than most office buildings of the period, the Heyburn has an air of gracious gentility. This comes partly from the pairs of arches and the rhythmic handling of the vertical piers, which are alternately broad and slender (fig. 180). Perhaps designed by Charles Beersman, also the designer of the Wrigley Building *(q.v.)* in Chicago,[1] the Heyburn's strong and weak piers (which are nonsupporting) are separated by elaborately decorated spandrel panels. These elements suggest the influence of Louis Sullivan's Wainwright Building (1890–91) in St. Louis, which Beersman knew. With its

[180] HEYBURN BUILDING, LOUISVILLE, KY., ELEVATION

blocks down the street—an urbanistic response in the spirit of the firm and appropriate for Louisville.[2]

1. Presentation drawing, 4 1/2 by 5 1/2 inches in pencil, ink, and blue, yellow, and pink tempera, signed GAPW, is framed in the office of the building. Other drawings are also located in the office of the building in Louisville.

2. See "Brown, Heyburn announce plans for buildings," *Louisville Herald Post,* June 16, 1916; "Plans filed for Heyburn Building," *Louisville Times,* January 5, 1927; "Plans of Building approved," *Louisville Times,* June 16, 1926; Kentucky Heritage Council Kentucky Historic Resources Inventory.

PITTSFIELD BUILDING

1926–27
55 East Washington Street
Chicago, Illinois

Cost in 1927: $5,972,606.28;
  pcf: $0.876
Status: extant

more slender proportions, the Heyburn exemplifies indeed the "proud and soaring thing" that Sullivan spoke of as the quintessential quality of the skyscraper.

Within the tripartite framework, the architect has provided a rich diversity of ornament—shells, shields, scrolls, rosettes, rinceaux, cartouches, and pinnacles—a harmonious and intricate design for a southern business community.

In plan the building is U-shaped, the interior lobby extending its entire length. Originally decorated with classical mouldings consonant with the exterior, this space was later remodeled in the Art Deco style.

Adjacent to a new theater complex and a distinguished old hotel, the Heyburn is still in service after more than sixty years, having recently undergone an extensive renovation program. Seen from the roofs of Louisville, the alternating rhythm of the facade echoes the alternating rhythm of the Starks Building *(q.v.)* four

In 1927, the skyline of downtown Chicago stretched from the Tribune Tower on North Michigan Avenue to the Straus Building on South Michigan Avenue. Midway between stood the Pittsfield Building, the tallest in the city. It was also at the commercial, retail, and symbolic center of the city. Including the classical colonnade in Grant Park, Chicago's frontyard, this part of the city was a cross section of a period in its architectural history ranging from the 1890s to the late 1920s, with the Pittsfield its towering climax (figs. 181, 182). Heralded as "Another Architec-

[181] PITTSFIELD BUILDING,
CHICAGO, ILL., ELEVATION

[182] PITTSFIELD BUILDING,
UPPER STORIES

At first, designers in Chicago responded to the new law simply by adding towers to the tops of the old building blocks, and the results sometimes looked additive. No doubt the powerful example set by Eliel Saarinen in his second-place design for the Chicago Tribune competition in 1922 played an influential role in the development of a fully unified skyscraper tower. Such a remarkable unity exists between the tower and the base in the Saarinen design that the very distinction between tower and base is dissolved. Four years later, Graham, Anderson, Probst and White's Pittsfield Building approached this unity using small, gradual setbacks in the tower. The telescoping forms of the tower building are, however, finished with the chateau roof associated with more traditional forms.[2] (In the Koppers Building in Pittsburgh [q.v.], the firm's designers responded more completely to the Saarinen influence, although here too they retained the chateau roof.)

The lower portion of the Pittsfield is twenty-one stories high, while the tower rises another seventeen stories.[3] Setbacks occur at the twenty-second, thirty-fifth, and thirty-eighth stories, and the whole is capped by a crown of weathered green copper. Finished in polished black granite at the base, the cladding sets off the bronze frames of the show windows and entrances to the shops on the building's two principal facades. Above, the walls are of terra-cotta, with decorated spandrel panels. Pointed finials or turrets cap the piers that terminate at each setback, and arched windows in pedimented gables provide the finishing touches. This

historicist Gothic mode had been accepted in the architectural community as especially appropriate for the vertical skyscraper for many years, and indeed the Fisher Building in Chicago (Daniel H. Burnham and Company, 1896) provided a precedent in the firm's own history.

The main entrance, of red Verona marble, is on Washington Street to the north and leads to the lavishly decorated elevator lobby with its specially designed mailbox (fig. 186). The Pittsfield was the first in Chicago to take

tural Triumph in the Loop," the monumental thirty-eight-story commercial and office building opened in September 1927.[1]

The stately tower emerges from the building block with a powerful thrust above the cornice lines of the surrounding buildings. Legally, the form had been made possible by the 1922 zoning ordinance that allowed building over the height limit of 264 feet provided the structure above the limit did not exceed 25 percent of the area below or one-sixth its volume, and also provided there was a setback of one foot in ten from all lines of adjacent property.

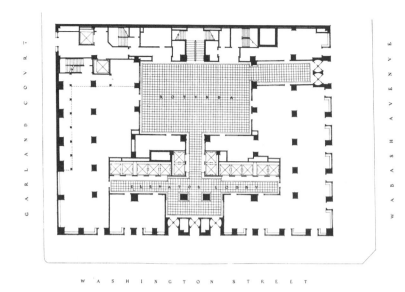

GARLAND COVRT

ROTVNDA

ELEVATOR LOBBY

WABASH AVENVE

WASHINGTON STREET

[183] PITTSFIELD BUILDING, PLAN

advantage of the provision of the zoning law that allowed direct special express service without transfer to higher floors. With deeply coffered ceilings, the marble walls set off the elaborately designed elevator doors and light and other fixtures. As visitors walk from the lobby along the corridor (fig. 183), they see glimpses of the five-story atrium beyond, one of the loveliest ever designed by the firm (fig. 184). Five stories high, surrounded by balconies and shop windows on all sides, the great space is embellished by glowing

[184] PITTSFIELD BUILDING, INTERIOR COURT

[185] PITTSFIELD BUILDING, LIGHT FIXTURE

marbles, gleaming brasses, and carvings in a Spanish Gothic style. The huge chandelier that hangs suspended in the center of the space casts light on the niches where flowering plants originally embellished the walls and an elegant octagonal seating area once marked the center of the floor (fig. 185). Long the building's trademark, much of this space is now used by service industries, such as travel agencies. On the south wall of this "rotunda," as it was called in the 1920s, a staircase leads to the lower arcade, a subterranean shopping area that once included a barbershop, a beauty parlor, a restaurant, and spaces for two private clubs, the Jewelers and the Chiselers.[4]

As a center for the jewelry trade even today, the building houses many dealers in precious stones, along with medical and dental offices, laboratories, and others. Because the office spaces were designed with these future tenants in mind, special plans were made to allow for extra plumbing and fixtures for compressed air and gas. An elaborate security system, in which a touch of an alarm set off a siren, stopped the elevators, and alerted guards to lock all doors leading out of the building, earned the Pittsfield a reputation for safety that soon afforded its jewelers lower insurance rates.[5]

[186] PITTSFIELD BUILDING, MAILBOX

The estate of Marshall Field erected the building to provide "fitting recognition to the far-seeing vision of the New England boy, who, in realizing that vision, was destined to play no small part in the . . . life of Chicago."[6] Since the Conway Building had already been named after the city of Marshall Field's birth, the trustees decided to name the building after the town where Field began his business career— Pittsfield, Massachusetts.

1. Joseph I. Karl, "The Pittsfield Building," *Building and Realty News*, September 1927, pp. 1–13.

2. *Architecture and Building* 60 (December 1928): 374, plates 239–40.

3. Original blueprints are available in the archives of the building, Chicago.

4. Rental brochure, archives of the building.

5. Ernest Fuller, "Famous Chicago Buildings," *Chicago Tribune*, February 7, 1959; ibid., "Pittsfield Turns 50," *Chicago Tribune*, December 18, 1977.

6. Karl, p. 1.

BUILDERS' BUILDING

1927
228 North LaSalle Street
Chicago, Illinois

Cost in 1927: $5,240,880; pcf: $0.622
Status: extant, remodeled

On and off since the days of the World's Columbian Exposition of 1893, the men of Chicago's construction companies had talked of collaborating to erect a monument to their industry.

More than thirty years later, several organizations bought stock in the new Chicago Builders' Building Corporation and decided to go ahead. Banding together under the leadership of

Adelbert E. Coleman, a manufacturer of ornamental metalwork, were the Builders' Association, the Iron League, the Electrical Contractors, the Terrazzo and Mosaic Dealers, the Steam Fitters, the Hoisters, and other trade associations. In addition, approximately sixty individual subscribers bought stock. They represented many of Chicago's leading companies in the field, including Patent Scaffolding, Central Asbestos and Magnesia, National Brick, Chicago Art Marble, Western Wire and Iron Works, Pittsburgh Plate Glass, National Fire Proofing, and Central Chandelier.

The building also shows the persistence of Daniel Burnham's view of an ideal building in an ideal city. Here, as late as 1927, the familiar tripartite, flat-roofed office block with a central light court appears again. Of course, no two of these buildings are exactly alike, but the differences are subtle. In the Builders' Building, giant Ionic pilasters unify the second through the fourth stories and appear again as great Ionic columns from the nineteenth to the twenty-first stories. The increased height, nearly double that of the previous decade, also distinguished the building from its predecessors (fig. 187).

In addition to erecting a monument to the building industry, the Chicago Builders' Building Corporation wanted a place to display building materials and equipment, an exhibition area that would be an impressive setting for the latest in design and technology. For this purpose, Graham, Anderson, Probst and White converted the usual cen-

[187] BUILDERS' BUILDING, CHICAGO, ILL., ELEVATION

tral atrium area that had worked so well as the lobby for office buildings, as the Banking Room for banks, and for the display of merchandise in department stores into a space for an indoor fair of exhibition booths for the tenants (fig. 188). That roster of authorities in materials and construction included the Kimball Brick Company; William A. Block, Electrical Contractors; Gray-Knox Marble Company; U.S. Blue Print Paper Company; Metal Door and Trim Company; and Federal Steel Sash Company. Hoping that such a building would attract thousands of men and women seeking ideas, for "a modest cottage, a bulking apartment building or hotel or a towering office structure," vendors backed up each display with construction offices on the upper stories to transform ideas into realities.[1]

Located conveniently at the heart of the city near the new bridge on LaSalle Street, the Builders' Building had direct access to the lower level of Wacker Drive for the shipment of merchandise and supplies by truck. Another attractive feature was a 200-car garage with four exits for tenants, which obviated rush-hour delays.

But the directors of the Builders' Building (Howard J. White among them) were not limited in their scope to business matters alone. They also spoke of their idea that the structure would provide an educational opportunity, that it would become a kind of a museum of the construction industry, a place where the exchange of ideas was encouraged. As an embodiment of this hope the architects gave over a whole

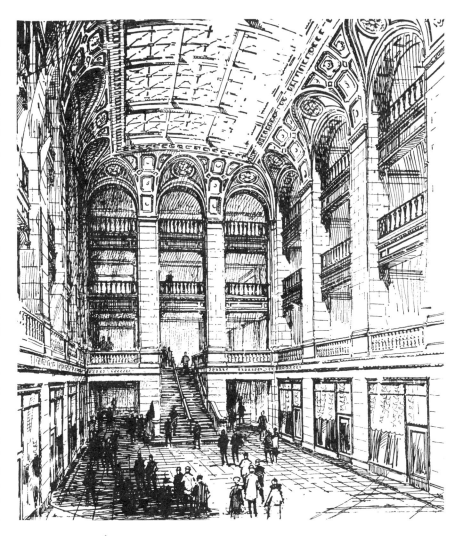

[188] BUILDERS' BUILDING, INTERIOR COURT

floor to an assembly hall and a series of conference rooms.

Sometime in the post–World War II era, the building was occupied by the Chicago Board of Education, and all but the two lower stories of the atrium were filled in. By November 1984, the building had deteriorated so badly that the new owners, Tishman Speyer Realty Company, engaged Skidmore, Owings and Merrill to remodel it and erect a new addition to the west. The new design, by Adrian Smith, links the old and new lobbies in the spirit of the original and has given new life to this venerable old structure. Above the cornice, a glass-enclosed structure with a mansard roofline connects the two buildings.

1. "Builders Building Big Civic Asset," *Real Estate News* 22, no. 1 (January 1927): 1.

O'NEIL'S DEPARTMENT STORE

1926–27
226 South Main Street
Akron, Ohio

Cost in 1927: $3,006,473; pcf: $0.298
Status: extant

On the northwest corner of the intersection of State and Main streets, O'Neil's is at the heart of downtown Akron. In the best department store fashion, the broad windows between its supporting piers display merchandise along 430 feet of the north-south axis on State Street and 216 feet along Main Street.

Tripartite in its divisions, the whole is crowned by a terra-cotta cornice of palmettes and honeysuckle motifs, and a flagpole atop each corner punctuates the blue of the midwestern sky. Protruding balconies further accent the corner piers, geometric spandrel panels provide a patterned relief in the sandstone cladding, a Greek key motif finishes the pilasters in the middle section, and elaborate urns adorn the piers at the attic story (fig. 189). The design had been simplified after it was first submitted by the architects.

The usual modifications to the air-conditioning system were made after World War II, and re-cently some restoration has been done to the elevator doors and other aspects of the interior to allow for conversion of one-half of the third floor and all of the fourth, fifth, and sixth floors to office space. A separate entrance to the office now exists on Main Street so the two parts of the building are differentiated. In 1946, Graham, Anderson, Probst and White added a parking deck and warehouse, solving the problems of the stream that borders the site to do so. Today, O'Neil's, in its adapted form and now owned by the May Company, continues to serve the Akron community.[1]

1. Blueprints, specifications, and construction photographs are located in the office of the building in Akron.

[189] O'NEIL'S DEPARTMENT STORE, AKRON, OHIO, EXTERIOR

[190] CHASE NATIONAL BANK BUILDING (EIGHTEEN PINE BUILD-ING), NEW YORK, N.Y., EXTERIOR

CHASE NATIONAL BANK BUILDING

(Eighteen Pine Building)

1926–28
Eighteen Pine Street
New York, New York

Cost in 1928: $7,491,159
Status: extant, extensively
   remodeled

Rising in dramatic stepped pyramidal setbacks against the backdrop of the earlier towers of lower Manhattan, and just behind the old Custom House, the building now called Eighteen Pine Street was the former head office of the Chase Manhattan Bank (fig. 190). The L-shaped site was not easy to deal with, but the designers, Alfred Shaw and Sigurd Naess, found that the limitations inspired them to create a form new to the vocabulary of the firm, and a shape that expressed the current architectural spirit in New York.

In describing the plot, a contemporary wrote in *Architectural Design:*

There is frontage on Nassau and Pine Streets, with a narrow L giving a frontage and entrance on Cedar Street, and only one square corner in the whole plan. In the architecture of yesterday, an architecture having to do mainly with facades, this would have been a desperately unhandy site. Under the terms of our architecture of today, which has to do mainly with masses, the matter finds a more natural solution. A building now can be piled up with all the rugged informality of a natural rock formation. Its diminishing masses may be set at

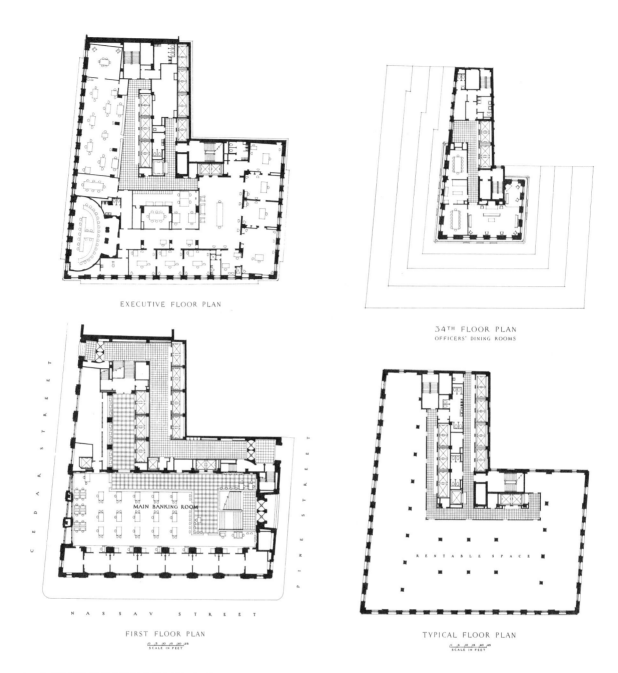

EXECUTIVE FLOOR PLAN

34ᵀᴴ FLOOR PLAN
OFFICERS' DINING ROOMS

FIRST FLOOR PLAN
SCALE IN FEET

TYPICAL FLOOR PLAN
SCALE IN FEET

[191] CHASE NATIONAL BANK, PLANS

angles oblique with the substructure, which would have played havoc with a conventional facade.[1]

Unlike some of their predecessors in the design department of the firm, Shaw and Naess were ready to respond to the latest trends in architectural circles. Many examples of the stepped pyramidal form that had appeared in New York as a response to the 1916 zoning ordinance were on the scene in 1924—the Shelton Hotel and the Barclay-Vesey Building to name just two of the most important. The Chanin Building was on the drawing board or going up in Midtown at about the same time.

The Chase was part of this series of spectacular setback skyscrapers, and it was followed by the Squibb Building, the Daily News Building, the Chrysler Building, and the Waldorf Astoria.

The narrow lot size on one side and the neighboring buildings impinging on the others and the requirements of the building code and the elevator machinery nettled the architects at every turn. Shaw usually designed buildings in mass and elevation and then gave them to Sigurd Naess, who developed the details in plan and section. The problems of the restrictive site for the Chase made it imperative that they reverse this procedure. Making the best of a difficult situation, Naess separated the building into two parts: a tall, narrow, L-shaped utility core and a broad office building.[2]

The core contains the elevators, plumbing and heating systems, and staircases, which rise uninterrupted on the William Street or east side to the full 478 feet. The terraces of the stepped pyramid surrounding this core are set back at regularly diminishing intervals on the other three sides according to the 1916 zoning law (fig. 191). When the building was completed, *The Chase* claimed: "The result is a step forward in the development of a characteristic American architecture. Though reminiscent of Egypt in the features indicated [the terra-cotta detailing] the impression is typical of New York and of the mighty forces of modern industry. The upward sweep of the Cedar Street wing seems to support the stepped heights of the Nassau Street profile like a mighty buttress. The effect is of massive solidity."[3]

Although the Chase was among the smallest of the new skyscrapers going up in New York in the late 1920s, in both height and volume, the bank itself had become the nation's leading lender to commerce and industry, with deposits from business sources totaling almost $320 million as early as 1922. By

1927, Chase National passed the billion dollar mark in total resources and by 1928 had become America's second largest bank. By contrast, the building was only the thirty-eighth tallest in New York.

In spite of its small size, the building was noticed by the contemporary French architect Henri Sauvage, who wrote that the "audacity of the design of the Chase" had influenced him in the design of the Hôpital Beaujon. Other French architects included the Chase when they spoke of emulating the "Babylonian palaces of New York," for their sculptural new forms, "at once picturesque, logical and beautiful."[4] Contemporary architect and writer Francisco Mujica wrote that the Chase, "erected opposite the Equitable Building, gives a clear idea of the hygienic and aesthetic results of the Zoning Resolution."[5]

Although the European modernists eschewed architectural ornament, American architects in the mid-1920s lavished attention over these details, and Shaw was no exception in his design of the Chase. Aware that classical mouldings and other Greco-Roman elements were now considered old-fashioned or inappropriate for setback skyscrapers, Shaw sought another historic source for the ornament of the building.

In his article for the July 1929 issue of *Architectural Forum*, Shaw wrote that the pyramidal massing of the building had suggested some of the characteristics of the architecture of Egypt to him, and that he therefore designed both the exterior and the interior "with a feeling for the simplicity of Egyptian detail, and

the color which is used in the more important rooms."[6] When the forms were interpreted a few years later, this Egyptian influence was passed over, and the building was celebrated as a truly indigenous American building because it seemed Mayan rather than Old World in inspiration. Clearly Egyptian in inspiration, sculptor M. H. Kock's great sphinxes at the corners and the mouldings beneath them seem to grow naturally out of the brick cladding, changing subtly from rectilinear to curved forms, and the cubic shape of the corner heads with their pharoahlike headdresses is both majestic and architectonic (fig. 192). Critic Matlack Price responded:

With the essential masses of his building determined, the modern architect has now only to concern himself with a manner of treatment, and this, it has been found, is best when it is simplest, and when it abandons, largely, the old "stock" architectural embellishments that have, after years of faithful service, earned a rest in quiet retirement. As was said in these pages last month about the Chanin Building, architects have wisely come to the conclusion that the copings of the great massive shoulders of the new buildings are not good places to set little urns and obelisks. So strong was the habit of using detail for detail's sake that it was first believed that set-backs needed some kind of extraneous embellishment in order not to look bleak or "unfinished." Fortunately, the immutable laws of scale asserted themselves, and demonstrated that no embellishment of set-backs can be trivial or unrelated, and that if any detailed treatment of the great masses is to be attempted, it must be of such heroic mould as that on the New York Telephone Building, the Shelton Hotel or the Chanin Tower. Thus, on the corners of the parapet of the first setback on the Chase National Bank Building, there is a great winged sphinx head, with the wings modeled into the coping, and in lesser setbacks above this these are repeated, an interesting motif, and one in conformity with the Egyptian detail used elsewhere.[7]

Monumental and simple in its form, the main entrance on Pine Street was also decorated with an elaborate Egyptian design in finely wrought bronze set in a frame of pink Tennessee marble. Carved with designs taken carefully from twenty-two old coins and an American gold dollar, these reliefs referred to Chase's "Moneys of the World" collection.[8]

The fourth floor originally held the bank's reception room, executive offices, and law library, all paneled in walnut and other fine woods and executed in a lighter classical style associated with the Adams brothers' eighteenth-century work in England. The Directors' Room, in the form of half an ellipse, was inspired by the Supreme Court Building in Washington, D.C. But these public rooms have all been altered. A contemporary account describes the old Directors' Room (fig. 193): "The whole atmosphere here is that of dignified repose—walnut panelling, carpeted floors, the feeling of a distinguished club as opposed to a commercial office environment. Portraits of the principal officers are framed architecturally in simple mouldings that match the

woodwork, instead of in heavy gold. A generation ago these interiors would have been pompous and ornate, heavy with grandiose impressiveness; here they are gracious, quietly well-bred, admirably expressive of the essential spirit of the organization."[9]

From the thirty-third to the thirty-fifth floors space was set aside for more dining rooms, a lounge, and a kitchen service area. Maneuvering up and down the elevators, and in and around the corridors of the L must have been disorienting, but at the top the rooms gave "magnificent glimpses across and over Manhattan and its rivers and environs."

Contemporary accounts indicate that the architects and the bankers worked in close cooperation with each other in planning the interior organization of the space. At that time the bank cleared checks totaling more than $250 million a day, and efficiency was a primary consideration. Lost motion in the use of files and records or in the contact of one department with another was reduced as much as possible. The five and a half basement stories contained the safe deposit department, the currency branch, and the great vaults that descended three stories into the ground, resting on rock eighty-five feet below the sidewalk. The telephone system had to allow anyone anywhere in the building to talk with any part of the United States and some parts of Europe at any time and was as large as the exchange in Hartford, Connecticut.

Writing an account after it was all over, Alfred Shaw suggests that the Chase National

Bank provided solutions for every essential problem of the modern American commercial building:

It was erected at the foot of Manhattan Island, which has produced the amazing pile of steel and stone that symbolizes America to most Europeans. . . . It was studied as to its economic possibilities during the period of real estate negotiations; and it was erected under the terrific pressure of mounting interest rates and demands for space and use. The engineering difficulties involved the problem of excavating to bed rock on the very toes of ponderous buildings, and of building foundations and basement floors while the bracing necessary to hold the adjacent walls was still in place. . . . The venerable tradition and present dignity of the Chase National Bank demanded an exterior design of fine architectural character. The officers of the bank as well as the architects realized the significance of creating a building which would not only be expressive of this dignity, but also individual and highly indicative of the new American architecture. . . . Great enterprises of this sort require the thought, enthusiasm and determined courage of many people. Into this structure have been built the ardor and spirit of all of them.[10]

In 1957, a number of changes were made to the building. The empty square within the old L-shape was acquired and filled in with an "annex" using the same cladding and general design as the original building. At the same time the bank decided to erect a new building to the east. The bank hoped to take advantage of

[192] CHASE NATIONAL BANK, DETAIL

new attitudes in both municipal and architectural circles that would allow taller buildings if public spaces were provided below. To facilitate the construction of a plaza, the City of New York agreed to cede to the owners a part of Cedar Street that ran between the two blocks. In exchange, the bank made somewhat larger parts of its property on surrounding streets available so that these thoroughfares could be widened. All of these successful efforts at cooperation between the municipal and the private sectors were possible in the new climate of public opinion in New York in the mid-1950s. Concerned about the deteriora-

tion of the financial district and believing that its revitalization was possible, a group of leading businessmen formed the Downtown–Lower Manhattan Association and named David Rockefeller, president of the Chase Manhattan Bank, as its chairman. In 1955, the Chase Manhattan purchased from the Guaranty Trust Company the block bounded by Nassau, William, Liberty, and Cedar, which had formerly been the site of the home office of the Mutual Life Insurance Company of New York. The Chase thus owned all of two adjoining blocks except two small parcels, which it acquired subsequently. Concerned

that the new design mark a radical departure from "the canyonesque construction that had been the hallmark of the architecture of lower Manhattan," Skidmore, Owings and Merrill began its designs for a new sixty-story building set back from the surrounding streets and sharing a public space with the older building. To facilitate this new approach to urban design, the city made the necessary accessions on Cedar Street.

Today both the old Chase National Bank Building (later owned by the Chemical Bank and the New York Trust Company and currently by the Morgan Guaranty Trust) and the new Chase Manhattan Bank have a shared L-shaped plaza that extends from Nassau Street to William Street. Both sections are raised up from the street and sidewalk area, isolating them somewhat from the pedestrian life of the city, a feature of the design now widely regarded as an error, but a mark of the early phase of this change in attitude toward city planning. In fact, the city's Zoning Resolution of 1961 promoted just this kind of plaza in many areas of New York, causing the authors of the *AIA Guide to New York City* to lament that the act had "brought barren plazas to the Avenue of the Americas: good intentions misdirected that present lifeless places without people, windswept and dull." At the Chase Manhattan Plaza efforts have been made to ameliorate the isolation by placing outdoor tables and chairs on the northwest portion, which add a festive note to the Wall Street area, while a Dubuffet sculpture enlivens the section to the southeast.[11]

[193] CHASE NATIONAL BANK, DIRECTORS' ROOM

1. Matlack Price, "An Appreciation," *Architectural Design,* n.d., pp. 6–8. Another contemporary account is in *Architecture and Building* 61 (April 1929): 198–200, illus. 119–24.

2. Edward Histed, interview, August 26, 1986. Histed was a draftsman in the GAPW design department, 1928–75.

3. *The Chase, A Monthly Magazine,* July 1927. The December 1928 issue also contains material about the building.

4. Isabelle Gournay, "Setback Skyscrapers in France: From Myth to Reality," paper delivered at the Society of Architectural Historians annual convention, Washington, D.C., 1986.

5. Francisco Mujica, *History of the Skyscraper* (Paris: Archaeological Architecture Press, 1930), plate 107.

6. Alfred Shaw, "The Chase National Bank Building, New York," *Architectural Forum* 50 (July 1929).

7. Price, "An Appreciation."

8. Starting at the bottom on the left the coins represented in bas-relief were a Roman sestertium, a stater from Metapontum, an early Greek coin from Poseidonia, a Spartan coin from Tarentum, a Hebrew shekel, an aureus of Augustus, a sixteenth-century Dutch coin, a testone of the Italian Renaissance, a colonial Pine Tree shilling, a testone of Francis I, a Spanish milled dollar, an American Peace Dollar, a Joachimthaler, an Elizabethan gold pound, a New York cent, a Japanese yen, a Russian two-kopeck piece, a florin, a Ptolemaic coin, an early Greek tetradrachm of Alexander the Great, a stater from Corinth, and a decadrachm from Syracuse. After these coins had been selected by the American Numismatic Society, enlargements were made from plaster casts for the marble cutters by the sculptor, M. H. Kock. Today this area is boarded up.

9. Price, "An Appreciation," p. 6.

10. Shaw, "The Chase National Bank Building," p. 3.

11. The Chase National Bank archives in New York contains many drawings, photographs, prints, letters, newspaper clippings, and other materials related to the history of the building, and a model is displayed in room 1927, Eighteen Pine Building.

STATE BANK OF CHICAGO BUILDING

(One Twenty South LaSalle Building)
1926–28
120 South LaSalle Street
Chicago, Illinois

Cost in 1928: $8,685,700; pcf: $0.887
Status: extant

Bright and strong, the physical character of the State Bank of Chicago has the alert and durable qualities of a conservative financial institution (fig. 194). The Continental and Commercial Bank (1912–14) (*q.v.*) just down the street at 208 South LaSalle is fourteen years older, but the signature of the same design team is unmistakable. Without apology, the continuity of Graham, Anderson, Probst and White's traditional style is firm and forthright. With no attempt at novelty, nor apology for conformity, the State Bank is a celebration of an urban cohesiveness, of being a subordinate part of a great financial district, of forming a vital link in an already well-established streetscape.[1] But the 1928 building is by no means a slavish imitation of the 1912 building. Taller, it also has slenderer proportions. A five-story base with rectangular openings supports the new height, and it is, of course, balanced by a five-story top, suitably lighter in mood with a three-story arcade and an attic story with Tuscan crown moulding.

Within this rectangular mass the formal design is one of mature refinement. The entrance in the center is emphasized by four giant-order Ionic columns in a portal that is allowed to project only slightly into the pedestrian space at sidewalk level. Horizontally and vertically the block of the building is subdivided to provide a balance between unity and variety. Stringcourses establish horizontal zones of varied proportions, and strong corner piers define the edges. The vertical supports are alternately wide and narrow, setting up a subtle rhythm in the facade and avoiding the monotony of extreme regularity.

By the same means, the proportions of the building can be clearly felt from a distance. Since architecture is an art of changing scale, up close the visitor's interest shifts to the play of light on the surface of the materials. A water table of polished rose granite speckled with dark gray gives way to light gray Bedford lime-

[194] STATE BANK OF CHICAGO BUILDING (ONE TWENTY SOUTH LASALLE BUILDING), CHICAGO, ILL., ELEVATION

[195] STATE BANK OF CHICAGO, BANKING ROOM

[196] STATE BANK OF CHICAGO, CHICAGO STOCK EXCHANGE ROOM

stone to the fifth floor, which is surmounted by a terra-cotta of lighter gray above.[2]

The great Banking Room filling the space from the second to the third floors is the climax of the interior (fig. 195). The blush of the buff Botticino marble is captured in the rose of the stencil decorations and the stained glass of the ceiling, combining to create an atmosphere of warmth and grandeur. Eight pairs of Doric columns separate this airy central space from the balconies, which divide into two stories screened by cast-iron railings of exceptional delicacy. Within this space, which hovers between the grand and the grandiose, the architectural decorations are luxurious, of the finest materials, and exquisitely wrought. Intricate and rich mouldings above the frieze go through eight changes in profile before reaching the elaborately carved ceiling, a field of rectangles embellished with a geometric motif similar to the frieze, but enriched by rosettes. The design changes from one of predominately rectangular spaces filled with stenciled patterns of rose, blue, and beige in the outer edges, to one of octagons filled with red and green stained glass in the center field, as varied as a Persian carpet. Indeed the whole room, nearly in its original condition, suggests a meeting of Moorish and classical decoration. Doorways, mailboxes, separating grilles, and standards for signs in intricate patterns, further enhance the lovely effect of the interior.

The second floor includes two other public rooms: the Chicago Stock Exchange Room (fig. 196) and a small private conference room. The Stock Exchange re-

tains its original ceiling, its geometric panels in low-relief designs as lacy and delicate as snowflakes, perhaps inspired by Louis Sullivan, but seeming too fragile for the melting atmosphere of cigar smoke. The walnut paneling is intact in the conference room. Above the Banking Room is the rental portion of the office building.[3]

Today the State Bank Building remains in excellent condition, continuing to serve Chicago's financial community through its owners, the Lurie Company; its two chief occupants, the Exchange National Bank of Chi-

cago and the Kemper Financial Services, Inc.; and its many other tenants.

1. The two buildings are now separated by a new building by Philip Johnson, a tall version of Burnham and Root's Masonic Temple of 1891–92, which stood on the northeast corner of State and Randolph streets until it was demolished in 1939.

2. Joseph I. Karl, "State Bank Building," *Building and Realty News*, December 1927, pp. 1–16.

3. Drawings and photographs of the original building are in the archives of the bank in Chicago.

THIRTIETH STREET STATION

1927–34
John F. Kennedy Boulevard and Thirtieth Street
Philadelphia, Pennsylvania

Cost in 1934, author's estimate: $10,439,146 for the main station, based on $0.70 per cubic foot for the portions handled by the architects.
Status: extant, in varying condition from poor to good in 1982 when extensive renovation was underway in compliance with National Historic Register constraints.[1]

The growth of Philadelphia and the dramatic increase in train travel brought huge challenges to the city and to the Pennsylvania Railroad in the mid-1920s. In 1924, Graham, Anderson, Probst and White drew up plans for the Philadelphia Terminal Improvements, with a new passenger station and a new suburban station—office building downtown. Congestion at the Pennsylvania Railroad's old Broad Street Station in the heart of the city and at its smaller West and North Philadelphia stations was acute. The Broad Street Station was a stub-end terminal about

one mile east of the road's main lines to the north and south, so all through trains had to be backed up to get to the center of the city, losing time at great inconvenience to all concerned. By 1927, more than 587 trains used the Philadelphia stations each weekday, and all but 30 of them stopped at West Philadelphia. It was clear that a new main passenger station in West Philadelphia was needed.[2]

It is interesting that the new station, called the Thirtieth Street Station, with its attendant changes in bridges, trackage, and other features, and a new suburban terminal beneath a twenty-two-story office building in the center of Philadelphia, became the central features of a program of beautification in Philadelphia that included underground passages for the trains, the construction of new boulevards and streets, the embellishment of the river's edge along the Schuylkill, and the electrification of all passenger and freight service coming into the city. Other improvements involved a central heating and auxiliary power plant and the complete rearrangement of the terminal trackage and signal and interlocking facilities, as well as the development of related city planning schemes that everyone hoped would revitalize Pennsylvania Boulevard the way Grand Central Station in New York had revitalized Park Avenue (fig. 38).

As a part of these improvements the Thirtieth Street Station's key role in Philadelphia's transportation network was emphasized by the surrounding wide streets and plazas that facilitated the arrival of automobiles from different sections of the city, and by a subway station connected to the city's regular subway system and to the four-track submerged electrified suburban lines. Two new loop tracks permitted all through trains from the north and west to head into the station at either end and then go from the station on a continuous route north or west (fig. 198). Topping it all off, the spacious flat roof of the station was designed to permit the landing of helicopters. One of the early schemes for the station even included a suspension bridge over the tracks to link an elevated roadway above the station to a new highway on the west. The

[197] THIRTIETH STREET STATION, PHILADELPHIA, PA.

new station in Philadelphia was envisioned as the vital nexus where all forms of transportation—ships, railroads, cars, and airplanes—would come together in a coordinated scheme.

For the climactic site on the river, at the end of a long vista, the architects dreamed of a station with grand proportions. Alfred P. Shaw, chief designer, proposed a flat-roofed rectangle with a projecting central pavilion and lower wings. A massive 639 feet long by 327 feet wide, the equivalent of two city blocks, with a maximum height of 116 feet, the station had classical porticoes designed to carry the traditional connotations of metropolitan arrival. When the station was finished, contemporary descriptions referred to it as a symbolic entrance, a "new gateway to the City of Philadelphia."[3]

Today the Corinthian columns, eleven feet in diameter and seventy-one feet high, form an impressive colonnade and, together with the subordinate wings at the sides, give Philadelphia a sense of dramatic closure on the west (fig. 197). On the north and south the facades are lower, but the tall windows separated by pilasters, capped with an attic story similar to the porticoes, bring harmony to all four sides, and mark a key point in the route along the Schuylkill Expressway. In every direction the building fits into the fabric of the city, playing an integral part in the idea of order in urban Philadelphia, as well as expressing its own particular, individual function as a railroad station.

In the great Waiting Room within, the feeling of the importance of travel is momentous.

Rectangular in area, 290 feet long by 135 feet wide, and rising 95 feet to a flat coffered ceiling decorated in red, gold, and cream, the whole is lit by sunlight filtering through the splendid banks of windows on both sides of the Concourse and reflecting on the Tennessee marble floors (fig. 40). Six massive fluted columns articulate the travertine walls, adorned only by a relief sculpted by Karl Bitter, *The Spirit of Transportation,* which was moved from the old Broad Street Station.

The basic idea of the plan was to put all the necessities of travel in the north wing, and all special, but less essential conveniences in the south wing (fig. 199). Directly north of the Concourse, and clearly visible today, are the ticket windows and the main Waiting Room, men's and women's toilets, a barbershop, and a women's restroom. In addition, a baggage room, a parcel checking room, and telephone booths are located at intervals. The suburban facilities, located in an elevated portion of the north wing, are reached by various ramps, staircases, and escalators, with mezzanine passages provided

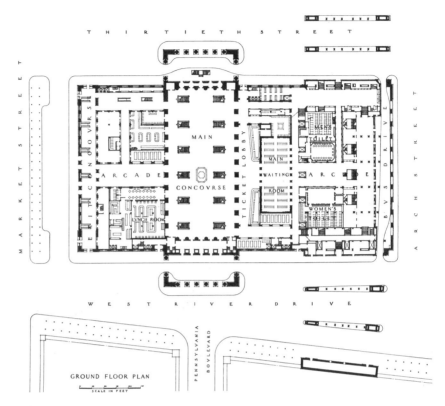

[199] THIRTIETH STREET STATION, PLAN

here and there. This suburban facility was built in conjunction with the new Suburban Station (now Penn Center [*q.v.*]) in the heart of Philadelphia, which opened April 1, 1930. From the Concourse, which extends over the tracks, all trains can be reached by stairs and escalators, and all the station service facilities are grouped around the Concourse.

Traveling light was not fashionable in the 1920s, when the common practice was to ship a trunk along for any journey lasting more than a week. Heavy valises were usually checked through or entrusted to redcaps for separate loading.[4] In some stations, a separate level was given over to baggage, but in Philadelphia the passenger platforms were used to handle some of the baggage, so trucking ramps were provided at both ends, leading down to baggage tunnels extending below the station tracks. These tunnels were connected by ramp with the mail-handling platform and continued beneath the east front of

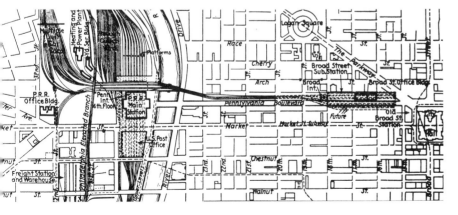

[198] THIRTIETH STREET STATION, MAP OF RAIL LINES

the building to the track-level baggage room. This baggage room was on the lower level by the river drive to give easy access to trucks and boats and was connected with the concourse-level baggage room and the suburban service platforms above by elevators.

In the south wing, separated by a central arcade forty-five feet wide, were provisions for a dining room, a lunchroom, a cafeteria, kitchen facilities, a drugstore, and other concessions and conveniences. In the restaurants, furnishings tacitly indicate that different classes of food service were offered, and contemporary menus reflect different price levels, geared for wealthy, middle-class, and lower-class travelers. Americans were constrained by their democratic traditions from using the terms "First Class," "Second Class," and "Third Class" that still described European train travel, but it was common practice in all American railroad stations of the period to provide three different types of eating accommodations. The architects aimed for "a quiet, conservative tone in the dining room" and specified walnut paneling and mirrors, while the lunchroom was finished more modestly, and the walls of the cafeteria were of glass brick. Contemporary attitudes toward women can be found in the architects' specifications, which provided "a more restful atmosphere in the women's rest rooms by the use of softer tones and more comfortable furniture." On occasion, railroad stations had to be used as mortuaries, and the Thirtieth Street Station was one of the first, if not the first, to include a chapel. Faced with Botti-

cino marble, the chapel also was decorated with soft mural paintings. An emergency hospital, approximately 3,300 square feet in area, was located on the fourth floor of the south wing.[5]

While writers of the 1930s praised the building, in the 1970s critics complained of the station that its exterior "lacked vitality," and helped to create "a strangely barren, large-scaled entrance to West Philadelphia." These authors' assessment of the interior is more favorable: "If the experience is not the same exhilaration once rendered by the old Penn Station in New York, there is still the feeling of Having Arrived."[6]

Viewed today from the air, from John F. Kennedy Boulevard, from the Schuylkill River, or from the plaza on Thirtieth Street, the railroad station takes its place as a subordinate but important part of the urban fabric of Philadelphia. Playing its roles well as the entrance to the city from the west and the climax of the view from the east, its severe form also expresses the spirit of the days when steamships, cars, railroads, and airplanes aimed at, among other things, an engineering purity of design, for speed was primary. But since time immemorial, travel has also been an occasion for ceremony. The classical porticoes proclaim the significance of travel by train bearing witness to its importance as few modern airplane terminals can. The lofty columns, gleaming marbles, and glowing lights of the interior transform the functional space into a ceremonial space, a setting worthy of human feelings, where railroad engineering rises to the humanistic art of architecture.

1. Funded by the U.S. Department of Transportation and the Federal Railroad Administration under the Northeast Corridor Rail Service Improvement Revitalization and Regulatory Reform Act passed by Congress in 1976, the work was being carried out in cooperation with Amtrak by DeLeuw, Cather, Parsons; Skidmore, Owings and Merrill; and I. Alper.

2. The complexities also involved special engineering solutions, including the construction of foundations to prevent the transmission of train vibrations into the buildings, which required all street footings to be constructed independently of building footings, the inclusion of air-gap expansion joints, and other precautions.

3. Neil D. Howard, "Philadelphia Improvements of the Pennsylvania Near Completion," *Railway Age*, July 28, 1934, pp. 92–110. A special feature of the new coach yard was the service facility, which included steam, air, water, and battery-charging outlets adjacent to each track. All of the outlets along the narrow service platforms left the wider platforms unobstructed for trucks. The magnitude of the problem was compounded by the need to lay thirty-four miles of track within about 500 acres.

4. Call buttons were located at points throughout the main floor, mainly at the checking rooms, for summoning porters. Indicator panels notified the porters where their services were required. In addition to the porter call system, a complex of special electrical systems included a clock and time-recording system, a burglar alarm connected to each ticket seller's space with an indicator in a police room on the third floor of the north wing, and a complete underfloor twin duct system for the operation of buzzer systems. The station also had its own telephone exchange and a pneumatic tube system, so that personal messenger service was unnecessary for conducting

most of the fast-paced daily routine of the station.

5. Specifications and drawings are located in the GAPW archives in Chicago. *See also* J. Walter May, "Pennsylvania Railroad's New Thirtieth Street Station," *U.G.I. Circle,* November 1930, pp. 9–12.

6. Edward Teitelman and Richard W. Longstreth, *Architecture in Philadelphia: A Guide* (Cambridge, Mass.: MIT Press, 1981). *See also* "The Pennsylvania Station, Philadelphia," *Building,* May 1933, pp. 7–9.

THIRTIETH STREET STATION STEAM HEATING PLANT

1929
Located 1,000 feet northwest of the Thirtieth Street Station
Philadelphia, Pennsylvania

Status: partially extant

Consolidating the work of five steam generating and three pumping and compressor plants into one modern plant, the new steam heating and auxiliary power plant was also designed so its capacity could be doubled, tripled, or quadrupled in the future. Anticipating that new construction in the area would be stimulated by the improvement program, the architects' drew up their proposal with four great smokestacks against the sky (fig. 200). Only the first of these was ever erected, but its output was prodigious. Its two boilers were of the inclined straight-tube, cross-drum type, each with a heating surface of 26,230 square feet and designed for operation up to 275 pounds per square inch gauge pressure. Each boiler was equipped with motor-drive, forced-draft, underfeed stokers. The main artery carried steam to the north end of the Thirtieth Street Station and from there across the Schuylkill River on the railroad's suburban track bridge to the Suburban Station and office building in the center of the city. An auxiliary electrical power plant was also included for emergency lighting and minor power requirements to supplement the railroad's primary source of power, a public utility.[1]

1. Neal D. Howard, "Philadelphia Improvements of the Pennsylvania Near Completion," *Railway Age,* July 28, 1934, pp. 108–9; *Steam Heating Plant, Philadelphia,* a brochure made for an inspection visit by the American Society of Mechanical Engineers on October 8, 1929, contains construction photographs, interior photographs, a cross-section drawing, progress photographs, and statistical information.

[200] THIRTIETH STREET STATION, STEAM HEATING PLANT, PROPOSAL

[201] BROAD STREET SUBURBAN STATION (ONE PENN CENTER AT SUBURBAN STATION), PHILADELPHIA, PA., ELEVATION

BROAD STREET SUBURBAN STATION

(One Penn Center at Suburban Station)

1924–29
John F. Kennedy Boulevard between Sixteenth and Seventeenth streets
Philadelphia, Pennsylvania

Cost in 1929: $6,027,735
Status: extant

According to the firm's 1924 plans for the Philadelphia Terminal Improvements, a new suburban underground terminal would be located beneath an office building at Arch and Fifteenth streets, immediately north and west of the old Broad Street Station. Eventually the suburban terminal–office building went up one block south and one block east of the original location. It served the old Broad Street Station as a suburban station, but few people in Philadelphia ever called it by its full given name. Also included was a plan for submerging the railroad tracks that ran at the surface east from Thirtieth Street along Pennsylvania Boulevard to encourage new development along this artery.

The new Suburban Station was almost at the apex of a triangle whose longest side stretched northwest along Benjamin Franklin Parkway toward the Philadelphia Museum of Art (fig. 38). The tall office building–suburban station might have acted as a link between the two boulevards had the small triangular tip to its east remained a park, but its appearance belied this connecting function. Contrary to the firm's usual practice, the office building–suburban station did not seem to fill a role in a larger urban scheme, rather it seemed an end in itself. This may be due to its tall, imposing form, or to the subsequent erection of the low, round Tourist Center in the small block to the east, which now plays the public role one might have expected from a railroad station in the late 1920s.

The terminal itself lies on a mezzanine floor fifteen feet below the street level, and the track level with its platforms is twenty feet further down. These two levels cover an area approximately 1,000 feet long by 200 feet wide, extending beyond the limits of the building above. When the station was first finished, the waiting rooms, ticket offices, information desk, and all of the auxiliary facilities were located on the depressed mezzanine floor. Four high island platforms and seven stub-end station tracks occupied the track level, but plans for adding more tracks were made in case demand increased in the future.

The efficient flow of traffic was praised in a contemporary issue of *Railway Age:*

One of the features of this terminal is the numerous means of entrance and exit provided to expedite the movement of passengers to and from the station. Each track platform is served by four broad stairways and an electric passenger elevator leading to the concourse floor, while 2 large elevators and 12 entrances and exits lead from the concourse to the street level or the Broad Street Station [*sic*] building above.[1] The latter exits and entrances include long wide ramps

[202] SUBURBAN STATION, DETAIL OF ENTRANCE

on easy grades leading from the east ends of the mezzanine and track levels to the City Hall station of the Broad Street City subway and beyond, and, temporarily at least, to the old Broad Street passenger station.[2]

The office building above seems tall, long, and narrow from Penn Center (fig. 201). Its slender verticality is heightened by the uninterrupted piers and recessed spandrels of the elevations. The polished black granite base ties the structure to the earth, while the slight setbacks, marked with tall piers topped with round balls at various levels, serve as a crown. The ever-present clock, the symbol of promptness, pride of every railroad man who knew how to run a railroad, still dominates the entrance on Sixteenth Street, but the sparkling little yellow lights that once spelled out "Pennsylvania Railroad" as dusk descended are now dark (fig. 202).

In plan the building is E-

[203] SUBURBAN STATION CONCOURSE, INTERIOR ELEVATION

shaped, and most of the street level space is given over to the Concourse or passages to the trains below on the east and west (figs. 203, 204) and to the elevator lobbies for the office building in the center. The lobby walls are clad in warm beige marble, the piers have shallow flutings and chevrons or zigzag mouldings, an Art Deco version of capitals.

This building reflects a subordination of the suburban commuter in the overall transportation network of Philadelphia in this era. Relegated to the underground in a structure that was primarily for offices, the daily traveler seems buried by the urban scheme. Since no aboveground space was allocated

around the station, none of the usual connotations of gateway to the city were attached to the building either. The station for through trains at Thirtieth Street subordinated the Suburban Station almost completely. The station at Thirtieth Street did have one disadvantage compared to the old Broad Street Station—it was not in the heart of Philadelphia, but across the river in West Philadelphia. Had it been located in the core of the city, like the grand old Broad Street Station, no extra suburban station would have been necessary. For this reason the Suburban Station was treated as a utilitarian necessity and an office building was erected over it.

1. Different names were used for this building in the course of its planning and design that are now somewhat confusing: Broad Street Suburban Station Building, Pennsylvania Underground Suburban Terminal, and Broad Street Station Building. Although the new station is not on Broad Street, it connects with Broad Street and the old Broad Street Station underground. The firm calls the new building the Broad Street Station in its 1933 book, but no one in Philadelphia ever called it this, reserving the name for the old station.

2. Neal D. Howard, "Philadelphia Improvements of the Pennsylvania Near Completion," *Railway Age*, July 28, 1934, pp. 92–110. *See also* an earlier article in the November 15, 1930, issue of *Railway Age*.

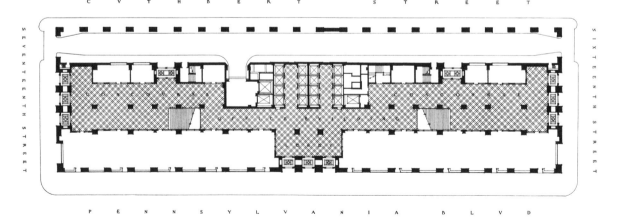

[204] SUBURBAN STATION, PLAN

PENNSYLVANIA RAILROAD OFFICE BUILDING

1926–27
Market Street and Lancaster Avenue, NE corner
West Philadelphia, Pennsylvania

Cost in 1927: $3,114,778.18; pcf: $0.446
Status: extant

Perhaps because the new railroad station at Thirtieth Street did not stimulate real estate development as anticipated with the undiluted optimism of the 1920s, this fourteen-story office building seems almost as isolated in West Philadelphia today as it did in the original model (fig. 205.) The E-shaped structure stands along with the Thirtieth Street Station, a steam heating plant, and an office building–station for suburban trains in downtown Philadelphia as part of the firm's work for the Pennsylvania Railroad during its improvement plan of the late 1920s.

Like the firm's other work of that busy decade, this building is tripartite in its divisions. In the shaft section in the middle, the piers rise uninterrupted to the eleventh story where simple capitals mark a transition to the giant order comprising the top three stories, which act as a crown. The flat pilasters, grooves, grids, circles, and squares that constitute the decorative motifs characterize the building's style as transitional between the classical and Art Deco styles the designers used in this period.

[205] PENNSYLVANIA RAILROAD OFFICE BUILDING, PHILADELPHIA, PA., EXTERIOR

KOPPERS BUILDING

1927–29
436 Seventh Avenue
Pittsburgh, Pennsylvania

Cost in 1929: $5,300,000
Status: extant

The industrial age is still embodied in the terrain and buildings of Pittsburgh. Railroad tracks and manufacturing complexes form an iron network over this valley in the earth where the Allegheny and the Monongahela rivers meet to form the Ohio River. Bridges to carry the materials of the age of iron and steel are cheek by jowl with the office buildings in the triangle between the rivers. The juxtaposition is invigorating, however, not jarring, earning the place its appellation "the city of Venus and Vulcan."[1]

In the midst of this triangular core are ten buildings designed by the men in Daniel Burnham's office, nine of which reflect the robust air of business in the first decade of the century. The office building over the Pennsylvania Railroad Station, for example is powerful and massive, its brown brick and terra-cotta cladding suggesting a ruggedness associated with railroading, whereas the Frick Building (437 Grant Street, 1898) and the Oliver Building (535 Smithfield Street, 1908–10) are clad in the sober limestone typical of the well-tailored "Burnham classicism" appropriate for the business aspects of industry.

By the late 1920s, however, automation played a larger role in Pittsburgh's industrial life, and

[206] KOPPERS BUILDING, PITTSBURGH, PA., ELEVATION

Graham, Anderson, Probst and White adopted features of the new Art Deco style to express the faster pace of this streamlined era for the Koppers Building.[2] While the firm had retained elsewhere its preference for classical forms until the middle of the decade, by 1929 it developed a compromise style that aimed at capturing

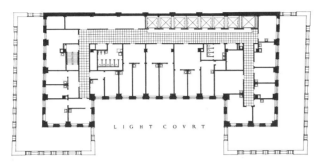

TOWER FLOOR PLAN

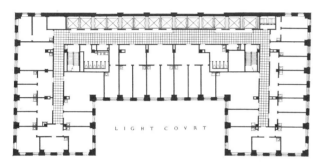

TYPICAL FLOOR PLAN

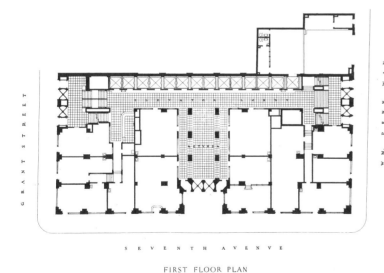

FIRST FLOOR PLAN

[207] KOPPERS BUILDING, PLAN

stripped classicism. From the side, the four setbacks of the slender profile resemble other modern stairstep buildings, but the green color, the semicircular openings at the twentieth and thirtieth floors, and the castellated forms of the top temper the contemporary with a traditional finish (fig. 206). The principal entrance on the Seventh Street side (fig. 55) is marked by a rectangular pavilion which opens into the arcaded lobby (fig. 56), where tiers of stores and offices off of the aisles and balconies create a shipshape modern impression, similar to the Field Building in Chicago.

Unlike the silver aluminum so common in other Art Deco buildings, the interior of the Koppers Building is trimmed in cast bronze. A matte finish on the elevator doors, mailboxes, clocks, and lighting fixtures is enlivened by the shiny cast-bronze balcony railings and handrails, in patterns of elegantly stylized leaves. The rest of the interior also has a balance between the old and the new. In plan, the U-shape of the building allocates the elevators to the rear, with double-loaded corridors in the wings and a terrace at the tower floor (fig. 207).[3]

1. Franklin Toker, *Pittsburgh: An Urban Portrait* (University Park, Pa.: Pennsylvania State University, 1986).

2. *Art Deco,* catalog to accompany an exhibition at Finch College, New York, New York, December 1974.

3. GAPW archives and the Kopper Building archives both contain construction photographs, drawings, and bound copies of the specifications.

something of the best of the old and the best of the new styles. With its chateau roofline clad in copper, the building recalls the earliest of steel-frame skyscrapers, such as Richard Morris Hunt's Tribune Building in New York (1875), but its setbacks and the sleek verticality of its uninterrupted piers are up-to-date

ALAMO NATIONAL BANK BUILDING

1929
154 East Commerce Street
San Antonio, Texas

Status: extant

In 1890, the old Alamo Mission was used as a storage house for the firm of Hugo and Schmeltzed who operated a store nearby. One day in November of that year, the two men decided that San Antonio needed another bank. They founded one and named it after the most famous monument in Texas.

By the mid-1920s, their first bank building was too small for a booming economy in what was then the largest and richest city in Texas. Discouraging words were seldom heard and expectations for the future were cloudless. Clearly a new building was in order, preferably one that would also overshadow the other two banks in town.

To express their client's wishes, Graham, Anderson, Probst and White erected a soaring skyscraper bank (fig. 208), but it was not like their usual big city, gray-limestone-clad office buildings. Instead the designers responded to the ambiance of the Southwest, using light beige brick on the piers and dark brown brick in an intricate, architectonic pattern that suggested a cityscape, on the spandrel panels.

The office lobby is decorated with a Spanish decor. Sage green and buff tiles provide a subtle contrast to the cool dark green and maroon marble of the doorjambs beneath the cast-plaster ceiling. Further on, inside the great Banking Room (fig. 209), sixteen majestic fluted piers encompass a space 133 feet long by 82 feet wide and 40 feet high, where the warm earth colors are repeated.

Unfortunately, when the bank opened on March 17, 1930, the great quantities of brass, Roman travertine, Botticino marble, and other luxurious materials in this grand space were embarrassing to its new owners. In the throes of the severest depression in

[208] ALAMO NATIONAL BANK BUILDING, SAN ANTONIO, TEX., EXTERIOR

[209] ALAMO NATIONAL BANK, BANKING ROOM

American history, banks needed to attract new clients, including working men, and the high style of the Banking Room seemed intended to do just the opposite. In the words of Ben Head, a former employee, it resembled "more a Claudian hall than a refuge to the man in overalls." [1]

Banks became increasingly unpopular in the dark days of the 1930s and were often the scapegoats of a desperate population. Accused of hoarding, they were charged by some with being the sole cause of the country's economic crisis. Luxurious bank buildings almost invited rock throwing, it seemed, and reports of broken windows and other acts of violence were frequent in some areas of the country. Nothing happened to the Alamo Bank in San Antonio, perhaps partly because it was also an office building.

The building appealed to professionals and businessmen. Local oilmen moved the San Antonio Petroleum Club from the Milam Building to the fourth floor of the Alamo National Bank Building, and lawyers, doctors, accountants, optometrists, architects, drilling companies, and detective agencies eventually filled the building nearly to capacity. Even after Black Tuesday and the severity of the depression, by 1934 "optimism was in the saddle," and throughout years of hope and despair the building and its occupants survived. [2]

Many of the banks of the 1920s were later remodeled radically to remove all traces of luxury and imperialism, but the

Alamo National Bank has undergone only modest changes. Old lamp fixtures were removed and given to an order of nuns in Boerne, Texas; tellers' cages were taken out; balconies were added on the two long sides. In addition, continuous light fixtures have replaced the old ceiling, and the air-conditioning, electrical, and ventilation systems were modernized in 1975. The original earth colors of the paneled frieze with its stars and zigzags, as appropriate to Texas now as they were in 1929, were carefully preserved. [3]

1. Ben Head, manuscript, Alamo National Bank, San Antonio, Texas.

2. Ibid.

3. Bradford R. Breuer to the author, February 3, 1984; and interview, April 10, 1984, at the bank.

NORTHWESTERN NATIONAL BANK BUILDING

1929–30
Marquette, between Sixth and Seventh streets
Minneapolis, Minnesota

Cost in 1930: $5,036,878; pcf: $0.573
Status: demolished

Handsome in its proportions, the E-shaped mass of the Northwestern National Bank Building was tripartite, with little ornament, in the mode of the stripped classicism of the times, except for the heavy swags at the top story, which was finished by a balustrade (fig. 210).

When the building was severely damaged by a fire in the early 1980s, its owners decided to tear the structure down to make room for a new business center. Accordingly, invitations for a buffet breakfast were sent by the Norwest Banks to view the "finale" of this building at its implosion on Sunday, March 11, 1984. CBS televised the "infotainment" on the news the same evening, carrying the image of the party held to view the collapse of the building.[1]

1. An invitation is in the GAPW archives in Chicago.

[210] NORTHWESTERN NATIONAL BANK BUILDING, MINNEAPOLIS, MINN., ELEVATION

FOREMAN STATE NATIONAL BANK BUILDING

1928–30
33 North LaSalle Street
Chicago, Illinois

Cost in 1930: approximately $9 million
Status: extant, with extensive remodeling of the Banking Room

[212] FOREMAN STATE NATIONAL BANK, ENTRANCE

Both up-to-date and distinguished, the silhouette of the Foreman National Bank creates the striking sense of an entryway to Chicago's financial district. The building successfully combines the old and the new by blending the setback modernity of the 1920s with many traditional touches (figs. 211, 212).

Rising rapidly to the thirty-eighth floor, the central tower is banked by symmetrical flanks to the north and the south. These flanks act as a base and help the building fit in with the older office blocks on LaSalle Street at the lower levels, while the tower relates to the newer spires elsewhere on the street.

In accord with the stripped classicism of the period, the shaft, or middle portion of the building shows little ornament. Only chevron flutings on the pilasters break up the light and give some definition in low relief to the verticals. The five-story base, however, is of rose granite speckled with light gray and black and is adorned with sculptural relief. Lines over the windows suggest pedimental openings at the fourth floor. At the top, the gradual taper is a streamlined version of the old chateau roof. From each side, two subsidiary towers act as transitions to the modern central tower, but recessed from the front plane, they are also reminiscent of buttresses.

The designer allowed the piers to sweep upward in the central tower without interruption by horizontals, a feature further accented by the suppression of the spandrel panels until the thirty-

[211] FOREMAN STATE NATIONAL BANK BUILDING, CHICAGO, ILL., EXTERIOR

third floor.[1] The spandrel panels in the center are of a darker terra-cotta than the piers and the other spandrel panels, which enhances the effect of the tower's rapid ascent. A five-story crown finishes the building majestically, like something out of a rendering by Hugh Ferriss. The suppression of the spandrels for soaring vertical effects is found in many other buildings of the period, including the nearly contemporary Board of Trade Building by Holabird and Root further down the street at Jackson Boulevard, giving continuity to the streetscape.

In plan, the building is a rectangle with the long side on LaSalle Street. Most of the second

[213] FOREMAN STATE BANK, BANKING ROOM

floor was originally occupied by the grand Banking Room. Its decorations, a sedate version of contemporary Art Deco motifs (fig. 213), were completely destroyed in a later remodeling and replaced by an American colonial decor. The public spaces of Graham, Anderson, Probst and White's nearly contemporary Twenty North Wacker office complex (part of the Chicago Civic Opera Building [*q.v.*]) now give a better idea of the firm's interior designs of this period.

Below the ground the vast area devoted to the safety deposit vaults is in the first sub-basement, while connections to the Chicago Tunnel Company's system were provided below. Across from City Hall and just a block from the Civic Center, the Foreman still dominates and pro-vides a sense of entrance to Chicago's LaSalle Street. From the second sub-basement to its place on the skyline, the building is integrated into the life of the city.

1. Working drawings, blueprints, and a model are located in the archives of the building in Chicago. The archives at GAPW contains a photograph of the presentation drawing and a bound book of twenty-five other photographs.

FIELD BUILDING
1929–34
135 South LaSalle Street
Chicago, Illinois

Cost in 1934: estimates vary from $12 million to $15 million. The cost of the site was $6 million.

Status: extant

As a stellar example of Graham, Anderson, Probst and White's office buildings of the turn of the decade, the Field Building (fig. 214) is discussed and illustrated in general terms in Part I. In addition, a number of other elements contribute to its success. The transportation system aloft, for example, was a point of pride.

Elevator service sets a new high mark of elevator efficiency with a fleet of forty high-speed elevators. Not only is the equipment of the most up-to-date design and construction, but the service far surpasses that of any other Chicago office building, with elevator requirements computed beyond the maximum estimated needs. Accordingly, duplicate elevator service is provided for the LaSalle and Clark Street entrances, each having eight local and eight express cars. Direct tower service is provided by a tier of eight elevators operating at a speed of one thousand feet a minute.[1]

A typical office floor was finished lavishly, with green mosaic terrazzo floors, shoulder-high wainscoting of white gray Arno vein marble from Colorado, and green verde antique marble bases from Vermont.

State-of-the-art heating and ventilating systems were the rule in the firm's practice, and the Field Building was no exception. It was the first Chicago office building to have enclosed radiators, which were completely concealed in metal fixtures finished to match adjoining cabinetwork, recessed under the windows, and made flush with the walls. All heating conduits were also concealed, eliminating the unsightly pipes common in most offices of the period. The Field Building used both coal and oil burners, the latter being provided in case a sudden drop in temperature in the spring or autumn required unusually quick heating.

At the time of the building's erection, Chicago's business district used only direct electrical current, but the Field Building provided alternating current. Proud of this exclusive feature, the rental brochure advised prospective tenants of its possibilities.

This enables the tenants to enjoy the advantages of electric clocks, which

[214] FIELD BUILDING, CHICAGO, ILL., ELEVATION

[215] FIELD BUILDING, LOBBY

ditioning was extended to the remaining floors in 1957.) The many advantages of this new science were extolled in the rental brochure.

Among the achievements of modern science is air-conditioning, or, more properly speaking, the invention of "man-made weather." This makes possible at all times an atmosphere that is ideal from the standpoints of health and comfort. Air-conditioning means far more than the mere introduction of good air, washed, vitalized and perfectly circulated. It means more than an automatic control of heat during the winter months. The science of air-conditioning provides for all this, and, in addition, regulates humidity and temperature during the summer months. . . . In the winter, a constant temperature, correct for ideal working conditions, is maintained with the right amount of humidity for health and disease-resistance. During the summer, not only is air filtered and washed clean of dirt and dust, but the temperature is cooler than outside, and the air is without the excessive humidity that causes so much discomfort and decreases working efficiency.[3]

are not available for direct current use. Radio is fast making a place for itself for business as well as for pleasure, and the presence of alternating current not only gives a better reception, but affords a greater range of models from which to select. Electric fans likewise are much easier to procure for alternating than for direct current, and the same is true of other

electrical devices which may be required. Needless to say, every office is supplied with an abundance of electrical outlets.[2]

At the time of its completion, the Field Building was the only large office building in Chicago having a central air-conditioning system, but it was confined to the first four floors. (Air-con-

While Americans were erecting their Art Deco buildings, the avant-garde Europeans were developing the emerging International Style. Both movements were concerned with the visual and cultural aspects of mechanization, and both rejected the classical, academic, official forms of the past in the search for a truly modern expression. On both sides of the Atlantic architects and designers were enamoured of the sleek utilitarian

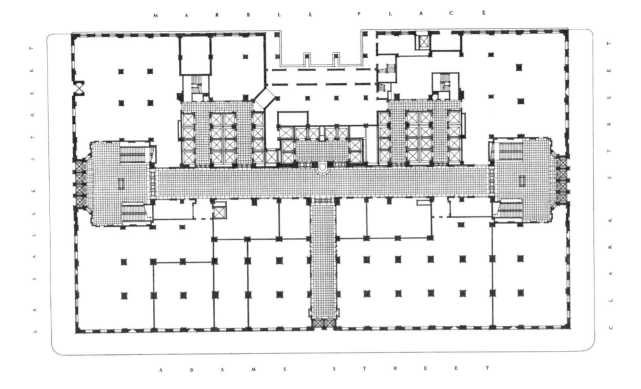

[216] FIELD BUILDING, PLAN

lines of ships, trains, locomotives, and airplanes, and they sought inspiration from the muse of transportation. The Field Building's use of nautical bridges on different levels in the lobby is a good example of this tendency (fig. 215). But the bases of European and American theoretical positions were different. The Europeans, having suffered the devastations of World War I on their own soil, were motivated by a need to provide a better world at a deep social level, and their architecture was related to an affirmation of a widely shared utopian vision. Their architecture and city-planning was radically different from what had gone before. Based on the expression of a new order, the new architecture was to make a better, more beautiful life possible for all classes. In New York and Chicago, and in the rest of the nation as well, few American architects had these social goals. Most were content

to continue to use the tried-and-true axial planning they had inherited from the academic tradition of the École des Beaux-Arts (fig. 216).

To bring their buildings up-to-date, they used every structural means to make them bigger and economically more productive for their clients. To compete with their rivals for tenants they used every new device in elevators and heating, ventilating, and air-conditioning systems. They embellished the exterior forms with fashionable motifs—this year, Egyptian; next year, Mayan; the year after, jaunty nautical imagery. Their *raison d'être* was to attract customers and to make a profit for their owners, but sometimes, in the best of circumstances, high aesthetic standards were reached as well. In the Field Building, erected during the darkest days of the depression, the architects' choice of materials, the perfectionism of their

planning and craftsmanship, their commitment to state-of-the-art service systems, and their stylish forms created a work of architecture among the best of its time and place.[4]

1. *The Field Building,* rental brochure, GAPW archives, Chicago, Ill.

2. Ibid.

3. Ibid.

4. Because of existing leases the building was erected in two sections. The first, on the site of the Home Insurance Building by William LeBaron Jenney on LaSalle Street, ran ninety-five feet east on Adams and was begun October 31, 1931. The second section, more than twice the area of the first, was begun sometime in 1932. When the tower was finished in the fall of 1934, this second section comprised about 80 percent of the whole project. *See also* "The Architects' Club Exhibition," *Treads & Risers,* March 1930, p. 16; "The Field Building," *Office Building World,* October 1931, p. 6.

CIVIC OPERA BUILDING

1927–29
20 Wacker Drive
Chicago, Illinois

Cost in 1929: $23,385,000
Status: extant, in good condition. Additions were made to the roofs of the central portion and the wings to provide for air-conditioning equipment in the 1950s. Some of the terra-cotta pediments were removed at that time.

One of Graham, Anderson, Probst and White's greatest works, and one of Chicago's finest buildings, the Civic Opera graces the western border of the Loop with its dynamic, elegant form (fig. 217). From its inception the building was conceived as part of a new, faster moving urban world. Since links to nearby transportation routes would serve both business and opera admirably, the easy connections to the building from cars, multilevel rapid transit, and locomotives seemed to assure its success to the scions of the Jazz Age. In addition, the new opera building would be at the center of the development anticipated in the western part of the Loop as soon as all the transportation systems were completed. "Wacker Drive was talked of for years and it has not fully arrived," a contemporary wrote, "but it bids fair to attain the glory of Michigan Avenue."[1]

Ease of access is perhaps an outstanding reason for the rapid growth of the area. Adjacent transportation facilities include the surface street car lines, the electric railways and the steam railroads using the North Western and Union Stations. The site is virtually the hub of a street and boulevard system that will make the building easily approachable by automobile from all parts of the city. From the north automobile traffic will use the already completed Wacker Drive. From the south, when the river straightening project is completed, Franklin Street will be virtually a continuation of Wacker Drive. Canal Street taps the southwestern part of the city, Washington Boulevard runs directly west. From the northwest motorists will use the 160′ wide Avondale Avenue artery, plans for which were recently approved by the city council.[2]

In addition, rapid transit lines stopping at Madison and Washington streets and the superhighways envisioned for the near future, would attract operagoers, commuters, and businessmen alike. If some conservatives felt that the location had not yet proved itself, ample evidence indicated that it was well on its way.[3]

At the river's edge the lowest story of the building is marked by suppressed arches. Here the deeply raked joins of the limestone cladding create darker shadows to give further weight to the base and to suggest its practical character servicing a loading dock.

The exterior of the auditorium portion is solid wall to the eighth floor finished with a row of grilled oriels and a course of giant-order windows that are followed by a frieze of theatrical masks, with piers extending above the roofline. The wings are given subtle vertical subdivisions by varying the design of the spandrels. Protruding or recessed bays give the tall central tower subtle subdivisions as well. Within this scheme the setbacks, transitions, and rooflines are embellished with terra-cotta finials, trumpets, lyres, masks, and laurel wreaths, which enliven the play of light on the varied surfaces. To set off the top, the spandrel panels and the window frames in the upper six stories are darker than those below adding deeper notes of finality to the growing crescendo. At last, great broken pediments allow the sky to come through at the top, and the brilliant copper green of the chateau roof proclaims the finale.

The plan (fig. 19) indicates the division of the main spaces on the first floor. There are three street entrances to the building, one near Madison which opens into the Civic Opera lobby, one in the center which serves as an entrance to the lobby of the office building, and one to the foyer of the Civic Theatre (878 seats). Elevators and stage equipment are carefully sandwiched in between. Since the western elevation is along the Chicago River, the stage doors open on Wacker Drive.

As the longitudinal section (fig. 20) shows, the lofty grand foyer, the pitch of the balconies, and the descending ceiling heights reach a climax in the framed setting of the proscenium arch (fig. 218). The space neces-

[217] CIVIC OPERA BUILDING (TWENTY WACKER DRIVE BUILDING), CHICAGO, ILL., EXTERIOR

sary for the stage equipment determines the height of the rear portion of the building to the west, while offices occupy the two wings. The low portion along the river, between the two wings, and the high back of rental suites to the west give the building its nickname, "Insull's Throne."

Samuel Insull, the leading entrepreneur in the enterprise, was the president of Commonwealth Edison, the nation's largest electrical company. He had assumed the presidency of the Chicago Civic Opera Company in 1922 and continued in that capacity until 1932.

The interior design, one of the greatest achievements of the firm and discussed in Part I (figs. 18, 21, 22), had many special features. Chief designer Alfred Shaw studied the designs of many theaters and opera houses, both in the United States and abroad, and consulted with many local theater groups. He spoke later of the stage area with considerable pride. "The stage . . . is by far the most modern in the world, a miraculous and thrilling installation. It has a gridiron 145' high and a mechanically movable floor and cyclorama; electrical equipment not equaled by any; storage for practically a whole season's repertory is provided in the house itself." [4]

As high as a fourteen-story building, the opera's stage is 75 feet deep and 120 feet wide, the largest in the country at the time. A 75-foot elevator carried backdrops to storage racks 35 feet below, where three thousand drops can be stored. The theater's light bridges, gridiron floor, and working curtains operated by hydraulic cylinders, were state-of-the-art mechanical equipment at the time. [5]

While Shaw was at work creating the design, Ernest R. Graham; Magnus Gundersen, the structural engineer; and Paul E. Sabine, the acoustical engineer, were hard at work on their respective problems. Sigurd Naess, who did the initial plans, had provided office space on the river side of the building for commercial income, but this added extra problems for the structural engineers. Graham arrived at a solution in his characteristic fashion. As retired designer Clifford Noonan reported:

One day Mr. Graham came in just loaded for bear and said, "We're going to start all over. Eliminate the office space on the river side of the building entirely and go up with a higher tower on the Wacker Drive side." [6]

[218] CIVIC OPERA BUILDING, MAIN AUDITORIUM

Several other conditions faced Gundersen, most of them caused by the building's adjacency to the Chicago River and the clear spans required on the first floor for the Civic Opera and Civic Theatre, both of them with large office buildings above. Since a mezzanine and two balconies extend across the auditorium, great skill and ingenuity were needed to maintain sight lines and erect the structure within the limited headroom. Both a cantilever bal-cony and fulcrum girders were used in the solution.[7]

Above all else, of course, the design of the interior had to conform to the primary consideration of acoustical engineering. The great reputation of the old Auditorium Theatre (Adler and Sullivan, 1889) made the problems acute. The Auditorium was not only one of the best models, but also the nearest, and it was close in size to the Chicago Civic Opera Building that was in-tended to replace it. (The Auditorium seated 3,400; the Civic Opera, 3,600.) Acoustical engineer Paul Sabine kept three essentials in mind.

First, contours should be such as to eliminate the possibility of there being undesirable reflections and concentration of reflected sound. Second, contours should be such that the reflection of sound from the bounding surfaces will serve the useful purpose of reinforcing the direct sound, particularly for those in the rear portion of the hall, and third, the total sound absorption in the hall should be adjusted to the volume, so as to give a desirable reverberation time. The first and second requirements are not independent. They are perhaps only the negative and positive statements of the same thing,—namely, to provide that the inevitable reflections from walls and ceiling shall promote rather than interfere with good hearing.[8]

In Sabine's view the spatulate shape of the Chicago Civic Opera Building's auditorium provided one advantage over the old Auditorium Theatre. The narrowness of the rectangular plan (necessary because the slight curve eastward in the Chicago River reduced the size of the block at the site) made reflections from the side walls stronger, improving the hearing conditions in the extreme rear seats of the main floor under the boxes and in the upper balcony.[9]

Finally, there was the matter of reverberation time to consider. If reverberation time is too long, the overlap blurs the fine effects of music. If it is not long enough, tone is dulled and volume is lost, an effect especially objectionable to the performers who do not sense the appropriate musical feedback. A golden mean between these two extremes is sought. Once again, the Auditorium Theatre was carefully studied and efforts made to copy its remarkable acoustics. Since the absorbing power of materials has an important effect on reverberation time, the architects consulted with Sabine to obtain results similar to those in the

Auditorium. By the appropriate installation of wall coverings, carpeting, and upholstered chairs, the empty auditorium of the Civic Opera was brought to a reverberation time of 1.88 seconds compared to the Auditorium's 1.90 seconds with a capacity audience. The average reverberation time among all the concert halls studied was 1.43 seconds. Ideally, reverberation time in smaller auditoriums is 1.4 seconds, with a tolerance of 0.2 seconds either way.[10] While the science of acoustics has come a long way since Sabine's time, many of the basics applied to the design of the Chicago Civic Opera auditorium remain the same.[11]

Today the Civic Opera auditorium is still somewhat short of an abstract acoustical ideal, but this is the case in most other halls with such a large capacity. To the average opera lover, however, the musical difference between the Civic Opera auditorium and smaller halls is not as great as the visual difference. The great distance between the stage and the upper row of the last balcony in the Civic Opera auditorium compared, for example, to the intimate distance between audience and stage in Covent Garden, London, is cause for the comment that in London you are in the same room with the performers, while in Chicago you share with them a covered space. Since American opera is not state supported, and the economics of modern stage production demand such large audiences, the huge size of the Civic Opera auditorium has probably, in the long run, played a more vital role in the fiscal health of both the

building and the company than its architects ever anticipated.

The Civic Theatre, in the Washington Street wing of the building, has a seating capacity of 878 and was specially designed for experimental or more intimate productions (fig. 22). Built as a possible setting for Insull's friends in theatrical circles, its stage area rises seven stories.

The rental offices begin on the third floor of the main tower and on the fourth and fifth floors of the wings, thus all the space above the seventh floor of this U-shaped building and in the tower is for offices.

The whole is both stately and majestic. The enduring quality of all aspects of the design seems to combine the best of the old with the best of the new, to modernize tradition without compromising it. The custom-designed light fixtures in the lobby, among many countless details, are a beautiful example of this creative combination of the traditional and the contemporary.

In spite of the dreams of its original guarantors,[12] the Chicago Opera Company never owned either its own home or any part of the building, but today, as the Lyric Opera, its regular season is fully subscribed in the sumptuous house designed for it in 1927. While the skyscraper office tower above provides income only for its owner, its name and its tower proclaim the importance of the opera on the skyline and mark its place in the fabric of the city. (For other aspects of the history of the building, see Part I.)[13]

1. "Big Business, Grand Opera," *Economist*, January 8, 1927, p. 112.

2. *Twenty Wacker Drive,* rental brochure, GAPW archives, Chicago, Ill., p. 1.

3. Buildings completed, under construction, or proposed for the area included the Builders' Building, the Morton Building, the Engineering Building, the Marshall Field Wholesale Building, the Chicago Daily News Building, the Chicago and North Western Railroad Station, Union Station, and the Chicago Mercantile Exchange.

4. Alfred P. Shaw, "Modern Opera Houses in Europe and America," in *Living Architecture,* ed. Arthur Woltersdorf (Chicago: A. Kroch, 1930), pp. 41–54.

5. Anne Lee, "The Chicago Civic Opera Building," *Architectural Forum* 52 (April 1930): 490–514.

6. Clifford Noonan, interview, 1987.

7. For a detailed explanation see Magnus Gundersen, "Structural Design of the Chicago Civic Opera Building," *Architectural Forum* 52 (April 1030): 595–98.

8. Paul E. Sabine, "Acoustics of the Chicago Civic Opera House," *Architectural Forum* 52 (April 1930): 599–604.

9. Ibid., p. 601.

10. Ibid., p. 604.

11. A re-evaluation was brought on by Maria Callas, who had asked that the orchestra be placed behind her rather than in the pit. The unfavorable results led to the hiring of Heinrich Keilholz, an acoustical expert, who made some other recommendations to improve the sound in his "Report on existing acoustical conditions in the auditorium of the Opera House in Chicago," March 11, 1958. This document is in the Alfred P. Shaw papers at the Art Institute of Chicago, Chicago, Ill.

12. A $10 million first mortgage loan from the Metropolitan Life Insurance Company and the sale of 100,000 shares of preferred stock at $100 a share were arranged by Samuel Insull, president of the Chicago Civic Opera Company in 1927. A portion was purchased in large blocks by some of the outstanding civic leaders of the Chicago business community. Insull then organized the Chicago Music Foundation for which all of the common stock of the building was held in trust. A second mortgage of $3,385,000 was obtained from the Continental Bank of Chicago, and Insull personally guaranteed the loan.

13. Other sources on the building include ink on linen drawings and photographs in the building and in the GAPW archives; a rendering of Insull's office in the collection of the Art Institute of Chicago; and the *Specifications Book* now in the office of the owner, Dino D'Angelo, at the Straus Building (*q.v.*) at 310 South Michigan Avenue, Chicago, Ill. *See also* R. D. Berry, "Stage Equipment and Lighting," *Architectural Forum* 52 (January 1936): 45–48; "Chicago Civic Opera," *Architecture and Building* 61 (December 1929): cover, 359–60, 363–65; "The Civic Opera," *Good Furniture* 34 (March 1930): 163–66; Michael Forsyth, *Buildings for Music: The Architect, the Musician, and the Listener from the Seventeenth Century to the Present Day* (Cambridge, Mass.: MIT Press, 1985); C. A. Frazier, "Mechanical Equipment of the Chicago Civic Opera Building," *Architectural Forum* 52 (April 1930): 610–14; "History of the Tower Club," manuscript, Chicago Civic Opera Building archives, Chicago; "The Lighting Fixtures in the Chicago Civic Opera House and Civic Theater Designed and Executed by Sterling Bronze Company," *Metal Arts,* March 1930, pp. 131–32; F. Loucks, "Electrical Installations 20 Wacker Drive Building," *Architectural Forum* 52 (April 1930): 608–9; "The Marble Halls of the Chicago Civic Opera Building," *Through The Ages* 7 (March 1930): 12–17; "The New Home of the Chicago Civic Opera Company," *Theater Arts Monthly* 12 (August 1928): 569; "Proposed Building for Chicago Civic Opera," *American Architect* 133, no. 2544 (May 5, 1928).

MERCHANDISE MART

1928–30
Wacker Drive between Orleans and Wells
Chicago, Illinois

Cost in 1930: reported as both $32 million and $38 million. In 1984, the Merchandise Mart was assessed at $101.9 million, the most valuable building on Chicago's booming Near North Side and the fourth most valuable building in the city.

Status: extant, in good condition. Recently the roof was repaired and the exterior cladding cleaned under the supervision of Graham, Anderson, Probst and White, William Surman, president.

America's two great transportation systems—waterways and railroads—meet and connect with each other in the heart of Chicago, the site of the Merchandise Mart (figs. 219, 220).

Linking the Atlantic Ocean, via the St. Lawrence River and the Great Lakes, to the canal system that led to the Mississippi River and the Gulf of Mexico, Chicago was the principal railway transfer point in the movement of cargo from Maine to California in the nineteenth century. Since it had become one of the largest freight centers in the world, it seemed possible to early entrepreneurs that the city could also become one of the largest wholesale centers in the world.

Chicago businessmen of the 1880s were not slow to seize an opportunity, but they needed a building type that was both a warehouse and a store, a structure that could handle many different functions—shipping and receiving, storage, display, and sales. As early as 1885, Marshall Field ordered a wholesale store from architect H. H. Richardson. By the mid-1920s, business had increased to such a degree that Marshall Field and Company outgrew the Richardson building and began the search for

[219] MERCHANDISE MART, CHICAGO, ILL., AERIAL VIEW. REPRINTED WITH PERMISSION, GEONEX CHICAGO AERIAL SURVEY

a good location for a new wholesale store.

A site in the bend of the Chicago River seemed an ideal place to provide access to the water system, and the five-acre parcel

[220] MERCHANDISE MART, ELEVATION

of land there was covered with the tracks of the North Western Railway. If the chairman of Marshall Field and Company could secure the air rights and build over the tracks, the new store would have direct access to both transportation systems. Fortunately, the North Western Railway was interested. It had been using the tracks for major operating purposes, but needed to develop the grounds further for a new in-city, less-than-carload freight terminal. The railroad felt it could make common cause with Marshall Field and Company. In the agreement the two parties worked out, the North Western sold its air rights over the level of twenty-three feet above the water surface and 450 parcels of land for column footings to Marshall Field and Company, reserving the rest for its new terminal.[1]

This railroad station connected with an already existing underground freight transportation system. Narrow-gauge tracks within this intricate network carried cargo to huge elevators that descended forty feet below the ground where the Chicago Tunnel Company's lines received it for delivery along sixty-two miles of tracks. Planned in interlocking rectangles underneath the city, these tracks connected all the major department stores and office buildings with all the major railroads.[2] This subterranean railroad not only transported merchandise, it delivered coal to heat the buildings and carried away the ashes for disposal. At its busiest, the system could move 70,000 cars a year, about 235 a day. When it was finished, the Merchandise Mart would have connections to

[221] MERCHANDISE MART, ENTRANCE ELEVATION

a nearly ideal delivery system, and the railway would have connections to the largest wholesale house in the world with a total gross floor area of 4,083,400 square feet.

This collaboration between Marshall Field and Company and the North Western Railway embodied Herbert Hoover's observation that "a significant modern development in the American system of business was organized cooperation." Consolidation and concentration were key ideas of the time, as businesses merged and one tycoon bought out several smaller ty-

coons to form an empire. Business on this imperial scale is powerfully suggested by the early illuminated nighttime view of the Merchandise Mart (fig. 221).

When the Merchandise Mart opened, an advertisement in the *Atlantic Monthly* declared "mass production, science and invention have rendered the 'old competition' (between manufacturers of the same type of product) futile, costly and therefore economically fatal."[3] The up-to-date manufacturer, interested in the benefits of organized cooperation and concentrated marketing, the ad continued, would

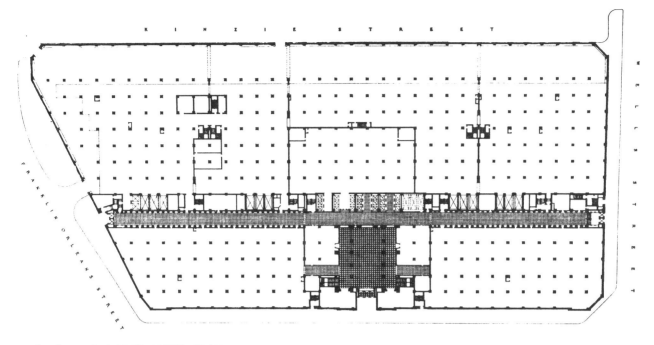

[222] MERCHANDISE MART, PLAN

[223] MERCHANDISE MART, LOBBY

be attracted to tenancy in the Merchandise Mart because this colossus of the marketplace exemplified the idea of a coalition among general merchandise manufacturers, wholesale distributors, and importers. In addition, they were all concentrated under a single roof at the center of one of the country's largest trading areas, at the transportation center of the nation. Focused like this, manufacturers could create a market where both the buyer and the seller saved time and energy. Out-of-town businessmen preferred a centralized facility that spared them expensive trips from city to city and taxi-hopping from place to place all over Chicago. Instead, the wide, 650-foot-long corridors of the Merchandise Mart, with its restaurants and other amenities, formed a city within a city, where the buyer could see and select from many different lines. The seller, in turn, saved the costs of travel trunks and other field-sales expenses. Speed of delivery seemed assured by the presence of the docks along the waterfront and the network of railway lines underneath.

The combination of two such facilities with their connection to an elaborate underground railway was unique to the city of Chicago. The tunnel system for freight and refuse, which seems like a model solution for keeping the streets above clear of delivery trucks and trash, transported as much as 650,000 tons in 1920, but is unusable for its original purpose today. The later construction of the subway system cut off vital sections of the tunnel system from each other, and the trucking industry took over the transportation of goods. When

Carl Condit wrote about the Chicago Tunnel Company in 1973, he remarked that its few remaining vestiges were "as completely hidden as the artifacts of ancient cultures."

The fate of the building above has been far better, and it stands in full use today. Its sturdy broad shape is like an anchor on the river for the more exuberant Palmolive Building, Wrigley Building, and Tribune Tower on nearby Michigan Avenue. By day it is more prosaic, but every effort was made to obviate the immensity of its great expanse. The central tower projects slightly, as do the towers on the corners. In addition, the top three stories are recessed, and corners everywhere are canted. The decorated surfaces are covered with a variety of stylized diagonals, diamonds, chevrons, and interlocking Ms.

The broad esplanade in front of the building allows a stream of visitors a view over the Chicago River, although the simple rostral light fixtures that once articulated the edge of the sidewalk have now been replaced by gigantic sculpted heads. The designers used heavy rustication and suppressed arches at the loading dock to indicate the more utilitarian function of the building at the river's edge.

In plan, the Merchandise Mart is an irregular trapezoid, because Orleans Street on its west side lies on an angle to the ruling grid of the city (fig. 222). The freight and passenger elevators that are such vital parts of the operation of the building lie along the long arcades that extend the whole width of the building from Wells Street to Orleans Street. Within these arcades on the two lower levels are

shops, restaurants, and other public services, including a barbershop. The main lobby (fig. 223) is defined by eight square piers of fluted marble, the frieze above composed of geometrized Native North American and Mayan decorative elements. The murals by Jules Guerin above the information desk depict "trade around the world," from camel caravans in Istanbul to Mississippi River steamboats.

Within the spaces of the Merchandise Mart many of the nation's most talented designers created settings fr the best furniture and other artifacts of the times. The barbershop itself might have served as a setting for an early 1930s Hollywood movie, a Busby Berkeley extravaganza of musical chairs (fig. 224). The Merchandise Mart was for many years the home of the National Broadcasting Company's Midwest studio (fig. 225), where such popular programs as "The Breakfast Club" originated.

During the Great Depression, Marshall Field and Company abandoned its wholesale operations in the Merchandise Mart and sold the building to Joseph P. Kennedy for about a third of its original cost. After World War II, business at the market expanded rapidly, greatly increasing the basis of the Kennedy family fortune. The railroad operations beneath the building did not fare so well. Trucking companies took over the merchandise freight business, and today the area beneath the Merchandise Mart is used largely for storage.

[224] MERCHANDISE MART, BARBERSHOP

[225] MERCHANDISE MART, NATIONAL BROADCASTING COMPANY STUDIO

Above, the vast warren of showroom spaces that comprises most of the building is in full use today by furniture companies and other manufacturers. Widely placed steel piers offer latitude in spatial treatment, and the building still accommodates showroom settings by some of the world's leading architects.[4]

1. Carl W. Condit, *Chicago, 1910–29: Building, Planning, and Urban Technology,* pp. 132–37, p. 173 notes 49, 50.

2. Ibid., p. 289.

3. "Merchandise Mart," *Atlantic Monthly,* September 1929, advertisement.

4. For further information see "Air Rights Office Building in Chicago," *Engineering News-Record* 102 (April 25, 1929): 664–67; Ernst Gerson, "Amerikanische Geschaeftsbauten und Wohnhauser," *Wasmuths Monatshefte* 14 (January 1930): 22; "Merchandise Mart," *American Architect,* June 20, 1928, p. 846; "Merchandise Mart," *Architecture and Building,* March 1931, p. 66; F. F. Sengstock, "The Largest Building in the World: The Merchandise Mart," *Western Architect,* December 1930, pp. 205–7; Carroll William Westfall, "Chicago's Wholesale Markets, 1885 to the Present," paper presented to the Society of Architectural Historians, Victoria, British Columbia, Canada, 1981.

JOHN G. SHEDD AQUARIUM

1925–30
1200 South Lake Shore Drive, on Lake Michigan
Chicago, Illinois

Cost in 1930, architects' figures: $2,811,446; Shedd figures:
$3,250,000, including furnishings.
Status: extant, in good condition; landmark, National Register of
Historic Places, February 27, 1987. A major addition by Lohan
Associates on the southeast part of the building was completed in
1991.

The Shedd Aquarium (fig. 9), a triumph of design, is Chicago's most brilliantly sited building. The potential of the project was fully realized through the cooperative efforts of its donor, director, architect, the commissioners of Chicago's South Park Board, and the Chicago City Council. Inspired by a vision they all shared, the World's Columbian Exposition of 1893, the men involved knew from their many visits to the White City what city planning could accomplish in superb siting, expansive promenades, striking vistas, and sparkling buildings.

In 1909, the men involved in these various groups had worked together to make this "City Beautiful" a permanent reality by promoting the Plan of Chicago. Calling for an arc of cultural institutions along Michigan Avenue, a portion of the Plan included an extension of the parks along the southern end of the Chicago harbor for museums. In 1919, the City Council enacted the Lake Front Ordinance, detailing the respective responsibilities of the Illinois Central Railroad and the Chicago Park District in the development of the lakefront south of Grant Park.

The Columbian Exposition was a model not only of cooperation among a great many business, political, and cultural leaders, but also for producing a dazzling array of exhibitions on a grand scale. Ever since the fair closed its doors, many of Chicago's affluent civic leaders had dedicated themselves to creating permanent institutions offering scientific and artistic exhibitions to enhance the attractiveness of the city. Chicago had become the source of great fortune for a number of entrepreneurs and merchants. Philanthropy and a desire to create a significant monument or cultural institution became a contagious trend in the decades following the fair. Marshall Field had given the city $8 million for a museum to house the collections assembled for the exposition, and his former stockboy, John Graves Shedd, hoped to give the city an aquarium.

John G. Shedd (1850–1926) was born in Alstead, New Hampshire, the son of a farmer. At sixteen he left home to work as a clerk in a fruit and bakery shop in Bellows Falls, Vermont, and in other stores in the area until 1872 when he arrived in Chicago and got a job as a stockboy and salesman in the linen department of Field, Leiter and Company. In 1893, he became a partner in the firm, and after Marshall Field's death in 1906, he became president. He was a member of the Commercial Club committee that supported Daniel Burnham's 1909 Plan of Chicago. After his retirement in 1923, he led an active life as a supporter of many other cultural institutions in Chicago.

In another example of the cooperation between public and private realms that made possible so much of the building of the 1920s, securing the aquarium's splendid location was the result of long negotiations. Acting as Shedd's agent, James Simpson, an executive with Marshall Field and Company, met with the man who had been Field's architect on so many occasions, Ernest R. Graham, and members of the South Park Commission for lunch at the Chicago Club on September 18, 1923. An excerpt from Simpson's letter to Shedd soon afterwards gives us insight into the diplomatic intricacies of these negotiations.

I have been moving rather rapidly on the aquarium project since I saw you Saturday noon. In the first place, I was driving home Saturday afternoon through Lincoln Park when a machine escorted by six to a dozen motorcycles buzzed through the park, and as they passed I turned around to see who the celebrities might be that were thus escorted and saw that Mr. William Hale Thompson [mayor of Chicago] was one of the occupants. We waved at each other and when they passed me a few hundred feet they stopped and Mr. Thompson signaled me to get out of

[226] JOHN G. SHEDD AQUARIUM, CHICAGO, ILL., ELEVATION

my car and come up to theirs. He got out and shook hands with me and asked me to have my machine follow and get in his and ride along with him. When I got in I found Governor Small in his machine and also John Dill Robertson.

Mr. Thompson had heard that I had called at the Lincoln Park aquarium a day or two ago and he wanted to talk aquarium. . . . He elaborated at great length on the desirability of an aquarium for Chicago located on the lake front, etc., and gave a lot of statistics and figures about the hatching of fish and other things which were of great interest to me. . . . To this Governor Small assented with considerable enthusiasm. . . . This morning, however, Mr. Charles L. Hutchinson called me up and said that he would like to talk with me further about the project. . . . I suggested to him that the ideal location for an aquarium would be at the foot of Roosevelt Road, with its axis in the center of the road. He debated for a while the possibility of doing

this, because of legal restrictions on the land, but he finally took out from his files . . . a letter from George P. Merrick written some years ago citing the Supreme Court's decision prohibiting buildings being constructed North of the North line of Park Row. This, of course, made possible the location of an aquarium on the site which I had suggested to him. . . . This noon I lunched with Mr. Sunny, Mr. Foster of the South Park Board, and Mr. Graham at the Chicago Club. Mr. Sunny asked me if I would state what was in my mind, and I talked to him about an hour outlining in general the following thoughts, predicated on interesting someone to supply the money for the construction of a building that will be satisfactory in every way to the South Park Commissioners:

First: That the South Park Commissioners should provide a site at the foot of Roosevelt Road for the proper location of such a building. Building to face west, but as all its exposure, south, north, east and

west, would be viewed from long distances on all sides, it would be necessary to construct such building with proper consideration to its very prominent location.

Second: That the South Park Board would agree to maintain and operate such aquarium, and tie up in some way by agreements that might be determined on so as to insure the perpetuity of such maintenance and operation. I named the sum of $100,000 a year or $150,000 a year as having been mentioned by people who were presumed to have some knowledge on the subject, but stated, of course, that this would be subject to verification, check and discussion.

Third: That I assumed the name of the donor of the money for the construction of such building would be attached to the project.

Fourth: That while I did not have an entire plan worked out in my mind, I recited the obstacles and difficulties that we have had in bringing the zoological garden project to a satisfactory conclusion only yesterday, after having surmounted a great many obstacles and agreeing on a contract with the Board of County Commissioners. I suggested that from my viewpoint it would probably be desirable to organize an aquarium society composed of some 200 members, representing the various religions, races and interests in our city, but dominated by the most substantial citizens of the very highest type. That such body would elect a governing or executive committee composed of perhaps 15 or 25 men, among whom should be a fair representation of the South Park Commissioners—say not to exceed five, possibly less, out of a total executive committee numbering 25.[1]

In addition to their fond personal memories of visits to the Fisheries Building (Henry Ives Cobb, 1893) at the World's Columbian Exposition, the men involved in the planning knew that aquariums were exceedingly popular tourist attractions. They knew that more people visited the aquariums at fairs in Chicago, Atlanta, St. Louis, Buffalo, and Omaha than any other exhibits. The New York Aquarium attracted more visitors than all the city's other natural history institutions together.

To help them draft and expedite the necessary enabling legislation with the state legislature in Springfield, Illinois, a group of local citizens organized as the Aquarium Society invited George F. Morse, a zoologist and director of the Boston Zoo, to be a consultant. The state legislature had power over the park districts in Chicago, an arrangement that had initially been made to protect the parks from the vi-

cissitudes of local Chicago politics. Legislative approval and passage of amendments to the Parks Museums Act securing tax revenues for partial support were received after some delay, and the society subsequently appointed Morse as its first director.

With the location,[2] financial,[3] and political problems solved, the designers began the planning process. In the fall of 1925, Walter H. Chute, associate director of the aquarium, and Leslie Stokes, engineer for Graham, Anderson, Probst and White, toured European aquariums in Naples, Nice, Monaco, Paris, Leipzig, Frankfurt, Amsterdam, Antwerp, Berlin, London, and Brighton. Later that year, Chute and Marvin Polk, construction architect for the firm, visited aquariums in New York, Philadelphia, Washington, D.C., and Detroit. In early 1926, Mario Schiavoni, project designer for the firm, visited aquariums on the West Coast, paying special attention to the newly built Steinhart Aquarium in San Francisco.[4] Before they were finished, the firm would present two plans to Shedd, a $2-million model and a much larger one costing $3 million. Shedd chose the larger.

The dazzling clarity of the marble octagon of the Shedd Aquarium (fig. 226) links Lake Michigan, Lake Shore Drive, and the other cultural institutions surrounding the southern arm of the harbor (see Part I). The orderly progression of three cultural institutions, from the rectangle of the Field Museum, to the octagon of the Shedd Aquarium, to the circle of the Adler Planetarium, completes the spirit, if not the letter, of

the 1909 Plan of Chicago as testament to a moment in Chicago history when the irregularities of political difference and personal gain were subordinated to the greater good of the harmony of the whole city.

Within, visitors may float through the spaces (figs. 12, 13) without a thought to their path or destination. One gallery opens into another, gently guiding people along, their minds free to concentrate on the exhibitions. Spectators move effortlessly around the undersea world. The flow of the space, like a gentle tide, moves through the displays, returning always, reassuringly, to the central pool under the octagonal dome (fig. 15) so that one never feels lost. Originally, light streamed through the central dome, diminishing as it flowed ninety feet into the thirty-foot-wide, deep-blue barrel-vaulted galleries at the perimeter. The dome is now tarred over.

Schiavoni spent many weeks in stone quarries selecting marbles for the interior, and the refinement of his sensibilities is apparent on every surface. Under the dome the white Georgian marble has the translucency of seashells; the gray marbles at the edges are veined like wet sand at the water's edge; and the wainscoting, of dark green Vermont marble, is ingeniously cut and laid so that its grain simulates waves.

A wealth of dolphins, octopi, marlins, sharks, tortoises, cappa shells, and starfish enliven the bronze fixtures, and the carved plaster and terra-cotta ornament on the interior and exterior (fig. 227) (see Part I). Sculptor Eugene Romeo carved many of the fish, including the sea creatures in the pediment. A bronze octopus supports the chandelier, tiles with saltwater fish surround the archways, and the face of the clock leading to the rotunda is marked with marine life: one o'clock is a seahorse, two a lobster, and so forth.[5]

Designing the storage and circulation system required for a large aquarium proved the biggest challenge of the building's mechanics. Each of the 200 exhibition tanks and each of the 175 reserve tanks, with a total capacity of 450,000 gallons, and four storage reservoirs in the basement with a total capacity of two million gallons had to be connected to the appropriate intake and outflow conduits. As water is the lifeblood of an aquarium, its temperature, filtration, salinity, aeration, and circulation must be constantly monitored. Water is divided into five groups according to the salinity and temperature: heated salt, chilled salt, heated fresh, chilled fresh, and natural fresh. Originally, the aquarium imported its saltwater from Key West, Florida, in 160 railroad tank cars built by George Pullman especially for the job. The last shipment of water arrived in 1970; it is now made on site. From reservoirs holding two million gallons, water is pumped through pipes to tanks near the roof. From there it flows by gravity to the fish tanks on the main floor and returns to reservoirs in the basement through filters. The seventy-five miles of pipes in the system are color coded by temperature and composition. Today these systems are computer operated.

Since the aquarium is not just

[227] SHEDD AQUARIUM, ENTRANCE DETAIL

an aquatic zoo, but a museum as well, the architects provided facilities not only for care of the fish, assorted coelenterates, echinoderms, cephalopods, and so on, but also for educational functions, a library, and a small auditorium.

Advances in technology have been introduced into the aquarium over the years, but the basic design has worked well for the fish, the staff, and the public for nearly sixty years. The Shedd continues to delight visitors with the variety and liveliness of its exhibitions (containing more than five thousand specimens), and by the spatial arrangements and surroundings that make viewing and moving within the galleries such an enchanting experience. Today the purpose of a museum visit is still admirably served by this functional, well-planned, beautifully executed building.

The Shedd Aquarium was, however, one of the last of the Beaux-Arts exteriors to be built in Chicago. The forms of the ancient world that had developed over many centuries were entering a long eclipse. American motifs of the Art Deco and Art Moderne styles that originated in the mid-1920s avoided any overt references to the worlds of Greece and Rome, although in many buildings architects continued to follow Beaux-Arts planning precepts. After World War II, modernist architects abjured everything that had a round column or a capital. Not far from the Shedd Aquarium, at the Illinois Institute of Technology, Mies van der Rohe and his disciples designed some of the greatest monuments in this spirit during the two decades between 1950 and 1970. Moving along Lake Shore Drive from Mies's campus toward the heart of Chicago, one passes the Shedd Aquarium, a reminder of our ancient roots that makes it possible once again for us to place ourselves in the stream of time.[6]

1. Simpson to Shedd, September 18, 1923, John G. Shedd Aquarium archives, Chicago, Ill.

2. In the meantime, the South Park District was finishing the landfill to complete the park system south to Fifty-seventh Street where it would join the older Jackson Park. In 1928, it created the 4,000-foot-long stretch of land that completes the Chicago harbor for cultural institutions on the south.

3. Always partially supported by funds from the Chicago Park District and city real estate tax levies, the Shedd, like the Field Museum, is

nevertheless an independent agency. Today about 50 percent of its operating cost is raised by admission fees, the Shedd endowment funds, and such customer services as book and gift sales.

4. Joan Campbell, "Shedd Aquarium Tour: History and Early Influences on its Development," paper prepared for the Chicago Architecture Foundation, 1984.

5. "Ornamental Bronze Work of the John G. Shedd Aquarium," *Metal Arts* 3 (May 1930): 217–19, 222, plates 29–30; "The Crowning Feature of the John G. Shedd Aquarium," *Metal Arts* 2 (October 1929): 162.

6. Drawings of the Shedd Aquarium are located in the GAPW archives, Chicago. Others in the Art Institute of Chicago include four

blueprints and microfilms of drawings. Construction and other photographs are located in the archives of the Shedd Aquarium and GAPW; Walter H. Chute, *The John G. Shedd Aquarium* (Chicago: John G. Shedd Aquarium Society, 1932) is an oral history transcription of Chute's experiences as director of the Shedd Aquarium, 1927–64 to be found at the Shedd Aquarium and Archi-Center, Chicago; Commission on Chicago Historical and Architectural Landmarks, "John G. Shedd Aquarium," preliminary summary of information; A. F. Kline, "The Shedd Aquarium," *Through the Ages* 6 (March 1929): 3–5; "John G. Shedd Aquarium: Greek Doric Style," *Building for the Future*, May 1930, pp. 4–5; "John G. Shedd Aquarium," *Western Architect* 39 (September 1930): plates 136–38.

MARSHALL FIELD AND COMPANY STORE

1929
1700 Sherman Street
Evanston, Illinois

Cost in 1929: $850,000
Status: extant; converted to apartments in 1988

To serve Chicago's rapidly growing suburbs in the 1920s, Marshall Field and Company hired Graham, Anderson, Probst and White to design two outlying stores, in Evanston and in Oak Park. Nearly identical, the designs of the Evanston and Oak Park buildings are a combination of two different styles, French mansard and Art Deco (fig. 228), evoking up-to-date Parisian chic. A subtle variety in the window treatment enlivens the rectangular massing of the buildings and clearly defines the parts. Broad display windows open up the ground level, three-story giant-order windows unite the middle floors, and the mansard roof is pierced with dormer windows.

Fitting in well with the substantial residential architecture of these prosperous suburbs, both buildings are clad in limestone, and the traditional Marshall Field clock keeps watch on the corners. The usual Marshall Field's green bronze trim with Art Deco motifs ornaments the canopies, spandrels, flagpoles, lights, and other fixtures.

The interiors reflect the steel-cage method of the buildings' construction, but the spaces are not mechanistically apportioned.

[228] MARSHALL FIELD AND COMPANY STORE, EVANSTON, ILL., EXTERIOR

The first floor is higher than the others for grandeur, and the top story, devoted mainly to office spaces, is lower.

As the one-hundredth birthday of Marshall Field and Company approached in 1952, Hughston McBain, then chairman of the board, announced plans for a suburban "State Street" complex in Skokie, a town just west of Evanston. This prize-winning shopping center, later called Old Orchard, stretched along a rectangular mall, housing the same sort of stores and shops that bordered the Marshall Field's stores in downtown Chicago, Evanston, and Oak Park. Customers could find anything they hoped to find in the city, it was easily accessible by automobile from the nearby Edens Expressway, and there was ample free parking. The completion of the $25 million ensemble was, however, the beginning of a slow end for the store in downtown Evanston. Another shopping center near Oak Park caused the same decline in sales there. By 1985, revenue had dropped off so radically in both the Evanston and the Oak Park stores that the company sold them to developers for conversion to other uses.[1]

1. Marshall Field's also opened a suburban store in Lake Forest, Illinois, in 1929 which is still in operation; drawings and photographs of the Evanston and Oak Park stores are in the Marshall Field's archives and at GAPW, Chicago.

MARSHALL FIELD AND COMPANY STORE

1929
1144 Lake Street
Oak Park, Illinois

Cost in 1929: $810,278; pcf: $0.542
Status: extant, closed in 1989 pending conversion to office or apartment use

Almost identical to the Evanston store (q.v.), the Oak Park store (fig. 229) is somewhat smaller, only three bays wide by five long. Evanston is three bays by nine. Evanston has three entrances, Oak Park only two.

[229] MARSHALL FIELD AND COMPANY STORE, OAK PARK, ILL., DETAIL

HUGHES BRYANT BUILDING

1929–30
1002 Grand Avenue
Kansas City, Missouri

Status: extant

At the corner of Grand and Eleventh streets, the soaring shafts of the Hughes Bryant Building express the streamlined aspirations of Kansas City in the railroad age (fig. 230). The three-story base is sturdy and dignified, then the dynamic verticals soar to the top suggesting the power of the locomotive. In this spirit the setbacks are not in steps, but in smooth, graceful arcs, each pier clad in white speckled vitricote. In contrast to the angular zigzags of many skyscrapers that move upward in awkward giant steps, the Bryant Building grows taller and slenderer in smooth, finely tuned stages. The inward curves of the pier finials contribute to the ease of the transitions, suggesting that the designer also anticipated an aerodynamic form from that icon of modernity—the Chrysler Airflow automobile. The color changes from white to tan where the finials curve, which increases the sense of depth. The spandrels are clad in darker black vitricote, which enlivens the design by providing a horizontal counterpoint. The rhythm of the 1-2-4-2-1 pattern also establishes both a center and a climax over the entrance.

Retail spaces greet the pedestrian at the sidewalk levels on both Grand and Eleventh streets. Entering the lobby the visitor is surrounded by marble—delicate cream on the floors and fluted panels of a boldly veined tan on the walls, topped by a lighted

[230] HUGHES BRYANT BUILDING, KANSAS CITY, MO., ELEVATION

barrel vault with ribs decorated with golden midwestern sunflowers. Bronze fixtures catch the light of the chandeliers and reflect on the panels of the elevators that carry people to the double-loaded corridors of the office spaces above.

Like most buildings erected in 1930, the Bryant had no built-in

air-conditioning system, and cooling devices of one kind or another were added piecemeal over the years. The hodge-podge of window units, together with layers of paint and grime that covered the metalwork and dingy carpets that obscured the marble floors, eventually made the building look shabby. Making matters

[231] BRYANT BUILDING,
ORNAMENT

moving layers of paint from the bronzework, which was then polished to its original splendor.[1] After the remodeling, tenants who were still in the building decided to stay, and new ones came in, including a law firm that leased five floors.[2]

The restoration of the Bryant Building and more than a dozen others in the area no doubt will have a positive effect on the long-term health of downtown Kansas City. The effort is also an important chapter in the history of preservation in the Midwest.

1. The old heating system needed no changes. Radiant steam heating with baseboard units in each office with valve controls to regulate the comfort of each tenant had been installed in 1930, and in 1976 it was still working well. Like others of the period it was found to be not only sensible, but economical and energy efficient as well.

2. George Ehrlich, *Kansas City, Missouri: An Architectural History, 1826–1976* (Kansas City, Mo.: Historic Kansas City Foundation, 1979); "New Look, Tenants for Building," *Kansas City Star*, September 19, 1976; "The Bryant Building turns a profitable corner," *Star* Real Estate, December 26, 1982, p. 5H.

BURLINGTON STATION

1930
1001 South Tenth Street
Omaha, Nebraska

Cost in 1930: $800,000
Status: extant. Project consisted of the extensive reconstruction of an 1898 structure originally designed by Thomas R. Kimball.

worse, suburban office space around Kansas City was plentiful and attractive, and gradually clients who did choose to locate downtown preferred new buildings, which they thought conveyed a more prestigious image. Slowly the Bryant lost its good tenants, and by 1975 realtors feared the building was no longer cost-effective.

In 1975, the Bay Colony Property Company of Boston recognized the structural soundness of the building and the elegance of its underlying design and original materials. The company bought the building and restored it, installing a computerized demand-control air-conditioning system; repairing the marble flooring; cleaning, painting, or regilding the ornament (fig. 231); and re-

The fourth largest rail transportation nexus in the Midwest, Omaha boomed as a wholesale trade center in the 1920s. Reconstructing and enlarging the old Burlington Station (fig. 232) to meet the new demands, Graham, Anderson, Probst and White altered the site and the old structure so radically that it emerged a new design.

The new site plan increased the efficiency of the traffic and lent a note of elegance to the area, which was elevated on a bluff far above the tracks. New ramps and stairs breached the difficult separation between trains and passengers gracefully, as did the new steps connecting the Burlington Station with the

Union Station on the other side of the bluff. The two stations then faced each other, with similar transition structures, and provided a strong sense of place for this part of Omaha. At the newly reconstructed Burlington Station, automobile traffic arrived at the upper level, and spacious driveways were provided at the north and south ends. The architects defined the edge of this plaza with a sidewalk balustrade adorned with light globes, Parisian in their nighttime effect.

In its remodeling of the exterior of the station, the firm removed the gabled porches, the columnar peristyle, and the pitched roof and ordered new Ionic columns for the central sec-

[232] BURLINGTON STATION, OMAHA, NEBR., ELEVATION

tion.[1] It also removed the porticoes and the lobby walls with their attached columns to make room for enlarged wings on both sides. The removal of these sculptural elements and the substitution of more planar forms transformed the station from a temple into an Italian palace.

The architects made other important changes in the ground plan. By removing a stairway from the middle of the old floor they were able to create the grand interior scale associated with waiting rooms of this period. By careful adjustments, however, most of the original marble mosaic floor with its circles and fan motifs remained.[2]

The ample space of the Waiting Room (fig. 233) is now articulated by five tall, slender windows on the north and south and by five panels with fluted mouldings on the east and west. The broad frieze that runs along all four walls is decorated with circular medallions that unite the ceiling with the mosaic design of the floor below.

Although the structure of the building looks sound and the limestone cladding is in fairly good condition, the rest of the station and its surrounding plaza and drives are in poor repair. The building was for sale in 1984 and its future uncertain.

1. The old Tuscan columns now stand near the football stadium of the University of Nebraska at Lincoln.

2. Drawings on microfilm, City of Omaha, Department of Planning; *Omaha Sunday World Herald,* August 3, 1930; Robert C. Peters, ed., *A Comprehensive Program for Historic Preservation in Omaha* (Omaha: Omaha City Planning Department). This book contains a photograph of the station before remodeling around 1910.

[233] BURLINGTON STATION, WAITING ROOM

[234] UNIVERSITY OF NOTRE DAME, SOUTH BEND, IND., AERIAL VIEW

EDWARD N. HURLEY COLLEGE OF FOREIGN AND DOMESTIC COMMERCE

1930–31
Notre Dame Campus, South Quadrangle
South Bend, Indiana

Cost: The architects' records contain an error. The cost is given as $471,547, the cost per cubic foot as $0.305, and the volume as 471,547 cubic feet.

Status: extant, in excellent condition. An addition on the back does not affect any of the principal facades.

Highlighting the international aspects of the curriculum, an ocean-going, three-masted clipper ship in copper was chosen to adorn the roof of the Edward N. Hurley College of Foreign and Domestic Commerce. Hurley, chairman of the United States Shipping Board during World War I and University Laetare medalist in 1926, felt that Notre Dame's newly created College of Commerce (1921) should be international in its course offerings and degree programs. Contributing $200,000 in 1930 for the erection of a new building, Hurley, a Chicagoan, requested that Graham, Anderson, Probst and White be given the commission.[1]

The long, low, two-story building was erected to fit into the corner of the campus where the Main Quadrangle intersects with the South Quadrangle (fig. 234). A tall entrance block in the center dominates the E-shaped mass. A single entrance door protrudes from the massive entrance block, which is lighted from above by three pairs of lancet windows (fig. 235).

A two-story memorial hall distinguishes the lobby where a dramatic, deep-tiered pit encircles an eight-foot terrestrial globe with the trade routes of the world inscribed on its surface. Above, neo-Gothic window frames and doorways lead the eye to the adjoining wings, which contain offices and classrooms (fig. 236).

[235] NOTRE DAME, EDWARD N. HURLEY COLLEGE OF FOREIGN AND DOMESTIC COMMERCE, ELEVATION

The style of the building, probably designed by Alfred P. Shaw,[2] suits Notre Dame and influenced Maginnis and Walsh in its law school building across the campus, and Kervick-Fagan in the Cushing Hall of Engineering where the same idiom and materials were used. When the College of Business Administration was expanded in 1968, Graham, Anderson, Probst and White designed a new building, which "turned out to be an extremely successful and harmonious use of the Gothic in a contemporary mode."[3]

1. Edward Nash Hurley Papers, University of Notre Dame Archives, South Bend, Ind.; Thomas J. Schlereth, *The University of Notre Dame: A Portrait of Its History and Campus* (South Bend: University of Notre Dame Press, 1976), p. 175; ibid, pp. 82–202.

2. *Notre Dame Scholastic*, May 20, 1932, contains photographs and comments, including a picture of Alfred P. Shaw as "superintendent of construction."

3. Schlereth, *Notre Dame*, p. 175.

[236] HURLEY COLLEGE OF COMMERCE, LOBBY

FIRST NATIONAL BANK OF ST. PAUL

1929–32
332 Minnesota Street
St. Paul, Minnesota

Cost in 1932, bank's records: $3,340,185.44
Status: extant, with complete alteration of the Banking Room and
   other floors and adjoining buildings erected on its flank

Situated in the heart of downtown St. Paul, the First National Bank's great height gives it a commanding position in the skyscape of the city (fig. 237). The thirty-two-story building is surmounted by a 100-foot supporting tower for the 50-foot

high "1st" sign on the top, its letters 14 feet tall. The pinnacled bank–office building also enjoys the company of some distinguished neighbors. Across the street is the Pioneer Building by Solon Spenser Beman, and next to it, the two six-story Endicott Buildings designed by Cass Gilbert (architect of the Minnesota State Capitol off in the distance).

Next door is the original home of the bank, still housing some of its offices. This hollow-square office building in the tradition of Daniel Burnham was to be connected with the new skyscraper, so Graham, Anderson, Probst and White opened the new Banking Room into the older one and indicated this on the exterior with cornice lines of the same height. The rounded openings of the old windows give way to the severe portals of stripped classicism in the newer building, but their level is the same. Thus both buildings had two-story Banking Rooms on the same floor, in harmony with each other.

Higher up, the newer building is a setback skyscraper of stripped classicism. Each pier rises slightly above the cornice line at each level where it terminates in a pyramidal form, giving these stages a castellated appearance.

The use of two different colored spandrel panels is an important device to help articulate the mass of the building. Within the uninterrupted vertical pier system, the dark spandrels seem

[238] FIRST NATIONAL BANK, BANKING ROOM

more recessed, allowing the light spandrels to act in two ways: first as suppressed stringcourses giving horizontal definition to the tall building, and second as assertive elements marking the corners. By contrast, the dark spandrels give depth, and emphasis, to the verticality of the central section. This careful use of spandrel panels to provide horizontal notes, massing, and texture is reminiscent of a similar role played by the stringcourses in the earlier classical tripartite office buildings of the firm, but here spandrel panels allow the verticals to dominate, in the spirit of the late 1920s. The sweep to the top is not so unmitigated that the building seems unanchored; it is still tied to the earth by strong horizontal accents.

The street level of the building is lined with shop windows, and within, the well-lighted arcades are finished in warm tones of marble. The variety of services

and merchandise available gives the building a "city within a city" quality enhanced by the black polished granite walls, with gold and silver zigzags, crown mouldings, and electric lights in the best Art Deco fashion. Near the elevators, the color scheme is softer. Two marbles, one a tan color with delicate maroon veinings and the other a tan color with bold, large-scale organic patternings, contrast and harmonize with each other.

The original Banking Room in the center of the U-shaped plan through the second and third floors was destroyed in a subsequent remodeling, but a contemporary photograph reveals a large room with tellers' cages on the periphery and balconies above (fig. 238).[1] All ornament was flat and geometrized. In black and white reproduction the room seems cavernous, but the historic imagination warms the image when reading a list of the colorful marbles used in the inte-

rior of the building. "Marble used in building was shipped from almost every marble-producing country in the world. Varieties used include Red Levanto, Yellow Lamertine, Breche Oriental, Premier Blue Belge, Premier Pyrenees Black and White, Roman and Siena Travertine."[2]

During the energy crisis of the 1970s, when the "1st" sign on the top of the bank went dark, a local newspaper reported that the bank had more questions about that sign than about any item related to banking. An intense lobbying effort to relight it ensued. When the effort succeeded in 1983, the new "1st" sign was red, as was the original, and its three sides were lit in rotating fashion. About four thousand feet of neon tubing were required to repair the sign.[3]

Crowned again by its original sign, the proportions of the First National Bank of St. Paul, its tall massing, and its play of horizontals and verticals form one of the most satisfying formal expressions of the spirit of the Art Deco period in St. Paul.

1. Photographs in GAPW archives in Chicago and in the archives of the bank in St. Paul.

2. *The First National Bank Building: Interesting Facts,* pamphlet (St. Paul: First National Bank of St. Paul, n.d.), available in the bank's archives. Also on hand are files of correspondence, drawings of four different schemes for the building, calculations for the projected annual income of each, and bills for travel costs for members of the firm.

3. Jim McCartney, "Flash: biggest '1' to be back on," *St. Paul Pioneer Press and Dispatch,* August 12, 1983.

CHICAGO HISTORICAL SOCIETY

1930–32
North Avenue and Clark Street, in Lincoln Park
Chicago, Illinois

Cost in 1932, architects' records: $570,000; newspaper accounts of the period: $1 million, probably including furnishings.

Status: extant, with two major changes. An addition in 1974 (Shaw and Associates) on the west changed the facade and moved the main entrance from the park to Clark Street. In 1988, another major addition (Holabird and Root) partially replaced the earlier one and wrapped around the north, south, and west, leaving the east facade as it was in the original.

In the 1920s, the focus of the Chicago Historical Society's collections was not the history of the city, as it is today, but American history in general. The Georgian style was appropriate for this purpose, and it was also a popular choice for college campuses and other cultural institutions in the period (see Part I). As was their practice, the architects provided a landscaped plaza at the Chicago Historical Society's western entrance. At the main entrance on the east, a ceremonial courtyard faced Augustus Saint-Gaudens's statue of Abraham Lincoln (fig. 239). Typically Georgian are the bilateral symmetry and strong central axis evident in the facade (fig. 240). This axis is marked by a central hall that once ran the full depth of the building and is expressed on the exterior by a two-story projecting pedimented portico with Roman Doric columns.

Horizontally, the building has the traditional tripartite division, the base of large blocks of limestone, the middle section of Virginia red brick with limestone trim, and the top stringcourse and balustrade also of limestone. All windows are twelve over twelve panes.

The interior spaces were laid out to simulate a walk through American history, from the fifteenth century to World War I, and the climax of the public spaces was Foyer Hall, a reproduction of Independence Hall in Philadelphia (fig. 24).

From here the visitor entered the past. The Spanish Exploration Room to the south was clad with coquina rock, a mixture of tiny shells and concrete frequently used in colonial Florida. Fifteenth-century Spanish anchors and a model of the *Santa Maria,* one of the three ships Columbus took on his first voyage across the Atlantic, filled this room. The French Alcove contained objects and documents associated with explorers LaSalle, Marquette, Jolliet, and others. Further on, the British Colonial Room reproduced the dining room from Mt. Pleasant, Philadelphia (John MacPherson, 1761), bought by Benedict Arnold in 1779, with an original Sheraton dining table, Chippendale chairs, and a portrait of George III.

Reproductions of the living room and master bedroom in Paul Revere's house in Boston, Massachusetts, occupied a portion of the spaces devoted to the American colonial period, but the climax of this section was a reception room copied after the Senate Chamber in Congress Hall, Philadelphia. Exhibited here were John Hancock's upholstered chair and the black velvet coat that George Washington wore when he delivered his Second Inaugural Address in the original hall. The Washington Room in the southwest corner followed the general design of the west parlor at Mount Vernon, Virginia, an appropriate environment for the society's memorabilia of the period.

A series of other rooms representing ensuing periods fol-

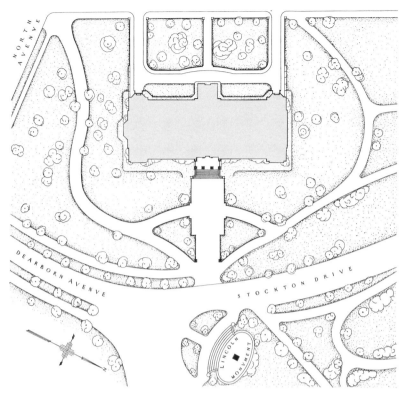

[239] CHICAGO HISTORICAL SOCIETY, CHICAGO, ILL., SITE PLAN

lowed: the New Republic Room displayed the French influence in the United States after the Revolution, the Western Expansion Room contained objects from the Gold Rush, the Mexican War, and the building of the railroads. A Marine Room reproduced Robinson Hall in the Peabody Museum of Salem, Massachusetts. With its panoramic view of Salem, it depicted other aspects of American adventures on the high seas. Confederate and Union portraits once lined the walls of the Civil War Room to the north of Foyer Hall, but now broadsides, newspapers, old maps, and photographs tell of Chicago's business and industrial history. Just beyond, bright flowered upholstery, rosewood furniture, and mannequins in flowing dresses enliven the popular Victorian Room in the northwest corner. Taking advantage of the

bay windows in the design, the museum's curators created a period room, copying its furnishings from the parlor of an 1850s Chicago house.

Exhibitions devoted to Chicago's history filled the remaining spaces. Relics of the early settlers, drawings of the Great Fire of 1871, a painting of the World's Columbian Exposition of 1893, flags, prints, paintings, medals, and objects from the Spanish-American War and World War I culminated in the Gold Star Room where the sons of members of the society who had lost their lives in the armed services were listed.[1]

One of the most popular museum forms of the period was the diorama, and eight of these sce-

[240] CHICAGO HISTORICAL
SOCIETY, EXTERIOR

nic depictions were the pride of the society's collection. Each of the deep display cases for these representations contains a picture at the back and sides that slant inward give a perspective effect for the figures, furniture, and other objects made to scale for their place in the orthogonal schemes. All eight were devoted to scenes from Chicago history, and all are still on display at the society.

The stairway that led to the lower story was copied from one in the Lee Mansion at Marblehead, Massachusetts, as was the chandelier above it. Most of this floor was devoted to Abraham Lincoln and other luminaries from Illinois and Chicago history. The bedroom in the Peterson House in Washington, D.C., where Lincoln died, was reproduced to provide an appropriate space for the furniture from the original room—bed, bureau, chair, picture, candlestick, and gas jet—that were given to the society by Charles F. Gunther,

who purchased them shortly after the assassination.[2] Today there are displays of pioneer life in the northern part of this ground floor, while offices and a large auditorium occupy the southern part. This lecture hall originally had a seating capacity of 430 that could be expanded to 1,000 by collapsing adjacent temporary partitions, but it can no longer be expanded. With its light yellow painted walls setting off the delicate white Adamesque trim, the room is still in frequent use for the society's many public activities.

An elevator to the third or top story opened on a foyer leading to the spacious Reading Room with its white railing reminiscent of a Quaker meeting house. Adjacent spaces led to the Atlas and Map Room, Manuscript Room, and Newspaper Room. All of these rooms serve different purposes today, but their ample proportions made them readily adaptable to new functions.

The requirements of the Chicago Historical Society have changed since 1930, when its collections were smaller and museums generally relied on historic reproductions and the exhibition of objects confined to display cases. Vastly expanded holdings, a new philosophy of museum practice, and technological improvements in storage and maintenance made another addition necessary in 1988. Designer Gerald Horn was concerned about preserving the best of the old building, but also faced the challenges of helping the society move toward its new goal of greater accessibility to the public. A decorative grid element in front may be hung with colorful banners, and display windows along Clark Street give passersby a glimpse of the exhibitions inside. An expanded gift and bookshop and a restaurant are all part of the new scheme, which wraps around and partially encloses the earlier buildings.

1. The Chicago Historical Society has about fifty blueprints of the original building, signed by Probst and White and dated August 7, 1930. The CHS Manuscript Collection contains a tentative ground plan, 1927–28, minutes of planning meetings, records of the fund-raising campaign, tabulations of the bids, and newspaper accounts of the laying of the cornerstone, Dedication Day, and the official opening November 12, 1932.

2. "Tour of the New Building," mimeographed, Chicago Historical Society Manuscript Collection, Chicago; "The Chicago Historical Society 1856–1946," *Chicago History* 1, no. 3 (Spring 1946): 57–85; "Chicago Historical Society Soon To Have New Home," *Museum News,* issues throughout 1928 and 1929; "Chicago Historical Society," *Chicago Herald American,* November 12, 1932; "A Monument to Chicago's History," *Townsfolk,* December 1932; Graham, Anderson, Probst and White, *Specifications for the Museum and Library Building for the Chicago Historical Society,* April 1931, CHS Manuscript Collection; Marc Waters, "The Chicago Historical Society Building," 1984, author's collection.

HOTEL MAYFLOWER

1930–31
Main and State streets
Akron, Ohio

Cost in 1931: $1,937,759.50; pcf: $0.592
Status: extant, now converted to low-rent apartments

The christening of the new Hotel Mayflower in 1931 was no mere bottle of champagne affair. At noon on the appointed day, a full squadron of Goodyear blimps and a fleet of airplanes soared overhead and showered the zeppelin dock on the roof of the hotel with rose petals. Ohio governor George White and the famous flyer Maj. James H. Doolittle watched from the Pilot's Room as the zeppelin *Akron*'s mobile mooring mast hooked on, and a host of airplanes gyrated through the skies above.[1] Below, the cheers of the crowd filled the air with an optimism rare in the United States in 1931.

At the time, three large rubber companies—Goodyear, Goodrich, and Firestone—and a number of cereal manufacturers had their national headquarters in Akron. The nation's obsession with automobiles, airplanes, and other vehicles using rubber tires filled the city with hope of expanding business opportunities, even in the early days of the depression, and a grand hotel was vital to its dreams of future growth.

Graham, Anderson, Probst and White's design for the fifteen-story, 450-room hotel was U-shaped in plan, with its mass divided horizontally into three parts: the base, the shaft, and the capital long associated with traditional design of the period (fig. 241). In keeping with a new ma-chine-age simplicity, the limestone base was ornamented only by decorative spandrel panels, a brightly lit canopy over the entrance, a swagged cartouch over the main portals, and stream-lined mouldings at the top. The designers tried to be both traditional and up-to-date in their work because the clients wanted the best of both worlds—the accoutrements of the grand hotel tradition and the flair of the latest designs.

Traditional details decorated the interiors (fig. 244). In the lobby, fluted pilasters articulated the wall and supported a classical frieze (fig. 242), and all windows were pedimented. The planning of the spaces, however,

[241] HOTEL MAYFLOWER, AKRON, OHIO, ELEVATION

[242] HOTEL MAYFLOWER, LOBBY

[243] HOTEL MAYFLOWER, BALLROOM

stage was provided where an orchestra might play for dancing on weekends. Modern aluminum chairs with green cord-woven upholstery and "temperatured air" made the room a popular place in Akron for many years.

The coffee shop, known as the Colonial Grill, was early American in style. The pine-board-covered walls had a four-foot tile base, and brass lighting fixtures with parchment shades surrounded the combination counter and table service. Two and one-half horseshoe-shaped counters with wooden stools accommodated forty-five patrons at a time. A soda fountain was also included.

The service areas of the hotel—kitchen, laundry, and linen rooms—were carefully planned with attention given to the smallest detail, as the working drawings indicate.[3]

The guest rooms in the U-shaped building were off a double-loaded corridor, all rooms having natural light. A special feature of the Hotel Mayflower was a radio in every room. Since fear of this invention's potential for disturbing the peace plagued every hotel manager, an ingenious device was imported from Chicago.

Each room has a built-in radio with a 4-panel control operating thru a centralized control board on the top floor. This equipment was installed by the Centralized Control Corporation of Chicago. A time clock control automatically turns service on and off at desired hours, so it is impossible for programs to be broadcast in the late evening hours and cause a possible disturbance to guests who have retired. The operator of the

facilitated the movements of a fast-paced businessman. The telegraph office, a host of public telephones, and a newspaper stand were all connected with the cashier by pneumatic tubes so that all charges for these communications services could be billed less than sixty seconds after completion.

The public rooms of the Hotel Mayflower followed a hierarchical pattern of decreasing levels of luxury, from the ballroom, down

to the dining room, and finally to the coffee shop. Crystal chandeliers and mirrored panels sparkled in the fifty-by-sixty-five-foot ballroom on the second floor (fig. 243), reflecting the series of arches that supported balconies above. Overhead, murals depicted the story of dance in various nations.[2]

In the dining room below, called the Puritan Room, classical pilasters suggested a more restrained atmosphere, but a small

[244] HOTEL MAYFLOWER, ORNAMENT

master set is able to determine the maximum volume of power distributed to all rooms. This also prohibits excessively loud reception at any time. It is said that four different programs may be received simultaneously in four adjoining rooms without any one of them interfering with the others. The installation can also be used to broadcast thru the hotel such programs as take place in the main dining room of the ballroom. Or the system may be used by the management to make announcements to guests in their rooms, or if desired, to page guests.[4]

Today the idea of "Big Brother" in the form of a hotel detective controlling the volume of the air-waves in our hotel rooms, or interrupting our sleep to make announcements, is alien, but in 1931 the fascination with new electric gadgetry was a welcome diversion to the traveler. The Hotel Mayflower followed the practices of luxurious hotels all over the world in providing full-length mirrors, racks for five different sizes of towels, hooks for shoe cloths and razor strops, and mahogany furniture "in accordance with Grand Rapids standards."[5]

The heating and ventilating systems were the best of the times. No boilers were needed in the Hotel Mayflower—"consequently no coal bins, no ash dumps nor reserve oil tanks." Steam was purchased from the Akron Steam Heating Company, metered as it came in, and conducted through a series of pressure-reducing valves to the various departments. Radiators were concealed. The copper heating unit was enclosed in a steel cabinet on the wall, with a grille permitting the heat to circulate. No exposed piping or cumbersome radiator units intruded into the rooms. Heat was controlled by the Warren Webster Moderator System, which regulated the flow of steam according to the temperature registered on a thermostat on the roof of the building.[6]

Ventilation for the public rooms and kitchens was maintained by seventeen multivane supply and exhaust fans. Fresh air passed through a series of filters for purification, then passed over heating coils before being distributed to the rooms. The equipment included an air-conditioning system for cooling air during the summer, which was made by the National Carbonic Machinery Company of Chicago.[7]

Although the old Hotel Mayflower has now been converted to low-rent apartments, and its public rooms converted to other purposes, people who have lived in Akron for many years remember its grand traditions.

1. *Official Souvenir of Opening,* brochure, GAPW archives, Chicago.
2. Ibid.
3. "The Mayflower Hotel of Akron," *Hotel Monthly,* September 1931, p. 32.
4. Ibid., p. 37.
5. Ibid., p. 38.
6. Ibid., p. 39.
7. Ibid.

UNITED STATES POST OFFICE

1914–34
433 West Van Buren Street
Chicago, Illinois

Cost in 1934: records vary from $16 million to $22 million
Status: extant, in fair condition

The history of Chicago's Post Office facility, which now consists of two buildings fused into one (the first part, the U.S. Mail Building [*q.v.*], was finished in 1921, the second in 1933), actually began with the Plan of Chicago (1909), when Congress Street was envisioned as Chicago's great western artery, providing a clear view to a climactic civic center at the intersection with Halsted Street. At the time, Congress Street was not the easiest place to imagine as a major new thoroughfare. It stopped at State Street, it did not begin again until Clark Street, and it existed only in fits and starts on the other side of the river.[1]

In the resolutely geometric scheme of the Beaux-Arts plan, however, the *logical* place for east-west express traffic in Chicago was at Congress Street because it was halfway between Wacker Drive and Roosevelt Road. In the Chicago grid, eight blocks make a mile, and the thinking behind the street plan was that Chicago's core should be centered within two great mile-wide, mile-long squares, the financial and retail section to the north and the wholesale and warehouse section to the south.

These two squares would be bordered by Wacker Drive on the north, Michigan Avenue on the east, Roosevelt Road on the south, and Market Street (now Wacker Drive) on the west, with Congress Street bisecting the whole. The publication of the dramatic drawings in the *Plan,* and the shared vision it embodied, kept the dream of a Congress Street thoroughfare alive for generations.

Railroad tracks serving lines coming in from the south covered the area of the proposed Congress Street west of the river to Canal Street, and the Enabling Ordinance for Union Station of 1914 was one of the major victories for the future of the street. Among the many provisions of this remarkable piece of constructive legislation was a requirement that the railroads would depress all tracks east of Canal Street and widen, recon-

[245] UNITED STATES POST OFFICE, CHICAGO, ILL., EXTERIOR

[246] UNITED STATES POST OFFICE, LOBBY

struct, and maintain viaducts in the central city. The 200-foot-wide viaduct over Congress Street now allows the east-west flow of traffic under it on the Congress Expressway.[2]

In the days when mail was handled chiefly by trains, the connections to the tracks below made this site a logical place for a post office, but there had been a big price to pay. When the U.S. Mail Building went up over this viaduct in 1921, the dreams of a Beaux-Arts civic center at Halsted Street were dashed.

In the decade following the erection of the U.S. Mail Building, the Plan proposals were eroded in other ways as well. In any case, in 1930, the U.S. Treasury Department planned to wrap a larger building around the old U.S. Mail Building and hired Graham, Anderson, Probst and White to design it. It was more than architect Edward H. Bennett could bear. Once a member of Burnham's firm, Bennett was a key figure in the design of the Plan and was for many years after Burnham's death its chief

defender. He denounced the new building as "Ernest R. Graham's insult to Congress Street."[3]

When it opened in 1932, Chicago's post office, with its 2.7 million square feet of floor space, was the largest post office building in the world. More than 125 trains and 6,000 trucks traveled in, out, and under this air-rights building each day, carrying more than 35 million letters, papers, and parcels. Hundreds of special machines, ten miles of conveyor belts, and forty-eight elevators moved mail through the nine floors of work space with extra high ceilings and the twelve office floors. A helicopter landing field on the roof awaited special cargo.

The long, broad proportions of the building stretch over Congress Street, with four large towers marking the ends at each of the corners (fig. 245). The rectangular mass of the building is further subdivided into three sections with base, shaft, and capital, or top section, all marked off by horizontal stringcourses. The piers of the steel-

cage frame rise uninterrupted within these divisions, so the verticality somewhat mitigates the severity of the horizontal mass. Like most other buildings of the period, the ornament is confined to restrained, geometric mouldings, spandrels, and capitals, the hard-edged quality that gave rise to the term "stripped classicism."

The lobby on Van Buren Street is T-shaped. The top section, 340 by 40 feet, stretches the entire width of the building, while the bars extend from Van Buren to Congress Street. The ceiling of the main lobby is 38 feet high, giving the room an awesome effect (fig. 246). The walls are clad in Alabama madre cream marble, with a base of imported Belgian black. Reliefs of ceramic tile with a green and yellow gold leaf baked on clear and black glass imported from France decorate the otherwise severe walls. Squares of Tennessee champion pink and tavernelle marble within a dark green marble border form the floor design.

Most of the customer services were located on the main floor. The second floor contained the receiving platforms and had offices in the corner sections. The third floor was given over to distribution matters, the fourth to handling the primary separation of mail. In the north part, a canteen, a bank for employees, a dispensary, and a branch of the Chicago Public Library were also included. The fifth to ninth floors were used for distribution of parcels, foreign mail, canceling, special delivery, the mechanical section, and spaces for other repair services.[4]

For many years after the post office was finished, the volume of mail in the United States kept getting ahead of the processors, and even the large post office in Chicago was scarcely adequate. But with the use of ZIP codes, optical character readers, automated devices, computers, and other electronic equipment to distribute the more than four billion items of mail that are processed in Chicago annually, the spatial needs of the post office have actually decreased in the 1980s. Today the building's nine workroom stories, which in the past required heavy and frequent use of elevators, are regarded as inefficient for modern mailing needs, and many postal operations have shifted to other locations. To consolidate its work for the new technology, the federal government plans to erect another building in the vicinity.

1. Map, Chicago Historical Society Library, 1899.

2. Chicago Plan Commission, *Discussion of the Proposed Site and Type of Building for the West Side Post Office in Chicago* (Chicago, 1915); Sally A. Kitt Chappell, "Urban Ideals and the Design of Railroad Stations," *Technology and Culture*, pp. 354–75.

3. Joan Draper, *Edward H. Bennett: Architect and City Planner 1874–1954* (Chicago: Art Institute of Chicago, 1982), p. 24. Rich in bibliographic material, this book is especially helpful on issues of planning.

4. Drawings are located in the archives of the post office, in the care of Thomas Dean, room 1002; "Chicago's General Post Office," mimeographed account of a description of the original layout, c. 1949 and "The Chicago Post Office," mimeographed account of the history of the postal service in Chicago, c. 1974, are both in the archives of the Chicago Post Office; Carl W. Condit, *Chicago, 1910–29: Building, Plan-*

ning and Urban Technology, p. 284; Charles DeLeuw, "Report on the Development of a Major Traffic Artery on the West Side of the City of Chicago," mimeographed, (Illinois Division of Highways, February 1935); W. A. Dudley to Edward H. Bennett, "Story of the Purchase of the New Post-Office Site," Bennett Papers, Art Institute of Chicago;

"Importance of Chicago's Postal Problem in the Scheme of Commercial Expansion," *Fine Arts Journal* 36 (March 1916): 99–111; "Near West Side Site Proposed for Civic Hall," *Chicago Tribune,* April 23, 1930; "Superhighway Developments in the Chicago Area," *Midwest Engineer* 2, (January 1950): 10–12.

ARMOUR EXHIBIT HALL

1934
Sixteenth Street Bridge, A Century of Progress International Exposition
Chicago, Illinois

Status: dismantled September 1935

The Armour Exhibit Hall was the last major piece of construction for Chicago's Century of Progress International Exposition (1933–34). It was erected just before the opening of the exposition's second and final year. Under ordinary circumstances the Armour building would have been a six-month job, but to meet the opening date of the second year it was erected in less than six weeks.[1] All exposition architects and engineers built according to stipulations for rapid assembly and minimal costs. Buildings were constructed in twenty-foot modules of light steel and timber framing and clad in prefabricated materials.

Occupying its own peninsula off Silence Bridge, the Armour Exhibit Hall was at the center of the fairgrounds. A dynamic exhibition hall and restaurant built to control and direct a continuous flow of spectators (fig. 247), the structure consisted of three geometric volumes. The first, a tall rectangular entrance lobby, was a rhythmic series of monolithic

shapes capped with a neon sign, "Armour," drawing the crowd to the exhibition. Once inside, the spectators passed into the second volume, the horizontal exhibition hall that decreased in width to funnel the crowd through to the circular restaurant. Two stories high, glazed with ribbons of windows, the restaurant was surrounded by a deck that ran along the periphery of the structure to a point overlooking the lagoon.

The Armour building exemplified the architectural theme of A Century of Progress, "Modern Invention and Science Through New Elements of Construction."[2] In addition to its structural methods, the fair combined three elements—color, light, and water—to give it a distinctive atmosphere. Color defined the main spaces and separated the masses of a given structure, intensifying some, subduing others to fit into an overall scheme. Glowing neon light took maximum advantage of the fair's site on Lake Michigan, reflecting on the many fountains, cascades, and other water elements to create what everyone called the "rainbow city."[3]

In this spirit, the Armour building also employed neon and floodlighting inside and out and fully exploited its location. It jutted out in the lagoon upon its own piling, and seemed to float upon the water. The building's geometry, color, lighting, and harmonious integration with the site prompted one local newspaper to call it "the good ship Armour."[4]

The ultra-modern building was an appropriate vessel for the scientific theme of the fair and the exhibit it housed. Muralist David Leavitt decorated the side walls of each exhibit hall with scenes illustrating the development of the company.

The solarium restaurant provided a panoramic view of the fairgrounds to the south, east, and west, and, along with the outdoor deck, created a pleasant resting place for fairgoers. Shortly after the close of the fair, in September 1935, Armour signed an order for the disassembly of the building.[5]

1. "For Immediate Release—Armour," press release, Century of Progress Publicity Office, April 13, 1934.

2. Louis Skidmore, "Planning and Planners," *Architectural Forum* 59 (July 1934).

3. Carl W. Condit, *Chicago, 1930–70: Building, Planning and Urban Technology* (Chicago: University of Chicago Press, 1974) p. 13.

4. *Chicago News*, May 31, 1934.

5. *See also* drawing by Walter Ohlson in the Manuscript Collection at the University of Illinois at Chicago; watercolors made into postcards by Art Tone, Curt Teich and Company, Chicago, 1934, University of Illinois at Chicago, Manuscript Collection; *Official Guide Book* (Chicago: Century of Progress and Cuneo Press, 1934). Kevin Latham contributed material to this entry.

[247] ARMOUR EXHIBIT HALL, 1933–34 CENTURY OF PROGRESS INTERNATIONAL EXPOSITION, CHICAGO, ILL., ELEVATION

[248] STATE LINE GENERATING STATION, HAMMOND, IND., PROPOSAL

STATE LINE GENERATING STATION

1921–29
103rd Street and Lake Michigan
Hammond, Indiana[1]

Cost in 1929, architects' figure: $4,650,000
Status: extant; National Historic Mechanical Engineering Landmark, April 19, 1977

In the fifty years between the invention of the incandescent lamp by Thomas A. Edison and the opening of the State Line Station, electricity grew from a phenomenon barely able to furnish light to houses within a half a mile to a system of plants servicing over a million customers in lines extending more than six hundred miles. From its earliest beginnings, Samuel Insull was at the center of this rapidly developing industry that was so closely tied to the industrial revolution and to the character of modern life.

From 1880 to 1892, he was Thomas Edison's secretary. He would later rise to the presidency of the Chicago Edison Company and its many subsidiaries and holding companies that evolved over the years. Insull's great strengths as a businessman were his ability to see the whole picture—technology, management, and finance—and to communicate his ideas and concepts to others.

By the first decade of the century, most of the technological changes necessary for the widespread use of electricity had been achieved, but the times called for increased entrepreneurial skills. Samuel Insull had the system-

building drive and organizational imagination to meet the challenges. Clearly, he thought on a large scale. Coming to Chicago in 1893, the year of the World's Columbian Exposition, the first great Chicago world's fair, Insull joined a community of other businessmen who were system builders, among them the railroad tycoons. Like many of them, when Insull needed an architect for a large project, he turned to Daniel H. Burnham, the man who had successfully brought about the wonder of the fair: the erection, in two years, of a city fit to entertain the world, a sparkling ensemble of buildings that brought international fame to Chicago. Burnham had showed remarkable sensitivity to the use of electricity as an architectural medium as well, for the sculptures, columns, and roofs of the White City were lit by arc lights, incandescent lights, and colored floodlights. Naturally, Insull would ask the man who

[249] STATE GENERATING STATION, DETAIL

said "Make no little plans" and who was able to anticipate future uses of electricity to be his architect. So Burnham won the commission for the Fisk Street Station, and his successor, Ernest R. Graham, won the commissions for the Crawford Avenue and State Line stations in the 1920s.

Graham, Anderson, Probst and White's design for the State Line Station (figs. 248, 250) expresses Insull's dreams for the future of electricity and for himself as a prince of industry (see Part I). The architectural envelope expresses the power plant's importance (fig. 249). As the citation for the National Historic Mechanical Engineering Landmark concluded:

From 1929 to 1954 the "State Line" turbine-generator was the largest unit of its kind in the world. Its 208,000 kw rating was 30% above the next largest unit at that time. In December of 1953 the Ohio Power Company's Muskingham #1 unit surpassed the "champ" with a rating of 213,000 kw. In an industry which had doubled its output at less than ten year intervals a 25 year reign represented a substantial engineering feat.

In 1929 the average kw capacity for a generating unit was 15,000–30,000 kw. The establishment of the "State Line's" 208,000 interconnected system evidenced a startling engineering breakthrough which set a precedent for future developments.[2]

According to Commonwealth Edison, at least one of the three shafts was in service from the beginning through February 1977. In addition, the turbine-generator is still in use today. In 1974 it had 7,015 service hours. State Line's Unit Number One has, therefore, not only established for itself a place in our technological history, but still remains an integral component of present-day energy service systems.[3]

1. Most of the site is in Indiana, but a small corner touches the border of Illinois, at the Chicago city limits. In 1924, application was made to the U.S. Department of War to fill in seventy-three acres in Lake Michigan. After the federal and state permits were obtained, the first contract for developing the riparian rights was awarded in May 1925, and site preparation began. By October 1926, the retaining wall was in place and sand was pumped in. Construction began in 1927. The cornerstone was laid April 14, 1928, and the building was complete by 1929.

Trial commercial operation began July 1, 1929.

2. American Society of Mechanical Engineers, "National Historic Mechanical Engineering Landmark, State Line Generating Unit No. 1, 1929," mimeographed dedication ceremony pamphlet, April 19, 1977.

3. See twelve boxes of blueprints in the archives in the gatehouse; some construction photographs, electrical drawings, and other photographs in the plant manager's office; Commonwealth Edison Co., "Announce Plans for Million Kilowatt Station," *Edison Round Table*, March 31, 1926, p. 2 (hereafter *ERT*); "Changing Times," *ERT*, November 15, 1928, p. 1; "Chicago's Development Dependent on Utilities," *ERT*, September 30, 1925, p. 2; "Development of Chicago District Generating Corporation Reviewed," *ERT*, August 31, 1938; Willis Gale, "Remarks at Fisk Anniversary Luncheon," October 1, 1953, typescript of address, Commonwealth Edison archives, Chicago; Rebecca Grill, "Shedding Light on the Past," *Edison*, Winter 1985, pp. 6–9; Thomas P. Hughes, "Electrification of America: The System Builders," *Technology and Culture* 20 (1979): 124–61; Alf Kolflat and Bernhard Schroeder, *The Sargent & Lundy Story* (Chicago: Sargent and Lundy, c. 1961); Forrest McDonald, *Insull* (Chicago: University of Chicago Press, 1962); "Order Two New Units for State Line Plant," *ERT*, January 31, 1930; "Plan to Complete Unit No. 2 at State Line," *ERT*, November 2, 1936; *State Line Generating Station Unit Number One* (Chicago: Commonwealth Edison Company, n.d.); State Line Generating Station, *State Liner* (July 1939) Tenth Anniversary Issue; State Line Generating Station, *State Liner*, (April 1954); Commonwealth Edison, "Still the Champ," April 7, 1954; "Two New Units at State Line," *ERT*, October 31, 1929, p. 2; Samuel Insull Papers, Loyola University, Chicago; Samuel Insull, *Central-Station Electric Service: Its Commercial Development and Economic Significance as Set Forth in the Public Addresses (1897–1914) of Samuel Insull*, ed. William E. Keily (Chicago, 1915); Samuel Insull, *Public Utilities in Modern Life: Selected Speeches (1914–1923)*, ed. William E. Keily (Chicago, 1924).

[250] STATE GENERATING STATION, TURBINE ROOM

[251] NATIONAL TRAILWAYS BUS DEPOT, CHICAGO, ILL., EXTERIOR

NATIONAL TRAILWAYS BUS DEPOT

1936–37
20 East Randolph Street
Chicago, Illinois

Status: demolished 1990.

The streamlined forms of the sleek automobiles and buses of the 1930s were incorporated into the forms of the Trailways Bus Depot, furthering the idea that a bus terminal was not a subgenus railroad station but worthy of its own imagery (fig. 251). The rounded corner of the Waiting Room and the use of a neon sign as an architectural mark of entrance were in the spirit of Art Deco, seen often at A Century of Progress International Exposition of 1933 in Chicago.

Inside, the travel motif switched to ocean liners, with porthole windows, chrome fixtures, and overhanging balconies (fig. 252). Railings appeared at every opportunity and each cubic foot was shipshape, with all the plaster surfaces painted blue and white. The chrome tube furniture upholstered in red leather, the wainscoting and countertops trimmed in red formica, and the floors of red, white, and blue terrazzo completed this salute to naval imagery.[1]

Alfred P. Shaw, the designer, had clearly left the traditional vocabulary of his elders behind and was speaking in the jazzier lingo of the 1930s. Using the color scheme of the buses as his motif, Shaw achieved a unity that expressed a new imagery for the growing bus company, marking a stage in the use of architecture as an advertising medium.

1. *American Architect and Architecture,* July 1937, pp. 37–40.

[252] NATIONAL TRAILWAYS BUS DEPOT, WAITING ROOM AND PLAN

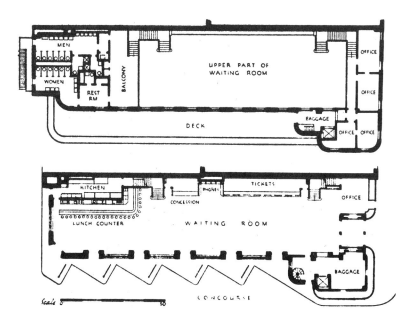

Architects with a Rich Heritage: The Legacy of Daniel H. Burnham; History of the Firm; Biographical Sketches of the Partners

Looking back on the prolific work of the firm, the observer realizes that there is no radical break in continuity from the turn of the century when Daniel Hudson Burnham (1846–1912) (fig. 253) was at the helm to the day Ernest Robert Graham died in 1936. Changes were gradual because the designers were almost all trained in the Beaux-Arts tradition, and the forms of buildings were determined by technological, social, and economic factors as much if not more than by stylistic considerations.

A report compiled by a government auditor in 1922 during a dispute about taxes gives the following profile of the firm between 1900 and 1917:

[253] DANIEL HUDSON BURNHAM

As of January 1, 1900, Burnham owned 70 percent of the firm and Graham 30 percent, but covered profit and losses only, not property. On December 31, 1904, this proportion changed to 60 percent for Burnham and 40 percent for Graham. Beginning in 1908, Anderson, Probst and White were given 2.5 percent of the profits each but no interest in the partnership. In January 1910 Burnham's sons Daniel H. Burnham, Jr. and Hubert Burnham were given a partnership interest, beginning with 1 percent and increasing over five years to 5 percent from Burnham's share, while Graham retained his 40 percent.

When Burnham died, $1,496,538.97 in profits due the firm were paid off. The Burnham estate received $730,000, Graham $299,419, and the Burnham sons each received $22,459. Anderson, Probst, and White each received $20,233. A new firm, Graham, Burnham and Company, which included Anderson, Probst, and White was begun July 31, 1912, with the understanding that it would last five years. Graham owned 51 percent of this firm, and the other five 9.8 percent each. This firm did not make its formal debut until May 4, 1914, because three of the members did not have architect's licenses [the report does not say which three] and were thus not permitted to use a letterhead bearing their names as architects before that time. The five year period following Burnham's death was a difficult one in the partnership. On June 4, 1917, Graham notified the others of his intent to dissolve the firm. On August 9 the Burnhams sold their rights for $175,000 and left to form their own firm. The remaining partners established Graham, Anderson, Probst and White at that time.[1]

The early work of what was to become the firm of Graham, Anderson, Probst and White was profoundly influenced by the ideas and principles of Daniel H. Burnham who had taken Ernest R. Graham into partnership in 1894. This influence is most apparent for the years before and just after World War I.

When Burnham died, he left his successors an active and successful architectural practice, a trained, well-organized staff capable of designing any contemporary building type, hundreds of satisfied clients, a well-accepted style, an international reputation, and a broadly shared vision of architecture and the city. There was enough work already in the office to keep more than two hundred men busy for months, and the promise of over a million dollars in more commissions to come, an enviable legacy for six younger men.[2] The new firm was established on the corporate model.[3]

Graham (fig. 254) was clearly ready to be the new chief. He was the oldest and had been with Burnham the longest—since 1891. In leadership ability and in temperament he resembled his mentor of more than twenty years. Seizing his opportunity, Graham immediately reorganized the firm by dividing it into four sections: Business, with himself as head; Design, with Anderson as head; Supervision of Construction, including work out of Chicago, with White as head; and Production, including the job of chief foreman of the drafting rooms responsible for all working drawings, with Probst as head.

Like Burnham, Graham was a conservative, careful architect with a deeply ingrained respect for tradition, craftsmanship, and sound business practice. Both men were midwesterners, undereducated by eastern standards, learning their profession by the time-honored apprenticeship method, a system common in their era.

ERNEST ROBERT GRAHAM
(1866–1936)

Graham was born in Lowell, Michigan, on August 22, 1866, the second son and the second of three children of Robert W. and Emma Post Graham. His father (1828–1889) was a stonemason, born in England, who left for New York in 1850. Four years later he settled in Lowell, Michigan, along the banks of the Grand River, where he farmed 160 acres.[4] In 1863 he met Emma, daughter of a Kansas City grain merchant. Shortly after their marriage, Robert Graham went into the boot and shoe business, keeping the farm as his home. During the post–Civil War building boom, Robert Graham returned to the construction business, soon becoming a small general contractor. His work included the Graham block in Lowell and other jobs in nearby Grand Rapids.

When he was sixteen, Ernest Graham went to work for his father in the daytime and attended high school at night. Work as a carpenter, mason, and jack-of-all-trades gave him a wide variety of experience in the construction field.[5] From his mother, a Bible school teacher, Graham acquired a sense of history and "a tendency to pious remarks." When his father died, Graham, by then at the beginning of his twenties, decided to seek greater opportunities. He left home with

[254] ERNEST ROBERT GRAHAM

the knowledge of how to put a building together and set out for Chicago. He received no more formal education, but was awarded degrees as an honorary Doctor of Letters by Notre Dame University and Coe College, nearly forty years later.

Graham would often talk of his early experience as a worker in overalls:

> Honest toil never hurt anyone regardless of age. My work with the trowel stood up with the best of them. Those were the days when a bricklayer laid three thousand bricks a day. The best men occupied both ends of the guideline with the fillers-in between them to keep the job rolling as a team. "Mortar up," was the foreman's cry. Besides a man earned his pay by the sweat of his brow without the aid of fringe benefits. We were a hardy lot free of confusion—organized or otherwise.[6]

Knowing that most midwestern architects learned their craft on the job, Graham was at first content to learn to construct rather than to design buildings. Like his father, he could follow models in "plan books," which contained "bedsheet drawings" that measured over five feet long, and "builder's handbooks," which could fit into a carpenter's overalls.[7] As he grew older and more experienced, Graham, wisely aware of his limitations, selected talented designers to do the work in the drafting room while he focused on drumming up business and supervising the men at the office and in the field. Nevertheless, Graham often played a decisive role in larger design matters, sometimes ordering major changes in a building.[8]

The midwestern climate, in which midwestern builders like Graham's father worked, was a demanding teacher, eliciting and forcing ingenuity. Facing temperatures that ranged from 30 degrees Fahrenheit to below zero in winter to 111 degrees Fahrenheit in the summer, builders boasted that "a man who could build here could build anywhere."[9]

Glowing visions of cities rising out of the forests and plains were part of the dream of many of the young farm boys of Ernest Graham's generation.[10] And midwesterners were particularly disposed to think in what Frederick Jackson Turner, the historian of the American frontier, called "large combinations."

Villages became towns overnight, towns became cities in one generation. These westerners were what we now call "rugged individualists," but they were at the same time the greatest "joiners" in America. The secret of leading these men was in knowing how to treat them as individuals, but as individuals of a team. Independent, ingenious, talkative, great jokers, hard workers, they formed a new breed of worker—the American workingman. Anyone who could learn to boss them could build well, and build at speeds which amazed the world. Although these workers were a tough and unruly lot they followed any boss who

could work beside them and who knew how to treat them as individuals and yet at the same time work them as a team. For the secret strength of the American workman was his capacity to subordinate his individuality in teamwork. He did this under a new kind of authority, the authority of rules which could be changed at will yet once agreed to were binding on all. Such rules represented the will of equals; they were an agreement, not a command.[11]

Within three years of his arrival in Chicago, Graham would be working on the construction of the World's Columbian Exposition, a project on a scale undreamt of even by the wildest real estate speculator in his home state. His first job on arrival, however, was modest, and it was not with Daniel H. Burnham, but with Holabird and Roche.

At the time, this firm was constructing the Tacoma Building, a perfect laboratory for learning the techniques of skyscraper construction. The Tacoma was built with traditional masonry walls on the sides and back; the rest of the building consisted of a combination of vertical steel H columns and girders and iron beams riveted together in a frame covered with terra-cotta fireproofing. The building had numerous windows and cast-iron or terra-cotta ornament. Thus Graham learned firsthand of the possibilities of metal skeleton construction early in the history of the tall building.[12]

Henry Ericsson, like Graham, was a supervisor of construction in those days, and in fact worked on the building next to the Tacoma. His description of the problems faced by these early skyscraper builders is enlightening.

One was left to meet new and trying problems by his wits and native resources right on the job. . . . How we did work in those days! I was contractor, superintendent, foreman, timekeeper and material clerk.[13]

Young supervisors like Ericsson and Graham worked "in the hole" alongside their men, who were often immigrants speaking no English.

None of them, foremen or workers, had ever set a steel beam—there were no "steel workers" in Chicago or anywhere else at the time—but some of the bricklayers had been sailors and knew about hoists and ropes, so they would lash the metal beams, hoist them up, and set them in place, doing "as good a job as willing hands always can do."[14]

If Graham chose his first employer well, he had also chosen his new city well. The Illinois-Michigan Canal had opened in 1848, and before long the city would become a railroad hub. Chicago teemed with life, talent, and opportunity. Between 1880 and 1888 when Graham arrived, the city's population grew from 500,000 to nearly 1,000,000. Louis Sullivan, William Le Baron Jenney, and young Frank Lloyd Wright were all working within a few blocks of each other. Innovation followed upon innovation as architects and engineers explored the possibilities of the metal skeleton as a building technique.

There were many solutions to the problems of plan too; from the "hollow doughnut" of the Rookery, its double-loaded office corridor surrounding a central light court; to the L-shape of the Tacoma; to the intricacies of S. S. Beman's Studebaker Building, its offices interspersed with studios and theaters.

A walk around town revealed many buildings with cast-iron fronts like the Page Brothers Building, Italianate facades like the one gracing the Delaware Building, great loft buildings, and impressive railroad stations. On Michigan Avenue, Adler and Sullivan's Auditorium Building was going up—combining a striking theater with a hotel and office building.

Elsewhere in the city, churches, rowhouses, workers' cottages, residences, and schools were being built at a rapid rate. There were examples of every building type and every style—Greek Revival, Gothic, Romanesque, Italianate, French Chateau, and Queen Anne to name the most common. A planned city was being built for railroad workers in Pullman, and large-scale plans were underway for the construction of the University of Chicago campus and a stately, citywide park system. If travel is for the architect what a

library is for the scholar, young Ernest had only to get on the trolley to round out his apprenticeship. For a small-town boy, a would-be architect, burgeoning Chicago was not only a teacher, but a new world.

As if that were not enough, around 1890 Chicagoans began planning to host a world's fair, the World's Columbian Exposition of 1893. Daniel Burnham was selected chief of construction. When his partner John Wellborn Root died unexpectedly on January 15, 1891, William Holabird recommended Graham highly and offered to let him go so that he could help Burnham out. It was the beginning of an association that would continue for twenty years.

Graham was only twenty-six when he began as Burnham's assistant chief of construction, supervising fourteen thousand men engaged in erecting a model city to dazzle the world. Burnham recorded in the scrapbook of the fair that Graham's title was later changed to assistant director of works; his duties, "to act for his chief in everything except in artistic designing for which he had no training."[15]

A natural boss, a man who liked to be in charge, Graham proved his mettle and showed his style by riding a white horse around the grounds while wearing a brown derby and giving orders left and right.

Seldom has a young architect had such an opportunity early in his career. He found himself in frequent contact with the nation's top ten architects involved in designing the main buildings; working on a variety of building types, from a railroad station to a fine arts palace; supervising the erection of the largest three-hinged arch building in history; and overseeing the completion of the Ferris wheel and dozens of pavilions representing the industries, arts, and crafts of nations from all over the world. This enviable apprenticeship gave Graham the confidence and experience that sustained him throughout his career.

Years later he wrote of the fair:

The World's Columbian Exposition, the building of which brought together the most eminent architects, sculptors and painters, had a wholesome and permanent effect on American Architecture. The entire country was stirred to a greater consciousness of beauty. Immediately afterwards the nation entered upon a period of tremendous industrial expansion, and architecture in America, stimulated aesthetically by the exposition, practically by the introduction of new steel construction, was called upon to inspire and direct the greatest era of building in the world's history.[16]

The hyperbole is revealing: here is Graham's naiveté and boosterism as well as his admiration of Beaux-Arts classicism and his view of the importance of the fair. Future historians may agree that the fair was to the history of city planning what French cathedrals were to the history of ecclesiastical architecture or Roman civil engineering to the history of vaulted construction, and they may one day yet concede that the World's Columbian Exposition of 1893 inspired the greatest era of building in the world's history. But that promise had not yet been fulfilled in 1933, when Graham wrote those words.

The fair was, however, a stunning success by the standards of critical review, revenue, and popular appeal. Henry Adams hailed it as a step in evolution. It cost $28.3 million and earned $28.8 million. Over 21 million people came and wrote the folks at home to "sell the cookstove if you must, but come, come to the fair."[17]

His experience with the fair convinced Graham that architecture needed more than the skills taught in departments and schools of architecture. It would also need the talents of men of affairs, of businessmen with highly developed administrative abilities. Burnham was a model of the new kind of architect who thought of building as a complex of activities in which the architect coordinates the skills of the engineer, contractor, promoter, and financier.

Pleased with his young assistants' work, Burnham took Graham, Edward C. Shankland (the fair's chief engineer), and Charles B. Atwood (the fair's chief designer) as partners in the firm that he renamed Daniel Burnham and Company on March 1, 1894. Atwood left in 1895 and four years later Shankland left to establish his own practice. Graham remained as Burnham's only partner until 1910, when Burnham divided his own share of the profits with his two sons, making them junior partners.[18]

Beginning in 1895 and for the rest of his life, Graham kept a record of his activities. More like a ship captain's log than a diary, these pages reveal little about Graham's thoughts, or the character of his professional relationships, but they are a conscientious list of where he went, whom he saw, and who called at the office, and they reveal an intensely active period between 1894 and 1912 when Burnham died.

It is interesting to compare this diary to the journals of other men. John Holabird, also a Chicago architect, included sketches, drawings, ideas, and reactions to what he saw on his journeys in his journals. Burnham left an archive of memoirs, notes, letters, and drawings, but in his diary noted no more than names or places. E. H. Bennett similarly confined himself to a form of log, and Graham did likewise. He would usually note the city, the date, sometimes the weather or the hotel, but the accounts of his travels were laconic: "Spent the day at Cambridge"; "Drove to Oxford"; "Visited Versailles"; "Visited Fontainebleau." A characteristic entry, made on June 27, 1920, read, "Spent the day quietly going about London." However, despite the absence of philosophical, theoretical, or aesthetic comments or references to larger affairs, Graham's sparse entries yield some telling information.

Since he was frequently at Burnham's side in negotiations on civic matters, Graham's initiation into Chicago politics began early. The diary entry for November 21, 1895, records one typical event.

> Mr. Burnham and I spent the afternoon in special committee chamber and Mr. Ellsworth and Atty. M——were present. Mr. Campbell, Chairman, . . . said when Field Museum and South Park Commission agreed the council would make proper ordinance.

Graham's daily work routine began regularly at 8:00 A.M. when he signed in at the office, almost invariably six days a week. Even when he had been traveling on business over the weekend he checked in promptly for work. A sampler of entries shows that his duties in the first decade after the fair were varied.

12/14/96 Spent the day in St. Louis with Mr. Parker and passenger agents of Frisco, Wabash and Vandalia lines. All anxious to concentrate on new building corner 7th and Olive.

7/20/97 Met St. Gaudens and went over Logan Monument.

1/24/98 Dr. Sheppard called and asked Mr. B. if he would do the university job for a reduced commission and he said no but would do it for full commission and then make a donation to the university.

3/28/98 Commenced work on revised studies Pittsburgh station. Commenced work on competitive studies for Toledo station.

The only hint of difficulty between Burnham and Graham occurs the next year:

7/5/99 Called on Mr. Selfridge this P.M. and he asked me if I were going to remain where I am after this year and I told him nothing as yet was decided. He then said he wanted to commence on drawings for a new State St. Bldg. at once but before going to D. H. Burnham he wanted to make sure he would have me to deal with, that he would not give the work to DHB & Co. if I were to leave. I am to settle this question the earliest date and report to him.[19]

After this there was no more talk of leaving.

Graham went to Europe in 1902 and his brief account reveals that he always traveled first-class and stayed at the best hotels: Claridge's in London, the Ritz in Paris, and the Biltmore (for which he was associate architect) in New York.

Another entry in the diaries reveals a lighter side to Graham:

10/20/04 Mr. Field asked when we could have a concert in the new Orchestra Building and I told him sometime in December. He said he would like to bet me it would not be until January. Therefore I wagered him a suit of clothes that the orchestra holds a session there before January 1.

As Burnham's assistant, Graham had a hand in almost every project that came into the office in those years. He prepared bids, closed contracts, talked with clients, went over plans, made site inspections, and negotiated labor disputes, among other duties. D. H. Burnham and Company erected a number of different building types—schools, libraries, hotels, department stores, banks, office buildings, railroad stations, warehouses, factories, residences, service buildings such as garages and parking docks, and public buildings. The emphasis, however, was on commercial buildings. Earning the firm an international reputation were such commissions as the Ellicott Building in Buffalo; the Flatiron Building in New York; and the Reliance, Fisher, and Railway Exchange buildings in Chicago.

The firm's offices were located on the seventh floor of the Railway Exchange Building. A model Burnham building with a square doughnut plan, it had a glass-covered lobby in the center clad with marble walls. On the exterior, the white enamel terra-cotta tiles covered the structural steel skeleton. In the eight years before Burnham's death, the Selfridge Department Store in London, the Union Station in Washington, D.C., Gimbel Brothers and the Hotel Claridge in New York, Wanamaker's in Philadelphia, and Filene's in Boston added new luster to the name of Daniel Burnham and Company.

Graham's flair and skill as a businessman emerge in the following anecdote by Andrew Rebori. It relates how the firm landed the commission for the Flatiron Building in New York.

According to reliable sources, George Fuller met Ernest Graham at the Chicago Club for lunch before boarding the Eastbound Century [the Twentieth-Century Limited]. The topic of conversation was the Fuller building contemplated for the corner of Broadway and 23rd Street on a triangular block noted for swirling winds. "When are you leaving for New York?" casually asked Graham. "Why, this afternoon," replied Fuller. "What a coincidence, my office has two reservations on the Century for this afternoon, let's go together," Graham said. And they did. Before the Century reached New York, Graham had the job for his firm's first big New York building.[20]

At this point Graham, the indomitable go-getter, really spread his wings—feeding new jobs to his associates: Peirce Anderson as top ranking designer, Edward Probst as practical head of the drafting force, and legal-minded Howard White in charge of contractual documents and legal matters. "Charlie" Murphy as personal aid and special partner to the President was always on the move trying to keep up with the head of the new firm.

All hands looked up to the steady skipper with deep regard and affection as the organization grew in size. Graham was the definite leader in a mass effort that operated with precision and force. Nonetheless, from the bridge he admired most the creative individual able to rise above the multitude to give expression in the shape of forms and things to come.[21]

During the twenty-four-year period (1912–36) in which Graham was its chief, the firm received over two thousand commissions. While many of these were for alterations, additions, and smaller jobs, as in any architectural practice, the office erected nearly a hundred important buildings of uniformly high quality in this era.[22]

Graham's skill in winning clients derived in part from his sociability. Membership in several elite clubs, such as the Chicago Commercial, Mid-Day, Old Elm, Racquet, Shoreacres, and Tavern clubs of Chicago and the Bankers and Metropolitan clubs of New York offered him many opportunities to meet prospective clients at lunch. Often mixing business with pleasure, he

would also schedule golf outings and fishing trips with his clients.[23]

Although he was only a moderate drinker, Graham was a frequent visitor at his favorite club, the Town House on Banks Street, in Chicago, a private club for executives where operating expenses were pooled monthly and allocated in proportion to the members' ability to pay. The Town House was destroyed for a high-rise years ago, but the north-south street remains and was later renamed Graham Court. During the 1933–34 Century of Progress International Exposition, Graham was also a regular guest at the Rendezvous Club at Twenty-third Street and the lake.[24] Graham was a firm believer in "Temperance, not Abstinence, using 'temperance' in the literal sense, meaning moderation, rather than in the sense intended by the advocates of the Temperance Movement."[25]

Graham was well known for being a good listener. "Let others do the talking," he would say to his associates, "and you will soon learn all they know without risk to your opinion. Experience teaches, the answer to ignorance is silence."[26]

There is evidence, however, that Graham was less amiable in dealing with contractors than with potential clients, at least in the early days. Paul Starrett, a Chicago building contractor, wrote about his observations of Graham when, as young men, they both worked with Burnham.

Graham and I were at outs. He was smart as a whip, but his ideas of fair dealing were so peculiar that I wondered at Burnham's confidence in him. Graham loved to see a builder lose money. He would go to almost any length to make him lose. As an example, on the Illinois Trust and Savings Bank a mason contractor named George Messersmith had put in the lowest bid on the masonry and Graham was authorized to give him the job. I was in the office when Messersmith came in. "How many brick did you figure on, George?" asked Graham. George gave his figure. "Now you know,

George," said Graham, "there aren't nearly as many bricks in the building as that. You take off 200,000. And what did you figure on to lay these brick?" Messersmith gave his figure, and Graham said, "Oh, you know you can lay them for $2 less a thousand than that!" So he went on through all the items, cutting the figures down. "Now, George," said Graham, "we have another figure much less than yours"—this was a lie—"but we want you to do the work. All this figures up to so much, but I'll allow you $10,000 more for good measure. If you want to take the contract for that, you can have it." Old George said: "Well, Mr. Graham, I guess you know more about it than I do. I'll take the job."

Graham turned to me and said: "Will you O.K. this?" "I will not," I said. "If Messersmith is bidding on this building, he ought to make his own figures." Well, Graham went ahead anyway, and he skinned the life out of old George on that job. He didn't get anything out of it personally, either, except the satisfaction of bragging to the owners of the extraordinarily low figure.[27]

Louis Horowitz, another general contractor, recalled

Graham's hair was red and he wore a wisp of red mustache. He always carried his head to one side and as he waddled swiftly, sharp-eyed, he reminded me of an alert duck. He was always hustling and much of his activity had to do with his efforts to make some contractor shave his price to a client of Ernest Graham. He loved to beat contractors with their own kind of sharpness. It was a game with him; indeed he delighted to skin their eye teeth by day and then skin them again at night around a poker table.[28]

There is other evidence, however, that Graham was fair-minded and evenhanded. The terms the firm worked out with the Federal Re-serve of Chicago show a system favorable to both client and general contractor: the contractor received a flat fee for assuming all responsibility for all subcontracts, with the understanding that the client would participate in any savings that might result later from a falling market or negotiations or trading with the subcontractors. In the case of the Federal Reserve of Chicago, for example, the contractors received 10 percent for the first $100,000 they could save, 15 percent for the second, and 25 percent for the third. All savings over and above $300,000 accrued to the client. In the end the bank had the benefit of a net saving of $475,383.60, out of which it paid the general contractor, John Griffiths and Son Company, an extra fee of $50,000 as agreed.[29]

The men who worked under Graham at the office invariably referred to him as "a perfect gentleman," "soft spoken," and "generous." Charles F. Murphy, his assistant for twenty years said "he was also a driver, a real worker . . . always a do-doer, wanting to get people to move."

During World War I, Woodrow Wilson put these qualities to use, charging Graham with the job of building gunpowder plants in West Virginia. Responsible only to the president, Graham was given seventy thousand men and soon set up a schedule that produced 3.5 million pounds of gunpowder a day.[30]

Generous, at times paternalistic toward the men in his firm, Graham tried to maintain feelings of good fellowship in the office, taking his associates out to lunch on their birthdays and seeing to it that paychecks for his employees continued even during long bouts of illness.[31]

His rivals in other architectural firms regarded Graham differently, however. At a meeting of the Chicago Architecture Club in 1984, Larry Perkins remarked that he remembered his father, Dwight Perkins, saying that William Holabird had once moaned aloud during a golf outing at the Glenview Country Club, "I did a terrible thing to Daniel Burnham, I introduced him to Ernest R. Graham."

Larry Perkins himself described Graham as "rough and tough. If he had his thumb in your eye then he could talk with you." Thomas Tall-madge recalled that Holabird referred to Graham as a "blankety blank red-headed young demon." A limerick accompanying a caricature of Graham in the Ryerson and Burnham Libraries of the Art Institute of Chicago proclaims:

And he said, If you think that my locks
Are the only thing like to a fox
Remember my guile and you'll see by my smile
That you've got yourself into a box![32]

At ease with wealthy and powerful men, Graham was a close friend of Harry Selfridge, the London department store owner; Samuel Insull, the utilities magnate; and Thomas Coleman duPont, the munitions manufacturer.[33] Contractor Louis Horowitz was also occasionally part of Graham's circle.[34]

Graham managed his private fiscal affairs well. Rental income from ownership of half of the Insurance Exchange and part of the Railway Exchange buildings provided the basis of his later fortune. His reputation was that of a practical financier and businessman who refused contracts for buildings that might prove financial failures and did not let the lure of profits unbalance his sound judgment.[35] As his last will and testament shows, he provided annuities for his widow, his stepson, his brother, his sister, his half brother, his cousin, and a friend. The rest he left in an endowment of over a million dollars to establish a school to be known as the "American School of the Fine Arts," later known as the Graham Foundation for Advanced Studies in the Fine Arts.[36]

A lifelong Republican, Graham was at ease with men in politics. He personally met four American presidents, Grover Cleveland, Theodore Roosevelt, William Howard Taft, and Woodrow Wilson. President Taft called on Graham in Chicago to discuss the city planning for Baguio, the summer capital of the Philippines, which had been annexed by the United States following the Spanish-American War of 1898. Graham's diary records yet another presidential meeting in connection with the firm's work on the Union Station in Washington, D.C.

2/7/11 Arrived in Washington in the morning. Went direct to General Bixby's office and spent the morning hearing arguments regarding the Metropolitan Bridge. Luncheoned with Mr. Peck and we together called on the Secretary of War and explained in detail the happy family we had gotten together in connection with the bridges. From there called on the President and spent some time. Took the midnight train back to New York.[37]

Graham was known for his skill in labor negotiations. If any problems arose on the job he would invite the labor leaders to his office for a meeting. Offering Corona cigars all around, Graham would settle matters with men like Mike Boyle, Pete Shaughnessy, and other Chicago labor leaders.

His reputation as a fair negotiator was so widely known that he would occasionally be asked to settle disputes among workers on projects with which his firm had no connections. In the spring of 1912, the plumbers and the steamfitters working on the McGundy Building were locked in disagreement. Skinny Madden and Simon O'Donnell, representing the laborers, asked Graham to act as arbitrator, hoping that he could help bring about a compromise, as he had when arguments had broken out on his firm's sites. A few days after a preliminary meeting, a bitter row erupted in Pat O'Malley's saloon and one man was killed. The following Monday morning the leaders waited at the door of the Railway Exchange Building for Graham. He was firm. "As long as there is violence and murder, I cannot do any good for you," he explained, refusing to meet with them. As always, Graham was aware of his own limitations. In fact, the dispute would continue to fester for another decade.[38]

Dealing with prospective clients Graham was a courtly entrepreneur in the initial contacts, a steadfast consultant throughout the planning process, and always a model businessman with facts and figures. His work on the commission for the Federal Reserve Bank in Chicago is a typical example.

When the newly appointed building committee of the bank met on January 28, 1919, to discuss its responsibilities in securing a new building, two different points of view emerged about how it should go about selecting an architect. W. A. Heath wanted to invite a number of architects to a hearing, but James Simpson argued that there were only two architects to consider seriously, "Mr. Graham's firm and Holabird and Roche," and that "more trouble, delay and dissatisfaction is always occasioned in dealing with a big competition than without." As Simpson himself favored Graham for his experience in large building projects, the group decided that it would meet with Graham "without incurring any obligation for the future."[39]

It was a familiar situation to Graham. He agreed to these conditions at a meeting two days later, saying that the architects would:

commence at once and prepare drawings and sketches, every conceivable plan, to work on this constantly until such time as you are ready to build and decide definitely on the plan you wish to adopt, when we will then proceed with finished working drawings preparatory to closing contract. Until such time . . . there is no charge on our part whatsoever and no obligation on your part.[40]

What arrangement could be more appealing to bankers? They could back out at any time. If they had paused to reflect, they might have considered that Graham would conduct the business so well it would seem ungentlemanly or unwise, or both, to go on with another architect without very good cause after the firm had spent so many hours laboring on their behalf. They might have gone back to the competition method to insure that they got the best of many good architects available but they did not.

The web of the courtship began in earnest in Graham's office on February 7. At that time Sigurd Naess, a member of the design team, asked for a temporary office in the bank "for the purpose of studying the organization, for facts and disposition of the different departments, vaults,

furniture, etc." Graham also asked that "all officers and employees offer suggestions in regard to the proper, efficient, or even ideal needs of present or future operations."[41]

On May 23, the building committee was invited to Graham's office (fig. 255) where the architects displayed their "designs, plans and tentative sketches and estimates of cost" with various elevations offered for the committee's consideration and to help them determine "whether to build an exclusive or monumental building or one of commercial design."

Graham was patient while the bankers mulled over these decisions for many months. It was not until November 5 that the matter was settled in favor of a commercial building. At no point in this long period did Graham have any written assurance that his firm would finally receive the commission. Graham apparently conducted the whole affair as a gentleman's agreement.

On December 5, the head of the Federal Reserve in Washington wired his instructions to hold off on any future construction because materials supply companies would soon be lowering their prices. The beleaguered bankers met with Graham, despairing of ever getting out of their present predicament in which the Federal Reserve in Chicago was forced to conduct business from four different buildings. Once more Graham helped the committee with his political *savoir-faire* and business acumen.

Backed by years of experience in dealing with government agencies negotiating contracts, Graham wrote a coolly reasoned memorandum to Washington in which he pointed out that labor was 80 percent of the cost of a building and that it was unlikely to go down; freight was 4 percent and that also was unlikely to do down. He conceded that building materials might go down, but asserted that they were not likely to go down much and that any savings would be offset by the rise in labor costs. Approval from Washington to go ahead came before the end of the month. There is no record in the minutes of any other architect being considered at any time, but the actual signing of preliminary plans in the archi-

[255] ERNEST R. GRAHAM'S PRIVATE OFFICE

tect's office did not occur until January 24, 1920, nearly a year to the date since the two parties had first met.

If he was a patient prospective architect, Graham was a deferential contracted architect. In the ensuing months he and the other partners sent dozens of letters to the building committee asking approval for this or that or recommending this subcontractor or that one on every aspect of the project. "Our recommendation is that you adopt travernell fleurie marble. . . . We submit for your approval the following hardware. . . . We suggest stack lining from the Central Asbestos and Magnesia Co. . . ." No one who dealt with Ernest Graham could complain that he wasn't consulted by his architect.[42]

The building committee, apparently completely satisfied with the work Graham had done, later hired him to build the Federal Reserve branch in Detroit, in spite of protests from the Michigan Society of Architects and the Michigan Chapter of the AIA. Before the decade was over, the firm had erected seven buildings for the Federal Reserve System, including those in Omaha, Oklahoma City, Denver, Dallas, and Kansas City, Missouri. Repeat business, a staple of the firm since Burnham's day, continued throughout Graham's tenure as senior partner.

Graham earned much of his fortune in the 1920s, an enormously active decade for the firm. The 175 to 250 men employed in the office turned out work at a prodigious rate. Graham was often out of town on business, traveling to Detroit, Omaha, New York, Dallas, Kansas City, Baltimore, St. Louis, Philadelphia, Pittsburgh, and San Antonio to keep up with the demands of new business.

Following the stock market crash of 1929, the firm sustained itself for several years with only three major Chicago commissions: the Field Building, the U.S. Post Office, and the Merchandise Mart. By 1935, the office staff had been reduced to fifteen men.[43] Charles Murphy said of this period that it was fortunate that when the crash occurred it was cheaper to finish the buildings already started than to tear them down.[44]

The decline of building activity during the depression years meant that the last six years of Graham's working life lacked the hustle and bustle of the preceding four decades. But in the meantime, he had come a long way from his days as a bricklayer to this longtime role as a leading figure in a major architectural firm.

About Graham's personal life we have rather sparse information. Graham was short and rather slender, his chief distinguishing physical characteristic being his hair, referred to as a lion's mane when it was red and as "abundant" when it turned white, and a moustache. He was a handsome man careful in his dress, with pants always well pressed, his three-piece suits well tailored, and his tie, watch chain, and hat well chosen. His energy and confident air gave him a powerful presence, augmented by his fondness for rattling gold pieces in his pocket.

Graham married Carlotta Hall, a Chicagoan, on May 17, 1893. The couple lived at 341 East Sixty-second Street until 1922, when they moved to 25 East Banks Street. Carlotta died December 12, 1923, and two years later at Stoke Poges, England, Graham married Ruby Fitzhugh Leffingwell (fig. 256), widow of William Leffingwell, the owner of a popular billiard parlor at Sheridan Road and Wilson Avenue in Chicago. Ruby's son William later changed his name to Graham. During his college years at Cornell, young Bill Graham frequently brought his friends home at holiday time. One of them, Robert W. Jorgenson,

[256] RUBY GRAHAM

was a frequent guest at the Graham mansion. He recalled:

Dinner at the Grahams' was always a formal occasion, attended by a butler, a footman, and a serving maid, with Mr. Graham sternly presiding at the head of the table.

He was probably in his sixties in those days—successful, rich and proud of his accomplishments. He seemed a friendly person, but one who was impatient with those who lacked ambition or expected to be compensated without themselves contributing.

He was especially fond of lecturing young people about how to "get ahead" in life. One of his favorite themes at dinner was the need for frequent self-appraisal, delivered in deep Stentorian tones to his captive audience. "Boys, write yourselves a letter! Ask yourselves what you have accomplished this day, and if you find yourselves wanting, resolve to mend your ways!"[45]

Robert Klark Graham, a nephew, also knew his Uncle Ernest during his college years. Although their relationship was not close, Graham sent Robert a regular allowance to support him while he studied to be a singer at Juilliard. Later Robert abandoned his musical ambitions, studied optics at Cornell, and made a fortune in plastic lenses.[46]

Graham's house at 25 East Banks Street had originally been commissioned by Potter Palmer. The architect was C. W. Palmer (no relation), who completed the design in 1888.[47] It is a handsome building.

Inside, an oval staircase rises four floors to a skylight and dominates the generous space of the foyer. To the left of the foyer, composite columns mark the entrance to the living room, which is adorned by rich mouldings and composite pilasters. Parquet floors and a marble fireplace further embellish the interior. The dining room, like the living room, has one curved side to the front and leads to a library, which Graham added to the house.

The library has a hidden door made of "shelves" of fake books leading to a staircase to a "Poker Room" in the half basement below. This was often the setting for lively card games.

Howard Thomas, a Chicago artist who made a drawing of Graham's living room fireplace to be used on the family's Christmas card, recalled some of the striking features of the luxurious house on Banks Street. One was a portrait by painter Howard Chandler Christy of Mrs. Graham attired in a pink gown and holding an ostrich fan (fig. 256); another was a piano finished in gold leaf. The dining room, distinguished by Middle Eastern decor, contained many objects later donated to the Field Museum, a portrait of

Graham by Sir William Orpen, and mementos of the Grahams' travels. A curving oval staircase led to Graham's study on the second floor, which was marked by two onyx pillars. To the left of the study was Mrs. Graham's room, which contained a sled bed that allegedly had belonged to Napoleon. A ballroom was located on the fourth floor, where the walls were hung with red velvet and embellished with reproductions of famous paintings, including the *Mona Lisa*.[48] Off to the side was Graham's wine cellar, with racks for over two thousand bottles.

Mrs. Graham's dressing room, hand painted in green and gold with cherubs, maidens, and flowers, is still in its original condition, but the other upstairs rooms were remodeled by Charles F. Murphy, who later occupied the house.

Although Graham's formal education had terminated in the public schools of Lowell, Michigan, he had a consuming interest in books for most of his adult life. In his later years, the urge to collect fine leather-bound volumes and first editions grew. While he was making plans for the private publication of the two volume monograph *Architectural Works of Graham, Anderson, Probst and White*, by Batsford, a London firm, he started to buy more books than ever. It is likely that he planned his purchases with the vision of a school library in mind. The library he eventually put together contained over three thousand volumes. They included, among other rarities, such items as Piranesi folios, a first edition of Palladio, eight volumes of the works of Augustus Welby Northmore Pugin, and some original John Soane drawings. The library did indeed pass to the Graham Foundation for Advanced Studies in the Fine Arts, founded by Graham's executors, and remained there until 1982 when the Canadian Center for Architecture in Montreal, Canada, purchased it.

Years later Andrew Rebori wrote about Graham's dreams during his last days—dreams of endowing a school.

> Seated alone or with friends before the open fireplace surrounded by his art treasures he became the great builder turned idealist

seeking to provide the means for advanced study in the fine arts that he could not afford to indulge in as a rugged dynamic individual in his own chosen field.[49]

The Graham Foundation for Advanced Studies in the Fine Arts, located at 216 East Superior Street [now at 4 West Burton Place] resulted from the legacy of Ernest R. Graham who disposed by will the bulk of his accumulated wealth for the benefit of talented men and women in the advancement of modern art.[50]

Graham died in November 1936. His funeral was held at the Fourth Presbyterian Church on Michigan Avenue, and he was buried in Graceland Cemetery near an oak tree and next to his first wife, Carlotta. In late afternoon in winter, the shadow of the tree reaches across Willowmere Pond to the boulder marking the grave of Daniel Hudson Burnham.

WILLIAM PEIRCE ANDERSON
(1870–1924)

For nearly all his long career, Graham had had the support of his three partners in one way or another. There is no doubt, however, that Peirce Anderson was by far the most important of these for it was he who had the qualities both Burnham and Graham lacked.

Thomas E. Tallmadge described Anderson as a big, spare man, "Herculean in build with a head like Beethoven." He was the opposite of Graham in temperament (fig. 257). Reserved and cautious, a bachelor all his life, Anderson was truly modest by nature. Like Charles Atwood, his predecessor as chief designer, William (a name he did not use in his professional life) Peirce Anderson was a well-educated easterner. Born February 20, 1870, in Oswego, New York, to Hugh and Hannah Louisa Peirce Anderson, he spent his boyhood in Salt Lake City, Utah. A five-year period at Riverview Military Academy, in Poughkeepsie, New York, followed. From there he proceeded to Harvard, where he received his

[257] WILLIAM PEIRCE ANDERSON

A.B. degree. In 1892, Anderson decided to continue his studies in either theoretical physics or electrical engineering. When he obtained a certificate in the latter two years later, he began to doubt the wisdom of his choice and traveled to Chicago to ask Daniel Burnham for advice. Burnham encouraged Anderson, then twenty-four, to continue his studies at the École des Beaux-Arts in Paris.[51] In Burnham's opinion, no better training for the practice of architecture existed, and entry was open free of charge to anyone in the world between fifteen and thirty years of age who could pass the entrance examinations.

The program was organized in five stages. To begin with, the applicant prepared for admission by studying under a designated master. Anderson began by becoming a member of Atelier Paulin. Then he listed himself as an *aspirant á l'École des Beaux-Arts,* took the entrance examinations, passed on the first try, and was admitted to the "second class" level. During this phase he attended lectures (which were elective) and soon afterward passed the examinations on scientific subjects. In addition to the usual courses and tests, the school used a point system to promote students to the first level. To earn points the student had to enter a contest, submit a sketch on an assigned project, and later expand it into a fully developed drawing. The better the design, the more points the jury awarded. Anderson reached the first level in 1897. In common with most of his fellow students, he was promoted after two years.

At this stage, the aspiring architects were required to complete six sketches and six complete renderings of complex building types—museums, theaters, or hotels—each year. In this phase, Anderson won four prizes in two years, about the average for his class. The final step up was a contest for the *Grand Prix de Rome*, but, as this was open only to Frenchmen, Anderson was not eligible.[52] He left the École des Beaux-Arts in 1899 with a coveted and much admired addition to his collection of degrees—*Architecte diplome par le Gouvernement*. Immediately after graduation, Anderson left Paris for a long-awaited year of travel in France, Italy, and Spain, sketching and visiting architectural monuments, thus finishing his education in the classical European manner.

For the rest of his life, Anderson looked back on his years in Europe as a golden period. In Paris he had worked alongside some of the most promising young architects of his era—Edward Bennett, Paul Cret, Chester Morrison Davidson, Theodore Lescher, Julia Morgan, Benjamin Wistar Morris, William E. Parson, George Robard, and James Gamble Rogers, to mention some of the Americans. He also came to know Louis Bourgeois, a Belgian who later immigrated to the United States, and L. F. Janin, who worked in the United States for a short time making renderings for the 1909 Plan of Chicago. Anderson lived in a commodious apartment on the Rue Jacob and on his daily walk to school passed the imposing buildings that distinguish Paris. Like so many

other architects trained there, he developed a lifelong and unfaltering preference for traditional architecture as exemplified in the buildings of the École des Beaux-Arts itself.

Anderson was also exposed to examples of classical works in the library there, through drawings tacked on the walls of the studios, sculpture in the courtyard, and theories expounded in lectures. Anderson's French masters had systematized the canons of the great European classical tradition, much as Napoleon had codified traditional law.

The historic ornamentation that Anderson preferred tended to be the heavy swags, urns, and coffers of the late Roman period. As Thomas Tallmadge put it:

> His inspiration was not Augustan, but the fuller, richer magnificence of the third century . . . the sweep of a great barrel vault, the majestic recessional of a glistening colonnade. Although possessed of an extremely logical mind and educated as an engineer he was never greatly interested in the metaphysics of architecture. The strict expression of function by form, or the development of an indigenous or an American style left him, to say the least, cold.[53]

While Anderson's architectural style has struck some critics as heavy-handed, his ability as a planner of architecture and urban spaces has been acknowledged. His plans for department stores, banks, and railroad stations exemplified the best of the classical tradition creatively adapted to the demands of new building conditions and types.

Compare Anderson's solution for Marshall Field and Company to Louis Sullivan's solution for Schlesinger and Mayer (1891–94 and 1899, now Carson Pirie Scott and Company). While no one disputes the appropriateness of the latter's horizontal massing and the beauty of the fenestration and its ornament, the interior spaces of Carson's are loftlike in their undivided simplicity. At Marshall Field's, the steel cage is manipulated so that three great vertical spaces emerge in meaningful counterpoint to the horizontal spaces. A thirteen-story arcade on the northeast corner provides a sense of climax, expressing the importance of the then largely feminine activity of shopping and fulfilling the social expectations of seeing and being seen on the balcony spaces surrounding it. A Tiffany mosaic vault (designed by Edward H. Bennett) adorns a five-story space in the southeast corner, and the four-story Walnut Room graces the northeast section.

The French lessons in planning and in the creation of ceremonial spaces Anderson learned in Paris and applied to a department store in Chicago have worked happily for generations. The climax of a visit to Field's comes in Peirce Anderson's dramatic, soaring spaces. The principles of proportioning and distributing rooms according to their use also holds true for the banks and the enormously complex railroad stations he designed. (See Part II for further discussion.)

Anderson's work for Burnham furthered his skill as a city planner. He was a member of the firm when Burnham was engaged in developing the plan for Washington, D.C. (1901–2), the Group Plan for Cleveland (1903), and a plan for San Francisco (1905), and he consulted with his fellow Beaux-Arts alumnus Edward Bennett (whom he personally had invited to join the firm) on the Plan of Chicago. After Bennett left the firm in 1910, Anderson did the city planning work, chiefly for the improvement of Manila and for the summer capital of the Philippines, the mountain city of Baguio. His chief aim in Manila was to keep the "mañana" atmosphere of the city while providing it with some straight streets.[54]

After the death of Daniel Burnham in 1912, Anderson had few opportunities to exercise his skill and training in city planning, largely because Bennett was widely regarded as Burnham's successor in this field. However, Anderson was responsible for the general plan for the disposition of buildings along the Chicago River, as Graham pointed out.[55]

Anderson's architectural training and cosmopolitan experience supplemented Burnham's and Graham's more limited backgrounds. Anderson was a member not only of the Architectural

[258] WATERCOLOR BY PEIRCE ANDERSON, VILLAGE SCENE

League, but of the National Sculptors Society, of the American Painters, and of the Harvard Club in New York. Thomas Tallmadge described him as "an accomplished and powerful draughtsman and the best water colorist in the architectural ranks that I ever knew."[56] Only two of the sketches Anderson made on his European tour have been found, but they support Tallmadge's judgment (figs. 258, 259). When Burnham died, President Taft appointed Anderson rather than Graham as Burnham's successor on the National Committee of Fine Arts.

Although he was reserved and modest by nature, Anderson could on occasion be aggressive and tough-minded. Graham was only four years older than Anderson, and two years after Burnham died, Anderson felt it necessary to let Graham know of his dissatisfaction with the way things were going. In an eight-page, single-spaced interoffice memorandum written in 1914,

[259] WATERCOLOR BY PEIRCE ANDERSON, DETAIL OF SIENA CATHEDRAL. PROPERTY OF BARBARA GRAHAM JAFFEE

he pointed out that the office organization was inefficient in several critical areas.[57] Given his powerful mind and his superb education and experience—all necessary to the firm—one wonders why Anderson was willing to accept only a 9.8 percent partnership arrangement after Burnham died. Perhaps it was his natural modesty, perhaps it was his bachelorhood, or perhaps he simply did not need more than his generous salary and percentage of the profits. At no time did any of the partners have to contribute capital to the firm. In September 1912, Graham's salary was $2,000 a month and Anderson and the others received $1,400.[58] Graham once complained to Charles Murphy that none of the other partners ever brought in a job. Perhaps Anderson wished to feel free of any sense of obligation in this respect.

When Anderson wrote a report for the "Record of the Class" on the occasion of his twenty-fifth reunion at Harvard in 1917, he listed the following as principal examples of his planning and design work: New York City, Equitable Building, Claridge's, Eighty Maiden Lane Building; Washington, Union Station and Plaza, Columbus Memorial, and post office; Chicago, Peoples Gas Building, Continental and Commercial Bank Building, Union Station; Boston, Filene's; and, in the Philippines, the planning of Baguio and improvements for Manila. Some of these were designed under Burnham's leadership, some under Graham's.

As the United States prepared to enter World War I, Anderson designed military training camps in fourteen different states and chaired the executive committee of the Central Department of the United States Army.

The postwar years were active ones, with plans for the Field Museum finally coming to fruition, and designs for the Straus Building in Chicago and a number of banks for the expanding Federal Reserve System on the boards.

From his earliest days, Anderson had hired or asked his chief to hire other designers to assist him, many of them also Beaux-Arts trained. These included Theodore Lescher, George Robard, and Edward Bennett from his own class, and later Charles Beersman, Louis Bourgeois, Frederick Dinkelberg, Mario Schiavoni, and Alfred Shaw.

Toward the middle of 1923 Anderson was diagnosed as having cancer and thereafter only left his home at 4858 South Blackstone Street for short trips to the office until he entered the hospital. During his final painful months, he worked from his bed. He died February 10, 1924.

"Andy is gone," said Graham, "his passing is a great personal loss to me. I shall miss him sorely more than words can express. He meant more than a partner to me—to

[260] EDWARD PROBST

EDWARD PROBST (1870–1942)

Like Graham and Howard White, Edward Probst (fig. 260) had only a public school education. A native Chicagoan born in 1870, he began his apprenticeship in the drafting room of architect Robert G. Pentecost and worked in a number of other offices for the next eleven years until he joined D. H. Burnham and Company in 1898. Gradually he assumed more responsibility and eventually took over supervision of the drafting room. Good at details, Probst had the reputation of being an exacting "task master." He oversaw three department heads: George Hubbard, in charge of plumbing and heating; Joachim Giaver and later Magnus Gundersen, in charge of structural engineering; and William Stevens, in charge of architectural drafting.

Edward Probst lived in his River Forest, Illinois, home until New Year's Day 1942, when he died at age seventy-one. His two sons, Marvin and Edward, Jr., headed the firm until it was sold to William Surman, the current president, in 1970.

HOWARD JUDSON WHITE (1870–1936)

Born on February 21, 1870, in Chicago, White (fig. 261) began his architectural training at the city's Manual Training School. After finishing the course in drafting, he entered Daniel Burnham's office as a junior draftsman at the age of eighteen.

When Burnham reorganized the office in 1908, White became superintendent of construction.[61] It was his responsibility to let bids, award contracts, and to be on the sites to oversee the work as the buildings went up. All the contractors, subcontractors, and superintendents in the field reported to him in the firm's offices on the fourteenth floor of the Railway Exchange or on his visits in the field. He was busiest between 1924 and 1929 when he was in charge of more than thirty structures.[62] His need to travel declined markedly during the depression bringing

lean on for support in fair or trying times. He was my right arm—always at my side." And the strong man's eyes were flooded with tears.[59]

In his obituary of Anderson published in the *Architectural Record*, Thomas Tallmadge wrote:

It has always seemed to me that the great marble gateway to the nation's capital, almost exclusively his work, best epitomizes his genius. It stands a peer, in that beautiful city, with the creations of Latrobe, Thornton, Hoban, McKim and Bacon. Over against the dome of Walter and the colonnades of Bulfinch, its triumphal arch gives back to the setting sun the glory that was Rome and to the sun in its rising the promise that is America.[60]

[261] HOWARD JUDSON WHITE

work of Graham, Anderson, Probst and White. The succession of well-trained, sometimes gifted designers who worked for the firm testify to Graham's ability to recognize and promote talent and to inspire loyalty in his employees. At the time of Anderson's death there were three especially gifted designers at work in the department—Charles G. Beersman, Mario Schiavoni, and Alfred Phillips Shaw.

When Graham died, tension in the office ran high. No one knew what would happen next. Alfred Shaw, the chief designer; Sigurd E. Naess, the planning expert; and Charles F. Murphy, Graham's longtime assistant, talked long into the night speculating about the roles each would play in the firm in the future. They need not have bothered. The next day, November 23, Probst called the three into the office and told them they had worked their last day at Graham, Anderson, Probst and White. In the depths of the depression Probst no doubt felt he could no longer support the large payroll Graham had managed to maintain. The three men went out to form their own firm, Shaw, Naess and Murphy, eventually one of the most successful in the city of Chicago. Later Shaw left to form Shaw, Metz and Dolio. Murphy's firm was later called C. F. Murphy and Company; it is now headed by Helmut Jahn and called Murphy/Jahn.

As the *Chicago Daily News* reported in 1937:

about a major change in White's work habits, which increasingly centered on ongoing construction in Chicago and alterations for old clients.

White was a soft-spoken man whose life revolved around his home. Since he did not socialize much at the office and left no papers, our knowledge of his personality and character is limited. But the working relationship of the four partners, and his vital role, is attested by the oeuvre of the firm. A photograph of the four with a presentation model of the Wrigley Building (fig. 262) commemorates the partnership. White died in 1936. His two sons both went to Princeton. One became a general contractor, and the other went into the insurance business.

Next to the partners, the designers and engineers played the most significant roles in the

A famous architectural firm, whose enterprises over the last fifty years ran into billions of dollars was reborn today with the formation of a new partnership retaining the name Graham, Anderson, Probst and White. The new set up occasioned by the death of two of the old partners [Graham and White] within the last two months leaves the firm under the guidance of Edward Probst, senior partner, and four co-partners, his two sons Marvin and Edward E., William E. Graham, son of the late Ernest R. Graham, and Wellington J. Schaeffer, a designer, all long associated with the firm.[63]

[262] GRAHAM, ANDERSON, PROBST, AND WHITE WITH MODEL OF THE WRIGLEY BUILDING

CHARLES G. BEERSMAN (1888–1946), MARIO SCHIAVONI (1883–1939?), AND ALFRED PHILLIPS SHAW (1895–1970)

Beersman was born and educated in the public schools of San Francisco until he entered the School of Architecture at the University of Pennsylvania. While there he won the LeBrun Traveling Scholarship for a period of study in Italy. In 1912, he worked in the office of James Gamble Rogers, where he assisted in work on the New Haven, Connecticut, post office. He next worked for John Russell Pope, assisting with the draw-

ings for the Scottish Rite Temple and the competition drawings for the Lincoln Memorial in Washington, D.C. Beersman seems to have been something of an itinerant draftsman in his early years. He worked for Tracy Egerton Swartout on the Missouri State Capitol, the Denver Post Office, the Mary Baker Eddy Memorial, Vincent Astor's Nurses Home, the Astor Public Market, the George Washington Memorial Competition, the Newark Memorial, the New York Court House, the Wilmington Courthouse, and the Francis Scott Key Memorial. Toward the end of World War I he joined the armed forces. For a short time he was a partner in the firm of Vollmer and Beersman, responsible for the Masonic Temple in Yonkers, New York, and serving as a consulting architect to the YWCA.

In 1919, Beersman joined Graham, Anderson, Probst and White and at once distinguished himself by his work on the Wrigley Building. Soon after, he designed the Straus Building on Michigan Avenue and also worked on the Federal Reserve Bank of Chicago, the State Bank of Chicago Building, the Builders' Building in Chicago, Foreman State National Bank Building in Chicago, and the interior of the Union Citizens National Bank in Baltimore. He designed the Central Station at the Century of Progress International Exposition in Chicago in 1933 and was a consulting architect for Commonwealth Edison. When the depression forced drastic cuts in the size of the staff, Beersman secured an assistant professorship at the Armour Institute of Technology (now Illinois Institute of Technology) in Chicago, where he remained until 1936. At this time he left to join the New York firm of Fellheimer and Wagner, where he remained until his death.[64]

Mario Schiavoni was born in Rome and entered the École des Beaux-Arts in Paris sometime in 1910. Credits and medals are recorded for him for two more years when he won the Prix de Paris given by the American Society of Beaux-Arts Architects. Little is known of his life except that he lived at 992 Tinton Avenue in New York in 1914 and in 1916 listed his office in the *Beaux-Arts Yearbook* as being in the Monroe Building in Chicago. Later he listed himself as living in Beachhurst, Long Island.[65]

Schiavoni was probably working in Chicago by the mid-1920s. Rarely, if ever, does the signature of the designer in an architectural office appear on the drawings, unless he or she is a partner in the firm. Mario Schiavoni's name, however, is inscribed at the bottom of the principal drawings of his greatest work, and one of Chicago's most striking buildings, the Shedd Aquarium. Schiavoni also signed the drawings for the Chicago Historical Society's building in Lincoln Park. Our last bit of information about

him is a note indicating that he lived in Flossmoor, Illinois, in 1939.

Alfred P. Shaw's long career is better known. Born in Dorchester, Massachusetts, on May 13, 1895, to Enoch and Ellen Phillips Shaw, he attended St. John's Preparatory School in Danvers, Massachusetts. His architectural education was at the Boston Architectural Club atelier, where his mentors were Constant Desiré D'Espradelle and Herbert L. Warren. Shaw's portfolio would have included very fine drawings, for the sketches he made of Longfellow House and Memorial Hall in Cambridge while he was a young man were published in *Western Architect* in 1928, as were travel sketches he made when he served as a representative of the Interallied Food Commission in Yugoslavia in 1919. Sometime in the mid-1920s, he joined Graham, Anderson, Probst and White. He was made a junior partner in 1929.

Imaginative and vivacious, Shaw would design buildings in mass and elevation and then give them over to Sigurd Naess, Ivar Naess's younger brother, who developed the details of the plan. In the years he was with the firm, Shaw gave it a startling fresh image, bringing the more contemporary Art Deco forms of the late 1920s into the repertoire of the office. With Shaw, the look of a Graham, Anderson, Probst and White building changed radically from the style associated with the firm in previous years.

The most stunning example developed by Shaw and Naess is the Chicago Civic Opera Building, where their expert planning and design were given a masterful finish by the decorative schemes of Jules Guerin. Other examples of Shaw's gifted pen include the Thirtieth Street Station in Philadelphia; the Chase National Bank in New York; the State Line Generating Station in Hammond, Indiana; and in Chicago, the Pittsfield Building, the Merchandise Mart, the Field Building, and the U.S. Post Office. After Graham's death, Shaw spent ten years in partnership with Charles F. Murphy and Sigurd Naess, and then formed his own firm, Shaw, Metz and Dolio. Shaw had two sons, Joseph and Patrick. Upon graduation from Harvard Patrick joined the firm his father had founded and now serves as president of Shaw and Associates. Patrick relates that his father always admired Ernest R. Graham, spoke of him with deep affection, and regarded him as a personal hero.

Statistics provide a clear indicator of the magnitude of the practice these men conducted. The log book shows more than two thousand commissions during Graham's tenure as head of the firm from 1912 to 1936; between 1913 and 1933 buildings costing more than $500 million were erected.

The legacy Daniel Burnham left to Ernest R. Graham was not only a rich and active practice and years of experience in erecting first-rate buildings, but the example of how to select talented men and inspire their best work and their loyalty. While Graham carried on these traditions, it was Anderson who continued Burnham's commitment to city planning on a grand scale. After Anderson's death in 1924, the firm concentrated on commercial architecture until Probst's death in 1942 brought an end to a partnership that had shaped important elements of the urban fabric of Chicago, Philadelphia, and Cleveland and erected public buildings, railroad stations, office buildings, hotels, museums, department stores, power stations, charitable institutions, lofts, manufacturing complexes, and other building types from New York to Pasadena. (For the accompanying changes in the idea of civic order, see the conclusion to Part I.)

Since the firm always used solid construction methods and fine materials and employed the best designers it could find, most of its buildings continue to enhance the cities they serve. During the late 1920s the firm responded to the increasing emphasis on the construction of commercial skyscrapers by relinquishing its earlier role as a leader in the design of railroad stations, and civic and cultural buildings. But a legacy of well-built, logically arranged, and handsome buildings endured as the firm adapted the canons of good architecture to meet the changing values of the early twentieth century. Enriched, nourished, and transformed by the great European classical tradition it inherited, the firm of Graham, Anderson, Probst and White in its turn transformed the traditions of architecture to meet the needs of its time and place.

NOTES

1. Paysoff Tinkoff, "Report on the Examination of the Books and Records of Graham, Anderson, Probst and White from January 1, 1917 to December 31, 1921 for Income and Excess Profits Tax Purposes Under Revenue Acts of 1917–1918." Tinkoff also included a history of the partnership agreements in the early part of his report. This valuable document is now at the Chicago Historical Society, Chicago, Ill.

2. Ibid.

3. Ibid.

4. *Dictionary of American Biography,* supplement 2, s.v. "Graham, Ernest R.," by Carl W. Condit, pp. 252–54.

5. Andrew N. Rebori, "The Work of Burnham and Root, D. H. Burnham, D. H. Burnham and Co., and Graham, Burnham and Co.," p. 17.

6. Andrew N. Rebori, "Ernest R. Graham: A Tribute to Greatness," manuscript in archives of the Graham Foundation for Advanced Studies in the Fine Arts, Chicago, p. 4.

7. Hugh Dalziel Duncan, "The Life and Times of Ernest R. Graham."

8. Ibid.

9. Ibid.

10. Ibid.

11. Ibid.

12. Robert Bruegmann, *Holabird and Roche, Holabird and Root.*

13. Henry S. Ericsson, *Sixty Years a Builder,* p. 30.

14. Ibid., p. 31.

15. "Burnham Scrapbook" (Chicago: Ryerson and Burnham Libraries of the Art Institute of Chicago), p. 13.

16. Ernest R. Graham, *Architectural Works of Graham, Anderson, Probst and White,* foreword.

17. For more on the World's Columbian Exposition, see David F. Burg, *Chicago's White City of 1893* (Lexington, Ky.: University Press of Kentucky, 1976).

18. Tinkoff, "Report on the Books."

19. Diaries of Ernest R. Graham, July 5, 1899, GAPW archives, Chicago, Ill.

20. Rebori, "The Work of Burnham and Root," p. 4.

21. Ibid., p. 6.

22. Commission Register, GAPW archives.

23. *Dictionary of American Biography,* supplement 2, s.v. "Graham, Ernest R.," by Carl Condit, pp. 252–54.

24. Rebori, "Work of Burnham and Root," pp. 11–12.

25. Ibid., p. 24.

26. Ibid., p. 15.

27. Paul Starrett, *Changing the Skyline* (New York: McGraw-Hill, c. 1936), pp. 54–57.

28. Earle Shultz and Walter Simmons, *Offices in the Sky,* pp. 77–78.

29. Deputy Governor S. B. Cramer to J. B. McDougal, Chairman, Building Committee, Federal Reserve Bank of Chicago, February 28, 1923, Federal Reserve Bank archives, Chicago, Ill.

30. *Coe College Courier* 17 (April 15, 1931).

31. Clifford Noonan, interview, September 1982.

32. I am indebted to the late Ann Lorenz Van Zanten for calling this to my attention.

33. C. F. Murphy, conversation with author, October 5, 1982.

34. Louis Horowitz, "The Towers of New York," *Saturday Evening Post,* March 28, 1936, pp. 49–50.

35. *Chicago Daily News,* January 2, 1937.

36. Ernest R. Graham, "Last Will and Testament."

37. Diaries of Ernest R. Graham.

38. C. F. Murphy, interview, October 15, 1983.

39. Minutes of the Building Committee, Federal Reserve Bank of Chicago, January 28, 1919, Federal Reserve Bank archives.

40. Ibid.

41. Ibid., February 16, 1919.

42. Graham to Building Committee, Federal Reserve Bank archives.

43. Clifford Noonan, interview, September 1982.

44. Rebori, "Work of Burnham and Root," p. 6.

45. Robert W. Jorgenson to author, August 8, 1985.

46. Robert Klark Graham, conversation with author, September 4, 1985.

47. Harold M. Mayer and Richard C. Wade, *Chicago: Growth of a Metropolis,* p. 150. Information on C. W. Palmer was provided by Tim Samuelson, Chicago Landmarks Commission, in conversation with the author, February 11, 1986. Mayer and Wade report that land values rose from $160 to $800 a front foot between 1882 and 1894 in the area.

48. Howard Thomas, interview, spring 1985.

49. Rebori, "Work of Burnham and Root," p. 13.

50. Ibid., p. 1.

51. Notice in the necrology section of *Report 10 35th Anniversary of the Class of 1892* at Harvard University, pp. 5–6.

52. Richard Chafee, "The Teaching of Architecture at the École des Beaux-Arts," in *Architecture of the École des Beaux-Arts,* ed. Arthur Drexler (New York: Museum of Modern Art, 1977), pp. 82–86.

53. Thomas Tallmadge, obituary of Peirce Anderson, *Architectural Record* 55 (May 1924):472a.

54. Anderson's ideas as a designer come to us through reports signed by Daniel Burnham, and it is impossible to be certain which man was originally responsible for the ideas. As Anderson was in the Philippines for months, received a salary for the work, and claimed it and the plan for Baguio in the report he wrote for the twenty-fifth anniversary of his class at Harvard, we may assume he played a key role. *See also* Daniel H. Burnham, "Report on Proposed Improvements at Manila," *Proceedings of the Thirty-Ninth Annual Convention of the American Institute of Architects* (Washington, D.C., 1906), pp. 135–51. Thomas S. Hines, *Burnham of Chicago: Architect and Planner,* pp. 197–216 contains valuable insights and documentation of the relevant archival materials in the Burnham Papers in the Ryerson and Burnham Libraries of the Art Institute of Chicago.

55. Rebori, "Work of Burnham and Root," pp. 20–25.

56. Tallmadge, Anderson obituary.

57. Memorandum, Anderson to Graham, GAPW archives.

58. Tinkoff, "Report on the Books," pp. 8–29.

59. Rebori, "Work of Burnham and Root," p. 25.

60. Tallmadge, obituary.

61. Tinkoff, "Report on the Books."

62. Edward Probst, obituary of Howard Judson White, *Illinois Society of Architects Bulletin,* January 1937.

63. *Chicago Daily News,* January 2, 1937.

64. Earl Reed, "The Department of Architecture of the Armour Institute of Technology," typescript, November 15, 1935, Henry Heald Papers in the Heald as Dean file of the Illinois Institute of Technology, p. 3. Kevin Harrington, professor at IIT, told me about this manuscript.

65. Richard Chafee, conversation with author, June 24, 1983.

Commission Register, 1912–36

Except for the dates, this Commission Register is taken verbatim from records in the current office of Graham, Anderson, Probst and White and covers approximately the years 1912 to 1936. Records for work during the Burnham years and after Graham's death also exist, but are not included here. As is standard procedure in most architectural offices, the firm assigned a number to each project, whether a large complex, one building, or a small alteration. Even if the project was abandoned early in the planning stages, the number was kept.

At no time did the architects assign dates, and in places the projects are not listed in strict chronological order. When other evidence, such as an account book or a competition deadline, exists, I have added dates. The last date that I can determine with certainty is 1934. As most of the work of the depression years after that involved minor alterations, I chose the year of Graham's death, 1936, as a stopping point. Commission numbers are easily datable from other evidence after 1941 when war-related government projects begin, but they are beyond the scope of this book. Numbers continue to be assigned by the firm to current projects.

Readers will find Appendix A in Thomas S. Hines, *Burnham of Chicago: Architect and Planner* (New York: Oxford University Press, 1974) useful for its lists of works done in the transi-

tional period between the death of Daniel Burnham and the founding of Graham, Burnham and Company. All but two of the "Buildings designed before, but completed after, the year of Burnham's death" in Hines were selected as principal works and appear in Part II of this book as they represent major works of Peirce Anderson. Hines also includes a useful table (Appendix B) on comparative building costs.

The Commission Register remains an important historic source since most of the drawings of the firm were discarded when it moved to its present quarters.

Building Title	Location	Building Title	Location
4981 Gutzon Borglum Stone Mountain Memorial	Stone Mountain, Ga.	4997 Lombard Hotel & Proposed Addition	Chicago, Ill.
4982 Buckingham Hotels Co.	Detroit, Mich.	4998 Union Trust Building	Cincinnati, Ohio
4983 Tacoma National Bank	Tacoma, Wash.	4999 Gimbel Brothers	New York, N.Y.
4984 Walter H. Wilson 16 & Wabash	Chicago, Ill.	5000 Conway Building Brevoort Hotel Stack [1912]	Chicago, Ill.
4985 Continental & Commercial Bank Building	Chicago, Ill.	5001 Chicago Union Station	Chicago, Ill.
4986 Reid, Murdock & Co. Warehouse	Chicago, Ill.	5002 Express Building, Chicago Union Station	Chicago, Ill.
4987 New Orleans Terminal	New Orleans, La.	5003 Field Museum of Natural History	Chicago, Ill.
4988 Edison Co., Fisk St. Ash Pit, Dock, etc.	Chicago, Ill.	5004 Eaton Warehouse	Winnipeg, Canada
4989 Edison Co., Fisk St. Machine Shop	Chicago, Ill.	5005 Selfridges Store	London, England
4990 Edison Co., Locomotive House	Chicago, Ill.	5006 Pennsylvania Station	Pittsburgh, Pa.
4991 Great Northern Hotel	Chicago, Ill.	5007 Union Station	Cleveland, Ohio
4992 Edison Co., Fisk St. Station	Chicago, Ill.	5008 Kimball Building	Chicago, Ill.
4993 Peoples Gas Co.	Chicago, Ill.	5009 American Brass Co. Office Building	Kenosha, Wis.
4994 Golf Course for Sir John Eaton	Toronto, Ontario, Canada	5010 First National Bank Building	Omaha, Nebr.
4995 Field Estate, 308 W. Madison	Chicago, Ill.	5011 Bethlehem Steel Office Building [1916]	Bethlehem, Pa.
4996 Cincinnati Traction Co.	Cincinnati, Ohio	5012 Continental & Commercial Bank Alterations	Chicago, Ill.
		5013 Crane Co., Corwith Plant Building D-4	Chicago, Ill.

BUILDING TITLE	LOCATION	BUILDING TITLE	LOCATION
5014 Crane Co., Corwith Plant Buildings D-5 & C-6	Chicago, Ill.	5036 James Simpson Residence, alterations	Glencoe, Ill.
5015 Crane Co., Corwith Plant Building E-8	Chicago, Ill.	5037 Tremont Building, alterations	Chicago, Ill.
5016 Crane Co., Corwith Plant Building E-5	Chicago, Ill.	5038 Masonic Temple Building, alterations	Chicago, Ill.
5017 Butler Brothers Building B	Chicago, Ill.	5039 Marshall Field & Co., S. Wabash alterations	Chicago, Ill.
5018 Joliet Township High School	Joliet, Ill.	5040 Thomas Rodd Residence, Southampton	Long Island, N.Y.
5019 Old National Bank, alterations	Spokane, Wash.	5041 Pennsylvania Lines Yard Masters Office, 63rd St.	Chicago, Ill.
5020 A. B. Jones Residence, alterations	Evanston, Ill.	5042 Pennsylvania Lines Yard Master Office, 59th St.	Chicago, Ill.
5021 Country Home for Crippled Children	Prince Crossing, Ill.	5043 Swimming Pool for James Simpson	Glencoe, Ill.
5022 Edison Building, alterations	Chicago, Ill.	5044 Garage, Bethlehem Steel Co.	South Bethlehem, Pa.
5023 Dime Savings Bank	Detroit, Mich.	5045 Equitable Building Vaults	New York, N.Y.
5024 Edison Co., Sherman St. Sub-station	Chicago, Ill.	5046 T. Eaton Co. Ltd. Store	Toronto, Canada
5025 Marshall Field & Co., alterations	Chicago, Ill.	5047 Aquarium Building	Chicago, Ill.
5026 Great Northern Hippodrome, alterations	(no city, no state)	5048 Duluth Natatorium for Julius H. Barnes	Duluth, Minn.
5027 Franklin MacVeagh & Co.	Chicago, Ill.	5049 Chicago Union Station Power House	Chicago, Ill.
5028 Merchants Loan & Trust, alterations & extension	Chicago, Ill.	5050 Cleveland Station, O. P. Van Sweringen	Cleveland, Ohio
5029 Stanley Field Gardens Cottage	Lake Bluff, Ill.	5051 Building for Wm. J. Berkowitz	Kansas City, Mo.
5030 Marshall Field & Co., repairs, Fulton St.	Chicago, Ill.	5052 Insurance Exchange Building	Omaha, Nebr.
5031 Marshall Field & Co. thread mill	Monticello, Ind.	5053 David Mayer Hotel	Chicago, Ill.
5032 Youngstown Sheet & Tube Co. office building	Youngstown, Ohio	5054 S.W. National Bank of Commerce, Hughes Bryant	Omaha, Nebr.
5033 Stores, Canal & Monroe Sts., C. L. Strobel	Chicago, Ill.	5055 Apartment Building for W. J. Chalmers	Chicago, Ill.
5034 Silversmith Building	Chicago, Ill.	5056 Board of Trade	Chicago, Ill.
5035 Stevens Building Grill Room	Chicago, Ill.	5057 T. S. Martin Co. Store	Sioux City, Iowa
		5058 Browning, King & Co.	Cincinnati, Ohio
		5059 Anheuser Busch Warehouse	Chicago, Ill.

Building Title	Location	Building Title	Location
5060 Wholesale Market (Picard)	Chicago, Ill.	5087 Memphis Station, I.C.R.R.	Memphis, Tenn.
5061 Michigan Railway Co. Building	Grand Rapids, Mich.	5088 Commonwealth Edison Fulton St. Substation	Chicago, Ill.
5062 Allied Bazaar, Coliseum	Chicago, Ill.	5089 Marshall Field & Co. Retail Store, South State St.	Chicago, Ill.
5063 Theatre Building, Randolph & Dearborn	Chicago, Ill.	5090 Field Estate, 174–184 N. State	Chicago, Ill.
5064 First National Bank Building	Milwaukee, Wis.	5091 Lasalle Bank, John G. Shedd & Federal Reserve	Chicago, Ill.
5065 Louis Fox Department Store	Fort Wayne, Ind.	5092 Robinson Building, O. W. Johnson	Racine, Wis.
5066 Barber Building	Joliet, Ill.	5094 Beidler Building, Washington & Union, J. G. Shedd	Chicago, Ill.
5067 Conway Building	Chicago, Ill.		
5068 Mrs. Eddy Party Wall	Chicago, Ill.	5095 Booth Warehouse (Inspection)	Chicago, Ill.
5069 Equitable Building [1913–14]	New York, N.Y.	5096 Corbin Residence	Chevy Chase, Md.
5070 Eighty Maiden Lane	New York, N.Y.	5097 Crane Co. Corwith Plant D-8 Building	Chicago, Ill.
5071 Field Estate, 215–219 S. Wabash	Chicago, Ill.	5098 Proposed Chicago Post Office	Chicago, Ill.
5072 John R. Morron Residence	Littleton, N.H.	5099 Continental Trust Co., alterations	Baltimore, Md.
5073 Putnam Building	Davenport, Iowa	6000 De Wolf Building	Chicago, Ill.
5074 Chicago Plan Commission	Chicago, Ill.	6001 Du Pont Residence & Garage	Wilmington, Del.
5075 46 Cedar Street (Henry Evans)	New York, N.Y.	6002 Biltmore Hotel [1913–14]	New York, N.Y.
5076 Insurance Exchange	Chicago, Ill.	6003 Marshall Field Annex	Chicago, Ill.
5077 Zion City Lace Works, Marshall Field & Co.	Zion City, Ill.	6004 Marshall Field & Co. Building, 15–17 W. Lake St.	Chicago, Ill.
5078 Gimbel Brothers	Philadelphia, Pa.	6005 Scheuttler Building, repairs (M.F. & Co.)	Chicago, Ill.
5079 Railway Exchange	Chicago, Ill.		
5080 Goddard Building	Chicago, Ill.	6006 Stanley Field Residence	Lake Bluff, Ill.
5081 Orchestra Hall Building	Chicago, Ill.	6007 Federal Reserve Bank	New York, N.Y.
5082 May Co. Building	Cleveland, Ohio	6008 Commission of Fine Arts	Washington, D.C.
5083 Chicago Club, alterations	Chicago, Ill.	6009 First National Bank	Odebolt, Iowa
5084 West Side Hotel, E. A. Howard	Canton, Ohio	6010 Queen City Club	Cincinnati, Ohio
5085 Canton Station	Canton, Ohio	6011 Gimbel Building	Milwaukee, Wis.
5086 Fleming Brothers Addition	Des Moines, Iowa		

BUILDING TITLE	LOCATION	BUILDING TITLE	LOCATION
6012 Garrett Biblical Institute, Alterations for Franklin MacVeagh & Co.	Chicago, Ill.	6041 Bank & Office Building LaSalle & Madison	Chicago, Ill.
6013 Harrisburg Speedway	Harrisburg, Pa.	6042 Pantages—O. J. Grace, Grand & Olive	St. Louis, Mo.
6014 Herald Exhibit	Chicago, Ill.	6043 Hughes Bryant	Kansas City, Mo.
6015 Illinois Central Station, Randolph Street	Chicago, Ill.	6044 Merchants National Bank	Cedar Rapids, Iowa
6016 Jelke Building	Chicago, Ill.	6045 O. H. Grace, Union Trust Co., 7th & Locust	St. Louis, Mo.
6017 Knauth, Nachod & Kuhn	Chicago, Ill.	6046 Illinois Trust & Savings Bank, Screen, Low Building	Chicago, Ill.
6018 Lehigh Valley Coal Co.	Wilkes-Barre, Pa.		
6019 Miners Bank Building	Wilkes-Barre, Pa.	6047 Enclosing Walls, Chicago Union Station	Chicago, Ill.
6020 Crystal Palace Rink, Mrs. E. J. Mariani	New York, N.Y.	6048 John C. Black Residence	Chicago, Ill.
6021 no record		6049 Walter H. Wilson, Robey & Jackson	Chicago, Ill.
6022 Building Material Exhibit	Chicago, Ill.	6050 Union National Bank	Muskegon, Mich.
6023 Rock Island Savings Bank	Rock Island, Ill.	6051 Textile Exchange, CB & Q Lot, also Federal Reserve	Chicago, Ill.
6024 Rollins' House	Chicago, Ill.		
6025 Stevens Store	Chicago, Ill.	6052 Mayor Preston of Baltimore	Baltimore, Md.
6026 Scanlan Warehouse	Houston, Tex.		
6027 Society Brand Building, alterations	Chicago, Ill.	6053 New Western Union Van Buren & LaSalle	Chicago, Ill.
6028 Society for Savings Building & Addition	Cleveland, Ohio	6054 C. I. Hogue, Continental & Com'l Bank	Chicago, Ill.
6029 Society Brand Building	Chicago, Ill.	6055 First National Bank	Muskegon, Mich.
6030 Spiegel Stack	Chicago, Ill.	6056 Dayton Hotel	Dayton, Ohio
6031 De Jonghe Restaurant	Chicago, Ill.	6057 Duluth Post Office & Group Plan	Duluth, Minn.
6032 Wilson Garage	Chicago, Ill.		
6033 Whitney Building	Detroit, Mich.	6058 Second National Bank	Minot, N. Dak.
6034 Western Union Building, alterations (old building)	Chicago, Ill.	6059 Wells Fargo Express Building	Chicago, Ill.
6035 Wilson Salesroom	Chicago, Ill.	6060 Fox & Co. Dept. Store	Hartford, Conn.
6036 Wilke Building	Chicago, Ill.	6061 Klearflax Linen Rug Co.	Duluth, Minn.
6037 Edmunds Mfg. Co. Warehouse	Chicago, Ill.	6062 Otto Young, Schulz	Chicago, Ill.
6038 Field Estate, 23–31, Franklin St.	Chicago, Ill.	6063 Fidelity Trust Co. (Wm. P. Gert, Pres.)	Philadelphia, Pa.
6039 Butler Building "A" (old building)	Chicago, Ill.	6064 Hotel Cleveland, Van Sweringen	Cleveland, Ohio
6040 Hughes Bryant, 10th & Grand	Kansas City, Mo.	6065 Gary State Bank	Gary, Ind.
		6066 Mooseheart Improvements	Mooseheart, Ill.

Building Title	Location	Building Title	Location
6067 Davis Theatre, 5th Avenue	Pittsburgh, Pa.	6090 Capitol Theatre, Broadway & 51st St.	New York City, N.Y.
6068 Insurance Exchange [1915]	Pittsburgh, Pa.	6091 Jackson & Clinton, Office Building. CM. St. P.	Chicago, Ill.
6069 Judson Bradway, Apartment Hotel	Detroit, Mich.	6092 Telephone Building	Cleveland, Ohio
6070 Illinois Central-Grand Central Station, Old	Chicago, Ill.	6093 Jackson Quincy LaSalle & 5th, Shedd	Chicago, Ill.
6071 Murphy Memorial	Chicago, Ill.	6094 T. Eaton Mail Order Bldg.	Toronto, Canada
6072 De Wolf Building Addition	Chicago, Ill.	6095 Club Quarters, O. P. Van Sweringen	Cleveland, Ohio
6073 Board of Trade Building	Duluth, Minn.	6096 Polk Street Widening	Chicago, Ill.
6074 Insurance Exchange, Fred G. Austin	Detroit, Mich.	6097 Post Office Alterations (Mr. Carlisle)	Chicago, Ill.
6075 Field Museum Sculpture	Chicago, Ill.	6098 Thos. Rodd Garage	Pittsburgh, Pa.
6076 Crane F-1 Building, Corwith Plant		6099 Federal Reserve—D. Mayer Van Buren & Federal	Chicago, Ill.
6077 E. A. Howard Residence	Chicago, Ill.	6100 Government Powder Plant "C"	Nitro, W. Va.
6078 Crane Co. Corwith Plant Boiler House	Chicago, Ill.	6101 Equitable—Bankers Club Roof Garden Ext.	New York, N.Y.
6079 Carson, Pirie, Scott, John Griffiths	Chicago, Ill.	6102 Marshall Field Retail Spc. Ext. Lighting	Chicago, Ill.
6080 Marshall Field & Co., Garage, Motor Service Building	Chicago, Ill.	6103 63rd St. Yard Office, Penn Lines	Chicago, Ill.
6081 Capitol Hill Improvements	Washington, D.C.	6104 Continental Comm. Bank Alts	Chicago, Ill.
6082 Marshall Field Wholesale, alterations	Chicago, Ill.	6105 California State Building Competition [1915]	Sacramento, Calif.
6083 Memorial for Thomas Rodd	Pittsburgh, Pa.	6106 Federal Reserve American Exp. Eckstein	Chicago, Ill.
6084 Chicago Union Station, Train Sheds	Chicago, Ill.	6107 Commonwealth Edison Display Cases 2nd Flr.	Chicago, Ill.
6085 C. C. Walker Lake Str. S. Michigan Ave.	Chicago, Ill.	6108 Merchants Loan Bldg. Entrance Grilles	Chicago, Ill.
6086 d'Humy-Strauss Garage	Chicago, Ill.	6109 Marshall Field Annex, New Elevators	Chicago, Ill.
6087 Childs Restaurant, next Palmer House, State Street	Chicago, Ill.	6110 Illinois Trust Co. Toilet Alts.	Chicago, Ill.
6088 W. H. Schmidlapp, Monitor Stove & Range Co. Building	Cincinnati, Ohio	6111 Federal Reserve—Present Site Extension	Chicago, Ill.
6089 Chicago Union Station, Mail Facilities	Chicago, Ill.		

BUILDING TITLE	LOCATION	BUILDING TITLE	LOCATION
6112 John G. Shedd, Madison & Franklin	Chicago, Ill.	6133 Library Bldg. & General Store	Mooseheart, Ill.
6113 Harrison & Clark Property 150 × 103	Chicago, Ill.	6134 Federal Reserve Bank Kansas City, MO [1919–20]	Kansas City, Mo.
6114 Harrison & Franklin Property	Chicago, Ill.	6135 Cleveland Peristyle Soldiers & Sailors Memorial	Cleveland, Ohio
6115 Theater—Levy Ladd Monroe Street	Chicago, Ill.	6136 U.S. Government War Exposition Grant Park	Chicago, Ill.
6116 Barnett Bros. Alterations Ry. Exch.	Chicago, Ill.	6137 Federal Reserve Bank, Dallas	Dallas, Tex.
6117 David Whitney Bldg. Detroit Lobby Signs	Detroit, Mich.	6138 Office Bldg. Cleveland Shops P.R.R.	Cleveland, Ohio
6118 Greene & Co. Alterations Ry Exch.	Chicago, Ill.	6139 Crane Co. C-5 Building	Chicago, Ill.
		6140 Crane Co. Nipple Shop	Chicago, Ill.
6119 Baby Nursery, Moosehart	Moosehart, Ill.	6141 51st ST. Rest Room P.R.R.	Chicago, Ill.
6120 Masonic Temple Alterations	Chicago, Ill.	6142 P.R.R. Colehour Office Bldg.	Colehour, Ind.
6121 Architects Committee	Chicago, Ill.	6143 Crane C-2, Generator Room	Chicago, Ill.
6122 Crane Company Corwith Plant Bldg. E-2	Chicago, Ill.	6144 Lincoln Memorial, Grant Park	Chicago, Ill.
6123 Marshall Field & Co. Siegel Cooper Bldg.	Chicago, Ill.	6145 Field Museum Hospital (Temporary)	Chicago, Ill.
6124 Terminal Warehousing at Atlantic Ports	Chicago, Ill.	6146 Field Museum Main Bldg. Additions & Alterations	Chicago, Ill.
6125 Train Shed. Ext. & Portion C-4, 5, 6 Crane Co.	Chicago, Ill.	6147 Illinois Merchants Bk. Bldg.	Chicago, Ill.
6126 Crane Co. Corwith Plant C-4 Bldg.	Chicago, Ill.	6148 Federal Reserve Bk. of Cleveland	Cleveland, Ohio
6127 Merchants Loan & Trust Co. Addition and Alterations for Ground Flr. Savings Bk. & Bond Dept.	Chicago, Ill.	6149 Memorial Building	Joliet, Ill.
		6150 Yarbrough	Fort Worth, Tex.
6128 Marshall Field & Co. Retail Miscellaneous	Chicago, Ill.	6151 Fourth National Bank	Macon, Ga.
		6152 Roosevelt Memorial	Chicago, Ill.
6129 Consolidated Ticket Off. (Insurance Exch.)	Chicago, Ill.	6153 American Railway Express Co.	Chicago, Ill.
6130 T. Eaton Co. Winnipeg Mail Order Bldg.	Winnipeg, Manitoba	6154 Post Office Facilities Parcel Post	Chicago, Ill.
6131 Womens Temple State Bank of Chicago	Chicago, Ill.	6155 Commonwealth Edison Electric Shop	Chicago, Ill.
6132 Crane Co. Corwith Plant B-2 Ext. North	Chicago, Ill.		

BUILDING TITLE	LOCATION	BUILDING TITLE	LOCATION
6156 First Trust & Savings Bank	Chicago, Ill.	6179 Tobey Lot—(Pittsfield Bldg.) [1923–24]	Chicago, Ill.
6157 Nebraska State Capitol	Lincoln, Nebr.	6180 Shaker Heights Development	Cleveland, Ohio
6158 The London Electric Ry, Co.	London, England	6181 National City Bank	Cleveland, Ohio
6159 Deering Estate	Minneapolis, Minn.	6182 Herrick, Myron T. Warehouse	Long Island City, N.Y.
6160 Boomer Hotel	Long Beach, L.I., N.Y.	6183 May Building, Additional Stories	Cleveland, Ohio
6161 Boomer Theatre	Long Beach, L.I., N.Y.	6184 MacKeen Building	Halifax, Nova Scotia
6162 Wells-Dickey Trust Co.	Minneapolis, Minn.	6185 Iowa National Bank	Davenport, Iowa
6163 The Harvard Club of Chicago	Chicago, Ill.	6186 Akron Hotel	Akron, Ohio
6164 Turner Memorial	Pittsburgh, Pa.	6187 Saginaw Land Co.	Saginaw, Mich.
6165 American Federation of Arts	Chicago, Ill.	6188 Marcus & Felt Office Bldg.	Philadelphia, Pa.
6166 Canal-Monroe St. Property Loft Bldg. (Robt. White)	Chicago, Ill.	6189 Cleveland Athletic Club	Cleveland, Ohio
		6190 Barber Hotel	Kansas City, Mo.
6167 Monte-Vista Bank & Trust Co.	Philadelphia, Pa.	6191 Citizens Bldg. as Federal Reserve	Cleveland, Ohio
6168 Provident Life & Trust Co.	Philadelphia, Pa.	6192 Evans, Henry Office	Brooklyn, N.Y.
6169 John & William St. Bldg. 110 Williany Street	New York, N.Y.	6193 Reynolds, Arthur—Residence Alterations	Glencoe, Ill.
6170 Insurance Exchange	New York, N.Y.	6194 Goodyear Tire & Rubber Co. Office Building	Akron, Ohio
6171 Rockhurst College (Gov. J. Z. Miller)	Kansas City, Kans.	6195 Union Station W. Kinzie Bridge	Chicago, Ill.
6172 Federal Reserve Ventilation, Hibernian Bank Bldg.	Chicago, Ill.	6196 Farmers National Bank	Princeton, Ill.
		6197 Rodes-Rapier Starks Bldg.	Louisville, Ky.
6173 First Nat'l Wisconsin Nat'l Merger	Milwaukee, Wis.	6198 Donaldson Department Store	Minneapolis, MN
6174 Citizens-Trust Union Commerce Bank Bldg.	Cleveland, Ohio	6199 Mooseheart 15 capacity Dormitory	Mooseheart, Ill.
6175 Belknap Hardware Mfg. Co. [1923]	Louisville, Ky.	6200 Wabash South Water St. Office Bldg.	Chicago, Ill.
6176 National Peace Celebration	Chicago, Ill.	6201 Wrigley Building South Section [1924]	Chicago, Ill.
6177 Two Bungalows, Convalescent Home for Crippled Children	Wheaton, Ill.	6202 Union National Bank	Wichita, Kans.
		6203 No record	
6178 Lawyers Building	New York, N.Y.	6204 Eaton Winnipeg Mail Order	Winnipeg, Man.

BUILDING TITLE	LOCATION	BUILDING TITLE	LOCATION
6205 Chase National Bank Alts.	New York, N.Y.	6230 Mooseheart Mother's House	Mooseheart, Ill.
6206 No record		6231 Riverside Park Memorial Flagstaff	Chicago, Ill.
6207 Kimball Wabash & 7th	(None given)	6232 Marshall Field Co. Cafeteria 12th Flr. N. Wabash	Chicago, Ill.
6208 M. O'Neil Department Store	Akron, Ohio		
6209 Putnam Estate	Davenport, Iowa	6233 Union Station New Plans	Chicago, Ill.
6210 French Salon	Chicago, Ill.	6234 Continental Comml. Bank Changes	Chicago, Ill.
6211 Whitney Building Alts.	Detroit, Mich.	6235 Michigan Avenue Bridge Plaza	Chicago, Ill.
6212 American Surety Co.	New York, N.Y.		
6213 D. O. Mills Property Broad St.	New York, N.Y.	6236 Randolph Street Arcade	Chicago, Ill.
6214 First National Fort Dearborn Bks.	Chicago, Ill.	6237 Southern Texas Comml. Nat'l Bk.	Houston, Tex.
6215 Waldeck Michigan & Grand Avenue (Wolbach)	Chicago, Ill.	6238 Memorial Auditorium	Louisville, Ky.
		6239 Southern Baptist Theological Seminary	Louisville, Ky.
6216 Gimbel Store	Philadelphia, Pa.		
6217 John P. Starks Theater Project	Louisville, Ky.	6240 J. F. Jelke Co. Office & Garage	None given
6218 Old Comml. National Bank	Oshkosh, Wis.	6241 Memphis Hotel	Memphis, Tenn.
6219 Republican National Convention 1920	Chicago, Ill.	6242 Booster's Information Booth City Hall	Chicago, Ill.
6220 No record		6243 Thos. Rodd Warehouse	Pittsburgh, Pa.
6221 Commonwealth Edison Co. Alts Marquette Bldg.	Chicago, Ill.	6244 Community Service Bldg. Standard Oil	Whiting, Ind.
6222 Penn R.R. Co. Office Wells & Van Buren	Chicago, Ill.	6245 Henry Evans Rush Street	Chicago, Ill.
		6246 Palmer House	Chicago, Ill.
6223 Goodrich Rubber Co. Michigan & 11th Sts.	Chicago, Ill.	6247 Thos Rodd Residence	Pittsburgh, Pa.
6224 Union Trust Co.	Spokane, Wash.	6248 Merchants Nat'l Bk. Addition	Indianapolis, Ind.
6225 Schoenstedt Theater & Apartment Building	Chicago, Ill.	6249 South Water Street Improvement	Chicago, Ill.
6226 Morden Building (Ins. Exch.) (Hogan)	Minneapolis, Minn.	6250 No record [Northwestern Nat'l Bank?]	Minneapolis, Minn.
6227 Goodyear Tire & Rubber Office	Toronto, Canada	6251 No record	
6228 Marshall Field S. Wabash Alterations	Chicago, Ill.	6252 Federal Reserve (Temp. Quarters) Federal Bldg.	Chicago, Ill.
6229 No record		6253 Federal Reserve Bank Branch	Houston, Tex.
		6254 Federal Reserve Bank Branch	Oklahoma City, Okla.

BUILDING TITLE	LOCATION	BUILDING TITLE	LOCATION
6255 Saks & Co.	New York, N.Y.	6280 Masonic Temple	St. Louis, Mo.
6256 Chamberlin Theater Drew & Campbell	Cleveland, Ohio	6281 Gate Lodge Office	Toronto, Ontario
6257 Twenty Wacker Drive (Opera Bldg.)	Chicago, Ill.	6282 Railway Exchange Fountain in Rotunda	Chicago, Ill.
6258 U.S. Mail Terminal Bldg.	Chicago, Ill.	6283 Joseph Bros. Co. Industrial Site	Chicago, Ill.
6259 Mooseheart Club House	Mooseheart, Ill.	6284 Milwaukee & St. Paul R.R. Co. Office Building Fullerton	Chicago, Ill.
6260 Silversmith Bldg. Alterations	Chicago, Ill.	6285 Remodel Residence into Flat Office	Toronto, Ontario
6261 Jewish Hospital	St. Louis, Mo.		
6262 Citizens Bank Building Alterations	Cleveland, Ohio	6286 Kentucky Female Orphans Home	Kentucky
6263 Union Trust Co.	Cleveland, Ohio	6287 Revell & Co. (Powers Bldg. Alts)	Chicago, Ill.
6264 Merchants & Savings Bank	Kenosha, Wis.	6288 Belmont Avenue Bridge (Rayen Co.)	Youngstown, Ohio
6265 Mooseheart Kindergarten	Mooseheart, Ill.	6289 North Michigan Avenue Hotel	Chicago, Ill.
6266 Crane Co. Bldgs. A1, B 4–5–6	Chicago, Ill.	6290 Mehornay Building	Kansas City, Mo.
6267 Union Trust Service Building	Cleveland, Ohio	6291 Wanamaker Building Alts.	New York, N.Y.
6268 Union Trust Bldg. Alts.	Pittsburgh, Pa.	6292 Wanamaker Building Alts.	Philadelphia, Pa.
6269 West Side Street Changes (M.F. Co. Warehouse)	None given	6293 Grant Park Widening & Lake Bowl	Chicago, Ill.
6270 Mooseheart Gymnasium	Mooseheart, Ill.	6294 North Pier Terminal	Chicago, Ill.
6271 Toronto Office Duplex Residence	Toronto, Ontario	6295 Capitol Building (Ahlschlager)	Chicago, Ill.
6272 Federal Reserve Bank	Atlanta, Ga.	6296 Illinois Masonic Nurses Home	Illinois
6273 City Plan Improvements	Chicago, Ill.		
6274 National Safe Dep. Co. Vaults First National	Chicago, Ill.	6297 Union Trust Col Broadway Branch	Cleveland, Ohio
6275 Graham, Anderson, Probst & White Monograph Book	Chicago, Ill.	6298 Mooseheart Women's Legion Club	Mooseheart, Ill.
6276 Freight Facilities Business District	Chicago, Ill.	6299 Union Trust Co. Pasadena Branch	Cleveland, Ohio
6277 Toronto Office Wily Residence	Toronto, Ontario	6300 Federal Reserve Bank Omaha Branch	Omaha, Nebr.
6278 J. F. Jelke, Jr. Private Garage	Chicago, Ill.	6301 Seymour Morris Residence Alts	Chicago, Ill.
6279 Boulevard Bridge Bank (Wrigley Building)	Chicago, Ill.	6302 Union Trust Co. Lorain St. Branch	Cleveland, Ohio

Building Title	Location	Building Title	Location
6303 Cleveland Public Library	Cleveland, Ohio	6327 Insurance Building Picard Lawrence Ave.	Chicago, Ill.
6304 Eaton Memorial	Toronto, Ontario	6328 Belknap Hdwe. & Mfg. Co. Power House	Louisville, Ky.
6305 Morton Building Washington & Wells	Chicago, Ill.	6329 Oak Park Country Club Alts.	Oak Park, Ill.
6306 McLoughlin Michigan & South Water	Chicago, Ill.	6330 Hoover Sweeper Co. Community Bldg.	Canton, Ohio
6307 John Barker, Ltd.	Kensington, London	6331 Wrigley Building North Section [1924–29]	Chicago, Ill.
6308 First National Bank	Canton, Ohio	6332 Cox Building	Lexington, Ky.
6309 Federal Reserve Bank Denver Branch	Denver, Colo.	6333 Rockford National Bank	Rockford, Ill.
6310 J. J. Turner Apartment Bldg.	None given	6334 Insurance Bldg. Franklin & Monroe Robt. White	Chicago, Ill.
6311 Bethlehem Steel Co. Offices Cunard Bldg.	New York, N.Y.	6335 Police & Municipal Court Building for City of Chicago	Chicago, Ill.
6312 Grand Canyon National Parks Improvements	None given	6336 Mercantile & Office Bldg. for Myer-Siegel Co.	Los Angeles, Calif.
6313 Standard Oil Service Stations Design	None given	6337 Warehouse for John T. Pirie (Penna System) C.P.S. & Co.	Chicago, Ill.
6314 Equitable Building 33rd & 7th	New York, N.Y.	6338 Insurance Building for Mr. Franham Upper Michigan Avenue	Chicago, Ill.
6315 John P. Starks Ramp Garage	Louisville, Ky.	6339 Union Station Power House	Chicago, Ill.
6316 Heart Office Building	None given	6340 C. C. Wormer, Jr. Park Boulevard Development	Detroit, Mich.
6317 Union Station Suburban St.	Chicago, Ill.	6341 Continental Trust Co. Alts.	Baltimore, Md.
6318 Chicago Athletic Assn. Alts.	Chicago, Ill.	6342 Union Savings Bank & Trust Co. Alterations	Cincinnati, Ohio
6319 Insurance Exchange Hughes Bryant	Kansas City, Mo.	6343 Higbee Department Store	Cleveland, Ohio
6320 Aldis Browne—Palmer Estate Adams & Wabash	Chicago, Ill.	6344 Palmer Estate Properties	Chicago, Ill.
6321 National Life Ins. (Johnson) Michigan & Pearson	Chicago, Ill.	6345 National Bank of Commerce Vault L. J. Horwitz	New York, N.Y.
6322 Exchange National Bank	Pittsburgh, Pa.	6346 Chase National Bank New Vault	New York, N.Y.
6323 Federal Reserve Bank of Chicago Detroit Branch	Detroit, Mich.	6347 First Trust & Savings Bk.	Hammond, Ind.
6324 Citizens National Bank	Baltimore, Md.	6348 Marshall Field & Co. McCormick Lot	Chicago, Ill.
6325 LaSalle St. Bridge Over River	Chicago, Ill.		
6326 Miscellaneous Prospects	None given		

Building Title	Location	Building Title	Location
6349 Hibbard-Spencer-Bartlett Condemnation	Chicago, Ill.	6367 New York State National Bank	Albany, N.Y.
6350 Amalgamated Trust & Savings Bank (Garment Works' Union)	Chicago, Ill.	6368 Pullman Property, S. W. Straus & Co.	Chicago, Ill.
6351 Bridge Building Gundlach J. W. Davis	Chicago, Ill.	6368A McDougall Residence	Chicago, Ill.
6352 Philip Peck, SW cor. Congress & Wabash Office Bldg.	Chicago, Ill.	6369 Ill. Trust & Sav. Bk. Bldg. for Chicago Hist. Soc.	Chicago, Ill. Lincoln Park
6354 Commonwealth Edison Co. Crawford Avenue Power Station	Chicago, Ill.	6370 Field Museum, Exterior Bronze Signs & Pedestals	Chicago, Ill.
6355 Union Stations Interlocking Tower	Chicago, Ill.	6371 Sesqui-Centennial Exposition	Philadelphia, Pa.
6356 Grand Opera Storage Bldg.	Chicago, Ill.	6372 Insurance Bldg. Palmer Lot W. Side N. Michigan Ave.	Chicago, Ill.
6357 Eitel Bros. Hotel Diversey & Outer Drive	Chicago, Ill.	6373 Insurance Bldg. Palmer Lot, E. Side N. Michigan Ave.	Chicago, Ill.
6358 Field-Shedd-Reid-Graham Private Garage	Chicago, Ill.	6374 Euclid-Superior Bldg. Van Sweringen Twin Bk & Office Bldg.	Cleveland, Ohio
6359 Silversmith Bldg. Sidewalk Alts.	Chicago, Ill.	6375 Bethlehem Office Bldg. Addition	S. Bethlehem, Pa.
6360 Farmers Deposit National Bank	Pittsburgh, Pa.	6376 Commonwealth Edison Co. Lake St. Property	Chicago, Ill.
6361 Starks Building Addition	Louisville, Ky.	6377 Residence of Jas. J. Davis, Esq.	Mooseheart, Ill.
6357 Eitel Bros. Hotel Diversey & Outer Drive	Chicago, Ill.	6378 Bronze Clock Union Trust Co.	Spokane, Wash.
6358 Field-Shedd-Reid-Graham Private Garage	Chicago, Ill.	6379 Insurance Bldg. Kirk Lot N. Michigan Ave.	Chicago, Ill.
6359 Silversmith Bldg. Sidewalk Alts.	Chicago, Ill.	6380 Penna. System Terminal	Philadelphia, Pa.
6360 Farmers Deposit National Bank	Pittsburgh, Pa.	6381 Moose Hotel (Jas. J. Davis, Esq.)	Chicago, Ill.
6361 Starks Building Addition	Louisville, Ky.	6382 Straus Building	Chicago, Ill.
6362 Botanical Garden	Washington, D.C.	6383 Sinclair Oil Co.	Chicago, Ill.
6363 Jones Syndicate (Textile Exchange)	Chicago, Ill.	6384 Ascher Bros. Washington St. Bldg.	Chicago, Ill.
6364 Chicago River Boulevard Scheme	Chicago, Ill.	6385 Eitel Bros. Hotel (Transcontinental Hotel) West Side	Chicago, Ill.
6365 Dearborn Station	Chicago, Ill.	6386 Oscar Friedman State near Lake St. Project	Chicago, Ill.
6366 Alworth Building Addition	Duluth, Minn.	6387 Old Edison Bldg. Alterations (Field Estate)	Chicago, Ill.

Building Title	Location	Building Title	Location
6388 Eitel Bros. NW Cor. Randolph & LaSalle Streets	Chicago, Ill.	6431 Crane Co. Corwith B4–5–6–7	Chicago, Ill.
6408 Old Men's Home	Mooseheart, Ill.	6432 Tower Office Bldg. Cleveland Union Terminals	Cleveland, Ohio
6409 Administration Building	Mooseheart, Ill.	6433 Cleveland Hotel Addition Building Cleveland Union Terminals	Cleveland, Ohio
6410 Alterations & Additions to S. Wabash & S. Bridges Bldgs. Marshall Field & Co.	Chicago, Ill.	6434 Moreland Court Apartments a/c Cleveland Union Terminals	Cleveland, Ohio
6411 Marshall Field & C. New Fixture Installation State St. Bldg.	Chicago, Ill.	6435 Crawford Air-Switch House	None given
6412 Ohio Dormitories	Mooseheart, Ill.	6436 through 6999—no record	
6413 Cotton Project Madison & Franklin Streets	Chicago, Ill.	7000 Chase National Bank Madison Ave. Bank Alterations	New York, N.Y.
6414 Radio & Fire Station	Mooseheart, Ill.	7001 Chase National Bank Park Ave. Branch	New York, N.Y
6415 Standard Bank Screens and Check Desks	Chicago, Ill.	7002 Alterations Davis Dry Goods Co.	None given
6416 Hoover Administration Bldg.	Canton, Ohio	7003 W. A. Wieboldt & Co. New Department Store	Chicago, Ill.
6417 Randolph & Michigan Schuyler I. C.	Chicago, Ill.	7004 Engineering Building	Chicago, Ill.
6418 Federal American Bank (R. F. Beresford)	Washington, D.C.	7005 Hoover Factory Addition	N. Canton, Ohio
6419 Chesapeake & Ohio Ry. Co. Passenger Station	Ashland, Ky.	7006 Appalachian Estates Country Club (Magid)	Tallulah Park, Ga.
6420 New York State Building	Mooseheart, Ill.	7007 Crane Co. Bldg. C-7	Chicago, Ill.
6421 Cuyahoga Building	Cleveland, Ohio	7008 Residence for G. C. Cleveland	Chicago, Ill.
6422 Hospital for Dr. Herman L. Kretschmer	None given	7009 Edison Bldg. Bridges	Chicago, Ill.
6423 Crane Co. Corwith Plant Extension to Boiler	Chicago, Ill.	7010 Peoples Gas Bldg. Revolving Doors	None given
6424 White Sulphur Springs	W. Virginia	7011 New Municipal & Criminal Courts Building	Chicago, Ill.
6425 International Exhibition (Ghetto, P.R.R. Property West Side)	Chicago, Ill.	7012 Hotel, Stevens & Wood 120 Broadway Camden, NJ	New York, N.Y.
6426 Woodland Avenue Branch Union Trust	Cleveland, Ohio	7013 Corn Exchange Bank Remodeling National City & Nat'l Bk. Republic	None given
6427 Dormitory for Kentucky Female Orphan School	Lexington, Ky.	7014 Commonwealth Edison Station McJunkin Building	Chicago, Ill.
6428 Garage North Side	Chicago, Ill.	7015 Commonwealth Edison Station Utilities Securities	Milwaukee, Wis.
6429 Toronto Power House Associate	Toronto, Ontario		
6430 No Record			

BUILDING TITLE	LOCATION	BUILDING TITLE	LOCATION
7016 Continental & Commercial National Bank Building Alterations 208 S. LaSalle	Chicago, Ill.	7037 Hotel Union Station West Side	Chicago, Ill.
7017 Brunswicke-Balke-Collendar Co. Stag Hotel	None given	7038 Pennsylvania Terminals Office Building Penna. R.R.	Philadelphia, Pa.
7018 Department Store Martin J. Lide	Birmingham, Ala.	7039 City Hall Suburban Station Penna. R.R.	Philadelphia, Pa.
7019 National City Bank	Akron, Ohio	7040 City Hall U.S. Post Office Penna. R.R.	Philadelphia, Pa.
7020 Cotton Mill Factory Marshall Field & Co.	Chicago, Ill.	7041 City Hall Amer. Rly. Express Penna, R.R.	Philadelphia, Pa.
7021 Post Office Pittsburgh, P.R.R.	Pittsburgh, Pa.	7042 City Hall Broad St. Station Penna, R.R.	Philadelphia, Pa.
7022 Pennsylvania Station Improvements	Cleveland, Oh.	7043 City Hall Auditorium Penna. R.R.	Philadelphia, Pa.
7023 Parke-Davis & Co. Bldg. (F. C. Austin Detroit, MI)	Chicago, Ill.	7044 Hotel Lake Otsego Dion Geraldine	Michigan
7024 Residence E. E. Strauss	Wilmette, Ill.	7045 Consumers Proposed Office Bldg.	Jackson, Mich.
7025 Cleveland Union Terminals Co. Bldg. S 1	Cleveland, Ohio	7046 Mr. Langley Sinclair Property	Chicago, Ill.
7026 Cleveland Union Terminals Co. Bldg. S 2	Cleveland, Ohio	7047 Garage Hoover Company	Canton, Ohio
7027 West Half (Air Rights Unassigned) Cleveland Union Term. Co. Bldg. P 3	Cleveland, Ohio	7048 C. C. Walker Property Shops & Club Bldg.	None given
7028 West Half (Air Rights Unassigned) Cleveland Union Terminals Co. Bldg. P 2	Cleveland, Ohio	7049 Dr. Albright Residence	Milwaukee, Wis.
		7050 Gimbel Bros. Eleventh Story	New York, N.Y.
7029 West Half (Air Rights Unassigned) Cleveland Union Term. Co. Bldg. O2	Cleveland, Ohio	7051 White Rock Mineral Springs Co.	Waukesha, Wis.
7030 No record		7052 Proposed Office Bldg. A. S. Schulman, Inc. Dearborn, Harrison & Plymouth	None given
7031 Gimbel Bros. Basements	New York, N.Y.		
7032 Peirce Anderson Memorial [1924]	None given	7053 Machingery Exposition Bldg. & Agricultural Mart West Side	Chicago, Ill.
7033 Alumnae Hall Kentucky Female Orphans Home	Midway, Ky.	7054 Study for a Garage for Development	None
7034 Commonwealth Edison Co. Chicago Trust Co. Bldg. Add. & Appraisals	Chicago, Ill.	7055 Standard Oil Co. Additional Stories	Chicago, Ill.
7035 First National Bank New Project	Chicago, Ill.	7056 Keeley Property, South Water St. & Michigan Ave.	Chicago, Ill.
7036 Cleveland Mail Terminal Nickel Plate	Cleveland, Ohio	7057 Elgin National Watch Co. Mfg. Building	Elgin, Ill.

Building Title	Location	Building Title	Location
7058 Deering Estate—Wacker Drive & Wabash Avenue	Chicago, Ill.	7081 Foreman National Bank Bldg. (Chamber of Commerce Lot)	None given
7059 Whitney Realty Co. Project (Witherell St.)	Detroit, Ill.	7082 Builders Building Wacker Dr.	Chicago, Ill.
7060 Apartment for Arthur Reynolds 209 Lake Shore Drive	Chicago, Ill.	7083 Chase National Bank	New York, N.Y.
7061 Cuneo—I. C. Randolph St. & Michigan Avenue	Chicago, Ill.	7084 L. S. Donaldson Co. N.W. National Bank & Office Bldg.	Minneapolis, Minn.
7062 Coe College [1924–29]	Cedar Rapids, Iowa	7085 Office Building Clark & Madison (Mr. Mann) Leiter Property	Chicago, Ill.
7063 C. & N.W.R.R. River Property Development	None given		
7064 W. J. Chalmers Property West Side	Chicago, Ill.	7086 Hotel (Jones Property) Canal & Jackson	Chicago, Ill.
7065 D. J. Schuyler Residence	Wisconsin	7087 Chicago Mercantile Exchange	Chicago, Ill.
7066 Randolph Street Pedestrian Subway	Chicago, Ill.	7088 Crane Co. Office Bldg.	Chicago, Ill.
7067 State Line Power Station	Indiana	7089 Insurance Exchange Addition Jackson & Wells Sts.	Chicago, Ill.
7068 Chicago Stock Exchange in State Bank of Chicago	Chicago, Ill.	7090 Chicago arena West Side Along Chicago River	Chicago, Ill.
7069 North Shore Channel	None given		
7070 Bank & Office Bldg.	Louisville, Ky.	7091 Printer's Building (A. R. Jones Property)	None given
7071 Eaton-Winnipeg, Additional Story Warehouse H-1	None given	7092 Garage Building (A. R. Jones Property)	Chicago, Ill.
7072 Stevens Memorial Site	Chicago, Ill.	7093 Marshall Field & Co. Warehouse Wacker Drive	Chicago, Ill.
7073 Alterations to Court Bldg. E-7 & E-8 Crane Co. Corwith	Chicago, Ill.	7094 Waite Phillips & R. O. McClintock Project	Tulsa, Okla.
7074 Crawford Avenue Station New Section	None given	7095 First National Bank	Trenton, N.J.
7075 Midland Bank Building	Cleveland, Ohio	7096 Elgin Clock Co. Factory Addition	Elgin, Ill.
7076 Office Building & Garages	None given	7097 Northeast Cor. Randolph & Clark Sts. Office Bldg. (Ettleson)	Elgin, Ill.
7077 W. H. Fuqua, First National Bank	Amarillo, Tex.	7098 Office Bldg. Michigan Ave. (Stop & Shop)	Chicago, Ill.
7078 Twelve Story Office Bldg. 4th & Jefferson Sts. (Hieatt)	Louisville, Ky.	7099 Chicago Yacht Club	Chicago, Ill.
7079 Fisk Bldg. Winston & Co. New Building Project	Chicago, Ill.	7100 Bryant Building	Kansas City, Mo.
7080 Industrial Exposition	Chicago, Ill.	7101 C. & O. Station	White Sulphur Spgs., W. Va.

BUILDING TITLE	LOCATION	BUILDING TITLE	LOCATION
7102 Office Shops Building (J. A. Carlson) Michigan & Eighth St.	Chicago, Ill.	7123 New York Central Office Bldg. P-2 Block (Air Rights)	Cleveland, Ohio
7103 Penna. R.R. Station	Akron, Ohio	7124 through 7142-no record	
7104 Office Building (James L. Stewart)	Pittsburgh, Pa.	7143 Chicago Produce Terminal	Chicago, Ill.
7105 Shops & Office Bldg. (H. A. Wheeler Union Trust Chicago)	Los Angeles, Calif.	7144 Jelke Garage Building	Chicago, Ill.
		7145 H-4 Block, Cleveland Union Terminal Co. [1924–29]	Cleveland, Ohio
7106 Office Building (Austin St. & Michigan Ave.)	Chicago, Ill.	7146 Marshall Field & Co. Suburban Retail Store	Oak Park, Ill.
7107 Marshall Field & Co. Motor Service Bldg. Alts. & Adds.	Chicago, Ill.	7147 Hoover Co., Factory Bldg.	Canton, Ohio
7108 Chicago Civic Auditorium	Chicago, Ill.	7148 Comm. Edison Co., E. Lake St. Sub-Station Addition	Chicago, Ill.
7109 Thomas Rodd Project	Pittsburgh, Pa.	7149 Marshall Field & Co., Suburban Retail Store	Evanston, Ill.
7110 Fox Theatre & Office	Chicago, Ill.	7150 Shop. Bank & Office Bldg. Central Trust Co. Property	Chicago, Ill.
7111 Housing Project	Chicago, Ill.		
7112 Wieboldt Office Building	Chicago, Ill.	7151 Board of Trade Bldg.	Duluth, Minn.
7113 Planetarium Adjoining Field Museum (Stanley Field)	Chicago, Ill.	7152 Jewish Hospital Dispensary Bldg. (Addition to Hospital & Eusemon Conv. Home)	St. Louis, Mo.
7114 Medical Arts & Garage Bldg. O-2 Block	Cleveland, Ohio		
7115 Office Bldg. Ontario St. & Huron Road O-2 Block	Cleveland, Ohio	7153 Central Trust Alterations Continental Bank Bldg.	Chicago, Ill.
7116 Chicago Union Station Property Next to Butler Bros. J. D. Esposito	Chicago, Ill.	7154 Inland Steel Co. Office Bldg.	Indiana Harbor, Ind.
		7155 Federal Pipe & Supply Plant	Chicago, Ill.
7117 Mail Terminal Bldg. Broadway & Central Avenues	Cleveland, Ohio	7156 Penna. R.R. Steam Plant	West Philadelphia, Pa.
7118 Crane Co. Building E-3 Corwith Plant	Chicago, Ill.	7157 Penna R.R. Warehouse	Philadelphia, Pa.
7119 Chicago Historical Society C. B. Pike Lincoln Park	Chicago, Ill.	7158 Simpson Estate, Stables	Chicago, Ill.
		7159 1st Nat'l Bank of St. Paul [1929–36]	St. Paul, Minn.
7120 Standard Oil Bldg. Alterations '28 Chicago attic	Chicago, Ill.	7160 1st Wisconsin Nat'l Bank	Milwaukee, Wis.
7121 Nurses Home (Moses-Shoenberg Mem.)	St. Louis, Mo.	7161 Edison Electrical Appliance Co. Bldg.	Chicago, Ill.
7122 Garage & Office Building Wacker Drive	Chicago, Ill.	7162 Dearborn Terminal Improvements	Chicago, Ill.

BUILDING TITLE	LOCATION	BUILDING TITLE	LOCATION
7163 Bowes Realty Property (For Chicago Plan Commission)	Chicago, Ill.	7221 Express Building, Illinois Central—16th & Indiana	None given
7164 Mayflower Hotel	Akron, Ohio	7222 New England Mart	Boston
7165 Marshall Field & Co., Alterations to Wholesale Bldg.	Chicago, Ill.	7223 Stockholm Plan	None given
		7224 Chicago Union Station— Addition to Headhouse etc.	Chicago, Ill.
7166–67—no record		7225 Montgomery Ward Chain Stores	Chicago, Ill.
7168 Bethelehem Steel Co. Office Building—Addition	None given	7226 James Simpson Sr. Estate (Tennis Courts)	None given
7169 thru 7176—no record		7227 Marshall Field & Co.— S. Wabash Project	Chicago, Ill.
7177 State Line Unit #2	None given	7228 Conway—Foreman Alterations (arcade)	None given
7178 through 7200—no record		7229 Housing Project	None given
7201 Power House—Chicago Union Station	Chicago, Ill.	7230 Averhill Property—Estate M. Field—Parking Deck	None given
7202 through 7205—no record		7231 Davis Co. 330 S. Wabash Ave.	Chicago, Ill.
7206 Whitney Building	Detroit, Mich.	7232 The Fair Store	None given
7207 Illinois Central Station— Randolph Street	Chicago, Ill.	7233 Medinah Bldg.—Mayer Estate	None given
7208 Garage—Grant Park	Chicago, Ill.	7234 John Simpson—house	None given
7209 Music Center	New York, N.Y.	7235 Armour Exhibit— Century of Progress [1934]	Chicago, Ill.
7210 Hotel—Union Station Property	Chicago, Ill.	7236 A. M. Castle Co.— Addition	None given
7211 Majestic Building (Maybley Bldg.) Alterations	Detroit, Mich.	7237 Field Wholesale Lot— West End (Int'l. Harvester)	None given
7212 Wrigley Memorial— Catalina Island	California	7238 LaSalle Theater Alterations Estate M. Field	Chicago, Ill.
7213 Mooring Tower & Gov't Bldg.—Grant Park (Airport)	Chicago, Ill.	7239 Stock Yards	Chicago, Ill.
7214 Wrigley Aquarium & Planitarium Catalina Island	California	7240 Field Inspection— Outside	None given
7215 Los Angeles Union Station	California	7241 Civic Center—North Bank Drive	None given
7216 Blackhawk Stadium	None given	7242 Northerly Island (Chicago Exposition authority)	Chicago, Ill.
7217 Mayer Estate—Scheme for Jackson & Wells	Chicago, Ill.		
7218 Rosenwald Museum Interior	None given	7243 Mayer Estate—Hilton etc.	None given
7219 Erickson Memorial	None given		
7220 Entrance Gates to Century of Progress [1933]	None given	7244 Field Garage—New	Chicago, Ill.

Building Title	Location	Building Title	Location
7245 Monroe & Franklin—Field Estate Loyola	Chicago, Ill.	7274 Santa Fe-Burlington Bus Station	None given
7246 Otis Estate—State & Jackson	Chicago, Ill.	7275 Triangle Restaurant	None given
7247 Office Randolph St. 105	Chicago, Ill.	7276 Building Trades Exposition	None given
7248 John Simpson House—Lake Bluff	Lake Bluff	7277 Manz	None given
7249 Richie Grocer Co.	Eldorado, Ark.	7278 Merchants National Bank	Mobile, Ala.
7250 Bermuda Bank—(Chase Nat'l)	None given	7279 A. M. Castle Co.—Garage	None given
7251 Decatur Cartage Co.—Truck Terminal	None given	7280 Archibald Residence	None given
7252 Adjoin 700 N. Michigan (Estate M. Field)	Chicago, Ill.	7281 Vilas Residence	None given
		7282 Roosevelt Theater Site	Chicago, Ill.
7253 S. Chicago German Restaurant	S. Chicago	7283 Kemper Insurance Bldg.	Chicago, Ill.
7254 Park Hotel	Madison, Wis.	7284 DeJong's Store	Evansville, Ind.
7255 Chicago & Northwestern Office Bldg. Jackson & Franklin	Chicago, Ill.	7285 Marshall Field & Co.—Air Conditioning	Chicago, Ill.
		7286 Bank Alterations	Muscatine, Iowa
7256 through 7260—no record		7287 Von Lengerke & Antoine	Chicago, Ill.
7261 Estate M. Field—71st & Oglesby	Chicago, Ill.	7288 Brunswick Balke Collender Co.	None given
7262 Fargo	None given	7289 Donnersburger—Bindery	None given
7263 American Manganese Steel Co.	None given	7290—no record	
7264 Decatur Cartage Co.—New Truck Depot Extension	None given	7291 A. M. Castle Co.—Warehouse Extension	None given
7265 Wrigley Field—Bleacher Addition	Chicago, Ill.	7292 Crane Co. E-5, 6, 7 Cooling Shed	Chicago, Ill.
7266 Washington National Life 608–10 Church St.	Evanston, Ill.	7293 Meis Dept. Store	Danville, Ill.
		7294 Warehouse (DeWolf)	None given
7267 Apparel Mart (wholesale lot)	None given	7295 Crane Co. D-5, 6	Chicago, Ill.
7268 Field Escalators—New	Chicago, Ill.	7296 Dearborn & Madison—Thompson	Chicago, Ill.
7269 Fisk Street Station—Alterations	None given	7297 Crane Co.—E-3 Transformer Vault	Chicago, Ill.
7270 M. O'Neil Co.	Akron, Ohio	7298—no record	
7271 Field Service Station	Evanston, Ill.	7299 Crane Co.—Office	Chicago, Ill.
7272 Field Retail—Elevator Modernization—S. State	Chicago, Ill.	7300 New England Church	None given
		7301 20th Church, Christian Science	None given
7273 West Town State Bank	None given	7302 Crane Co.—E-7 Office	Chicago, Ill.

Building Title	Location	Building Title	Location
7303 Warehouse (DeWolf)	None given	7318 Williams Apartment	None given
7304 Field Retail—Leopold	None given	7319 Subway	None given
7305 Dean—Residence—Garage	None given	7320 J. P. Harding Apartments	None given
7306 Logan	None given	7321 Mercantile Building LVD	None given
7307 21st Church	None given	7322 Nixon Houses—W. E. Graham	None given
7308 20th Century Fox Film Studio	None given	7323 Airport	Chicago, Ill.
7309 thru 7311—no record	None given	7324 Medical Arts	Ottumwa, Iowa
7312 Washington National Ins.	Evanston, Ill.	7325 St. Anthony Hotel	San Antonio, Tex.
7313 Edward Probst—Housing (Davis)	None given	7326 Fort Wayne National Bank	Ft. Wayne, Ind.
7314 Kimball	None given	7327 Seven Up	Joliet, Ill.
7315 thru 7316—no record		7328 Insurance Bldg.	None given
7317 General Electric X-Ray—Bldg. 5	None given	7329 Schulze Baking Co.	None given
		7330 Joyce Seven Up	Chicago, Ill.

BIBLIOGRAPHY

A CONVENTIONAL BIBLIOGRAPHY would duplicate the notes to the text unnecessarily. Some of the major sources relating to the principal figures and the history and architecture of their times are listed below.

MANUSCRIPTS

The archives in the office of Graham, Anderson, Probst and White contains the diaries Graham kept from 1896 to 1936 and vertical files of correspondence, memoranda, newspaper clippings, journal articles, photographs, account books, specifications, and other materials that were the primary sources for this book. In addition, the Ryerson and Burnham Libraries of the Art Institute of Chicago's holdings on Daniel Burnham, Alfred P. Shaw, and Edward H. Bennett provided background material and other contemporary views. The archives of the Graham Foundation for Advanced Studies in the Fine Arts, Coe College, the Chicago Historical Society, the University of Notre Dame, Loyola University (Samuel

Insull's papers), Harvard University (Peirce Anderson material), DePaul University (for the Kimball Building), Filene's Department Store, the Continental and Commercial National Bank, the Chicago Title and Trust (for the Conway Building), the Equitable Life Assurance Company, Mount Wilson Observatory, the Charles A. Stevens Company, the David Whitney Building, the Civic Opera Building, the S. W. Straus Building, Marshall Field and Company, the Loyal Order of Moose, the Jewish Hospital of St. Louis, Commonwealth Edison Company, the Chase National Bank, the Alamo National Bank, the First National Bank of St. Paul, and the United States Treasurer's Office in Washington, D.C., were invaluable.

DRAWINGS, PHOTOGRAPHS, MODELS, AND OTHER IMAGES

For the art historian, images are a principal resource. Although the firm discarded many drawings when it moved to its present headquarters, hundreds of tubes of presentation drawings, working drawings, sketches, and other materials still remain in the archives. Building managers or owners often kept a set of working drawings or construction photographs, or these records were deposited in the building's archives. These small collections, discovered on trips to each building, provided information otherwise not available.

INTERVIEWS

Employees of the firm interviewed, some on several occasions, include Charles F. Murphy, Carter Manny, Jr., Clifford Noonan, Edward Histed, Gerald Eisel, and William Surman, current president of the firm. Current owners or managers of buildings, local preservation officials, and historians provided insights otherwise not possible, and they are cited in footnotes whenever possible.

JOURNALS

Contemporary journals consulted for the period included *American Architect, Architectural Review, Brick Builder, Craftsman, Architectural Record, Inland Architect, Journal of the Society of Architectural Historians,* and others cited in the notes. Because they have indexes, the *New York Times* and the *Chicago Record-Herald* were used frequently. The *Economist,* published in Chicago, was helpful.

BOOKS AND ARTICLES

Alberti, Leon Battista. *On the Art of Building in Ten Books.* Book 7, section 1. Translated by Joseph Rykwert, Neil Leach, and Robert Tavenor. Cambridge, Mass.: MIT Press, 1988.

Anderson, Peirce. "Notes on the New Union Station at Washington, D.C." Graham, Anderson, Probst and White archives, Chicago, Ill.

Axelrod, Alan, ed. *The Colonial Revival in America.* New York: Norton Press, 1985.

Babcock, R. *The Zoning Game.* Madison: University of Wisconsin Press, 1966.

Bach, Ira J. *Chicago On Foot.* Chicago: Follett, 1969.

Banham, Reyner. *Concrete Atlantis.* Cambridge, Mass.: MIT Press, 1986.

———. The *Architecture of the Well Tempered Environment.* Chicago: University of Chicago Press, 1984.

Bruegmann, Robert; Chappell, Sally; and Zukowsky, John. *The Plan of Chicago: 1909 to 1979.* Chicago: Art Institute of Chicago, 1979.

Bruegmann, Robert. *Holabird and Roche, Holabird and Root: An Illustrated Catalogue of Works, 1880–1940.* New York: Garland Publishing in cooperation with the Chicago Historical Society, 1991.

Burnham, Daniel H., and Bennett, Edward H. *The Plan of Chicago.* Edited by Charles H. Moore. Chicago: Commercial Club, 1909.

Chappell, Sally A. Kitt. "A Place for Everyone: Burnham's Hierarchical Order." *Inland Architect* 31 (November/December 1987): 50–60.

———. "As If the Lights Were Always Shining: Graham, Anderson, Probst and White's Wrigley Building at the Boulevard Link." In *Chicago Architecture: 1872 to 1922,* edited by John Zukowsky, pp. 291–301. Chicago: Art Institute of Chicago; Munich: Prestel-Verlag, 1987.

———. "Another Top: The Board of Trade Proposal." *Chicago Architectural Journal* 3 (1983): 20–21.

———. "Beaux-Arts Architecture in Chicago." *Inland Architect* 24 (October 1980): 17–23.

———. "Dream City, Downtown." *Chicago Architectural Journal,* 1986.

———. "The Equitable Building in New York Reconsidered." *Journal of the Society of Architectural Historians* 49 (March 1990): 90–95.

———. "Urban Ideals and the Design of Railroad Stations." *Technology and Culture* 30 (April 1989): 354–75.

Clay, Grady. *Close-up: How to Read the American City.* London: Pall Mall Press, 1973.

Condit, Carl W. *Bibliography of the Design, Construction, and Operation of Railroad Passenger Stations, 1875 to Date.* (Crete, Nebr.: Railway History Monograph, January 1982).

———. *American Building Art: The Twentieth Century.* New York: Oxford University Press, 1961.

———. "Ernest R. Graham." In *Dictionary of American Biography,* edited by Robert Livingston Schuyler, vol. 22, supplement 2. New York: Charles Scribner's Sons, 1958.

———. *Chicago, 1910–29: Building, Planning, and Urban Technology.* Chicago: University of Chicago Press, 1973.

———. *The Chicago School of Architecture: A History of Commercial and Public Buildings in the Chicago Area, 1875 to 1925.* Chicago: University of Chicago Press, 1964.

Craig, Lois A. *The Federal Presence.* Cambridge, Mass.: MIT Press, [1978].

Delafons, John. *Land Use Controls in the United States.* Cambridge, Mass.: MIT Press, 1969.

Domosh, M. "The Symbolism of the Skyscraper: Case Studies of New York's First Tall Buildings." *Journal of Urban History* 14 (May 1988): 321–45.

Drexler, Arthur, ed. *The Architecture of the École des Beaux-Arts.* New York: Museum of Modern Art, 1977.

Duncan, Hugh Dalziel. "The Life and Times of Ernest R. Graham." Graham Foundation for Advanced Studies in the Fine Arts Archives, Chicago, Ill., c. 1955.

Ericsson, Henry. *Sixty Years a Builder.* Chicago: A. Kroch and Son, 1942.

Fitch, James Marston. *Grand Central Terminal and Rockefeller Center: A Historic-Critical Estimate of Their Significance.* Albany: State of New York, New York State Parks and Recreation, Division of Historic Preservation, 1974.

Fogelsong, Richard. *Planning the Capitalist City.* Princeton, N.J.: Princeton University Press, 1986.

Gibbs, Kenneth Turney. *Business Architectural Imagery in America, 1870–1930.* Ann Arbor, Mich.: UMI Research Press, 1984.

Goldberger, Paul. *The Skyscraper.* New York: Knopf, 1981.

Goodsell, C. *The Social Meaning of Civic Space.* Lawrence, Kans.: Kansas University Press, 1988.

Graham, Ernest R. "Last Will and Testament." Graham Foundation For Advanced Studies in the Fine Arts Archives, Chicago, Ill.

Graham, Ernest R. *Architectural Works of Graham, Anderson, Probst and White.* London: Batsford, 1933.

Greenberg, Alan. "Urban Detail and the Urban Street." *Threshold* 3 (Autumn 1985): 16–30.

Harvey, David. *The Urbanization of Capital.* Baltimore: Johns Hopkins University Press, 1985.

Herschensohn, Michael J. "Idealism in Industry: Chicago's Pioneering Contribution to American Urban Planning History in the Central Manufacturing District." Paper accompanying an exhibition of the same name at ArchiCenter, Chicago Architecture Foundation, 1984.

Hines, Thomas S. *Burnham of Chicago: Architect and Planner.* New York: Oxford University Press, 1974.

Hitchcock, Henry-Russell. *Architecture: Nineteenth and Twentieth Centuries.* Baltimore: Penguin Books, 1958.

Horowitz, Helen Lefkowitz. *Culture and the City: Cultural Philanthropy in Chicago from the 1880s to 1917.* Lexington, Ky.: University Press of Kentucky, 1976.

Horowitz, Louis I. *The Towers of New York.* New York: Simon and Schuster, 1937.

Hughes, Thomas P. "Electrification of America: The System Builders." *Technology and Culture* 20 (1979): 124–61.

Huxtable, Ada Louise. *The Tall Building Artistically Reconsidered: The Search for a Skyscraper Style.* New York: Pantheon, 1984.

Interstate Commerce Commission Reports 70 (June to December 1921): 351

Jaher, F. C. *The Urban Establishment: Upper Strata in Boston, New York, Charleston, Chicago and Los Angeles.* Urbana, Ill.: University of Illinois Press, 1982.

Johannesen, Eric. *Cleveland Architecture 1876–1976.* Cleveland: Western Reserve Historical Society, 1979.

Jordy, William, and Coe, Ralph. *Montgomery Schuyler (1843–1914) American Architecture and Other Writings.* Cambridge, Mass.: Harvard University Press, Belknap Press, 1961.

Jordy, William H. *American Buildings and Their Architects: Progressive and Academic Ideals at the Turn of the Twentieth Century.* Garden City, N.Y.: Doubleday, 1970.

Kaufmann, Edgar, ed. *The Rise of an American Archi-*

tecture. New York: Metropolitan Museum of Art and Praeger, 1970.

King, Anthony, ed. *Buildings and Society: Essays on the Social Development of the Built Environment.* London: Routledge and Kegan Paul, 1980.

Krinsky, Carol Herselle. *Rockefeller Center.* New York: Oxford University Press, 1978.

Leedy, Walter Jr. "Cleveland's Terminal Tower—The Van Sweringens' Afterthought." *Cleveland State University Gamut* 8 (1983): 7.

Lewis, Russell. "Everything Under One Roof: World's Fairs and Department Stores in Paris and Chicago." *Chicago History* 12 (Fall 1983): 28–47.

Manieri-Elia, Mario. "Toward an 'Imperial City': Daniel H. Burnham and the City Beautiful Movement." In *The American City: From the Civil War to the New Deal,* edited by Giorgio Cuicci, et al. Cambridge, Mass.: MIT Press, 1979; London: Granada, 1980.

Mayer, Harold M., and Wade, Richard C. *Chicago: Growth of a Metropolis.* Chicago: University of Chicago Press, 1969.

Meeks, Carroll L. V. *The Railroad Station.* New Haven: Yale University Press, 1955.

Monroe, Harriet. *A Poet's Life, Seventy Years in a Changing World.* New York: Macmillan Company, 1938.

Moore, Charles. *Daniel H. Burnham, Architect, Planner of Cities.* Boston and New York: Houghton Mifflin Company, 1921.

Morss, Robert Lovett. "A Non-Union Union Station." *New Republic,* June 27, 1923, p. 120.

Mumford, Lewis. "New York vs. Chicago in Architecture." *Architecture* 56 (November 1927): 244.

Pevsner, Nikolaus. *A History of Building Types.* Princeton, N.J.: Princeton University Press, 1967.

Probst, Edward. Obituary notice for Howard Judson White. *Illinois Society of Architects Bulletin,* January 1937.

Rebori, Andrew N. "The Work of Burnham and Root, D. H. Burnham, D. H. Burnham and Co., and Graham, Burnham and Co." *Architectural Record* 38 (July 1915): 33–168.

Roth, Leland M. *McKim, Mead & White, Architects.* New York: Harper and Row, 1983.

Schultz, Earle, and Simmons, Walter. *Offices in the Sky.* New York: Bobbs-Merrill Company, 1959.

Schuyler, David. *The New Urban Landscape.* Baltimore: Johns Hopkins University Press, 1986.

Scully, Vincent. *American Architecture and Urbanism.* New York: Praeger, 1969.

———. *Modern Architecture.* New York: G. Braziller, 1974.

Searing, Helen, ed. *In Search of Modern Architecture: A Tribute to Henry-Russell Hitchcock.* New York: Architectural History Foundation; Cambridge: MIT Press, 1982.

Starrett, Paul. *Changing the Skyline.* New York and London: McGraw-Hill Book Company, Whittlesey House, 1938.

Stern, Robert, et. al. *New York 1900.* New York: Rizzoli, 1983.

Stilgoe, John R. *Metropolitan Corridor: Railroads and the American Scene.* New Haven and London: Yale University Press, 1983.

Sullivan, Louis. *Autobiography of an Idea.* 1924. Reprint. New York: Dover Publications, 1956.

Summerson, Sir John Newenham. *The Classical Language of Architecture.* Cambridge, Mass.: MIT Press, 1981.

Tallmadge, Thomas E. *The Story of Architecture in America.* New York: W. W. Norton and Company, 1936.

Tinkoff, Paysoff. "Report on the Examination of the Books and Records of Graham, Anderson, Probst and White from January 1, 1917 to December 31, 1921 for Income and Excess Profits Tax Purposes Under Revenue Acts of 1917–1918." September 16, 1922. Graham Foundation for Advanced Studies in the Fine Arts Archives, Chicago, Ill.

Toll, Seymour I. *Zoned America.* New York: Grossman Publishers, 1969.

Turner, Frederick Jackson. "The Significance of the Frontier in American History." In *Proceedings of the Forty-first Annual Meeting of the State Historical Society of Wisconsin.* Madison: State Historical Society of Wisconsin, 1894.

Turner, Paul. *Campus: An American Planning Tradition.* New York: Architectural History Foundation; Cambridge, Mass.: MIT Press, 1984.

Van Zanten, David. "Beaux-Arts Gothic." *New Mexico Magazine of Art,* 1982.

Weisman, Winston. "The First Landscaped Skyscraper." *Journal of the Society of Architectural Historians* 18 (May 1959).

Westfall, Carroll William. "Manners Matter." *Inland Architect* 24 (April 1980): 19–23.

———. "Chicago's Wholesale Markets, 1885 to the Present." Paper delivered to the Society of Architectural Historians, 1981.

Wilgus, William J. "The Grand Central Terminal in Perspective." *American Society of Civil Engineers Transactions* 106 (1941): 992–1029.

Wille, Lois. *Forever Open, Clear and Free: The Struggle For Chicago's Lakefront.* Chicago: Henry Regnery, 1972.

Willis, Carol. "Zoning and *Zeitgeist:* "The Skyscraper City in the 1920s." *Journal of the Society of Architectural Historians* 45 (March 1986): 47–59.

Wilson, Richard Guy. "Architecture, Landscape and City Planning." In *The American Renaissance 1876–1917* Brooklyn, N.Y.: Brooklyn Museum, 1979.

Zukowsky, John, ed. *Chicago Architecture: 1872 to 1922.* Chicago: Art Institute of Chicago; Munich: Prestel-Verlag, 1987.

———. *Chicago and New York: Architectural Interactions.* Chicago: Art Institute of Chicago; 1984.

ILLUSTRATION CREDITS

THE MAJOR PORTION of the illustrations for this book are from *The Architectural Work of Graham, Anderson, Probst and White, Chicago*, published privately for the firm by B. T. Batsford, London, in 1933. These are listed below under Graham, Anderson, Probst and White. Other contributors are Sally A. Kitt Chappell, figs. 71, 116 (courtesy of William Wrigley, Jr.), 130–31, 133, 256, 258 (courtesy of Christine Susman); Chicago Historical Society, fig. 188; Civic Opera (Dino D'Angelo), fig. 16; Coe College, figs. 161–64; Commonwealth Edison, figs. 73, 158; Dwight Cendrowski, Inc., fig. 49; Eaton Collection, Archives of Ontario, fig. 109; Federal Reserve Bank of Dallas, fig. 125; Field Museum of Natural History, Chicago, figs. 3, 5, 7; Geonex

Chicago Aerial Survey Company, fig. 219; Graham, Anderson, Probst and White, figs. 1, 2, 4, 6, 8, 10–13, 15, 17–33, 35–48, 50–56, 58, 59, 61–64, 66, 68–70, 72, 74–108, 110–15, 117, 118, 120–24, 126–29, 136–37, 139–57, 159–60, 165–80, 182–87, 189–97, 199–213, 216–218, 220–21, 223–33, 236–46, 248–49, 251–52, 255, 261–62; Barbara Graham Jaffe, fig. 259; Koppers Company, Inc., fig. 57, LaSalle Bank Building, Archives, figs. 60, 214–15; Mooseheart, figs. 132, 134–35; Mrs. Marvin Probst, fig. 260; Ryerson and Burnham Libraries, Art Institute of Chicago, fig. 222; University of Illinois at Chicago, University Library, A Century of Progress Records, fig. 247; University of Notre Dame, Archives, figs. 234–35.

INDEX

Numbers set in italic indicate pages where illustrations appear.